ART *of* ESTRANGEMENT

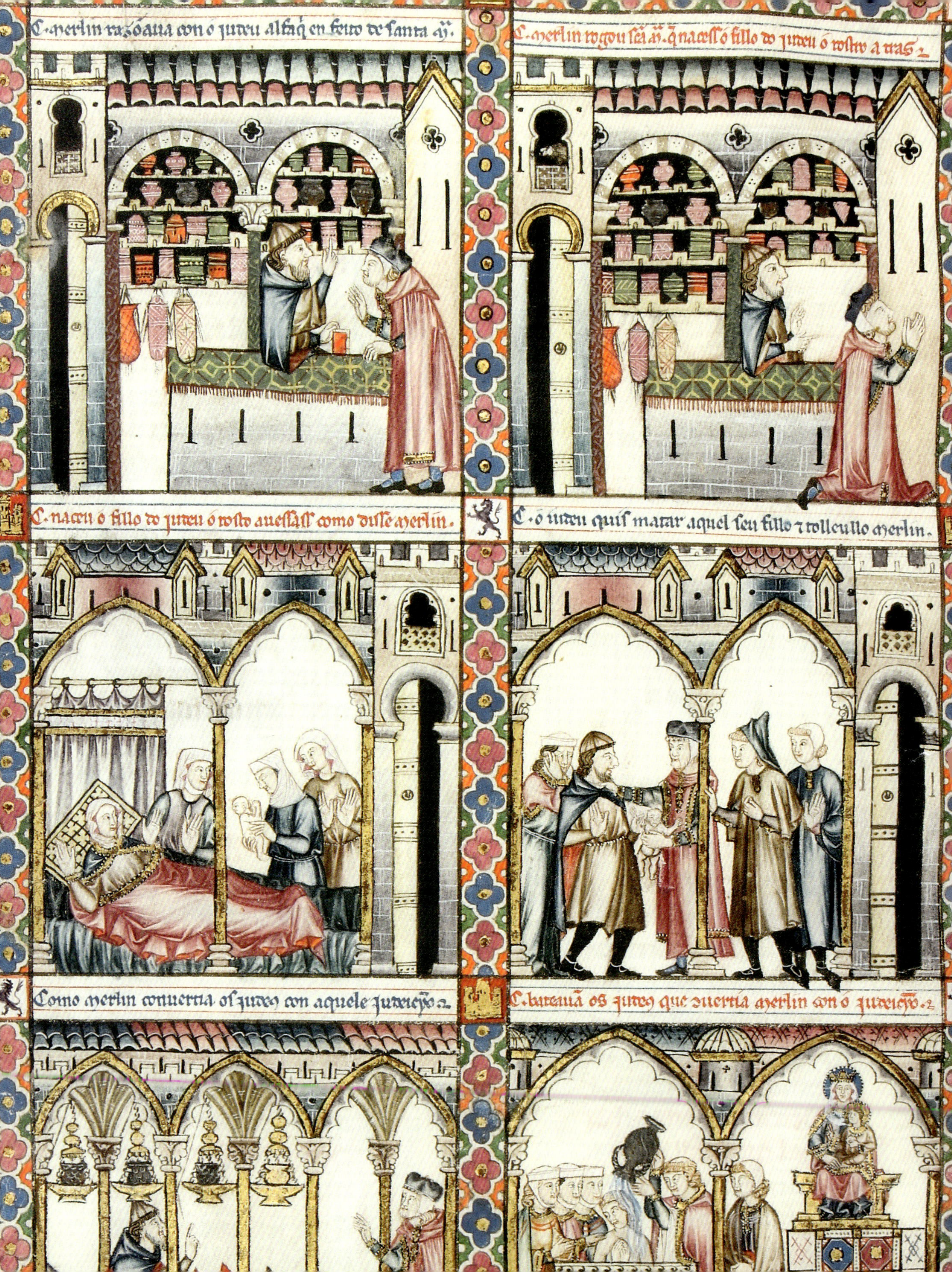
C. Merlin razõaua con o iudeu alfaq̃ en feito de santa M̃.
C. Merlin rogou sca M̃. q̃ nacesse o fillo do iudeu o rostro a tras.
C. naceu o fillo do iudeu o rosto auessas como disse Merlin.
C. o iudeu quis matar aquel seu fillo e tolleullo Merlin.
Como Merlin conuertia os iudeus con aquele iudeiço.
C. bateaua os iudeus que cõuertia Merlin con o iudeiço.

PAMELA A. PATTON

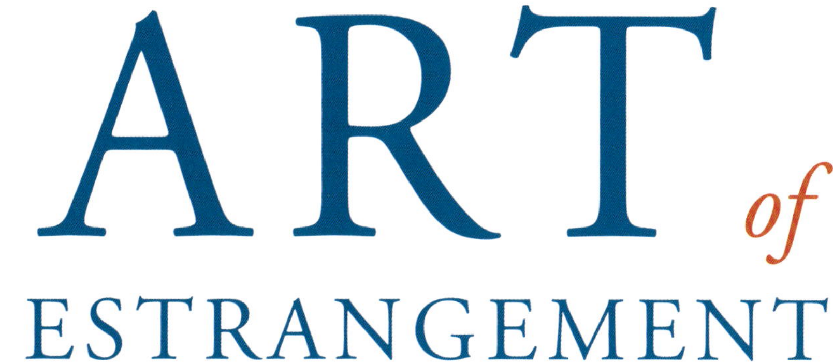

REDEFINING JEWS IN RECONQUEST SPAIN

The Pennsylvania State University Press
University Park, Pennsylvania

Publication of this book has been aided by a grant from the Program for Cultural Cooperation Between Spain's Ministry of Culture and United States Universities.

Publication of this book has also been aided by a grant from the Millard Meiss Publication Fund of the College Art Association.

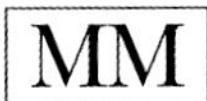

Library of Congress Cataloging-in-Publication Data

Patton, Pamela Anne.
Art of estrangement : redefining Jews in reconquest Spain / Pamela A. Patton.
p. cm

Includes bibliographical references and index.

Summary: "Examines the influential role of visual images in reinforcing the efforts of Spain's Christian-ruled kingdoms to renegotiate the role of their Jewish minority following the territorial expansions of the twelfth and thirteenth centuries"—Provided by publisher.

ISBN 978-0-271-05383-7
(cloth : alk. paper)

1. Jews in art.
2. Art and society—Spain—History—To 1500.
3. Jews—Spain—Identity.
4. Spain—Ethnic relations—History—To 1500.
5. Spain—Civilization—711–1516.
I. Title.

N8219.J49.P38 2013
704.9'493058924046—dc23
2012003778

Printed in China by Everbest Printing Ltd., through Four Colour Print Group, Louisville, KY

Designed by Jason Harvey

Published by The Pennsylvania State University Press,
University Park, PA 16802-1003

The Pennsylvania State University Press is a member of the Association of American University Presses.

It is the policy of The Pennsylvania State University Press to use acid-free paper. Publications on uncoated stock satisfy the minimum requirements of American National Standard for Information Sciences—Permanence of Paper for Printed Library Material, ANSI Z39.48–1992.

FOR EMILY AND EVAN, WHO KNOW THEIR HISTORY

CONTENTS

ILLUSTRATIONS

ACKNOWLEDGMENTS

Thanks are owed to many institutions and individuals for supporting the completion of this book. Among the earliest must be counted an NEH Summer Institute on Jews in medieval Christendom, led by Irven Resnick at the Oxford Centre for Hebrew and Jewish Studies, in which I participated in 2003. I could hardly have hoped for a better beginning to my then-nascent project, and I owe deepest gratitude to the National Endowment for the Humanities, to Professor Resnick, to his remarkable faculty, and to my genial Institute colleagues for that stimulating, challenging, and memorable experience. I am grateful to the NEH also for a subsequent Summer Stipend that allowed me to advance my work, as well as to the Program for Cultural Cooperation Between United States Universities and Spain's Ministry of Culture, the University Research Council of Southern Methodist University, and the Dean's Office of Meadows School of the Arts at SMU for generously supporting the travel, research, and writing time that this project required. Finally, I thank the University Research Council of SMU, the Meadows Dean's Office, and the Division of Higher Education and Ministry of the United Methodist Church for supporting my acquisition of images and publication rights.

Gratitude is due as well to the many individuals, both abroad and in the United States, who facilitated my access to materials central to my study and often shared their own expertise. These include José Luis del Valle Merino at the Biblioteca Real de El Escorial; Manuel Castiñeiras then at the Museu Nacional D'Art de Catalunya; Juan Antonio Yeves at the Museo Lázaro Galdiano in Madrid; Mercé Obón Alonso at the Fundació Francisco Godia in Barcelona; Nadia Fernández and Manel Riera at the Collecció "El Conventet" in Barcelona; Miquel S. Gros at Arxiu i Biblioteca Episcopal de Vic; Nancy Turner at the Getty Museum; and Charles Ryrie of Dallas. Particular thanks are owed to Carmen Godia and the Mayor's Office in Valencia for special permission to publish works held in their collections.

Many other scholars were kind enough to share their reactions to my developing project and especially to papers and publications in which I debuted ideas presented in this book. Although I have no hope of naming all the wonderful minds to whom I am indebted, I am especially grateful to Ali Asgar H. Alibhai, Pablo Ancos, Annemarie Weyl Carr, Michael Curschman, Jerrilyn Dodds, James D'Emilio, Angela Franco Mata, Mercedes García Arenal, Colum Hourihane, Deirdre E. Jackson, Katrin Kogman-Appel, Therese Martin, the late Donna Mayer-Martin, Mitchell B. Merback, Cynthia Robinson, Connie Scarborough, John Williams, David Wulstan, and the countless seminar students who so willingly permitted me to test some of my ideas in the classroom. I owe thanks in particular to several colleagues whose early critique of the manuscript in progress greatly sharpened my arguments: Jessica Boon,

Alessandra Comini, Melissa Dowling, Jane Elder, and Marcia Kupfer. I am grateful as well for the insights and suggestions of Debra Strickland and Marc Michael Epstein, who reviewed the work for Penn State Press, and of Eleanor Goodman and John Morris at the Press itself. Their advice greatly facilitated my final revision of the work, any remaining faults of which must of course be attributed to me alone.

Quite as important to this project was the support of staff and faculty at Southern Methodist University. Thanks are owed to Beverly Mitchell in Hamon Arts Library, Billie Stovall in the Interlibrary Loan Office, the staff of Bridwell Library, and Gillian McCombs, Dean of the Central University Libraries, for their gracious and responsive understanding of my research needs and their extraordinary efforts to acquire and maintain these resources. In the Department of Art History, Joy Richardson must be thanked for her persistence and creativity in helping me to navigate the many administrative minefields connected with travel, research funding, and photo acquisitions. Janis Bergman-Carton, department chair for most of the period during which the project was completed, supported my research agenda with characteristically generous goodwill.

The preparation of this book for press was, perhaps predictably, a family affair. My husband, Eric Marshall White, was, as always, the first to whom I entrusted my working drafts and their most important critic. His expertise in book history made him an indispensable guide at many points in my research, and his comments on my writing were sensible, perceptive, generous, and sometimes very funny; it has been a joy to share this work with him. My parents, Gary and Lenore Patton, offered encouragement, perspective, and, in those moments when academic and family schedules collided, much-appreciated child care. My children, Emily and Evan, are now old enough to display not just good-humored tolerance of their mother's eccentric interests but also a gratifying degree of enthusiasm for them. Each contributed concretely to the preparation of the manuscript: Emily lent her eagle eye to proofreading, and Evan's knack for order aided measurably in checking citations. I dedicate this book to the two of them in gratitude for their encouragement, their patience, and their genuine understanding of why history matters.

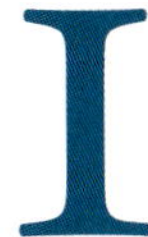

"ALIENS IN THEIR MIDST"

REIMAGINING JEWS IN MEDIEVAL IBERIA

A little Jewish boy, native of the town, came
for the pleasure of playing with the children;
the others welcomed him, they caused him no grief;
they all took delight in playing with him.
—GONZALO DE BERCEO

He who is neighbor to a Jew will never be a good Christian.
—VINCENT FERRER

Composed in the Christian-dominated northern kingdoms of Spain in the thirteenth and fifteenth centuries, respectively, the two passages above manifest a series of contrasts that might be considered paradigmatic of the Jewish-Christian relationship in central and late medieval Iberia. The first, drawn from a poem composed by Gonzalo de Berceo (ca. 1198–after 1252), recounts how a young Jewish boy, accustomed to going to school with his Christian friends, innocently joins them in taking communion at Easter.[1] When his enraged father reacts by throwing him into a furnace, the boy is rescued by the Virgin Mary and promptly converts, to the delight of the townspeople. Although this narrative has international roots—it originated in Byzantium and in subsequent versions often is set in the French city of Bourges—in Berceo's hands it derives much of its force from the guileless camaraderie between the Jewish boy and his Christian schoolmates, a relationship that might be perceived as peculiarly reflective of the poet-cleric's context in thirteenth-century Iberia, a land where Jews, Christians, and Muslims regularly shared geographical, cultural, and social space, with varying degrees of comfort.

Berceo's idyllic *convivencia* is to some extent demanded by the narrative. The Christian boys' "pleasure" and "delight" in their playmate not only sets the stage for the child's acceptance of communion; it also creates an effective foil for his Jewish father's murderous outrage at this act. Yet Berceo's strategy was not entirely abstract. To succeed, it depended upon a social factor that was far more concrete: the willingness of a medieval Iberian audience to accept the boys' carefree disregard for religious and cultural difference as not merely possible, but normative.[2] That they did so seems very likely: not only do other literary narratives of the same era, such as those in the *Cantigas de Santa María,* regularly begin their tales with similar moments of cultural porousness, but actual Jews and Christians in medieval Iberia found abundant and varied opportunities for interaction in nearly every sphere of medieval life, from agriculture and business deals to festivals and folk dancing.[3] While such opportunities could ebb and flow with the vicissitudes of local culture, their existence was a fact of which Berceo's Christian listeners and readers could not have been unaware.

A similar awareness underlies the second passage, but its impact here is strikingly different. This text derives not from a story, but from a sermon delivered in the Valencian town of Onda on 6 May 1416 by the famous Dominican preacher Vincent Ferrer (1350–1419).[4] Vincent's terse denunciation of neighborly contact between Christians and Jews was pronounced as part of a homily in which the friar demanded total separation between the daily business of Jewish and Christian communities, from housing and baking to the sale of meat and the operation of taverns. Its pithy rejection of the very social contact evoked by Berceo's lighthearted portrayal of Jewish and Christian children at play reveals Vincent's own consciousness of the frequency with which such situations obtained in many parts of Iberia, and particularly in his native Valencia.[5] His sharp response can be ascribed to many things: its hortatory, rather than narrative, context; its concern with whole communities of actual Jews, rather than a fictitious individual; and its foundation in the enormous social pressures caused by high rates of Christian conversion among the Jews of Aragon at the end of the fourteenth century.[6] Yet, like Berceo's poem, Vincent's denunciation is effective both in evoking a convincing social context and in elucidating a point of view that must have been widely shared. Moreover, like Berceo's more casual, if also calculating, evocation of the everyday friendliness between two faith groups, Vincent's markedly harsher response has just as sturdy a foundation in medieval Iberian thought.[7]

These two texts contribute to a broad tapestry of evidence that offers modern scholars insight into the complex, mutable relationships formed by Christians and Jews in the northern kingdoms of medieval Iberia, and particularly into the place held by Jews in a Christian world that during the central and late Middle Ages found itself in an especially dynamic state of development. The study of these relationships involves not just the untangling of the many theological threads by which the two faith groups had been both yoked and differentiated for centuries, but also the confrontation of their intertwined social fortunes in Iberia and the extraordinary variety of results that these could engender. Against this complexity, even such contradictory documents as those with which this chapter opened offer invaluable insight: when examined closely against the backdrop of

Spain's equally complex medieval history, they can elucidate the conceptions, stereotypes, social structures, and patterns of behavior underpinning these relationships. In this sense, they say as much about the complexity of their cultural matrix as they do about the fragmentary nature of the evidence through which medievalist historians now seek to understand it.

Yet the medieval Iberian tapestry still lacks many threads. Chief among these is the evidence that still remains to be provided by visual culture, an area that at this writing has only recently begun to be incorporated seriously into the study of Christian-Jewish relations in medieval Spain. That visual images can offer significant insight into the medieval relationship between Christians and Jews in particular has been demonstrated abundantly for other areas of Europe, where a dynamic recent scholarship has shown how images in sculpture, stained glass, and particularly manuscripts addressed and helped to shape relationships between Christians and Jews that have until this point been studied primarily through the evidence of texts.[8]

The potential of visual culture to enrich the study of medieval Iberia specifically is suggested by a pair of images that may seem as contradictory as the two passages with which this chapter opened. Like them, these images derive from larger works of contrasting context and function, and they manifest commensurately vivid differences in their representation of Jewish figures and their place within Christian society. The first image appears in the *Libro de ajedrez, dados y tablas* (Escorial, MS T.I.6), a richly illustrated manual concerning chess and other board games that was produced for King Alfonso X of Castile (r. 1252–84) toward the end of his reign, in 1283.[9] One of about 150 illustrations depicting diverse combinations of players, including Christians, Muslims, and Jews of various ranks, the image on folio 75r depicts a Jew and a Christian engaged in a game of backgammon, their board tilted vertically to display the positions of the game pieces to the reader (fig. 1). The Christian wears a slight smile as his right hand follows the dice he has just thrown, while the Jew points intently at the game board, counting his opponent's score.

Both figures are distinguished by visual conventions that would become increasingly common in Iberia from the last quarter of the thirteenth century onward. The Christian appears in three-quarter view; he is blond and bareheaded, with a light and neatly trimmed beard. The Jew wears a close-fitting, slightly pointed cap and a dark, wispy beard; his profile orientation emphasizes his enlarged eyes, strongly marked brows, and sharp nose, features reminiscent of the exaggerated physiognomies already assigned to Jews elsewhere in western European imagery. The incorporation of these features is subtle: they blur persistently with more individualized, portraitlike traits that seem to identify the figure as a specific individual, perhaps a member of Alfonso's court—as indeed a number of these figures may be.[10] His individualization, his intent but tranquil expression, and his relaxed interaction with his opponent suggest that the signs that mark this figure as a Jew functioned primarily in a denotative sense, signifying his identity but lacking the negative or alienating nuances so often implicit in such features.[11] His differences of dress and physiognomy from the Christian courtier deepen, if anything, the egalitarian

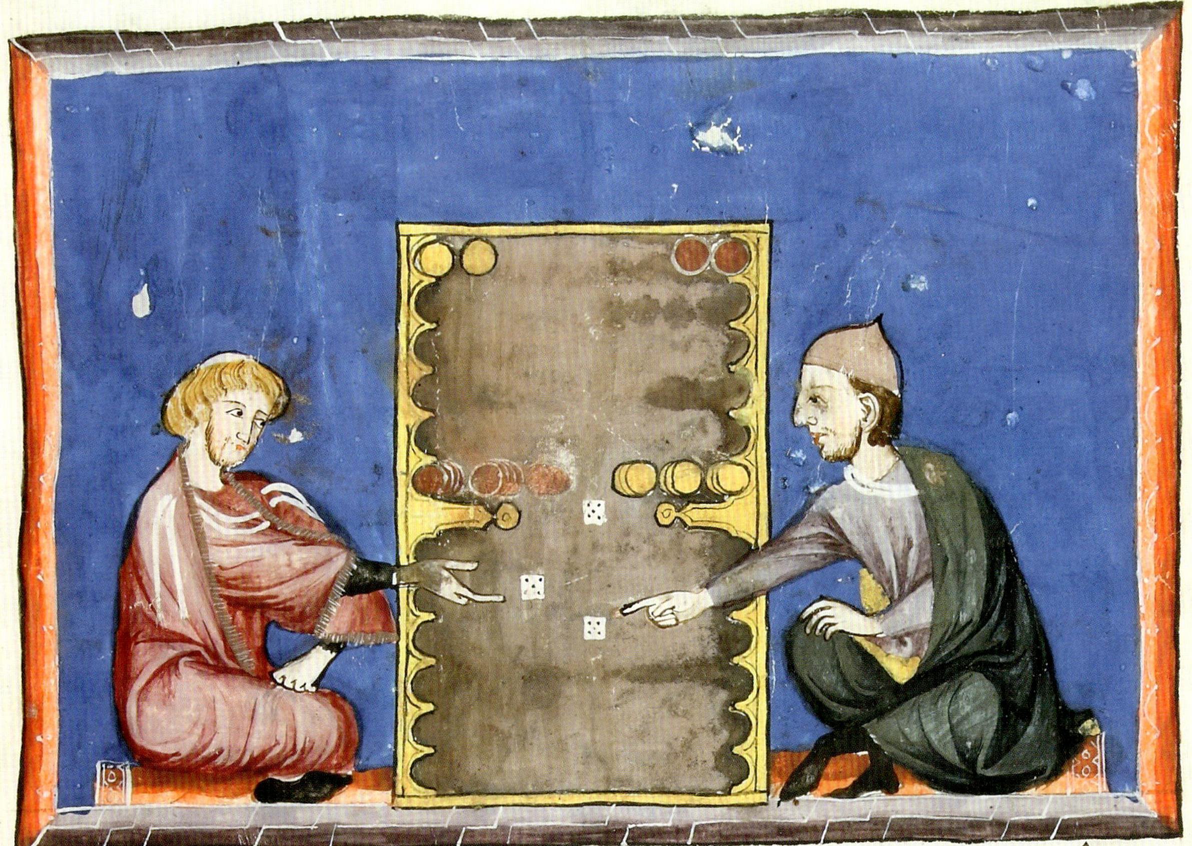

Este es el iuego que llaman el seys dos ⁊ as.

Otro iuego ay que llaman el seys dos ⁊ as. ¶ Et entablan los iogadores en la una quadra del tablero. ⁊ el que uence la batalla a la mano. deue poner sos quinze tablas en esta guisa en la casa del seys. ⁊ de dentro del tablero en la una quadra ocho tablas ⁊ en la casa del dos en essa misma q̃dra quatro tablas ⁊ en la del as tres. ¶ Et ell otro iogador deue poner las suyas en essa misma quadra en la casa del cinco ⁊ del quatro. ⁊ del tria en cadauna cinco cinco tablas. ¶ Et por que aquel que uence la batallas a las casas del seys dos ⁊ as: llaman a este iuego assi. ¶ Et deue iogar primero ⁊ tomar las mas casas que pudiere en la otra quadra que esta de lado. ¶ Et ell otro que iogara empos el otrossi tomara las mas casas q̃ pudiere en essa misma quadra. ¶ Et si en tomando las casas fiziere ell uno all otro una tabla o mas. deue las tornar no a la quadra quel esta en derecho ni a la casa quel esta de lado mas a la quel esta en pospunta. ¶ Et desq̃ las metiere en esta quadra deuelas traer en derredor por todas las quadras fasta aq̃lla quadra donde se deuen leuar. ¶ Et el que mas ayna las leuare ganara el iuego. ¶ Et este es el departimiento deste iuego. que de suso diximos.

FIG. 1
Jew and Christian playing backgammon. *Libro de ajedrez, dados y tablas.* Real Biblioteca de El Escorial, Madrid, MS T.I.6, fol. 75r. © Patrimonio Nacional.

quality of the image: seemingly no more concerned with cultural difference than were Berceo's schoolboys, the two grown men play together just as the aristocratic Christians and Jews of Alfonso's court probably did.[12]

A contrast to this ludic image is provided by an illustration from a late fourteenth-century Catalan manuscript of the *Breviari d'amor*, written by the Franciscan monk Matfre Ermengaud (London, British Library, Yates Thompson MS 31, fol. 132r). Composed in Occitan around 1288, this encyclopedic exposition on the various forms of spiritual love, from love of children to love of God, had quickly gained a cycle of illustrations closely tied to its idiosyncratic text. By the first decades of the fourteenth century, both the text and its images had been transmitted to Iberia, where they came to be produced repeatedly in both Catalan and Castilian translations.[13] The imagery in question appears in a section of the text that concerns the refusal of Jews to accept Christianity's fulfillment of Old Testament prophecy. Like others in this section, this illumination accompanies Ermengaud's vernacular commentary on the short passages of Hebrew scripture, each copied with painstaking care into its own text panel, that appear in the margins (fig. 2).

Two of the three illustrative panels set within the text columns concretize Ermengaud's charge that the Jews have remained blind to the New Law implicit in their own scriptures. Each depicts a doleful Jewish figure, enveloped in the red, hooded cloak and narrow slippers by which Jews were commonly denoted in the visual traditions of the Aragonese Crown, and each is beset by eager demons. In the first panel, two demons with curved goat's horns draw a blindfold tightly across the eyes of the Jew, who raises one hand ineffectually as a small codex droops in the other. In the second, a demon with large bat wings covers the ears of a heavily bearded Jew as he gazes uncomprehendingly at the scroll in his hands. A third panel in the lower left corner provides a counterpoint to these befuddled figures, depicting Saint Jerome gazing at his own long scroll with placid comprehension.

These are very different Jews from the mild-featured backgammon player of Alfonso's manuscript. Stripped of individualizing features and identified primarily by the generic markers of slippers, hood, and beard, these figures stand for all Jews in their torpid inability to comprehend the higher truths behind the letters of their own sacred texts.[14] The demons'

FIG. 2
Demons blinding Jews. *Breviari d'amor.* British Library, Yates Thompson 31, fol. 132r. © The British Library Board. All rights reserved 01/05/2011.

oppressive gestures call to mind the litany of grievances over Jewish resistance to the truths of their Law that had become a constant in medieval Christian polemics, as crisply exemplified by the reproachful words of the French Cluniac Peter the Venerable: "Open your eyes at last, open your ears, and be ashamed that you are clearly the only blind people in the world, the only deaf people to remain."[15] The agency of demons in perpetuating this Jewish insensibility, as we shall see, has a similarly rich ideological pedigree and an even wider cultural reach, since it evoked popular superstitions about Jewish association with the devil and necromancy that lay well beyond the limits of acceptable church doctrine.[16]

The contrastive visions of the Jewish-Christian relationship that these images present, like those offered by the two texts with which this chapter began, exemplify the diversity of roles played by Jews in the temporal and the spiritual worlds of Iberia's medieval Christians. They likewise bear with them cultural nuances accrued within their respective ideological frames: one image was shaped by the peculiar flexibility of an aristocratic court culture, the other by generations of exegesis, religious polemics, superstition, and popular lore. Each thus offers a perspective on the Jewish-Christian relationship in Iberia that is very rich in potential and that deserves incorporation into a wider scholarly discourse.

The present book aims to effect this incorporation by examining the potential of visual imagery to enrich modern understanding of the place and perception of Jews in the Christian kingdoms of medieval Spain during the twelfth through mid-fourteenth centuries, during and just after the most active phase of the phenomenon that is imperfectly, but for this period justifiably, labeled the "Reconquest."[17] My efforts are grounded in the belief that the scrutiny of such imagery can expand and refine, to an extent impossible through study of texts alone, modern understanding of the ways in which Jews figured in the Iberian Christian imagination, and of the ways in which these ideas were expressed and reinforced during the central and late Middle Ages. This period, as we shall see, was one of particular dynamism for medieval Iberian Christians, whose growing hegemony within the Iberian Peninsula and deepening engagement with European culture outside it prompted widespread changes in their perceptions of, and behavior toward, the religious minorities with which they had shared space for so long. At the same time, it heralded

Nostra dona fo figurada en la uergua de aaron.

ויניח משה את כל
המטות לפני יי באהל
העדות ויהי ממחר
ויבא משה אל אהל העדות
והנה פרח מטה אהרן
לבית לוי ויוצא פרח
ויצץ ציץ ויגמול
שקדים ויראו ויקחו
איש מטהו

Dix moyses q̄ la uergua de aaron en lo tabernacle p(er)uitut de deu sens humor de t(er)ra flori e feu fuyles e fruyt.

Lo iueu encegat p(er) enten.

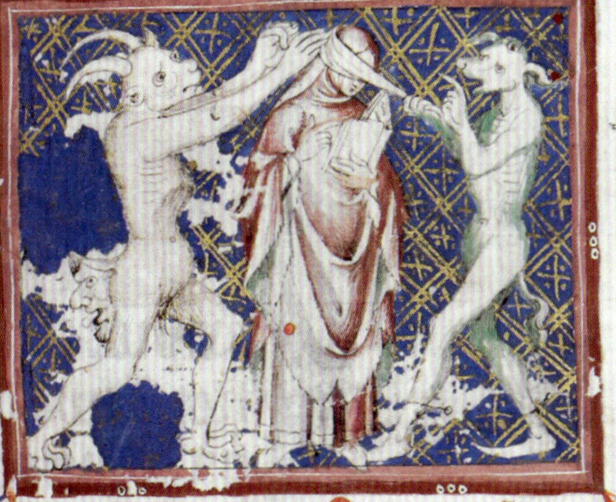

Ieronimus.

Quod beata maria debet de(us) mu(n)di parere fuit ostensum ezechieli in figura illum cap(itulo)

Dixit ezechiel et conuertit me ad uiam porte sanctuarii exterioris que respiciebat ad orientem et erat clausa et dixit d(omi)n(u)s ad me. Porta hec clausa erit et no(n) aperietur et uir no(n) transibit p(er) ea(m). q(uonia)m d(omi)n(u)s deus isr(ae)l ingressus est per eam.

Que nostra dona deguees esser uerge en figura deu e fo monstrat a ezechiel propheta en figura de la p(re)sent [illegible] capitol.

החיצון הפונה קדים
והוא סגור ויאמר
יי אלי השער הזה
סגור יהיה לא יפתח
ואיש לא יבא

Dix ezechiel yo giue a la una de la porta del santuary de fores q(ue) reguarda uers orie(n)t e era closa. e dix n(ost)re senyor a mi. Aquesta porta sera closa e ho(m) no passara p(er) ella. car n(ost)re senyor deus de isr(ae)l es passat p(er) ella. Lo iueu encegat no entén la figura.

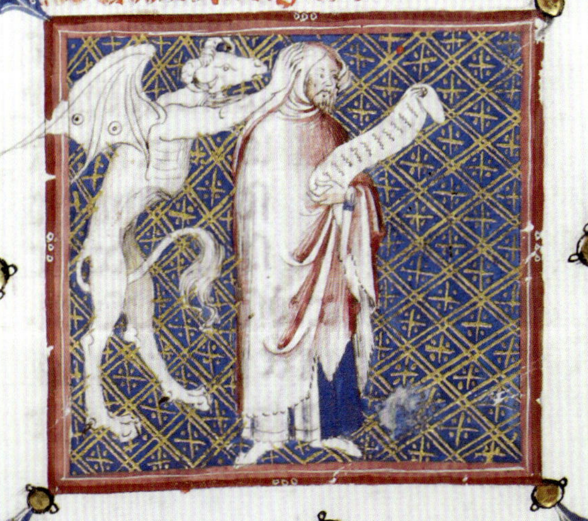

significant changes for the Jews of the peninsula, whose status under both Muslim and Christian majorities, while neither static nor monolithic, would be irreversibly reshaped by the new Christian dominance. It is in visual culture, I believe, that this transformation can be traced at its richest and most expansive.

The broader study of religious and cultural relationships in Christian Spain has reached a point at which work of this kind can be particularly fruitful. Shifting from the wide, teleological perspective characteristic of much early scholarship, recent historians of medieval Iberian cultural relations have begun to refine such arguments by sharpening their focus to specific historical events, sites, monuments, and issues, an approach that permits closer attention to the variability of conditions and forces that obtained in a land that was far from unified in politics, culture, or language. The most successful of these studies have scrutinized the dynamics of individual communities to elucidate Christian perceptions of religious minorities in medieval Spain and to understand how such perceptions affected daily relationships.[18]

David Nirenberg has argued for the importance of this shift as a corrective to the distorted perspectives forged by those who, on the one side, have presented the history of Jews in Spain as a gradually progressive decline paralleling that of Jews in western Europe as a whole, and those who, on the other, have emphasized episodes of social tolerance and cultural exchange as evidence of a fundamentally peaceful coexistence that, until the fifteenth century at least, was marred only exceptionally by interreligious tension.[19] The latter have taken Américo Castro's classic concept of *convivencia,* originally intended to acknowledge a more variable coexistence and exchange of cultural and especially linguistic forms, to an optimistic, misleading extreme, using it to imply the existence of a peaceful pluralism.[20]

The interpretive difficulties posed by Spain's complex political and cultural history clearly render this polarization untenable. In a land divided unstably among feuding Christian and Muslim political authorities, both of which hosted a Jewish minority that lived for centuries under a very wide range of circumstances, social relationships and attitudes varied widely, and they could change as quickly as a border shifted or a castle fell.[21] The resultant diversity demands the scrutiny of a great range and depth of evidence, and recent scholarship on Iberian cultural relations has responded by looking beyond traditional disciplinary boundaries in order to analyze legal and ecclesiastical texts, court and economic records, theological and philosophical works, and even literature and drama as grounds for a more textured conception of the ways in which Jews figured in a changing Christian worldview. The result has been a fuller and certainly more accurate picture of medieval Iberian life than was offered by more conventionally framed studies, a picture that opens the way to the important contributions to be made by the study of visual culture.[22]

Despite its inherent anachronism in a medieval context, I have chosen to use the term "visual culture" alongside terminology more traditional to the field of medieval Iberian studies. While for medieval artists and viewers the term's dependence upon a perceived division between "high" and "low" art would have been of questionable relevance, for modern readers more accustomed to such a division it is a usefully expansive descriptor in that it emphasizes the extraordinary breadth of visual forms that will be examined here, from deluxe court manuscripts and limestone sculptures to lusterware dishes and hasty scribal doodles.[23] Because the makers and viewers of such works expanded well beyond the literate royal and religious circles from which much other historical evidence has tended to emanate, study of this wide range of objects provides a perspective on the Jewish-Christian relationship in Spain to which traditional textual sources may not fully attest, and with this a chance to perceive more accurately the textures and complexities of medieval Iberian society: its popular tensions and local habits; its stereotypes; its ingrained superstitions.

The present book undertakes to do just this for a pivotal period of Iberian history, stretching from the last decades of the twelfth century into the middle of the fourteenth. This period represented a phase of dramatic social change for the Iberian Christian kingdoms, whose increasingly organized efforts to claim Muslim-held lands in the course of their Reconquest had begun to see marked success. During the twelfth and early thirteenth centuries, key military victories expanded Christian political authority over great swaths of new land in central and southern Spain, and with this over thousands of new Muslim and Jewish subjects.[24] The need to assimilate these religious minorities in a manner that would preserve their social and economic utility without threatening the stability of Christian rule became a perpetual preoccupation for their northern conquerors. So too, under the influence of a church increasingly active in the drive to eradicate heterodoxy in all forms, did the desire to articulate theologically the place of these minority religions with respect to Christianity. In both endeavors, as this book will show, Iberian rulers and theologians alike found ammunition in the texts, practices, and images of their nearest European neighbors, where the lack of religious minorities in equally significant numbers had done little to discourage an explosion of polemics, legislation, and restrictive social practices aimed at controlling such groups' status in both theology and public life.

The tensions that accompanied such changes bore heavily on all of Spain's inhabitants, but perhaps never more poignantly than on Iberia's Jews, who since the Roman era had survived, and sometimes thrived, as a minority within both Christian and Muslim spheres.[25] In both cases, Jewish status had depended in great part upon how the ruling culture understood and attempted to control both perceived and actual differences between itself and its minority populations. Jews living in recently assimilated Christian lands now found themselves part of a transformed and irregular social landscape, within which their perceived value as an administrative and economic resource was easily overbalanced by suspicion of their acculturation to Muslim ways and their rejection of the majority faith.[26] The complexity of their situation provoked an equally complex Christian response, which was driven above all by the need to craft a new conception of Jews and their faith that would function effectively within this radically transformed world. This response can be observed on many fronts, from legal initiatives and religious polemic to social practices and literature. It is also attested, however, by a new wealth of visual imagery—found in manuscripts, sculpture, ceramics, and other media—that was generated by and for the newly confident Christian majority during this pivotal phase. These images, and the unique perspective that they offer on the transformed relationships of Jews and Christians during this time, will be the focus of this book.

The Study of Visual Culture and Medieval Jewish-Christian Relations

Since the appearance in 1966 of Bernhard Blumenkranz's influential study of the depiction of Jews in Christian art,[27] a number of publications have addressed the ways in which Christian representations of Jews help to illuminate the attitudes and day-to-day realities that characterized the dealings of the two medieval communities. To date, such studies have focused primarily on northern European medieval culture, if also recognizing, and in doing so often deliberately avoiding, the social and cultural complexities of the Iberian arena. They nonetheless provide a usefully adaptable model for the extension of this work into the Iberian Peninsula.

One of the most important claims inherent in this literature concerns the rise, during the twelfth and thirteenth centuries, of a newly hostile visual language that seems to parallel the heightened religious tensions felt throughout Europe during this period. The emergence of such signs has been related by many to new social and economic pressures that in this period strained an already complicated relationship between Jews and Christians in western Europe. These included widespread resentment of the new Jewish monopoly on moneylending as canon law increasingly restricted Christian usury; the imposition, formalized at the Fourth Lateran Council in 1215, of identifying dress to prevent Jews and Christians from mingling too freely; and increasingly intense fears of Jewish predation in the form of infanticide, well poisoning, and host desecration. Accompanying and inspiring these social tensions, as Jeremy Cohen in particular has shown, was a widespread theological shift from an Augustinian view of Judaism as the root of a vital new faith to the condemnation of Jews as Christ-killers and heretics.[28]

For medieval France, England, and Germany, the regions on which most modern study has focused to date, the analysis of visual culture has both deepened and revolutionized modern understanding of these developments, but for Iberia such study has lagged. There the scrutiny of visual and material culture has tended to focus more fully on elucidating the relationship between the peninsula's politically dominant cultures of Islam and Christianity, for which abundant visual evidence exists and which has understandable appeal for modern scholars.[29] To direct similar questions to the Jewish-Christian relationship in Spain is equally feasible, as has been well attested by several important museum exhibitions on Jewish life in Spain that have appeared since the early 1990s.[30] It has been attested as well by consequential scholarship on art produced by Jews, which amply demonstrates such works' potential to elucidate the status of Jews within a culturally Christian majority whose sense of self-identity was expressed with increasing force in the central and latter Middle Ages.[31] However, the same depth has not been attained in the study of how such developments might be represented in Christian-made works of art in Iberia, and especially of the complex ways in which such images intersected with broader social and cultural trends during key periods such as the one to be considered here. More often, such scholarship has taken the form of broad surveys whose extended chronological focus impedes a synthetic view.[32]

The present study aims to be both tighter in chronological span and more expansive in cultural and disciplinary scope. It will examine the birth of a new visual language used to represent Jews, their faith, and their place within Christian society as it began to emerge just as and just after the Christian successes of the Reconquest reached their height in the late twelfth and early thirteenth centuries. It will posit that these two developments were by no means coincidental: that the explosion of new ways of representing—and, by extension, of new ways of conceptualizing—Jews and Judaism in Iberia was facilitated by, and often directly responsive to, the near-universal social and ideological upheavals that accompanied the rise to power of Christian rulers and church authorities throughout the peninsula during this period. Recognizing that the origins of this imagery often lay well outside the Iberian sphere, it will examine the importation and adaptation of these predominantly foreign forms as a key aspect of this response. Its ultimate goal is to trace conclusively the ways in which visual culture articulated, supported, and even advanced the transformation of Jewish-Christian relationships in an equally transformed Iberia.

It is challenging, to say the least, to venture broadly synthetic conclusions about any aspect of culture in a land so diverse as medieval Christian Iberia. The northern kingdoms differed significantly from each other in everything from political organization to ethnic makeup and language, and individual local contexts could differ even more dramatically, prompting potentially very different medieval readings of images and objects that might to modern viewers seem similar. Because of this, my study will aim less for comprehensiveness or teleological momentum than for an analysis that is founded on the scrutiny of individual works within their equally individual social and cultural settings. Doing so, especially within the context of a deliberately tightened chronological frame, will permit a deeper examination of those examples that bear most fruitfully on this book's larger questions, teasing out the preoccupations and patterns necessary for a more textured understanding of them.

To analyze visual images in relation to community ideology is not, of course, the same thing as to analyze them as historical documents themselves. Images, like literature, present a constructed reality that draws freely on the perceptions and agenda of the artist and the prevailing expectations of his or her audience. The tendency of medieval artists to rely on convention and tradition, rather than direct observation, renders the "archaeological" reading to which medieval images are sometimes submitted very risky. Rather than succumbing to the temptation to read such images as veritable snapshots of medieval life, we must recognize that they testify primarily to what Iberian Christians, and then perhaps only one or some Christians, merely thought about their Jewish neighbors: how they understood Jews to function, and what they thought they represented, within their own world and worldview.

This notion draws substantially upon Jeremy Cohen's famous concept of the "hermeneutical Jew": a conceptual image of the Jew as constructed not on the basis of lived experience, but "in the discourse of Christian theology."[33] Whereas Cohen's hermeneutical Jew was formed within the writings and preaching of Christian churchmen and within a primarily theological sphere, a flowering of scholarship inspired by this argument has proven that its impact could be felt well beyond the boundaries of traditional theology. Visual images of Jews, just as much as literary, historical, and conceptual ones, underwent a hermeneutical process of their own as they were made meaningful to the readers, hearers, and viewers for whom they were intended, and in the course of that process their meaning could change in accordance with the varying preoccupations or anxieties of this audience.[34] The constructed character of the images analyzed here, which responds as much to traditional ideology as to the needs, values, and perceptions of a contemporaneous viewer, thus remains central to our understanding of how these images reveal the transformations of medieval Iberian society during this pivotal historical phase.

The Historical Frame

The chronological frame encompassed by this study opens at the end of the twelfth century, a moment marked both by a lull between two highly active phases of the Reconquest and by the emergence of the first Christian images in which the Jewishness of particular figures and themes first seems to have earned the conscious attention of patrons and artists. It ends with the onset of the Black Plague ca. 1348, the social disruptions of which so transformed the place of Jews in medieval Iberian society, as elsewhere in Europe, as to warrant a conclusion here.[35] This span thus encompasses the most territorially expansive period of the Reconquest in the early thirteenth century and the new settlement that followed this expansion, prompting an unprecedented shuffling of relationships between the conquering Christians and the religious Others with whom this process brought them into increased contact. Just as the Crusades provoked for Christendom a new awareness of the differences between itself and the cultures beyond its Mediterranean boundaries, the Reconquest seems to have prompted a new drive to explore such differences within medieval Spain.

By the end of the twelfth century, the Christian kingdoms of Iberia had reached a turning point with regard to both their individual political and cultural formation and their relationships with the rest of Europe.[36] The success of increasingly unified attempts to capture Muslim-held territory for the expanding northern kingdoms of Leon-Castile, Navarre, and Aragon had accelerated markedly after centuries of slow and sporadic effort. In the five preceding centuries following the Muslim invasion of Visigothic Iberia in 711–14 C.E., Christian and Muslim polities had both fought and forged alliances in the struggle for political stability. Each had treated its religious minorities, including the Jews, who had lived in Spain at least since the late Roman period, with everything from grudging tolerance to outright persecution.[37] Now, following the collapse of the Umayyad caliphate in the eleventh century and the military successes of the Christian kingdoms in the twelfth, the balance of power had shifted decisively.

By the first decades of the thirteenth century, more than half of the Iberian Peninsula, along with substantial populations of Muslims and Jews, had come to rest in the hands of Christian rulers. By 1248, this would increase to encompass all but the small tributary kingdom of Granada at the southern tip of the peninsula. The kings of these suddenly expanded realms now looked northward toward their counterparts in other European kingdoms, not only for sources of money and manpower in the conquest and settlement of previously Muslim lands, but also for cultural models in the formation of a proper Christian realm. Rulers intermarried increasingly with the other royal houses of Europe, as did Fernando III of Castile when he took Elizabeth of Hohenstaufen (known in Spain as Beatriz de Suabia) as a bride.[38] Iberian kings and their courtiers increasingly crossed the Pyrenees for education and diplomacy in foreign courts. When they returned, these travelers often brought with them both examples and producers of those courts' latest forms of cultural expression: writers, troubadours, artists, and architects who mingled freely with the native physicians and philosophers of the Iberian courts to forge a culture newly transfigured by a European cultural stamp. In visual culture, this phenomenon is best exemplified in the great cathedrals of Burgos and Leon, both begun in the second quarter of the thirteenth century and modeled heavily on French Gothic examples.[39]

New contacts with Europe were effected along other routes as well. As early as the eleventh century, Iberian kings had encouraged monks from France, first Benedictines from Cluny but eventually also Cistercians, regular Augustinians, and other religious communities, to travel to Spain to aid in religious revival and reform.[40] The establishment of new monasteries, and the regularization of existing ones, was seen as essential to the stability of territories recently taken from Al-Andalus, as well as to the support of the historically profitable pilgrimage to Santiago de Compostela—itself a powerful highway for the transmission of culture and ideas.[41] From the thirteenth century onward, the introduction into Iberia of newly founded orders with a distinct missionizing agenda, chiefly Dominicans and Franciscans, heightened this effect, as did increasing trade with both northern Europe and the Mediterranean.[42] The twelfth through fourteenth centuries thus witnessed the importation into the Christian kingdoms of all manner of new cultural products from beyond the Pyrenees, including Romanesque and Gothic architectural forms, new kinds of liturgical performance, and a wide range of theological and secular literature.

These cultural importations carried with them conceptual ones, especially new ways of thinking about the world and the various peoples within it. In much of Europe, these conceptual patterns were marked by a century of engagement in the Crusades and by the deep concern of the Latin Church with heresy, both within its ranks and beyond them. Such phenomena added urgency to the threat, whether theological or social, that Judaism and Islam were seen to pose to western Christendom.[43] The church's expansive battle to control and convert or eliminate such nonbelievers was waged on many fronts, from theological polemics to an insistence first on the separation of non-Christian minorities, as at the Fourth Lateran Council in 1215, then on their outright elimination or conversion. Such efforts took root much earlier and more actively in countries like England, France, and Germany than they would in Iberia, where the long-standing coexistence of multiple religious cultures surely muted the perceived urgency of the church's concerns. Nonetheless, by the middle of the thirteenth century, with such developments as the entry of the Dominican Order into Spain, ecclesiastical efforts to purge and unify western Christendom had gained a foothold on the peninsula.

Christian Iberia's new openness to, even appetite for, ultra-Pyrenean culture included a receptiveness to new ideas about the place of Jews and other religious minorities within a majority Christian culture, just at a time when Europeans themselves were developing a new awareness of their relatively circumscribed place in a larger world and a new desire to clarify the terms of their own identity. Their intensifying discomfort with those who stood outside their cultural norms,[44] whether Muslims, Jews, heretics, lepers, Byzantines, or Tartars, would powerfully shape Iberian Christians' views of their own intercultural relationships.

The developments described here did not progress monolithically throughout Iberia: political, cultural, religio-ethnic, and linguistic differences among the Spanish kingdoms remained strong throughout this period, as is reflected also in the individualization of each one's legislative, social, and cultural history. These differences, as we shall see, often included sharp contrasts in policies toward, ideas about, and images of Jews, who themselves played different roles with respect to the populations of each polity. Such differences are particularly marked between the two most powerful and extensive Iberian crowns, that of Castile, unified with Leon from 1230 onward, and that of Aragon, which had merged with Catalunya in 1137 and absorbed the kingdom of Valencia after 1238. One challenge undertaken in this book is to recognize this variability as a component of broad conclusions that apply beyond a single realm.

Connections with Northern Europe

Because the changing status and perception of Jews in Iberia remained consistently intertwined with the conditions for Jews elsewhere in Latin Christendom, these developments must be outlined here as well. During the central Middle Ages, the position of Jews in Europe had reached its own turning point. Although the degree to which this should be viewed as a unified phenomenon might be questioned, a general deterioration of Christian tolerance for Jewish minorities has been documented in many European communities from the late eleventh century onward.[45] Jeremy Cohen and others have argued that during this period, the relatively benign Augustinian view that Jews were witnesses to Christian history whose continued presence on earth as "living letters of the law" was acceptable, even necessary, to a dominant Christian society was gradually replaced in Christian thinking by a heightened perception of Jews as actively antagonistic to Christians and their faith.[46] Central to this shift was a reconceptualization of Jews as outright enemies of Christianity—as killers of Christ, as heretics, as allies of the devil, and as authors of all manner of societal ills, from usury and plague to child murder.

This shift was not merely theological; it was accompanied by, and to some extent sprang from, other social, political, and economic factors that emerged during the same period: the increased mobility of medieval society with the rise of trade and pilgrimage; the repeated moral and economic setbacks of the Crusades; the development of large urban centers such as Paris, with their flourishing bourgeois classes; the growth of international trade; and the rise of a money economy. The place of Jews, along with that of other incompletely assimilated outgroups, within this precarious social order became increasingly difficult for many Christians to articulate and justify as their own social roles began to change, and a once tolerated, if disparaged, religious minority came to be perceived as threatening both the social hierarchy and the individuals who composed it. Some fears of Jews had a concrete foundation, as when the enforcement of usury laws prohibiting Christian lending at interest to other Christians left mainly Jewish lenders available in this role; others, such as the accusations of well poisoning or predation upon Christian children that emerged repeatedly from the twelfth century onward, drew on fantasy and rumor.[47] Both signaled a sea change in the terms on which Christians and Jews would interrelate for centuries to come.

This change may be most easily traced in the actions of political and ecclesiastical authorities. Many would point first to the watershed of the Fourth Lateran Council of 1215, in which rules regarding the visual differentiation of Jews from Christians by distinctive dress were among a number of efforts promulgated throughout Christendom to segregate Jews and other minorities.[48] Secular rulers, although often hesitant to pressure excessively a population from which they customarily derived significant financial profit, weighed in with their own increasingly restrictive legislation, which was often aimed at controlling not only social interaction but also economic and legal dealings between Christians and Jews. Yet in many areas mere separation was not seen as sufficient: papally sanctioned efforts to convert Jews through enforced sermons and other strategies found increasing support from secular authorities from the mid-thirteenth century onward.[49]

Ultimately, even these measures proved insufficient for many European rulers, for whom the outright expulsion of Jews from their lands represented a means of simultaneously eliminating a vexing minority problem and annexing their remaining wealth and goods. Jews were expelled from England in 1290 and from France several times before their permanent expulsion in 1394; small local expulsions also took place in German and Italian lands over the course of the fifteenth century. Such policies eventually reached Iberia, as is well known, although Jewish populations survived in the kingdoms of Aragon and Castile until 1492, in Portugal until 1497, and in Navarre until 1498.[50]

The tightening policies of church and state authorities were interwoven with increased tensions at the popular level as well. Indeed, the most significant episodes of popular violence against Jews in Europe had roots in local reaction to political and religious developments: the infamous attacks on Jewish communities along the Rhine in 1096 were perpetrated by Christian troops just setting out on the First Crusade, while the accusations of ritual murder that emerged throughout Europe following the mysterious death of William of Norwich in 1144 were often fostered, as Gavin Langmuir has shown, by local clergy.[51] The latter charge was only one of several key *topoi* that began to emerge in popular imaginings about Jews as expressed in local rumor and superstition. Now not simply killers of Christ, nor even merely pragmatic obstacles to the running of an orderly society, Jews became linked with more ominous stereotypes: allies of the devil, practitioners of black magic, and authors of all manner of societal ills, from usury and well poisoning to sexual deviance and child murder.[52] Whereas specific historical accusations of this kind are sometimes documented in legal texts or church records, such "actual" cases of Jewish predation on the Christian faithful had important conceptual analogues in the stereotypes and stock narratives that at this point began to emerge in other forms of verbal and visual expression, including religious philosophy and polemic; the narratives of liturgical drama, song, and poetry; and various forms of visual imagery. Such works, springing from a rich admixture of tradition, rumor, and fantasy, offer a fertile ideological backdrop against which to scrutinize the works of visual culture that are examined in this book.

Most of these developments found a place in medieval Christian Iberia, but here their extent and trajectory differed. Despite a powerful appetite for many things European, Spanish Christians seem to have been slower to adopt many of the policies and attitudes toward Jews that prevailed elsewhere. Moreover, despite the increased production and availability of religious polemics on the subject, as well as growing pressure from religious leaders both within and outside the peninsula, secular authorities within Spain often resisted imperatives to segregate or restrict Jewish communities. Exemptions from canon and local laws regarding distinctive Jewish dress that were firmly enforced elsewhere in Europe, for example, were routinely granted by the kings of both Aragon and Castile during the thirteenth century.[53] As we shall see, Iberian rulers, whose court retainers often included Jewish scholars and scientists and whose economic livelihood came to be tied closely to their Jewish communities, could also be highly skeptical or even dismissive of popular accusations against "their" Jews.

Such reactions must be attributed less to such leaders' enlightened attitudes than to their interest in maintaining a status quo that had thus far served both Crowns well. The taxation of the Jewish *aljamas* consistently brought in welcome revenue, while the Jews' knowledge of Arabic and engagement in commerce were of significant utility in settling and administering newly conquered Muslim lands.[54] For scholars who, like Alfonso X, possessed loftier cultural goals, Jews also represented a key cog in the machinery that brought Eastern philosophy and science into the Latin-speaking sphere.[55] Jews simply represented too useful a resource for their survival to be jeopardized by excessive external pressure.

At the popular level, too, Iberian Jews enjoyed a stabler existence than did their ultra-Pyrenean counterparts for much of the Middle Ages. Anti-Jewish violence on a large scale was rare here before the end of the fourteenth century, and in at least one instance an attack on the Jews of Toledo by foreign soldiers preparing for the battle of Las Navas de Tolosa was stopped by local troops.[56] Yet at the same time, there is some evidence that popular society, and the clergy that served it, was more permeable to the shifts in ideology so rapidly transforming northern Europeans' views of religious relations. This is witnessed, as we shall see in the next chapter, by the early assimilation of anti-Jewish narratives already popular elsewhere in Europe, like the story of Theophilus and the Jewish boy of Bourges, both translated into the vernacular by Gonzalo de Berceo in the middle of the thirteenth century, as well as by the slow but eventual penetration of once-rejected claims of Jewish violence by the beginning of the next century.

The apparent Iberian resistance to anti-Jewish policies and attitudes changed dramatically at the middle of the fourteenth century. Already weakened by successive years of famine in the first half of the century, the population of northern Spain fell easy victim to the Black Death, which struck Europe with enormous force in the year 1348.[57] Civil war between Castile and Aragon, as well as internal battles over the succession to the Castilian crown, caused widespread social disruption and economic pressures that emboldened an already rebellious nobility to resist the kings' attempts to exert power. All this had disastrous results for Iberia's already pressed minorities, not least of which was the unprecedented wave of pogroms that began in Seville in 1391 and spread to nearly every major Iberian city that same year.[58] These events left both the social landscape and the visual culture of Spain very different indeed from what they had been over the preceding two centuries, and for this reason they mark the end of the period examined in this study.

Tracing the struggle of Christian rulers, church leaders, and the Christian populace to reconcile the conflicted position of Jews in a changing social order and in the process to define their own status within it is a central goal of this book, and that struggle is closely reflected by the changes that took place in Iberian visual culture precisely during the period in question. Not only do Christian images of Jews and other outgroups become more abundant from the late twelfth century onward, but they also display an increasing self-consciousness and complexity: characteristically generic images, such as the beardless, tunic-clad Jews of the early twelfth-century Girona Creation Tapestry (fig. 3), now gave way to more deliberately structured and hostile images responsive to specific points of tension between the Jewish minority and its increasingly dominant Christian overlords.

One of the signal characteristics of such imagery is its strong link with the visual traditions of the wider European arena. Iberia's centuries of shared hegemony between Muslim and Christian rulers, its geographical dislocation from the European mainstream, and its proximity to north Africa and the *Dar-al-Islam* had resulted in a culture that was more layered and idiosyncratic than that in many areas of Europe. However, the successful expansion of the Christian kingdoms into traditionally Islamic lands in the twelfth and thirteenth centuries, and the involvement of French and other northern rulers in these efforts, now facilitated a deepened engagement in many aspects of European culture. As we shall see, many although not all of the motifs and *topoi* employed by Iberian artists to construct their images of Jews, such as the "Jewish nose" and the deceptive usurer, had their

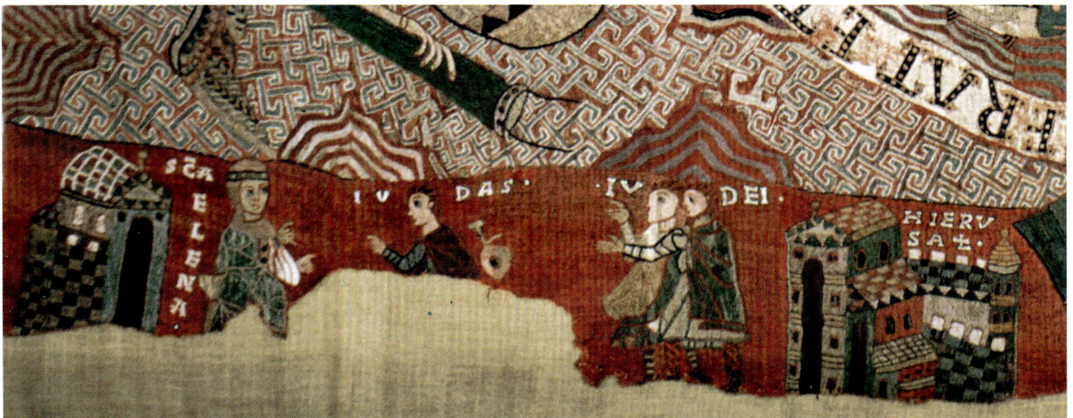

FIG. 3
Jews questioned by Helena. Detail of the Girona Creation Tapestry, Girona Cathedral. © Erich Lessing / Art Resource, NY.

origins in art outside the peninsula.[59] For the Christians of northern Iberia, changing ideas about Jews thus went hand in hand with a new cultural orientation, and by extension with changing ideas about themselves.

Given these developments, a central question of this book will be if, and if so how, Spanish Christian imaginings about Jews and their faith differed from the conceptions emerging concurrently elsewhere in Europe. If in Europe as a whole, as has been argued, a critical reversal in Christian attitude from general tolerance of Jews to a pattern of hostility toward them led to sharply increased social and economic restrictions, mass violence, and outright expulsion, did northern Iberia follow a similar conceptual trajectory? Or did the deep cultural, political, and linguistic differences that separated the medieval Christian kingdoms of Iberia from much of trans-Pyrenean Europe, not to mention the deep familiarity with Jewish culture that characterized at least the major urban centers of the kingdom, engender alternative viewpoints here? How did Iberian Christians conceive of the place of Jews in both the real and the theological world? And how did visual culture record and promote these new conceptions? Addressing these questions represents the first stage of an inquiry aimed at a fuller understanding of the means by which Iberian Christians negotiated their relationships with, and expressed their differences from, the Jews with whose presence they would continue to grapple until their expulsion at the end of the fifteenth century.

Jews, Christians, and Images in Medieval Iberia

The first of this book's central chapters traces the earliest, often sporadic efforts of Iberian artists to develop a visual lexicon capable of expressing prevailing preoccupations regarding Jews and their place in both temporal and salvation history. Initially, such signs took the form of widely known visual conventions that had been imported, virtually unaltered, from abroad and that served to point up long-held theological concerns, such as the question of Jewish involvement in the Crucifixion or disbelief in key doctrinal points. In time, and in tandem with the increasing efforts of political and religious authorities to more sharply demarcate social and cultural boundaries between Christians and Jews in general, these signs would come to be tailored more specifically to an Iberian milieu, with its particularized expectations and concerns. The insertion of new elements of Iberian Jewish dress, the manipulation of heretofore traditional symbols like Ecclesia and Synagoga, and overt references to doctrinal and social controversies that were particular to the Iberian sphere all contributed specialized meaning to these adopted signs.

Chapter 2 will also consider the Iberian response to popular and literary stereotypes, such as the greedy usurer or the beautiful Jewess, that drew on European visual traditions, textual exempla, sermons, poetry, and liturgical drama. Particular attention will be given to the question of which of these stereotypes seem to have been adopted readily and which were disregarded or even observably resisted. Asking not just whether and whence such themes were imported, but also when, how, and by whom, will reveal that these were by no means passive adoptions. Instead, Iberian patrons and artists approached such *topoi* with striking selectivity. The logical conclusion, that some formulae simply remained untenable in the Iberian visual lexicon, attests to the persistence of social and ideological differences between the Iberian kingdoms and their counterparts north of the Pyrenees in spite of their new cultural ties.

Chapter 3 considers the human figure as a site upon which Jewish alterity began to be inscribed and inflected by Iberian artists. Although such stereotyped Jewish features as an enlarged nose and long beard, widely used elsewhere in Europe by the end of the twelfth century, are found in both Castile and Aragon by the middle of the thirteenth, they do not always carry the overtly negative charge that characterizes many ultra-Pyrenean works. Instead, as in the backgammon scene examined earlier in this chapter, they sometimes seem to have functioned as essentially neutral descriptors much like the formulaic likenesses often used by both Christian and Muslim Iberian artists to denote Africans or Arabs. Nonetheless, such morally neutral images often coexisted with others in which a negative value is quite clear, attesting to the variability with which Iberian artists deployed these and other physiognomic and somatic conventions. This dichotomy also introduces the controversial possibility that, at this very early date, Jewishness was coming to be seen in Iberia as a manifestation of religious identity that was to some extent physiological, foreshadowing early modern Spanish concerns regarding *limpieza de sangre,* or "purity of blood."

Chapter 4 analyzes a phenomenon with a powerful legacy in medieval Spain: representations of Jews that are shaded by references to Muslims and Islam. The continuing presence of Muslims in high-medieval Iberia, both as rulers of a rapidly shrinking Islamic polity in the south and as an often populous minority in the Christian north, necessarily affected how Iberian Christians and Jews constructed their own cultural identities. The impact of these political and social stressors on Christian perceptions of Spain's *other* cultural Others, the Jews, can be seen in a number of works of art in which the line between Jewish and Muslim figures has been either unconsciously or deliberately blurred. Analysis of these elisions necessarily will remain attentive to their varied interpretive possibilities: while some seem to parallel similarly meaningful conflations in religious polemic and law, others may simply reflect the degree to which actual Iberian Jews had adopted recognizably Islamic cultural practices by this period.

Chapter 5 addresses the depiction of Jews in the abundantly illustrated codices of the *Cantigas de Santa María,* produced for Alfonso X of Castile toward the end of his reign. While these extraordinary and oddly precocious manuscripts might justifiably be presented as unique works in the history of medieval Iberian art, they in fact draw together many of the same thematic strands that so powerfully shaped the imagery of other works under consideration here. Rather than scrutinizing the *Cantigas de Santa María* illustrations, as previous studies sometimes have, as either literal catalogues of Castilian social life or the personal bully pulpit of their royal patron, this chapter will present this imagery instead as a collection of quasi-independent visual narratives that reveal their artists' struggle to reconcile highly abstracted European stereotypes of Jews with the immediate social experience of thirteenth-century Castilians. The multiple voices revealed during this process, as we shall see, speak powerfully of the tensions between authoritative and popular that were central to the production of many of the images in which the Jewish-Christian relationship would be negotiated during this period.

Ideally, the study of Jews in Iberian art and thought would extend beyond the Christian realms to examine Islamic Spain as well. Although few if any Islamic visual representations of Jews exist, ideas about Jews and Judaism among the Muslims of Al-Andalus shaped the ideas of Iberian Christians in ways too powerful to be overlooked. At the same time, however, the study of Jewish status in Islamic thought both generally and in Al-Andalus in particular and the study of Jews in western Christendom draw on such a different range of sources and disciplinary methods that it would be difficult to encompass both in a single volume.[60] Thus, while my study will draw upon the Islamic material whenever relevant and possible, its center necessarily will remain in the Christian kingdoms of the Iberian north.

The contradictory messages inherent in the texts and images with which this chapter began speak to the depth that the study of images can lend to modern understanding of the shifting historical fortunes of the Jews in Reconquest Iberia, of the changing Christian perspective that lay behind these events, and above all of the extraordinary variability of the changes that took place. As we shall see, alterations in the Christian perceptions of Jews did not emerge at the same rate, nor with equal vigor, in all areas of Iberian society. Instead, they followed varying trajectories within each kingdom, and even more within the varied ecclesiastical, popular, and royal circles to which they were made available. Each of these communities possessed its own motivations for the relationships it forged with the minority cultures with which it came into contact, and each found its own way of expressing these concerns.

Despite their formal, functional, and regional variety—or indeed because of it—the images examined in this book have the potential to furnish a more extensive and authentic view of the changing Jewish-Christian relationship in Spain than more traditional historical evidence allows. While many works, like the luxury manuscripts that make up a high percentage of the objects examined in the following chapters, were produced for royal or ecclesiastical patrons and might reasonably be taken to reflect an elite point of view, their artists often had more direct experience of the mentality outside the castle walls, and they sometimes drew upon a far greater diversity of sources, from clerical preaching to popular superstition, than their aristocratic patrons might have imagined. Other works, such as the scribal doodles considered primarily in chapter 3, will offer an even more direct glimpse into the ways in which Jews and their culture were seen by segments of society that only rarely recorded their perceptions in written or visual form. Taken together, such works promise an enriched understanding of the Iberian view of Jews in this period.

In bringing to light works of art whose significance has eluded sustained scholarly attention, in examining the intersections of these objects with the nonvisual arts and texts that surrounded them, and in setting this inquiry against the idiosyncratic social landscape of Iberia's Christian kingdoms during and following the apex of the Reconquest, this study seeks to add depth and texture to an investigative process that is already well advanced in many respects. My hope is that in demonstrating how Iberia's newly preeminent Christians reframed and articulated their understanding of the Jewish place in a rapidly changing political and social arena, this work will also clarify how Iberian society came to redefine itself through such understanding—a redefinition so radical that, in the wake of the pogroms of 1391, the Portuguese-Jewish ethicist Solomon Alami could lament that Iberia's Christians had rendered his once-assimilated people "aliens in their midst."[61]

2

TOPOS AND NARRATIVE

NEW SIGNS AND STORIES FOR IBERIAN JEWS

A lateral panel in the retable dedicated to St. Stephen from Santa María de Gualter, attributed to the Catalan artist Jaume Serra and now in the Museu Nacional d'Art de Catalunya in Barcelona, endows the saint's persecutors with a gamut of familiar Jewish signs (fig. 4). Distinguished from the fair-skinned, smooth-featured martyr Stephen by their dark complexions, bifurcated beards, exaggeratedly long noses, and sagging hoods, they grimace and gesture disjointedly, tearing up pages of their Hebrew texts in fruitless objection to the saint's preaching. Although these features were by the late fourteenth century firmly established in Iberian visual tradition, their roots lay in a semiotic vocabulary developed centuries earlier in other parts of Latin Europe, especially England, France, and Germany, where they had already served to articulate new Christian conceptions of, and anxieties about, the proper place of Jews in a rapidly changing society.[1]

Such European images ranged widely in character, in complexity, and in the intensity with which they commented on the contemporaneous Jewish-Christian relationship. Some are seemingly straightforward: on a late twelfth-century copper-gilt and enamel portable altar from Westphalia, the exaggerated hawk noses and distinctive pointed hats of three Jews observing the Crucifixion simultaneously denote their identity and imply their guilt as disbelieving participants in the violence against Christ (fig. 5).[2] Others, such as the illuminations of the *Bibles moralisées,* offer richly multivalent commentary on the place of Jews in the Christian world (fig. 6).[3]

Among the most important conclusions to emerge from study of such images is the rarity with which specific visual motifs or formulae traditionally considered to be "anti-Jewish" bore fixed or formulaic meanings. Instead, like those of most medieval signs, their symbolic implications varied along with each work's physical, conceptual, and ideological context. Even visual signs that in Western art came to be associated strongly with Jews, such as beards, enlarged noses, pointed hats, or yellow clothing, continued simultaneously to designate other categories of persons—not just negative types, like fools or heretics, but also occasionally positive ones, such as Old Testament patriarchs.

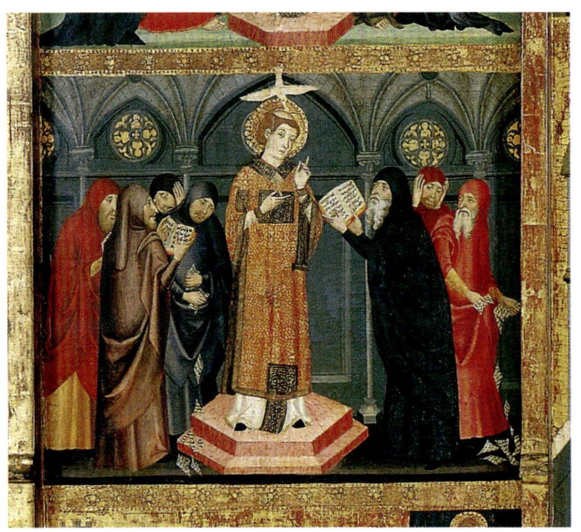

FIG. 4
Saint Stephen preaching to the Jews. Detail of Jaume Serra (?), Retable of St. Stephen from Santa María de Gualter. © MNAC, Museu Nacional d'Art de Catalunya, Barcelona. Photo: Calveras/Mérida/Sagristà.

Such signs thus could not automatically be assigned pejorative connotations; once established, they could perform a role that was primarily denotative and neutral, or even positive.[4]

Recognizing this multivalency is key to the study of Iberian depictions of Jews, which demonstrate especial flexibility in adapting and deploying a lexicon of visual signs that often originated abroad and thus were subject to a selective process consistent with the cultural fluidity of the northern Iberian kingdoms. Such adaptations were central to the function of these motifs for a local audience whose concerns and experience often differed sharply from those of the European mainstream. So too, as we shall see, was the outright rejection of other motifs that found little or no footing within the Iberian cultural frame.

Those formulae that did gain acceptance in high and late medieval Iberia emerged earliest and most enduringly in those areas of Christian Iberia, such as Catalunya, in which the Christian-Jewish relationship itself was subject to particularly sharp political, social, or religious tensions. This is hardly surprising, since Christian images that facilitated new ways of thinking about Jews presented an ideal vehicle for the negotiation of such conflicts. Although they must also be understood as part of the broad process of social readjustment that occurred throughout Europe in the high Middle Ages, the Iberian examples reveal themselves at times to be direct and even idiosyncratic local responses to a variety of highly specific contextual circumstances. An assessment of these responses stands to offer insight not just into the works themselves, but into social and ideological structures that shaped the fortunes of Iberian Jews at this pivotal historical moment.

This chapter will examine some of the earliest visual motifs to be imported or invented by Iberian Christian artists as they grappled with the need to articulate new ideas about Jews in the late twelfth through early fourteenth centuries. Although it will include such familiar northern European signs as the so-called Jew's hat or the stereotype of the Jewish usurer, it also will explore unique local motifs that express concerns peculiar to their Iberian milieu. The latter images draw on a rich and varied local tradition and powerfully illuminate Spanish Christians' evolving conceptions of their Jewish neighbors in a rapidly changing Iberia.

Because one especially sensitive set of Jewish signs—the formulaic exaggeration of facial features to create what has been called a "Jewish profile," as well as other physical idiosyncrasies that came to be associated with Jews—raises a host of its own issues when considered in relation to Iberian society, discussion of these will be reserved for a separate chapter.

Sartorial Signs

The development of a visual language aimed at articulating Jewish difference progressed sporadically in Iberia, emerging when called for by a particular ideological agenda, but easily forgone in cases where Jewish presence or identity required less elaboration. Offering a case in point are the beardless, tunic-clad Jews who are confronted by Saint Helena in the Girona "Creation Tapestry," introduced in chapter 1 (fig. 3).[5] Within an elaborate radial composition in which an enthroned Christ is surrounded by a cycle of the Creation, the four winds, and the four seasons, these figures form part of a fragmentary cycle of the Legend of the True Cross that appears on the lower edge of the textile. As is consistent with the work's early date, the short tunics and short hair of the two figures questioned by the empress are nearly indistinguishable from those of the pagan and Christian figures that appear elsewhere in the work; only the inscription IUDEI and their traditional role in the narrative identify them as Jews.

As the impulse to articulate Jewish difference intensified in many Iberian locales toward the turn of the thirteenth century, a variety of new signs began to appear. As elsewhere in Europe, costume was among the first of these. Frequently deployed was a distinctive pointed cap similar to

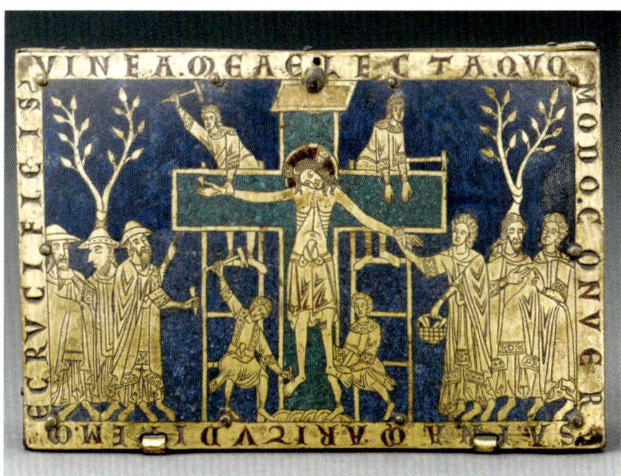

FIG. 5
Crucifixion. Portable altar from Westphalia. Louvre, Paris. © Réunion des Musées Nationaux / Art Resource, NY.

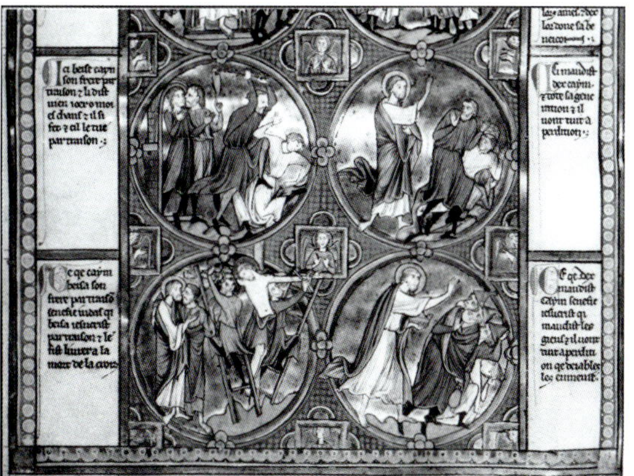

FIG. 6
Cain's exile compared with Christ's rejection of the Jews. Detail from the Old French *Bible Moralisée.* Österreichische Nationalbibliothek, Vienna, MS 2554, fol. 2v. © Österreichische Nationalbibliothek.

the type that had been employed in northern European art since the eleventh century.[6] Perhaps because of its similarity to iconographic conventions already known and used in Iberia, such as the Phrygian cap, such headgear seems to have borne a wide range of meanings for Iberian artists, and some of these might be read as neutral or even implicitly positive. Such is the case in the early twelfth-century nave frescoes of Santa María de Taüll (fig. 7), where the young David wears a pointed cap that marks the youthful hero as Jewish while still permitting him to act as a savior of his people and, through this, a prototype of Christ.

Pointed hats could play a primarily denotative role in Iberian imagery well into the thirteenth and fourteenth centuries, most often in the depiction of Old Testament patriarchs or other positive Jewish figures. In a fourteenth-century Bible now in the Archives of the Crown of Aragon in Barcelona (Sant Cugat MS 28, fol. 64r), the Israelites who populate many Old Testament initials wear red or blue conical hats much like those found in Parisian Bibles of the same date (fig. 8). These pose a contrast to the multivalency of similar signs in many French manuscripts, where such caps could evoke layered allusions to heretics and other outgroups as well as to Jews per se.[7] Instead, the Jew's hat in such Iberian manuscripts often seems intended simply to identify Jews *as* Jews, and sometimes Jews of a particularly positive class. This could range from Jews mentioned in the Gospels as abandoning their traditions to follow Christ, such as Nicodemus, Joseph of Arimathea, or Joseph the husband of Mary, to Christologically

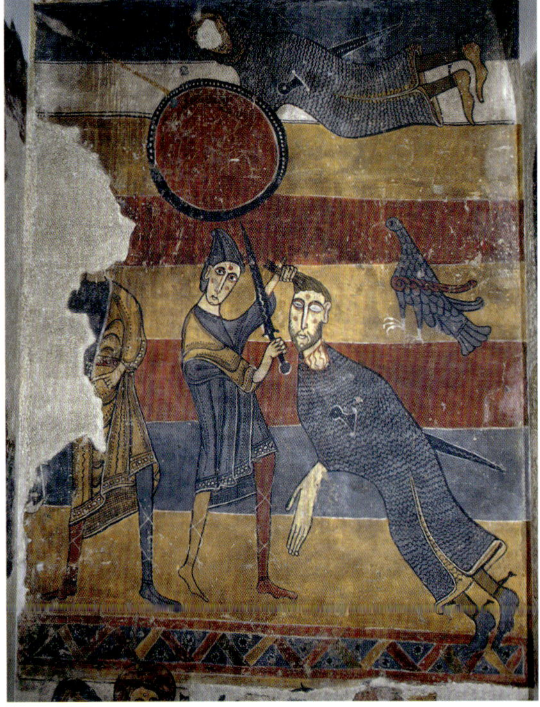

FIG. 7
David battling Goliath. Detail of a fresco from Santa María de Taüll. Museu Nacional d'Art de Catalunya, Barcelona. © MNAC. Photo: Calveras/Mérida/Sagristà.

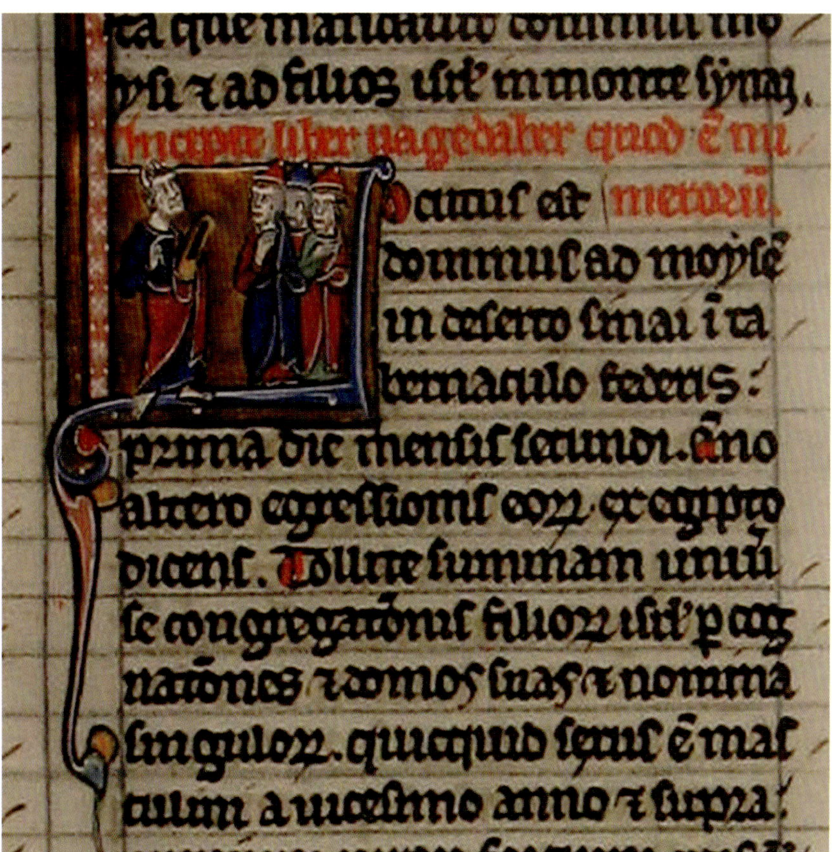

FIG. 8
Initial L (Numbers) depicting Moses and the Israelites. Archivo de la Corona de Aragón, Sant Cugat MS 28, fol. 64r. © España, Ministerio de Cultura.

significant prophets like Isaiah, who on the Pórtico de la Gloria at Santiago de Compostela wears a distinctive, close-fitting cap (fig. 9).

At the same the potential of the Jew's hat to raise sharper moral or theological concerns was quickly apparent to Iberian artists, who in some contexts explored it quite profitably. One such case is the late twelfth-century cenotaph of SS. Vicente, Cristeta, and Sabina in the Church of San Vicente in Ávila.[8] Designed to commemorate the three sibling saints in their recently rebuilt basilica, this unusual, shrinelike structure incorporates a series of reliefs illustrating the life and martyrdom of Vicente and his two sisters. The saints' legend, initially recorded in Prudentius's fourth-century *Peristephanon,* preserves many elements typical of such early Christian hagiographies. It recounts that, having refused to participate in pagan rituals, Vicente was imprisoned in his home town of Talavera. Then, following a persuasive visit from his sisters, he fled with them to Ávila, where the three were captured, tortured, and executed at the order of the Roman governor Dacian.[9]

Prudentius's version lacks any reference to Jews, but by the time of its incorporation into tenth- and eleventh-century versions of the Mozarabic liturgy, the legend had acquired an

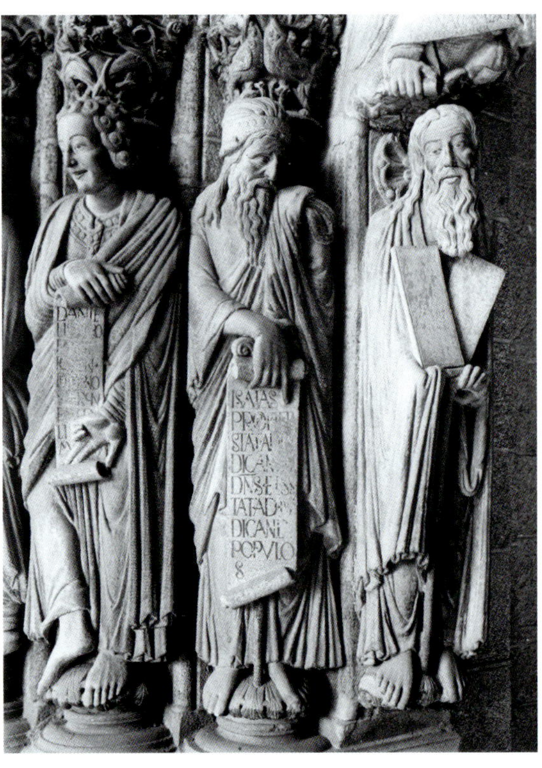

FIG. 9
Moses, Isaiah, and Daniel. Santiago de Compostela, Pórtico de la Gloria. © Fundació Institut Amatller d'Art Hispànic. Arxiu Mas.

entirely new episode featuring a Jewish character. As told in these versions, the Jew discovered the martyred siblings' unburied bodies and was immediately attacked and immobilized by the giant serpent guarding them.[10] Divinely inspired, he prayed to Christ for assistance, promising to convert and to build a basilica in which the saints could be buried properly; he was promptly released and went on to fulfill his pledge. This new subnarrative, with its emphasis on the Jew's recognition of Christ's salvific power and, perhaps more important, his willing conversion to a new faith, has been interpreted as responding to an increase in anti Jewish sentiment within Visigothic Spain during the seventh century, when the episode was likely added.[11]

By the twelfth century, the episode of the converted Jew had become fundamental enough to the saints' story to be immortalized in the visual narrative of the Ávila cenotaph. Resting beneath a gabled Gothic baldacchino, the shrine presents the story of Vicente and his sisters in a series of eight episodes, four on each of its long sides. On the north, Vicente is called before Dacian, refuses to worship idols, is visited by his sisters in prison, and flees with them to Ávila. On the south, the siblings are tortured on X-shaped crosses, then placed between heavy blocks that crush their heads, sealing their martyrdom (fig. 10). The next scene depicts the Jew lifting his hands to heaven as the serpent winds around his neck, while the last shows him bending with a palette and level to seal the central of three sarcophagi beneath a trio of round arches representing the new basilica he has built (fig. 11).[12] In both scenes, the Jew wears a large, lobed hat much like that worn by Isaiah on Santiago's west portal. Emphasizing the figure's alien faith, this headgear lends impact to the moment of conversion and redemption represented by the building of the new basilica.

The hat, however, accomplishes significantly more than this: it also permits the backward extension of the Jew's role into episodes of the narrative preceding his conversion. On the shrine's northwest corner, the same figure in his lobed cap stands in a turret to watch the three saints' flight from Talavera to Ávila before taking his place among the Roman executioners who crush the young Christians' heads on the shrine's south side.[13] The visual repetition of the Jew at these crucial narrative moments transforms him from the happenstance observer of the Visigothic tale to a persecutor who nurtures an active hostility to the young saints. No surviving text of the period accounts for this elaboration, nor indeed do comparable visual images exist. Instead, the Jew's expanded role may represent a

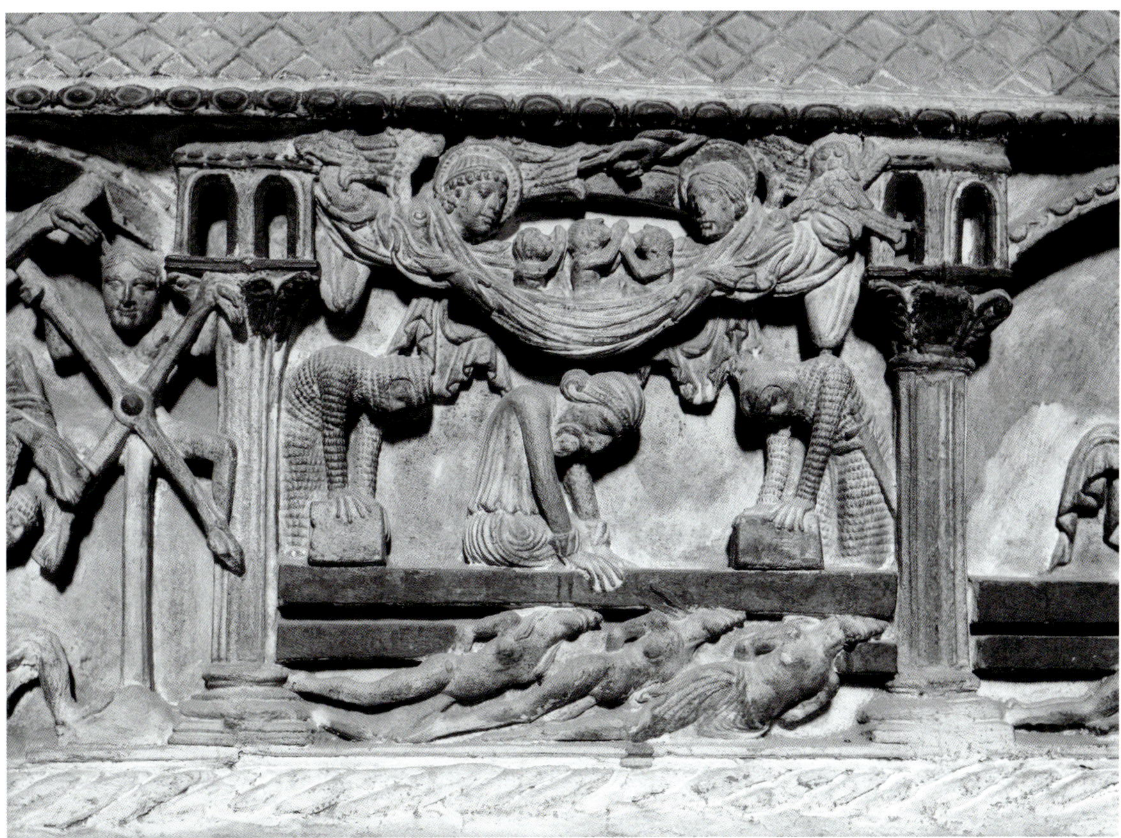

FIG. 10

The Jew participates in the martyrdom of S. Vicente and his sisters. Shrine of SS. Vicente, Cristeta, and Sabina, Ávila, Basilica of San Vicente. Fundació Institut Amatller d'Art Hispànic. Arxiu Mas.

local variation on the tale, perhaps one inspired by oral traditions that have not survived in written form.[14]

The hat that marks the Jew's engagement in the narrative is indistinguishable from that worn by Joseph, the husband of Mary, who appears in an Adoration of the Magi on the aedicula above the cenotaph. Its repeated appearances in the hagiographical narrative underscore the premeditated nature of the Jews' collusion with Roman authorities to cause the young martyrs' deaths, much as the Jews of Jesus's time were understood to have collaborated with Pilate's soldiers. This parallelism echoes the ideological shift described by Jeremy Cohen in his analysis of twelfth-century polemics, in which the once-prevalent view that the Jews had killed Christ in ignorance was eclipsed by accusations that they had knowingly murdered their Messiah.[15] Such thinking had gained strength throughout Christian Iberia with the repopulation and monastic expansions that accompanied the Reconquest, and it might have found an especially receptive audience in Ávila, where Jews

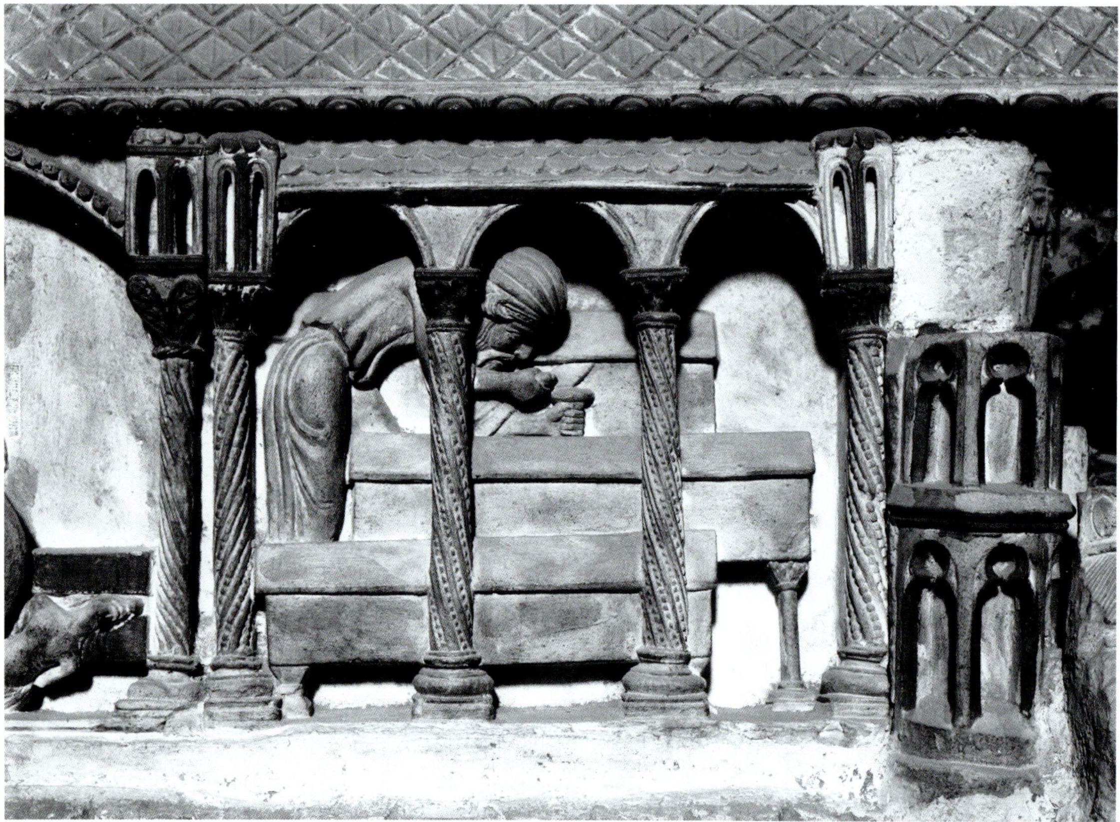

FIG. 11

The Jew builds a basilica and tombs for S. Vicente and his sisters. Shrine of SS. Vicente, Cristeta, and Sabina, Ávila, Basilica of San Vicente. Fundació Institut Amatller d'Art Hispànic. Arxiu Mas.

appear to have played a significant role following the city's Christian conquest and settlement in the last quarter of the eleventh century.

Jews certainly formed part of Ávila's population after its Christian occupation: a formulaic statement of Jewish rights appears in its twelfth-century *fuero,* and in documents of 1144 and 1176, respectively, the Castilian kings Alfonso VII and Alfonso VIII promised a percentage of their annual Jewish rents to the city's cathedral.[16] By the first decades of the thirteenth century, the city's Jewish population was substantial enough to merit a visit from the aged Jewish scholar David Kimḥi as he traveled through Spain in the course of the Maimonidean controversy. By 1295, the *aljama* had even produced its own pseudo-Messiah, an illiterate shepherd named Abraham, whose written revelations attracted the attention of the prominent rabbi Solomon ibn Adret. Cathedral records attest that by 1303, no fewer than forty Jewish families occupied ecclesiastical lands.[17] This development is consistent with Jonathan Ray's broad analysis of Jewish communities on the Iberian frontier, the growth of which seems to have derived largely from new immigration in the wake of Christian conquests, rather than merely the revival of preexisting populations.[18] It offers a revealing context for the creative transformation of the bumbling Jewish convert of the Visigothic legend into the active persecutor of the cenotaph, whose literal construction of a new basilica for the saints exemplarily applies the tithes then imposed on the city's actual Jews. Far from merely recording a legend, the cenotaph reliefs articulate visually the anxieties prompted by Jewish ascendancy in Ávila, and likely in other recently conquered cities.[19]

Iberian artists responded more diffidently to another motif used widely elsewhere in Europe: the Jewish badge. This sign has firm historical roots: whereas the unusual headgear associated with Jews in medieval art cannot be conclusively connected with either actual Jewish dress or the practices and policies of European rulers, the emergence of the badge as an iconographic element can be related directly to the Fourth Lateran Council of 1215, one result of which was the well-known decree that Jews be distinguished from Christians by a visible mark of some kind.[20] Response to the new rule varied widely throughout the Latin West, but in many cases it resulted in the requirement that Jews attach to their clothing some form of badge, which could range from the large white replica of Moses's tablets favored by English rulers to the yellow or red ring-shaped emblems, or *rotuli,* mandated in the Mediterranean sphere.[21]

The Spanish kings were irregular in enforcing the Lateran regulation.[22] In the Crown of Aragon, James I attempted to impose a Jewish badge in 1228 but withdrew his efforts in the face of widespread Jewish protest. Instead, and in spite of periodic papal attempts to enforce the imposition of a badge, he permitted Jews to wear a specially shaped mantle that eventually came to satisfy the same purpose.[23] Only in the fourteenth century was the wearing of a badge required more consistently, and even then a continued emphasis on the mantle in Jewish legislation suggests that this continued as a viable alternative.[24]

In Castile, Jewish reaction to the Lateran Council requirement was so strong that in 1219 Fernando III petitioned for an exemption, arguing that the regulation was causing Jews to flee to Al-Andalus and costing the Crown a valuable source of revenue.[25] His successor Alfonso X did include the requirement of a distinguishing mark in his great law code, the *Siete partidas,* but this work was not promulgated until 1348, and there is little evidence that much of the Jewish legislation that it contained was actually enforced in Alfonso's time.[26] Numerous subsequent complaints of noncompliance with the Lateran IV requirement, such as those raised by the Cortes of Palencia (1313) and Toro (1371), suggest that it continued to be disregarded by Alfonso's successors as well.[27]

Iberian artistic practices seem to have paralleled these social ones in that they only rarely utilized the badge as a Jewish sign. Those few Iberian images that do so appear mainly in times and places where either the unusually rigorous observance of such rules or unusually high religious tensions would have made the appearance of the badge more meaningful. Two such examples derive from fourteenth-century Catalunya. The first is found in a fourteenth-century manuscript containing a compilation of legal privileges known as the *Llibre verd de Barcelona* (Barcelona, AHCB, MS Gen., 6–225).[28] In a section of laws added by James I (r. 1213–76) appears a minute bearded figure wearing a blue, hooded mantle on which is affixed a faint red *rotulus* (fig. 12).[29] The six thin white lines that dangle from beneath his hood may represent *tzitzit* (fringes) of the traditional prayer shawl known as a *tallit.* Wedged into the narrow initial I of "In nomine domini . . . ," the tiny Jew forms part of the introduction to a section of laws concerning moneylending, a practice that preoccupied Aragonese Christians throughout and beyond James's long reign.[30]

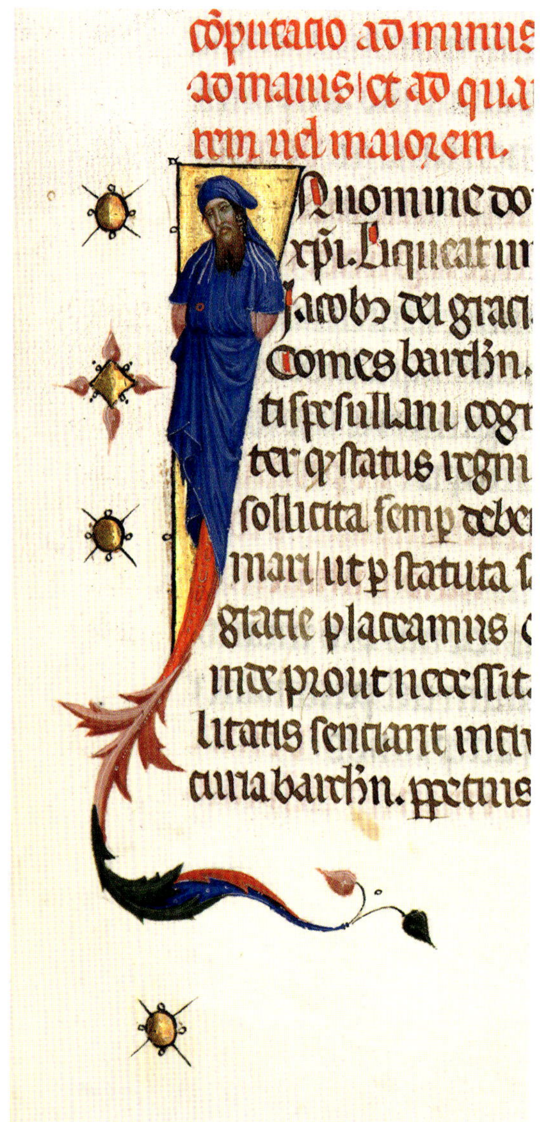

FIG. 12
Initial I depicting a Jew wearing a rotulus and *tzitzit* (?). *Llibre verd de Barcelona.* Barcelona, Archives of the History of the City of Barcelona, MS Gen. 6-225, fol. 79r. Ajuntament de Barcelona, Arxiu Històric de la Ciutat de Barcelona, by permission.

As we shall see, the visual link between Jews and moneylending that is activated here by the rotulus and shawl would become one of the most powerful symbolic forces in the Iberian visual lexicon.

A Jew wearing a rotulus also appears in the mid-fourteenth-century fresco cycle of the Discovery of the True Cross, a series now incompletely preserved in the retrochoir of Tarragona Cathedral.[31] A key participant in the narrative is a hooded figure wearing a prominent white circle on his garment (fig. 13), presumably the cooperative Jew whom the *Legenda aurea* describes as having aided Empress Helena in her quest for the Cross. The Jew's figure appears twice, first lowered into the pit where he claimed the Cross would be found, and then standing nearby as it is excavated, episodes that parallel those later preserved in a breviary printed for Tarragona Cathedral in 1485.[32] The inclusion of a badge is sufficiently justified by the need to identify the legendary figure as Jewish, but its prominence might also represent a response to the increased enforcement of the actual Jewish badge in the Crown of Aragon, which began in the first years of the fourteenth century: a red-and-yellow wheel was imposed at the Corts of Lleida in 1300, while in Barcelona in 1312 an ordinance was passed that made a red or yellow rotulus the size of a person's palm an alternative to the customary Jewish cloak.[33]

The cloak itself proved a far more resonant image for many Iberian artists, especially those in the Crown of Aragon. Such mantles had been worn voluntarily by Jews in parts of Spain for centuries before their adoption as a specifically religio-cultural marker, and they are associated with Jews in visual images even before the 1215 Lateran Council decree. In the Navarrese cloister of Santa María la Mayor in Tudela, begun ca. 1186, Pharisees and other Jews are depicted wearing not only these hooded mantles, but also baggy trousers and a peculiar form of slipper possibly derived from Islamic dress (fig. 14).[34] When, toward the end of the thirteenth century, the cloak's association with Jews came to be fixed by law as well as custom, its deployment as a Jewish signifier in art quickly outpaced that of the essentially foreign hat and badge.[35] In Castile, it penetrated quickly the fantastical Jewish iconography of the *Cantigas de Santa María;* in Catalunya, it became a widely used shorthand for Jews in a variety of visual contexts, most strikingly in the informal genre of imagery traditionally referred to as scribal doodles.

Jews make frequent appearances among the casual drawings that were added by medieval scribes to the notarial and legislative texts so abundantly preserved in Aragon. Many appear in fourteenth-century copies of the *Usatges de Barcelona,* a compilation of Catalan laws and customs first promulgated by count Ramón Berenguer (r. 1035–76) and decisively compiled by King James I. Although customarily endowed with more formal decoration, such as filigreed or even historiated initials, manuscripts of the *Usatges* often also accrued more informal scribal drawings either during their production or in subsequent revisions of the text.[36]

One such manuscript, now in Paris (BnF, MS lat. 4670A), includes several marginal images apparently added either during or shortly after its completion, probably in Barcelona, in 1321–23.[37] Although many of these doodles, which include a variety of human figures, animal heads, architecture, and even a *spinario,* have little to do

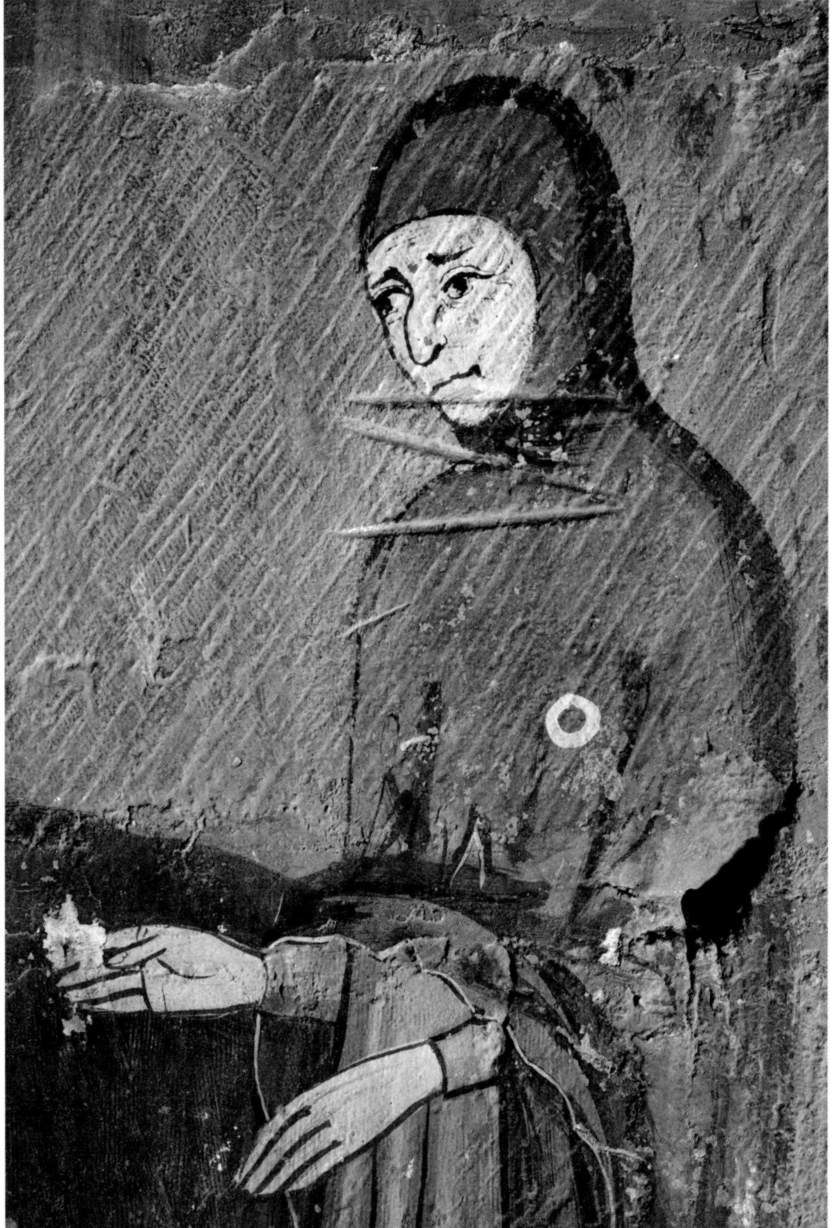

FIG. 13
A Jew wearing a rotulus. Detail from a fresco cycle of the Discovery of the True Cross. Tarragona Cathedral, retrochoir. Fundació Institut Amatller d'Art Hispànic. Arxiu Mas.

with Jews, several others are clearly identified as such by characteristically Jewish hooded mantles, enlarged noses, and occasionally beards. These sketches most often appear in the margins of passages referring specifically to Jews. Pen sketches of a Jew's head and a standing figure in a Jewish hood appear adjacent to one passage that stipulates the length of time that a letter of

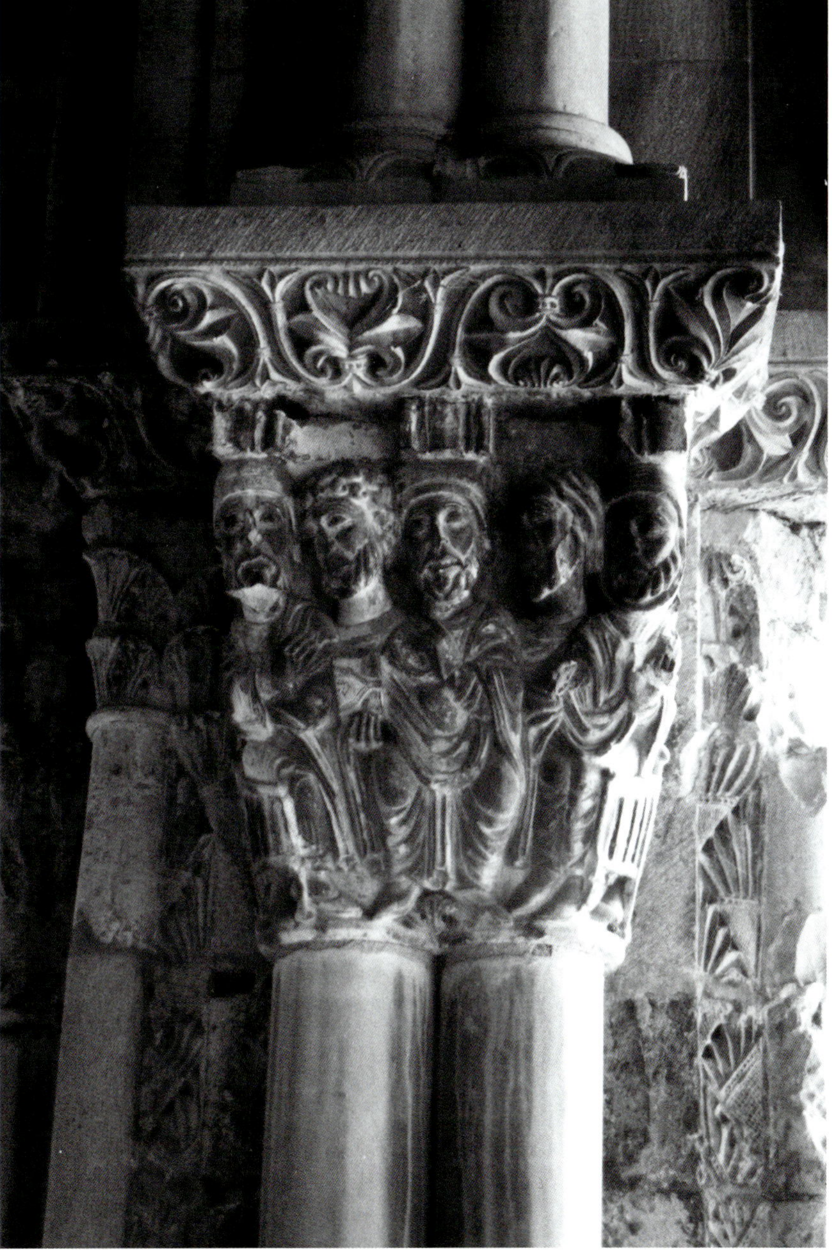

FIG. 14
Priests and scribes conspire in Caiaphas's house. Detail of a capital from Tudela, Santa María la Mayor, cloister. © Pamela A. Patton.

usury from a Jew will remain valid; a hooded, beardless figure with a pointed nose and protruding lips flanks a section outlining the penalty for luring a baptized Jew back to his old religion (fig. 15).[38] The implications of such pairings, which spring from powerful associations of Jews with money and duplicity, will be explored more extensively below.

Old Forms and New Meanings

In many European contexts, such signs as the rotulus or Jew's cap often bore pointed implications about the perceived place of Jews in Christian society, heightened as they were by the social and economic tensions that in many areas of Europe had sharpened dramatically by the turn of the thirteenth century. While a similarly decisive shift cannot be traced as easily within the various Christian kingdoms of Iberia, during this same period a growing acculturation to ultra-Pyrenean ideas about Jews and their place in Christian society does seem to have rendered patrons and artists more receptive to stereotypes already common in much of the Latin West.

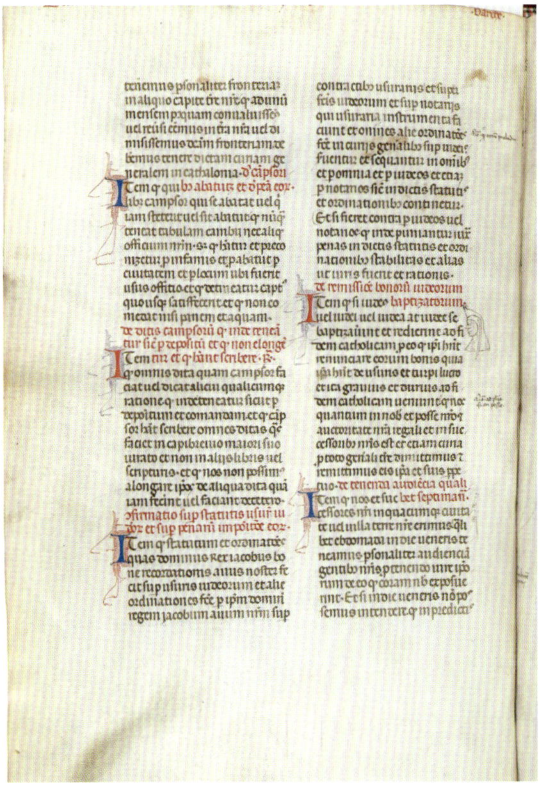

FIG. 15
Scribal doodle of a Jew. *Usatges de Barcelona*. BnF, Paris, MS lat. 4670A, fol. 213v. Bibliothèque nationale de France, by permission.

The first such images to appear in Iberia were directed at reevaluating the role of Jews in salvation history generally, and more specifically in the events surrounding Christ's death on the cross. Where once Christian scholars had followed a fundamentally Augustinian model that conceived of Jews as necessary, if uncomprehending, witnesses to Christian history, by the twelfth century they had begun to lay the guilt for Jesus's murder directly at the feet of a fully complicit Jewish people. As argued by these churchmen, Jews had abundant evidence within their own texts that their Messiah had come, but rejected and betrayed Christ despite their awareness of his divine role.[39] While this charge purportedly was leveled at the Jews of Jesus's own time, it took little to extend their historical culpability more universally to the Jewish people, whose continued resistance toward Christian doctrine seemed to underscore their enmity toward Christ.

Outside the Iberian sphere, this perspectival shift speedily found visual expression in such works as the well-known English ivory cross now in the Cloisters in New York (fig. 16). Here, the implication of Jewish guilt in the death of Christ is made evident in such details as a central

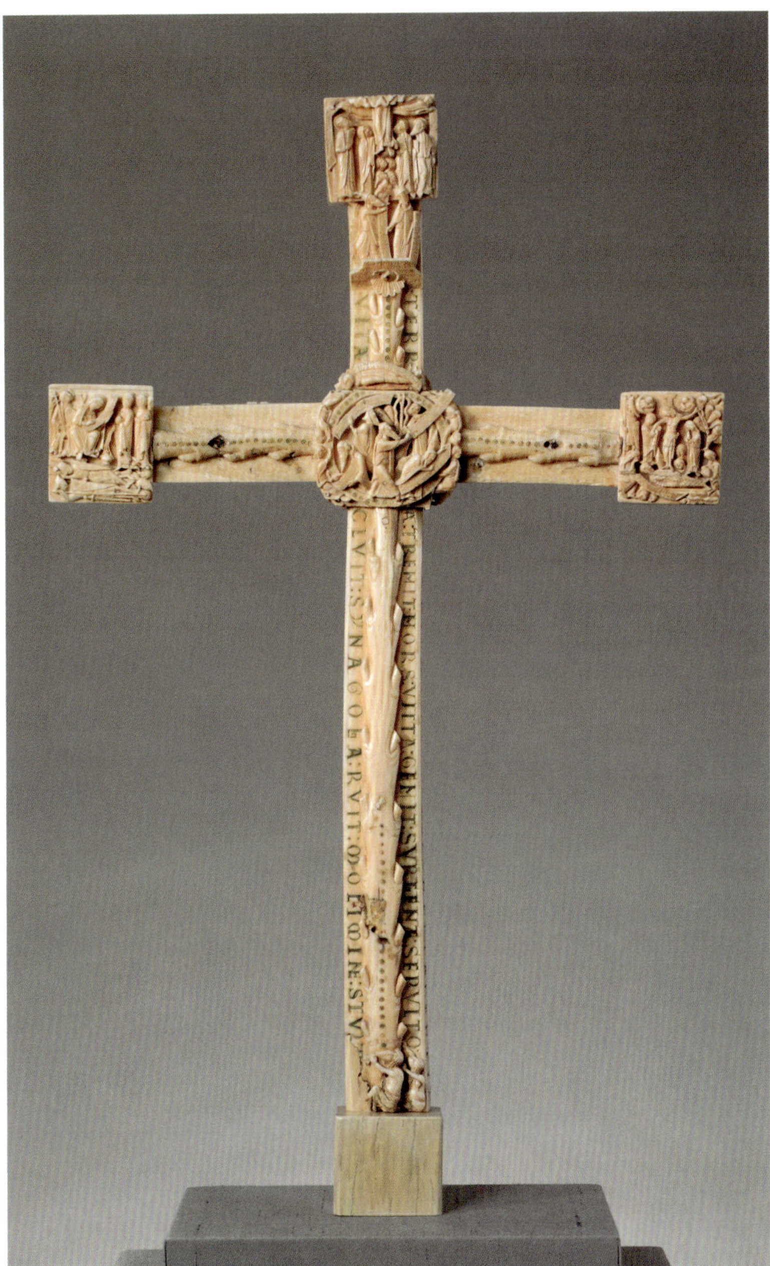

FIG. 16
Cloisters Cross, obverse. New York, Cloisters Collection. © Metropolitan Museum of Art / Art Resource, NY.

roundel in which Pilate and Caiaphas debate the content of the *titulus* for the Cross, another in which the drooping personification of Synagoga impales the Lamb of God with her spear, and the dozens of tiny Jews who press in at the margins of the Passion scenes on the work's finials. Their culpability is further emphasized by inscriptions on the shaft and banderoles of the cross, which include such barbs as "The Jews laughed at the pain of God dying" and "Synagogue has collapsed with great foolish effort"—overall, an extraordinary infiltration of then-current anti-Jewish polemics into a work of visual art.[40]

Textual rhetoric of this kind was slower to flourish on the Iberian Peninsula, where religious polemicists native to Spain, such as the Jewish convert to Christianity Petrus Alfonsi (ca. 1080–after 1120), initially kept their focus on key doctrinal differences that distinguished the two faiths, such as belief in the Incarnation and the Trinity.[41] In so doing, they drew upon a local history of polemical debate among Jewish, Muslim, and Christian writers for whom such distinctions were critical to maintaining religious and cultural boundaries frequently threatened by physical proximity. However, as engagement with European religious culture intensified in the thirteenth century, and especially with the arrival in Spain of the preaching orders, these doctrinal debates were intensified by new claims that the Jews had not merely rejected, but had deliberately murdered, their Messiah. These arguments emerged especially pointedly in the writings of the Catalan Dominican Ramon Martí (ca. 1215–ca. 1285).[42] Reflecting his exposure to the work of Thomas Aquinas and many other ultra-Pyrenean writers of his day, Martí made the case for Jewish culpability in Christ's death with an acidity then still unusual for an Iberian author: "The first villainy in the Jews' actions causing that final expulsion was the reprobation, reproaching, and repulsion of our messiah, as well as the persecution of him, the pointless hatred with which they have hated him until now and hated him then."[43]

Martí's text stands out as one of the earliest Iberian polemics to express so vividly an idea that would remain rare in textual form before its emergence in vernacular Passion narratives of the fourteenth century and later.[44] Yet visual renderings of the Passion story attest to the currency of this notion in Iberia even before the friar wrote his words. In the capitals of the Tudela cloister, introduced earlier in this chapter, biblical Jews in characteristic hooded cloaks take an active role within an sculpted program centered around an extensive Passion narrative, acting as conspicuous participants especially in scenes of betrayal and violence against Christ.[45] The effect is especially striking in two juxtaposed capitals on the cloister's northeast pier, which depict the Conspiracy of the Priests and Pharisees in the

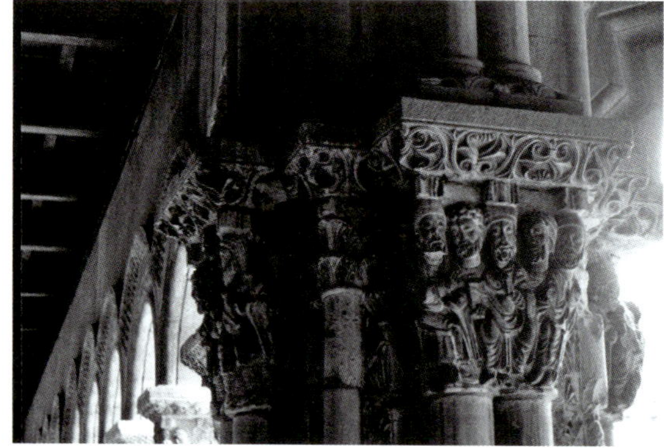

FIG. 17
Conspiracy and Payment of Judas capitals on the northeast cloister pier. Tudela, Santa María la Mayor, cloister. © Pamela A. Patton.

House of Caiaphas and the Payment of Judas, respectively (figs. 14, 17). Neither of these episodes appeared often in Iberian Passion narratives, and their joint inclusion was rarer still. Here, they are paired so as to interrupt the traditionally seamless sequence from Christ's Entry into Jerusalem to the Last Supper. Echoed as they are by similarly dressed Jewish figures in successive episodes of Christ's Arrest and Burial, they craft a compelling visual argument for Jewish agency in the Passion.

This unusually early articulation of Jewish enmity may be attributable to social and religious tensions peculiar to Tudela, an originally Muslim city that came under Christian rule only when Alfonso I of Aragon and Navarre entered the city in 1119.[46] While Alfonso and his successors offered significant inducements to retain the city's Jewish population, neither the townspeople nor the Augustinians brought in to support the city's new cathedral were as friendly toward their Jewish neighbors. By the last third of the century, the Jewish community had been relocated to a fortified quarter for its own protection, and royal privileges increasingly began to include a range of defensive rights, such as immunity for acts of self-defense, that suggest a growing desire to control and protect Jews in their interaction with the Christians of the town.[47] In the cloister of Santa María la Mayor, the institutional heart of Tudela's Christian community, the proleptic conflation of the cloister's images of biblical Jews with Tudela's own medieval ones, and the new prominence of their role in the Passion cycle, seem to reflect this wider shift.

Visual references to Jews as active agents in Christ's death increased in frequency over the course of the thirteenth century, as is especially well exemplified by two powerful images of the Crucifixion in the Escorial manuscript of the *Cantigas de Santa María,* a work that will be examined more extensively in chapter 5. Most striking is the one that accompanies Cantiga 50, a song that lauds both the Virgin Mary herself and the veracity of the Incarnation.[48] The subject of the Incarnation readily invited consideration of Jews, whose disbelief in the doctrine remained a chief point of contention in polemical exchanges; however, it should be noted that the *cantiga* text makes no mention of them.[49] The association is animated only in the song's illustration (fol. 74v), which includes a scene of the Crucifixion in which several leering Jews have gathered maliciously around the crucified Christ, some lifting their eyes to watch a coreligionist hammer nails into Christ's hand as the Virgin, nearly forgotten below, embraces her son's feet (fig. 18). Although ostensibly referring to a line in the *cantiga*—"He assumed flesh within the Virgin and, moreover, allowed himself to be killed for us"—the artist here seems to have welcomed the opportunity to envision Jews as active perpetrators of the crime and to concretize their unconcern with the Virgin's maternal anguish.[50]

The *topos* of the Jews as Christ's enemies facilitated the emergence in Iberia of a second and closely related conception: that of Judaism as akin to heresy, and thus as requiring the same active opposition in preaching and missionary work. This idea may be traced first to the tendency of twelfth-century Western churchmen to group Jews with heretics, along with Muslims and other outgroups, as opponents of Christianity; it developed further in the hands of those orders, like the Dominicans, which had

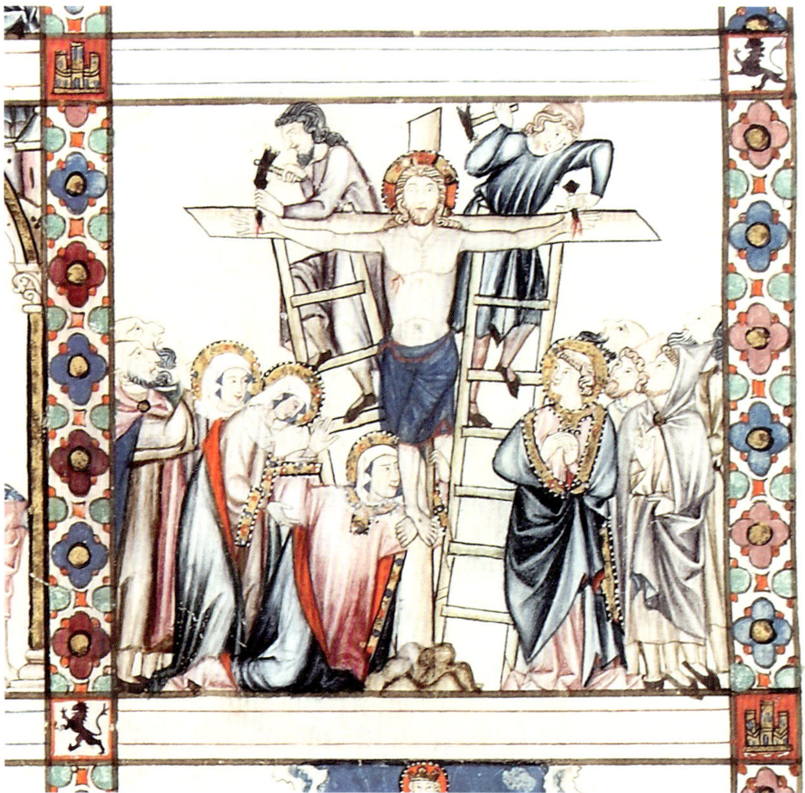

FIG. 18
Jews participating in the Crucifixion. Detail from the illustration to Cantiga 50 (*loor*), *Cantigas de Santa María*. Real Biblioteca de El Escorial, Madrid, MS T.I.1, fol. 74v. © Patrimonio Nacional.

been formed with the pursuit of heresy as their primary goal.[51] It may indeed have been the Dominicans who most strongly developed the notion in Iberia, where their missionary efforts quickly came to encompass the Jews and Muslims they encountered there.[52]

Prominent in this regard was the Catalan-born churchman Ramon de Penyafort, third General of the Dominican Order, confessor and advisor to James I and a strong advocate of preaching, as he himself put it, to "those who dishonor God by worshiping vilely, namely Jews, Saracens, and heretics."[53] Penyafort's initiatives, assisted by the Jew-turned-Dominican Pablo Christiani and the learned polemicist Ramon Martí, were particularly forceful in the Crown of Aragon. They included the foundation of special *studia* in which friars were taught Hebrew and Arabic to facilitate their understanding of their opponent faiths, as well as the imposition, occasionally supported by the Aragonese kings, of forced sermons among Jewish communities in particular. Penyafort's writings, as well as those of Martí and others in the Aragonese sphere, reflect a strong desire to engage with these groups in the course of Dominican preaching, one which was supported, if not always consistently, by local rulers.[54]

Perhaps the most famous result of the Dominican efforts in thirteenth-century Spain was the historic disputation staged in Barcelona between Pablo Christiani and the famous

Catalan rabbi Moses ben Nachman of Girona, better known as Nachmanides, between 20 and 27 July 1263.[55] The aptly named Pablo Christiani had converted from Judaism to Christianity around 1229, later joining the Dominican Order.[56] Like Ramon de Penyafort, with whom he became closely associated, he directed much of his missionizing toward Jews. The debate was called by James I at the Dominicans' request; to represent the Jewish side, the king summoned Nachmanides to Barcelona. The written accounts left by both parties offer significant insight into the debate's content, if less clarity as to its outcome, since each side claimed a victory. What is clear is that a significant proportion of the debate centered around what Christiani intended to characterize as the Jews' own theological errors, especially those passages in the *aggadot,* or homiletic rabbinic texts, that seemed to run counter to Jewish belief, such as an *aggadah* that predicted the Messiah's birth on the day of the destruction of the Temple. In focusing on the apparent errors of Jewish belief and practice, it has been argued, Christiani effectively shifted Judaism into the realm of heresy.[57]

Visual renderings of the confrontation of Christian churchmen with Judaism often were dialectically conceived as well, extending a tradition that had been established in Iberian polemical literature since the eleventh century.[58] Such visual disputations earn pride of place in the Castilian manuscripts of the *Virginitate perpetua sanctae Mariae adversus tres infideles.* Composed by Ildefonsus, archbishop of Toledo from 657 to 667, and frequently recopied in the twelfth and thirteenth centuries, the work comprises a series of six lections regarding the position of the Virgin Mary within the doctrine of the Visigothic Church. Three of these take the form of disputations between Ildefonsus and three successive nonbelievers identified as Iovinian, Helvidius, and Judaeus ("A Jew").[59]

In two manuscripts of this work that were produced in Toledo around 1200, both now in Madrid (Bib. Nacional de España, MS 10087, and Fundación Lázaro Galdiano, MS 14424), these disputations are introduced by full-page illustrations of each debate. Each image follows the same simple formula, depicting the archbishop and his opponent seated face to face, flanked by their respective supporters. Their adaptation to an Iberian milieu, in contrast to the better-known and earlier Parma Ildefonsus, is evident in such details as the disputants' individualized attire, which, in the case of the Lázaro Galdiano manuscript, has been linked by some with contemporary Islamic costume.[60] More striking still is that in both manuscripts, all three figures also display long noses and beards resembling the facial stereotype assigned in northern European art to Jewish figures more exclusively. This apparent lack of discrimination between heretics and Jews suggests that in this context at least, such features had not yet acquired a consistent or exclusively Jewish connotation. Instead, both physiognomic markers and local costume function mainly to draw a distinction between the Christian Ildefonsus and the theological outsiders with whom he debates.

The fluidity with which these motifs were deployed is at its clearest in the rendering of Helvidius in the Biblioteca Nacional manuscript (fig. 19). Here, the non-Jewish heretic not only displays the long beard and cap later associated more exclusively with Jews, but he also holds a scroll bearing a tiny line of faintly visible pseudo-Hebrew. The salience of this pseudo-writing, which elsewhere would be expected to refer specifically to Jews, must have lain in its foreignness to Christianity, which it associatively imputes to Helvidius as another category of nonbeliever. Such imprecision might seem surprising given the presumed familiarity of Hebrew in a milieu such as Toledo, where it served as both the sacred language and a living alphabet for local Jews and surely was not unrecognizable to the literate Christians for whom this manuscript was made. Nonetheless, it must be assumed that whatever familiarity these Hebrew letters held for their viewers was outweighed by their power to mark their bearer as alien to the Christian faith.

Both Hebrew and pseudo-Hebrew writing served as a powerful sign of distance from the majority culture in Iberia, as in many parts of Europe.[61] It was used in this way as well in a single-volume Latin Bible from the Catalan city of Vic, now in the British Library (London, BL, Add. MS 50.003). A colophon on fol. 451v records this work's completion in 1273 by a canon of Vic named Iohannes Poncii, or Joan Pons, for a prelate (*presul*) whose name is now erased, but who at this date could only have been the cathedral's current bishop, Ramon d'Anglesola (r. 1265–98).[62] This Bible, like others produced in the Vic scriptorium in this period, is conventional in many respects: its single-volume format, running headers, and historiated initials ally it with the reduced-scale, single-volume Bibles produced in centers like Paris and Bologna from the first half of the thirteenth century onward, often for the use of the mendicant orders.[63] Although its decoration in many respects resembles that of other such manuscripts, it differs from them in including several unconventional historiated initials that reflect a concern with Jews and their perceived challenge to a Christian world order.

One such initial, the P of "Post mortem Iosue . . ." that opens the Book of Judges (fol. 84r), depicts the Israelites gathering after Joshua's death (fig. 20). The deceased Joshua sits in the upper zone of the initial, his mild facial features and jaunty pink cap a distinctive contrast to the crudely stereotyped, hook-nosed faces and Jewish cloaks of his followers. These latter converge over a scroll on which one figure painstakingly inscribes from left to right, reversing the proper direction of Hebrew writing, a series of tiny Hebrew letters. Combined with the figures' distorted features and local dress, this writing both demarcates the misguided Jews of the temporal world from their idealized patriarch in the heavenly zone above and plays on the centrality of this language in the clerical confrontation with Judaism.

It is the latter theme—that of disputation—that predominates in several other initials in the same Bible. In these, traditional Old Testament motifs have been displaced by vignettes depicting contemporary Jews and Christians engaged in actual disputations. In the initial A of "Anno," which opens Daniel (fol. 320r), the depiction of the prophet in the lions' den that is customary in historiated Bibles of this type has been replaced by a medieval disputation scene, in which a massive, elegantly gowned cleric points authoritatively toward the small codex in his left hand as an angry Jew lifts his eyes to heaven with an exasperated gesture (fig. 21). The disputants' pointing fingers and the childlike agitation of the

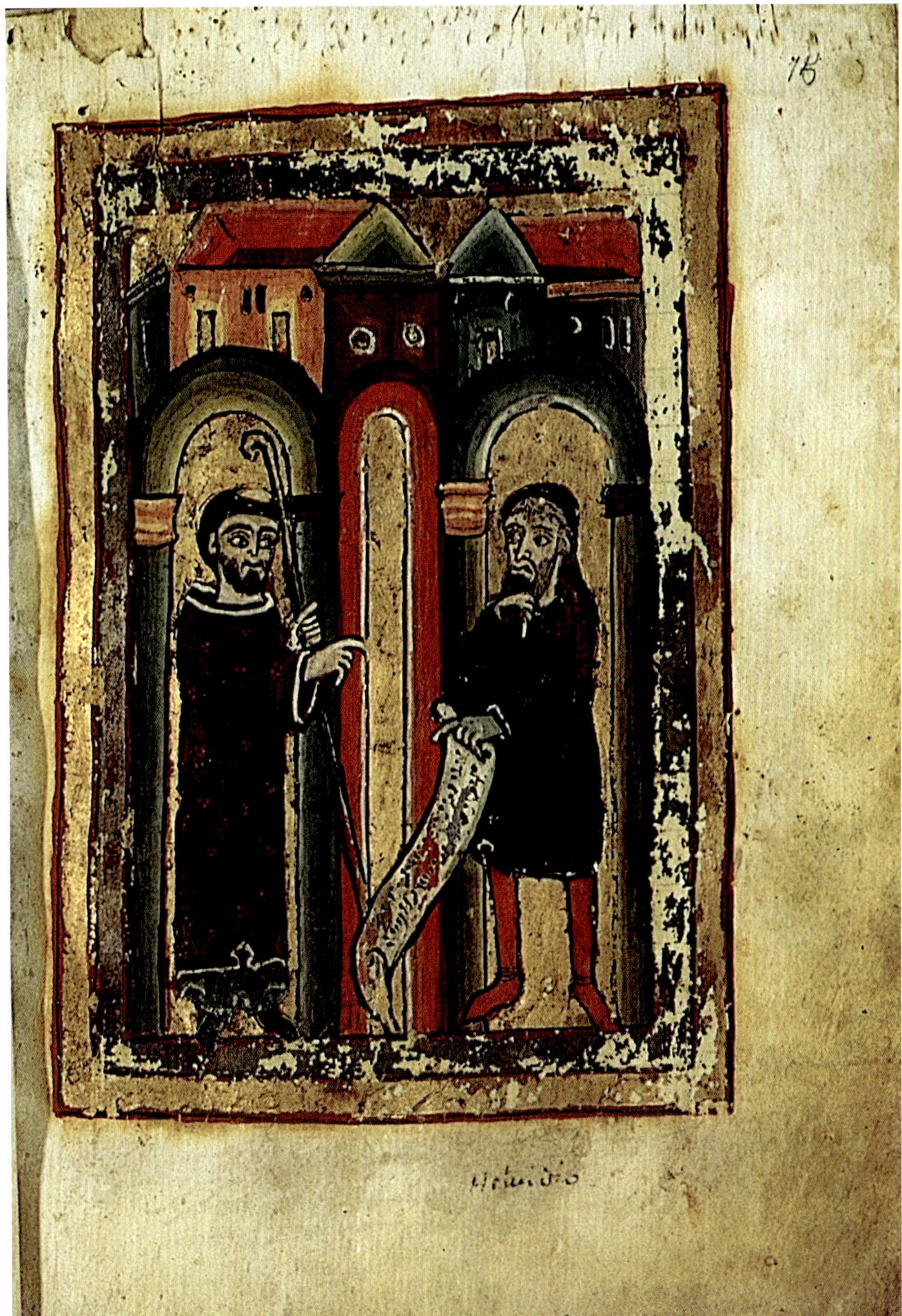

FIG. 19
Ildefonsus disputing with Helvidius. *Virginitate perpetua sanctae Mariae*. Biblioteca Nacional, Madrid, 10087, fol. 15r. © Madrid, Biblioteca Nacional.

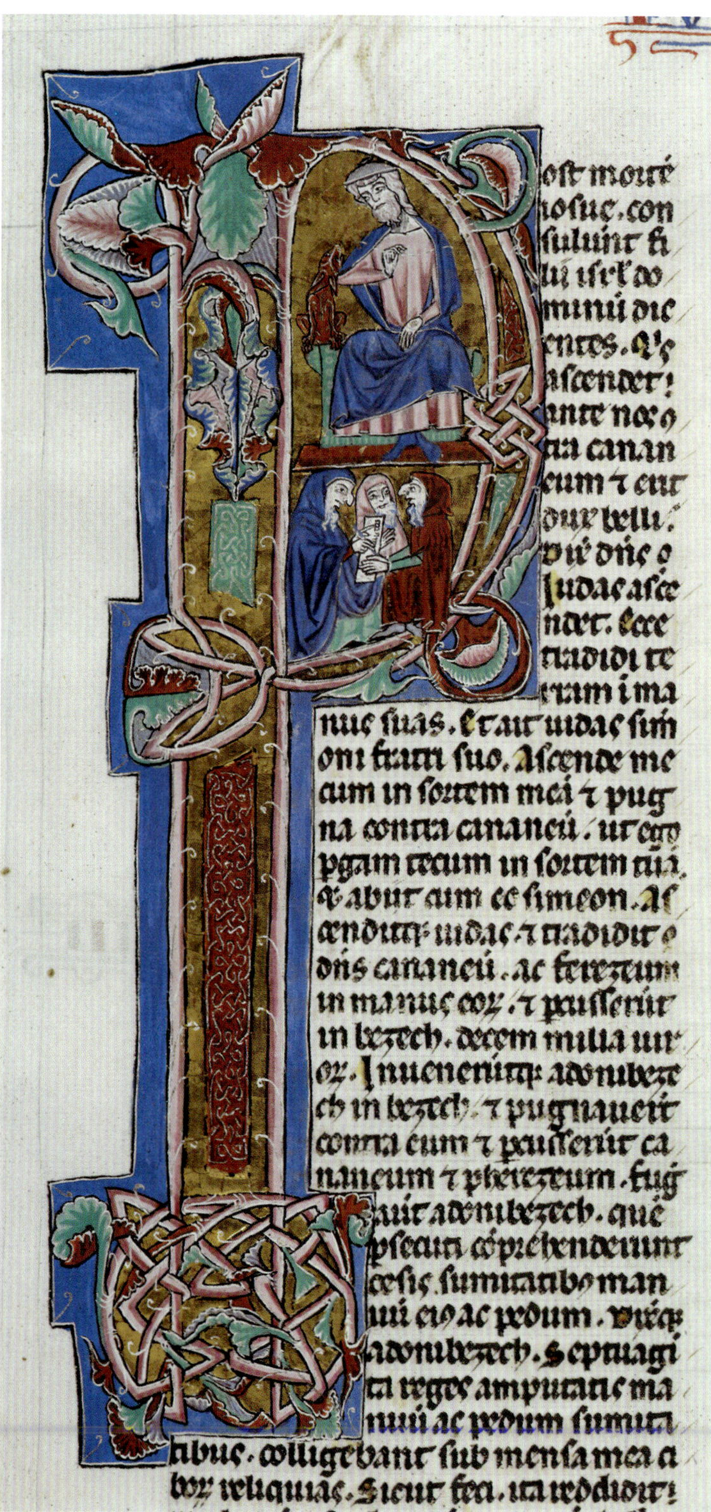

FIG. 20
Initial P (Judges) depicting Joshua and the Israelites. Vic Bible of 1273. British Library, Add. 50.003, fol. 84r. © The British Library Board. All rights reserved 01/05/2011.

losing party loosely echo those of the Ildefonsus images just discussed. As in a similar disputation in the initial to Joel, it glorifies the struggles not of scriptural but of contemporary churchmen.[64]

Whether such images brought to mind the widely popular dialectical literature of medieval writers like Peter Abelard, Petrus Alfonsi, and Ramon Llull or triggered memories of actual confrontations such as the Barcelona disputation of a decade earlier,[65] they must have resonated powerfully in Vic, which at just this time had become the site of conflict between the city's Christians and a newly flourishing Jewish *aljama.* As in many cities in Old Catalunya, James I's encouragement of Jewish settlers after the conquest of Valencia had led to a dramatic increase in Jewish inhabitants from the mid-thirteenth century onward.[66] Whereas these

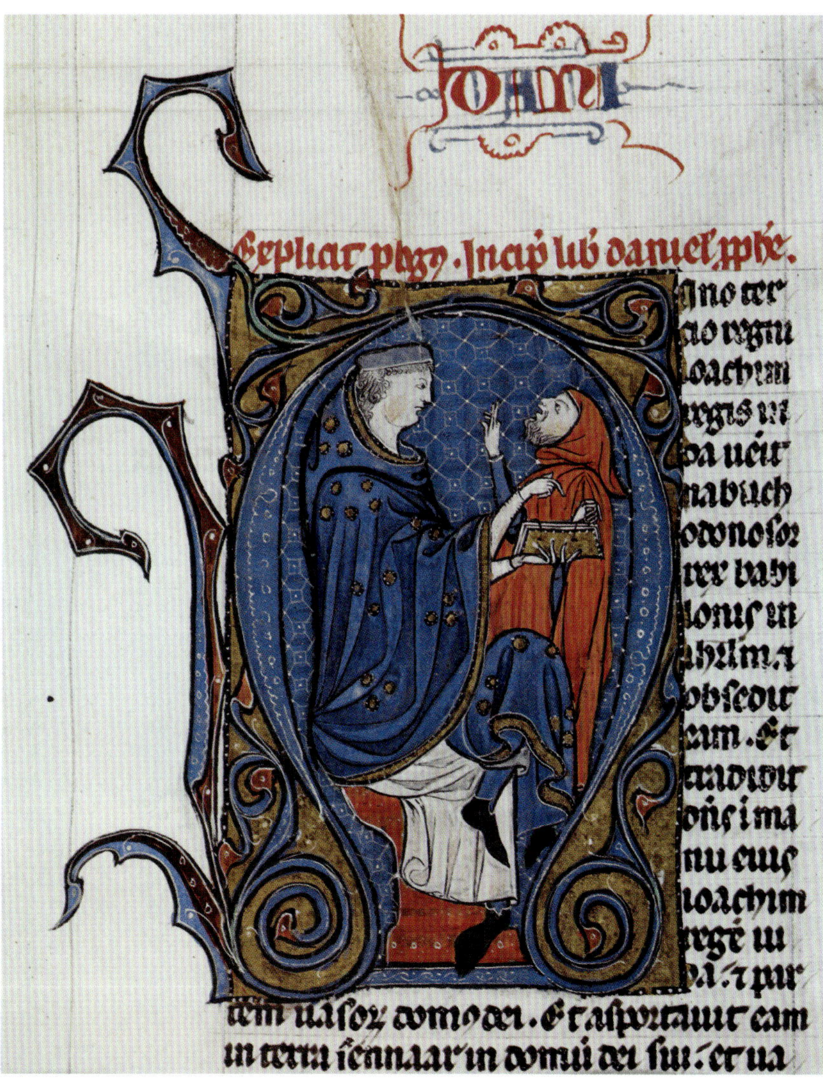

FIG. 21
Initial A (Daniel) depicting a disputation scene. Vic Bible of 1273. British Library, Add. 50.003, fol. 320r. © The British Library Board. All rights reserved 01/05/2011.

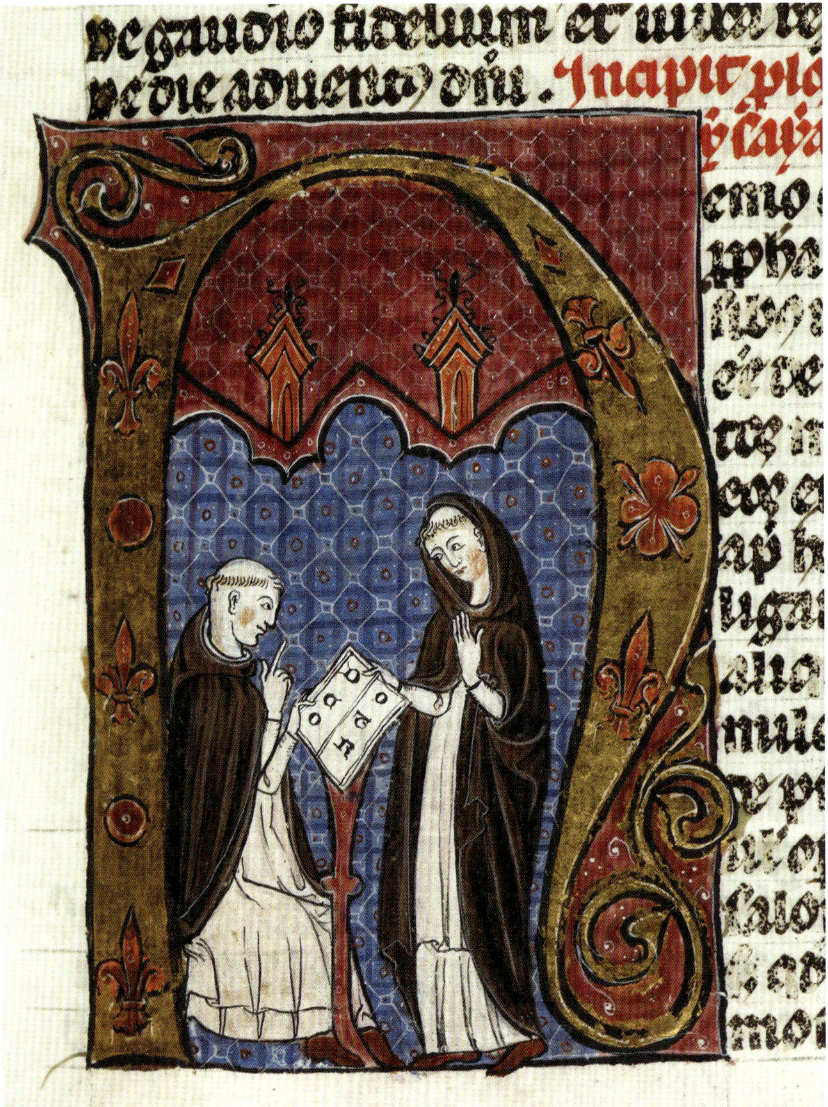

FIG. 22
Initial N (Prologue to Isaiah), two Dominicans. Vic Bible of 1273. British Library, Add. 50.003, fol. 259r. © The British Library Board. All rights reserved 01/05/2011.

settlers played a variety of roles in many of their adopted cities, the great majority in Vic, already a thriving financial center, were occupied as moneylenders. The first mention of a Jewish individual living in the city is dated 1240; records of debts to Jews both within and outside the city begin in 1248, and these increase markedly over the rest of the thirteenth century.[67]

By 19 August 1277, enough families were resident in Vic to encourage the purchase of a plot on which to build a new synagogue.[68] This last act, however, raised strong protest from the archdeacon of the cathedral, Ramon de Messerata, who in early 1278 denounced the intended construction of the synagogue as a scandal to all of the Catholic faith, whose acquiescence to this supremely evil work (*opus nefandissimum*) had been made at the risk of their souls.[69] In speaking for the church and its clergy, it may be assumed, the archdeacon must at least have had the imprimatur of the bishop, the same Ramon d'Anglesola for whom the 1273 Bible apparently had been made five years before. While it is always possible that his invective represented an isolated response to a momentary civic crisis, the fact that the synagogue was to be built within episcopal jurisdiction, not to mention the bishop's indebtedness to Jewish lenders at this time,[70] suggests a more systemic discomfort with Vic's newly flourishing *aljama.*

An intensifying factor here may have been the local activity of the Order of Preachers. Although no Dominican foundation would exist in Vic for several centuries more,[71] the order by now held powerful sway in Catalunya generally, thanks in part to native son Ramon de Penyafort. Penyafort's collaboration with the Dominican archbishop of Tarragona had resulted in the establishment by the mid-thirteenth century of Dominican bishops at Barcelona, Lléida, Girona, and Vic itself, whose bishop, Bernat de Mur, elected in 1243, was the immediate predecessor of Bishop Ramon d'Anglesola, patron of the 1273 Vic Bible.[72] Although d'Anglesola himself was not a Dominican, he had studied canon law at the University of Bologna, which also housed a major Dominican *studium.*[73] He thus must have possessed a strong awareness of the Dominican agenda, with its strengthening conception of Jews as among the mass of misguided unbelievers who needed, as Pablo Christiani is said to have put it, "to be brought to redemption and perfection."[74] The relevance of this context is reflected in another unorthodox vignette ornamenting the N of "Nemo . . ." beginning the prologue to Isaiah (fig. 22). Replacing the customary image of that prophet's martyrdom is a depiction of two Dominican clerics reading from an open book containing the word "DOCTOR." Little further evidence is needed to suggest the influence of the friars on this manuscript, as on the policies and attitudes of a cathedral community that now found itself seeking a frame through which to conceptualize and articulate its resistance to Jewish immigration.

Ecclesia and Synagoga in Spain

Paired representations of Ecclesia and Synagoga stand among the most common visual formulae by which the Jewish-Christian relationship was addressed in northern European visual culture from the twelfth century onward.[75] Laden with emblems of their respective faiths, these two allegorical figures encapsulated the essential elements of the Christian attack on Judaism. In the famous thirteenth-century sculptures on the south portal of Strasbourg Cathedral, Ecclesia's familiar chalice promises eternal life, while Synagoga's tenuous grasp on the Mosaic tablets suggests their obsolescence; Ecclesia's upright stance, direct gaze, and triumphal cross-staff convey the confidence of her new faith as Synagoga's blindfold, broken spear, and drooping posture reveal her abject defeat (fig. 23). Like the many other monumental pairings of these figures that emerged in medieval Germany and France, these sculptures embodied for a receptive public a social and religious relationship more idealized than real, one in which Jews and their faith took their expected place as inferior witnesses to a triumphant Christian present.[76]

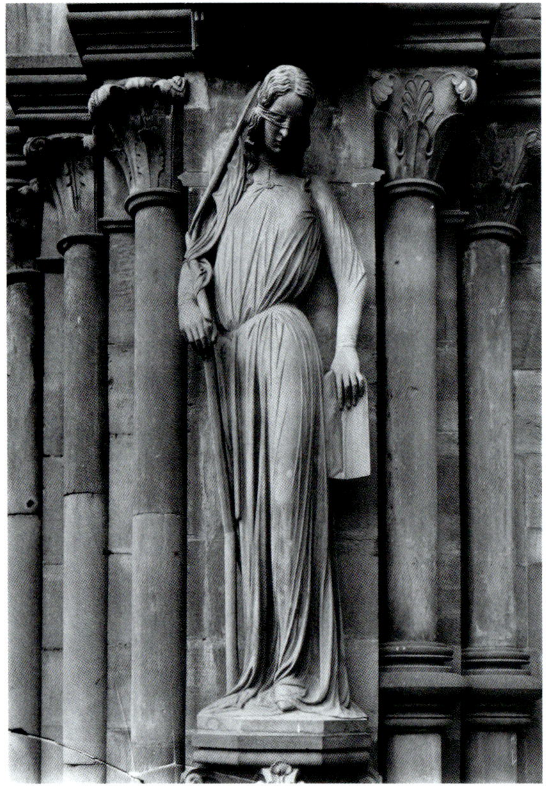

FIG. 23
Synagoga. Strasbourg Cathedral, south portal. © Foto Marburg / Art Resource, NY.

The Ecclesia-Synagoga motif emerges only occasionally in Iberian liturgical manuscripts, often in those whose decorative traditions maintained consistency with works produced in France and elsewhere. In a missal from Sant Cugat del Vallès, made for Barcelonese use in 1315 (Barcelona, Archives of the Crown of Aragon, Sant Cugat MS 24), the pair appears within the initial V at the beginning of the Common Preface ("Vere dignum et justum est," fol. 90v) of the Ordinary of the Mass.[77] Flanking a cross bearing a roundel containing the lamb of God, Ecclesia triumphantly raises her chalice as the blindfolded Synagoga falls limply backward, her staff shattered and the tablets of the law falling from nerveless fingers (fig. 24). The placement of this motif in the *Vere dignum* initial, like the layout and figure style of the manuscript in general, derives from and strongly resembles French manuscript traditions of the thirteenth and fourteenth centuries and was doubtless derived from them.[78]

Other Iberian depictions of Synagoga took more idiosyncratic form. The monumental pairings with Ecclesia so popular in thirteenth-century Germany remained extremely rare in Spain, and when they did appear, it was usually within a larger narrative of the Passion or Resurrection. Such was likely the case for a pair of polychromed wooden figures produced probably in Palencia or León toward the end of the thirteenth century and now in the Godia Collection in Barcelona (fig. 25). Along with a number of stylistically similar figures depicting the Deposition, the Entombment, and the meeting of Christ and the Magdalen that survive along with them, they likely formed part of a relief ensemble of the Passion and Resurrection that would have been displayed within a chapel.[79] Ecclesia can be recognized by her traditional accoutrements of crown and bishop's miter; her left hand, which probably held a cross-staff, is missing, while the right contains a large cylindrical opening that probably once held a chalice. Synagoga wears a blindfold, and her drooping head rests on her right hand; the missing left hand presumably held a broken spear. The posture and orientation of the standing figures suggest that they faced each other, most likely across a central Crucifixion.[80]

While at first glance these figures seem to replicate the ultra-Pyrenean type with minimal alterations, their intricate polychromy is thoroughly Iberian. Gilding, silver, and expensive blue and red pigments permit a strong contrast between the bright but simple patterns of Ecclesia's costume, which include castles suggestive of the Castilian coat of arms, and Synagoga's brilliantly striped robes, which intersperse strips of gilding and diamond shapes with vivid reds and blues in a distant echo of the Andalusi textiles that had become fashionable at the highest levels of Castilian society. This is an opulence to which an Iberian viewer would have been keenly attuned: no sterile limestone cipher, this Synagoga flaunts the love of the worldly luxuries that was held to have diverted her from the sobriety of Christian truth.[81]

The effort to translate for local viewers the essentially unfamiliar Ecclesia-Synagoga formula is further evident in a pair of picture Bibles made in Navarre around 1197 for King Sancho VII (r. 1194–1234). Each book contains an extended pictorial cycle comprising close to one thousand full- and half-page sequential illustrations, accompanied by brief Latin captions, that summarize the major events of the Old and New Testaments, the lives of several hundred saints,

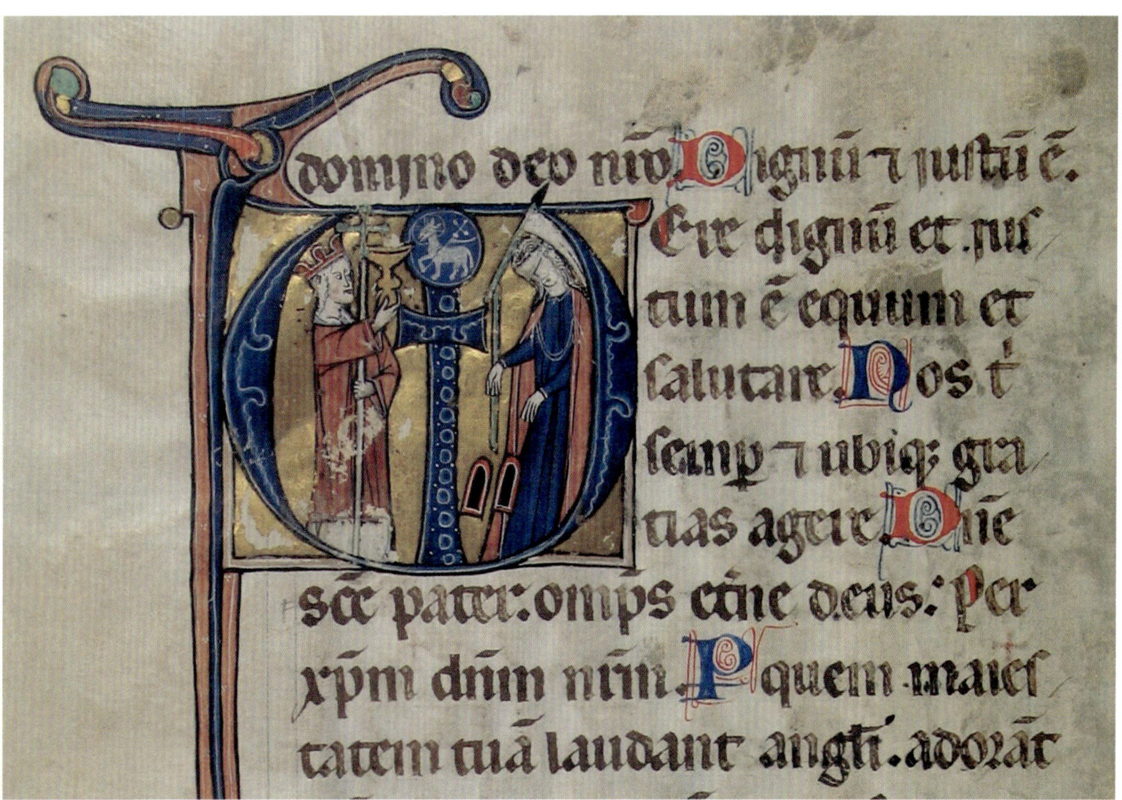

FIG. 24
Initial V depicting Ecclesia and Synagoga. Missal of 1315. Archivo de la Corona de Aragón, Sant Cugat MS 24, fol. 90v. © España, Ministerio de Cultura.

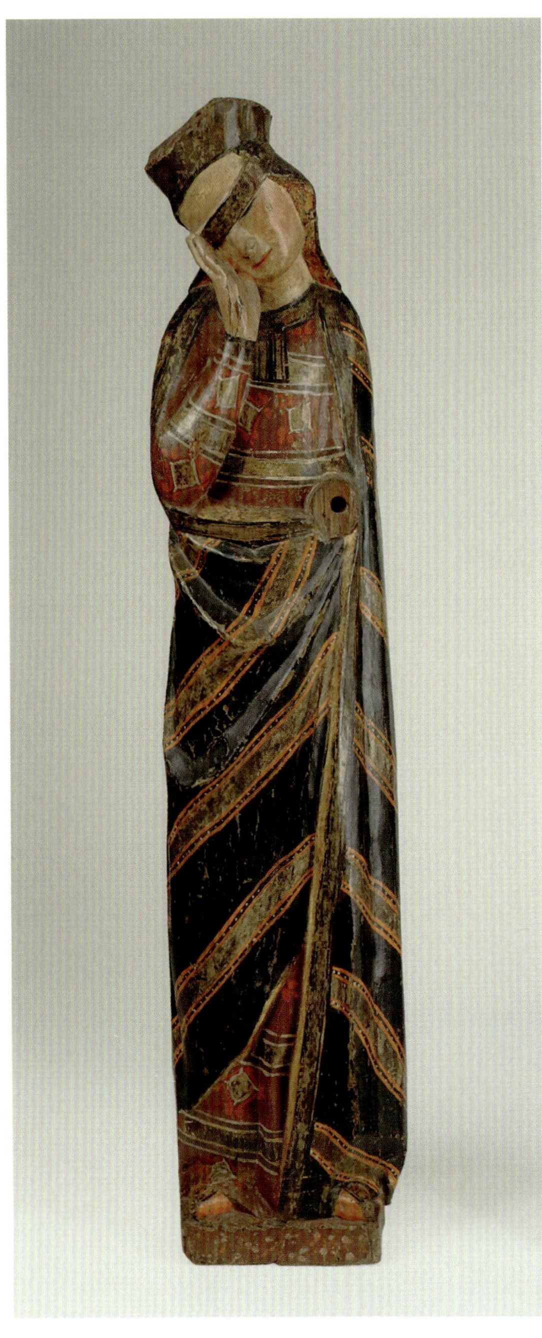

FIG. 25
Polychromed wood sculpture of Synagoga. Barcelona, "El Conventet" Collection, by permission.

and the second coming of Christ.[82] Navarre maintained close ties with France throughout the high Middle Ages, through both French settlement following the Reconquest and a complex network of dynastic alliances with Aquitaine and Champagne that peaked with the Champenois count Thibault's ascension to the Navarrese throne in 1234.[83] The uniquely extensive format of the Pamplona Bibles surely reflects this openness, as may their inclusion of Ecclesia and Synagoga as part of the image cycle. Nonetheless, the challenge of inserting the allegorical pair into an otherwise fairly literal biblical narrative clearly presented a puzzle for the artist, who solved it by inserting the image between Christ's descent into hell and the appearance of the angel of the Resurrection at Christ's empty tomb, placing the figures within the broader context of Christ's victory over death and also, implicitly, over Jewish disbelief.

Like the other sparsely colored line drawings that characterize King Sancho's Bible, the Ecclesia and Synagoga image is highly economical. The version in the presumably earlier copy, now held in Amiens (Amiens, Bib. municipale, MS lat. 108, fol. 193r),[84] depicts two seated female figures holding bannered staffs (fig. 26). Ecclesia, exceptionally placed to the viewer's right rather than to the left, raises her free hand in a gesture of rejection as she glares at Synagoga. The latter bows her head, her broken staff threatening to tumble onto her head as a fat serpent coils over her eyes in place of a blindfold. The inscription above the pair emphasizes the break with the Old Law that would be heralded by Christ's resurrection: "Isaiah foresaw, the synagogue remembers, but it never ceases to be blind. The Church separates itself from Synagogue."[85]

Several unorthodox features signal the newness of this motif to the Bible's illustrator. Most idiosyncratic is Ecclesia's placement to the proper left, or sinister side, rather than the customary right, and the yellow color of her banner, a hue more often associated with her Jewish counterpart.[86] Indeed, in a second copy of this Bible produced shortly after 1197 and now in Augsburg (Universitätsbibliothek, MS Cod. I.2.4°.15, fol. 210r), Ecclesia has returned to the

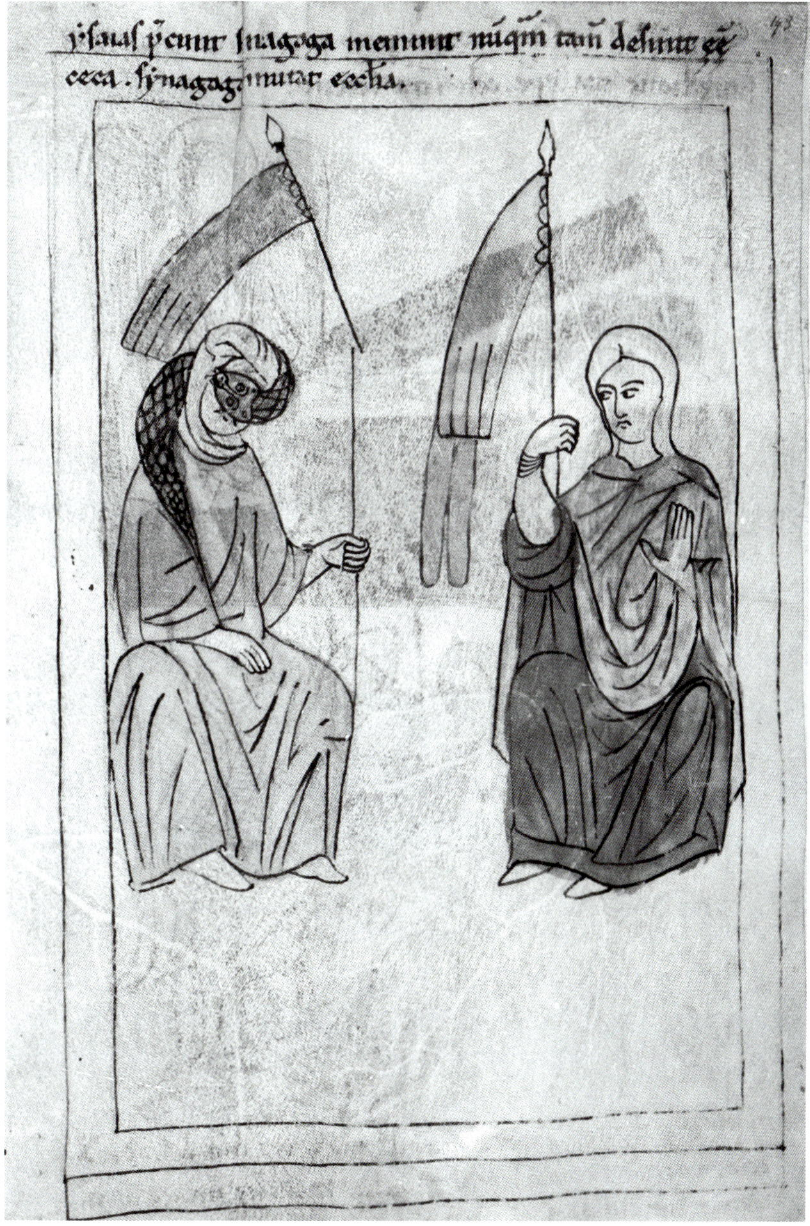

FIG. 26
Ecclesia and Synagoga. Picture Bible. Bibliothèque municipale, Amiens, MS lat. 108, fol. 193r. © Fundació Institut Amatller d'Art Hispànic. Arxiu Mas.

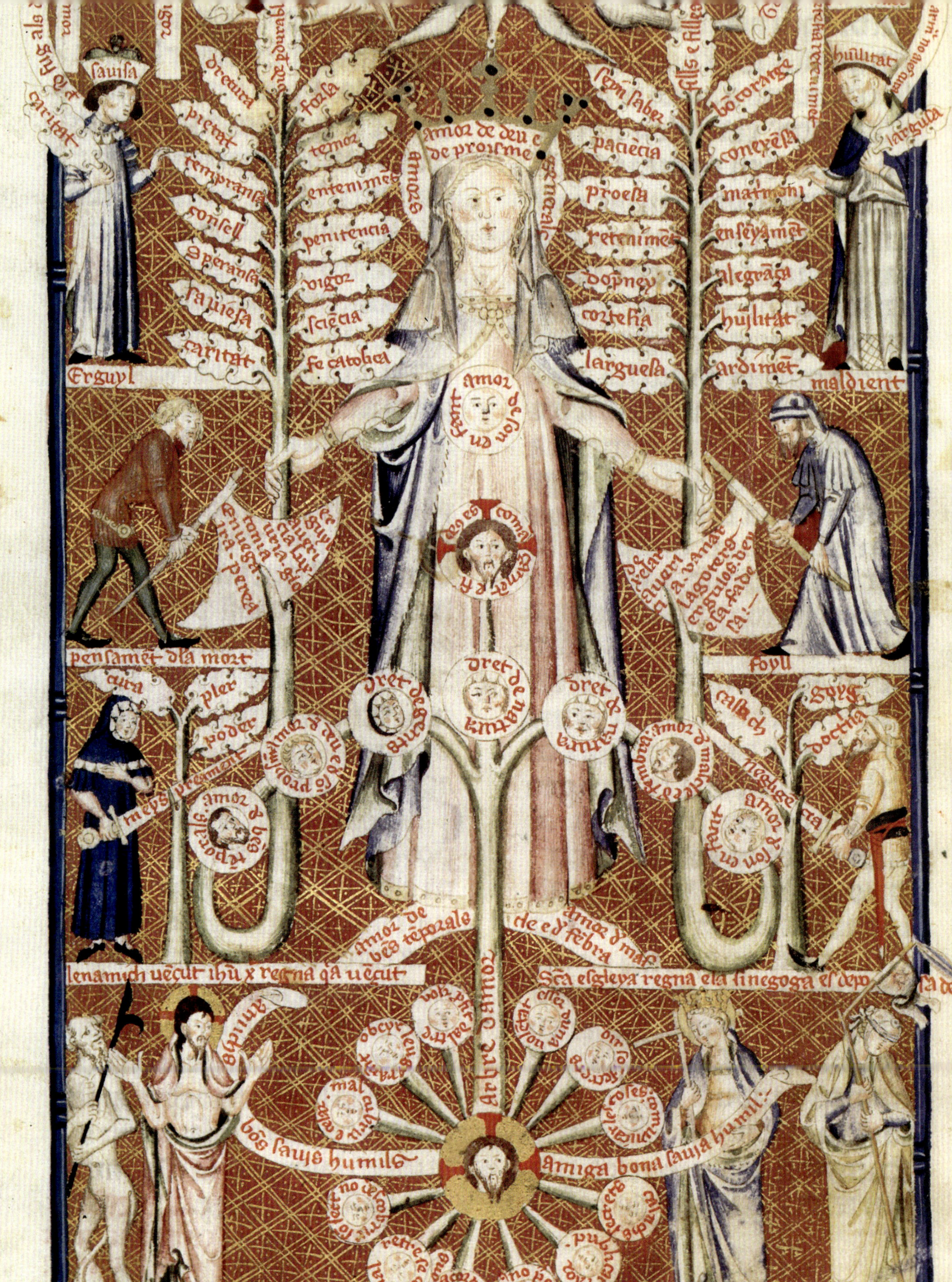

Amor de deu e de proisme
sauisa
humilitat
largueza
dreitura
forsa
pietat
temor
consell
penitencia
Esperansa
vigor
sauiesa
sciecia
caritat
fe catolica
seny saber
boncorage
paciecia
conexesa
proesa
matrimoni
retenimet
enseyamet
dopney
alegransa
cortesia
humilitat
larguesa
ardimet
Erguyl
maldient
Amor de son enfant
pensamet dla mort
foyll
dret de gentz
dret de natura
dret de natura
amor de bes temporals
amor d mascle e de fembra
Arbre damor
bos sauis humils
amiga bona sauia humil

FIG. 27
Diagram of the Tree of Love with Ecclesia and Synagoga. *Breviari d'amor.* BnF, Paris, MS esp. 353, fol. 7v. Bibliothèque nationale de France, by permission.

"good" side of the image, as if its artist had corrected an earlier misinterpretation.[87] Also unusual is the serpent that replaces the blindfold covering Synagoga's eyes, an element with no known precedents and few surviving parallels in the art of western Europe.[88] While its implication of satanic ties seems logical in this context, both this unexpected element and the confusion over Synagoga's proper position within the image suggest that the fine points of the European formula may have remained obscure to Sancho's artists.

More idiosyncratic still is the deployment of Ecclesia and Synagoga in Iberian manuscripts of the *Breviari d'amor,* introduced in chapter 1.[89] The standardized cycle of illustrations that became attached to this encyclopedic Occitan text appeared earliest in southern French manuscripts of the work and presumably originated there, but by the fourteenth century the same cycle had begun to emerge in Catalan translations of the work as well.[90] Especially distinctive is the portrayal of Ecclesia and Synagoga within a full-page diagram of the Tree of Love, a motif found in both Provençal and Iberian manuscripts. In a Catalan manuscript now in Paris (BnF, MS esp. 353, fol. 7v), the two allegories flank the Tree in complementary pairings with Christ and the devil (fig. 27): at left, Christ raises his hand in blessing as a demon slinks off into the margin, while at right, Ecclesia returns his gaze as a downcast Synagoga stands by.[91]

Whereas most aspects of this illustration closely follow the Provençal model, it is inflected by two subtle Iberian additions. One is the small ring affixed to Synagoga's headdress, which resembles those sometimes worn by Jewish women in Catalunya in response to the demand for distinguishing dress.[92] More complex is the eight-pointed star that marks Synagoga's banner, an element that (along with its relative the hexagram, as chapter 4 will show) was used indiscriminately by Iberian artists to denote non-Christian Others. The latter motif frequently appeared in military contexts, as it does on a Muslim standard in a wall painting of the conquest of Mallorca from the Palau d'Aguilar

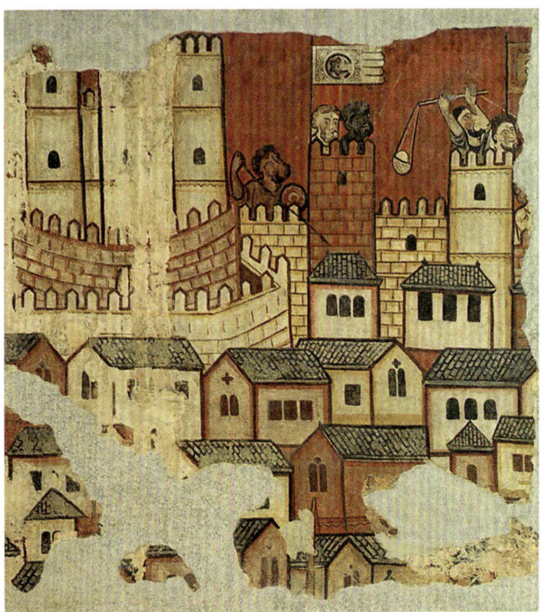

FIG. 28
Muslim soldiers at the battle for Mallorca. Detail of a fresco from the Palau d'Aguilar. Museu Nacional d'Art de Catalunya, Barcelona. © MNAC. Photo: Calveras/Mérida/Sagristà.

in Barcelona, now in the MNAC (fig. 28). Transferred to Synagoga's banner, the hexagram serves simultaneously to signal Synagoga's alterity and to suggest her potential violence toward those of the Christian faith, an insightful adaptation of this foreign motif in response to local expectations.

Jews and Money in Aragon and Castile

The influx of polemical images and ideas that crossed the Pyrenees from northern Europe could only have fueled Iberian Christians' desire to resolve the contradictions between the increasingly abstract religious opponent that such images presented and the actual Jews with whom they dealt daily on the street, in the market, and in the square. This discordancy surely was greater in Iberia than in those locales, such as England or France, in which an actual Jewish population had dwindled or disappeared by the turn of the fourteenth century, and as indeed is suggested by the often self-contradictory aspects of the imagery that did take root in Spain. This is nowhere more apparent than in the reception and dissemination of images related to Jews and money.

Iberian images linking Jews with money are distinctive in that they were grounded so predominantly in social and economic, rather than theological or philosophical, concerns. They drew not on a desire to locate Jews within the history of salvation, but upon the need to articulate the role and status of Jews within their own society. Throughout Europe in the eleventh and twelfth centuries, the revival of a money economy had raised new tensions in medieval society, especially in urban areas where most transactions were carried out, and these challenged the authority of a medieval church for which money and its handling posed an especially thorny moral problem. Of greatest concern to many was a rise in the practice of usury, the taking of monetary profit in exchange for the loan of money. The mere desire for such profit had traditionally been considered opposed to Christian morality, based on an understanding of the biblical proscription of taking profit from another's need as implying a kind of theft, a sin against justice, or even a sin against nature. As the economy of the medieval West became more heavily based on monetary exchange, legislation restricting usury among Christians mushroomed from the twelfth century onward.[93]

A well-known result of this legislative crackdown was an increase in Jewish involvement in moneylending throughout Latin Europe. Since usury between Christians had been prohibited—just as intrafaith lending was proscribed in Judaism and Islam—Jews found themselves encouraged into the practice of lending to Christians at just the time when the exchange and manipulation of money had become central to the functioning of the medieval economy. In much of Latin Christendom, the increasing exclusion of Jews from other trades by the emergent guild system, the growing curtailment of Jewish property rights, and the encouragement of rulers who enjoyed a percentage of the profit on such loans aided in inducing Jews into moneylending at so great a rate that, in 1145, Bernard of Clairvaux refashioned the word *judaizare* to refer specifically to the lending of money at interest.[94]

In northern Europe, these abstract concerns quickly found both formal and informal visual expression. An unusually elaborate example is an English scribal drawing at the head of an exchequer's roll produced in Norwich in 1233 (London, Public Exchequer's Office, n. 87: Hilary Term, 17 Henry III).[95] Designed to record tax payments made by the Jews of the city, it is the most complex of several such doodles preserved in English tax records of the period (fig. 29). It depicts two Jews at a counting table, accompanied by a hooded man with a balance and a demon labeled Colbif, who points to the pair's prominent noses as other demons advance with bags of money. Presiding over this scene is a surreal, crowned figure with three contiguous faces.

Inscriptions identify the central three figures as known individuals: the triple-faced figure is Isaac of Norwich (d. 1241), a wealthy moneylender whose debtors included the abbot and monks of Westminster, while the pair below are his collector Moshe ("Mosse Mokke"), who was executed for coin-clipping in 1242, and a woman named Abigail ("Avegaye"), thought by some to represent Mosse's wife and a moneylender in her own right.[96] The trio's questionable character is expressed by a number

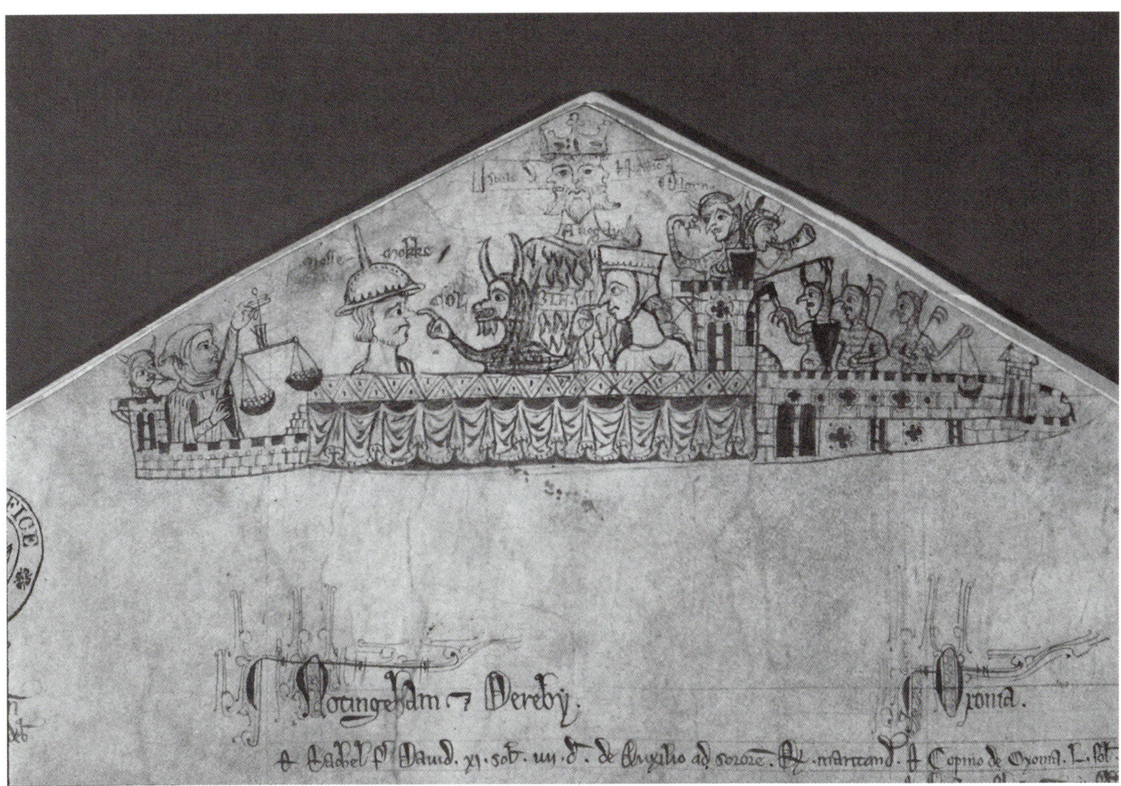

FIG. 29

Scribal doodle of Jewish tax collectors. Exchecquer's Roll. London, Public Exchecquer's office, n. 87, Hilary Term, 17 Henry III. © HIP / Art Resource, NY.

of equally negative signs: their enlarged eyes and noses resemble those of the demons that surround them; the presence of a figure labeled "Dagon" conjures connotations of idolatry; and Isaac's triple face and crown embody the same conventions as those commonly used in depictions of Antichrist. Although presumably little more than the impulsive doodling of an otherwise unoccupied scribe, this unusually complex image evokes many of the abstract concerns about moneylending that occupied medieval canonists and polemicists, such as the association with the devil—a theme to be discussed further in the following chapter—with Antichrist, and with idolatry.[97] Here, it intensifies these themes by applying them to specific individuals.

By contrast to the situation in many parts of Europe, the involvement of Iberian Jews in the economic life of their cities remained comparatively diverse during the thirteenth and fourteenth centuries. The relative weakness of the guild system in Spain, the long-standing engagement of Jews in agriculture and a variety of trades, and, in many parts of Iberia, the sluggish enforcement of canon laws restricting Christian moneylending slowed Jewish involvement in the money trade in many areas—although in some cities, such as Vic, this engagement did occur very quickly.[98] Iberian images that play upon the Jewish role in moneylending emerged at a commensurately tardy pace.

In their earliest form, stereotypes linking Jews with money were often embedded in imported narratives, including hagiographical legends. One such is the tale of Saint Nicholas, portrayed on a series of early thirteenth-century pier capitals in the cloister of Tarragona.[99] Embedded among several more familiar miracles associated with the saint is a capital depicting Nicholas's restitution of funds to a Jew who had lent money to a Christian (fig. 30). As the tale goes, the Christian, who had sworn by Saint Nicholas that he would repay the funds promptly, refused to do so and was brought before a judge. Having hidden the coins in a hollow staff, he asked the Jew to hold this as he swore that the latter was in possession of the money as he spoke. After deceiving both judge and Jew, he left for home, only to be struck and killed by a cart, which broke open the staff to reveal his hidden wealth. The Jew, impressed by what he took to be divine retribution, refused to touch the money until the victim had been revived by Saint Nicholas; he then converted to Christianity.[100]

The Tarragona capital presents the two critical moments in this narrative, the Christian swearing before the judge and the accident with the cart. In this, it follows an iconographic tradition also common in France, the likely source of this imagery.[101] It is notable that the figure of the Jew receives relatively little emphasis here: he is distinguished from the Christian only by a pointed hood, and his negative role as a moneylender is easily outweighed by his victimhood and subsequent conversion. Instead, in this tale, his primary function seems aimed at demonstrating the authenticity and conversionary power of the saint.

Such ambiguity would soon change: in both Navarre and the Crown of Aragon, the growing prominence of Jews in economic life was fostered by access to Mediterranean trade in the latter half of the thirteenth century, as well as by the encouragement of the Aragonese kings, for

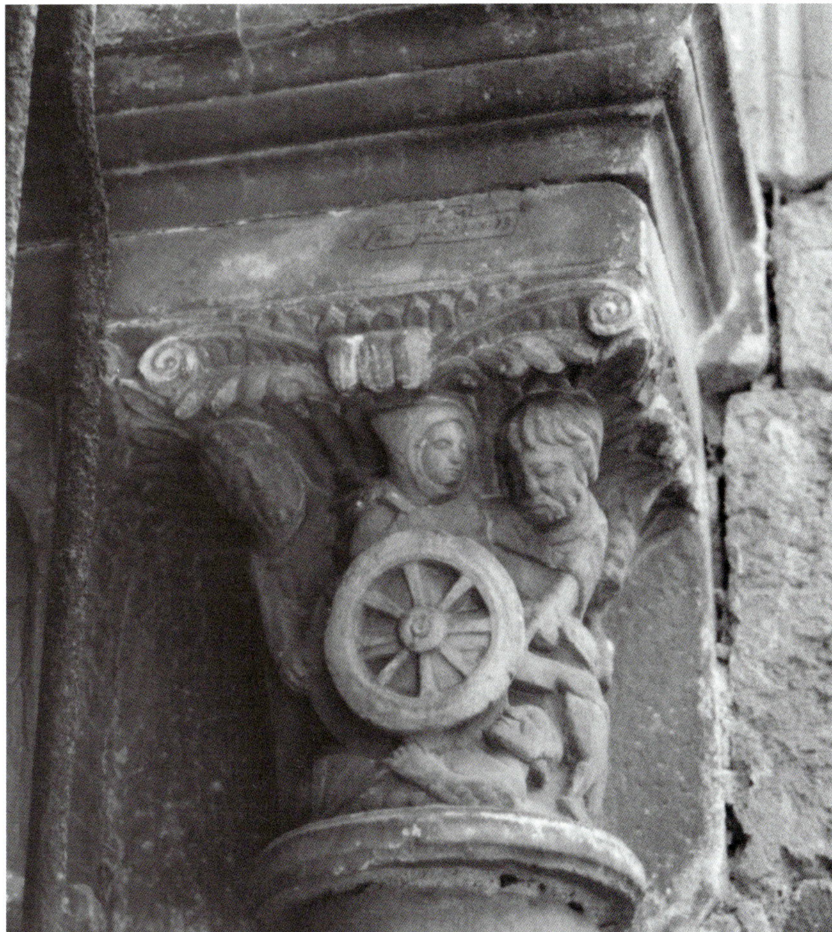

FIG. 30
Saint Nicholas punishing a man who deceived a Jewish moneylender. Detail of a capital, Tarragona Cathedral cloister. © Pamela A. Patton.

whom Jewish communities and moneylenders both represented a dependable source of income.[102] This new role is suggested by an illuminated initial in a late thirteenth- to early fourteenth-century manuscript of the *Corpus iuris civilis,* produced in Catalunya and now in Paris (BnF, MS lat. 8936). Introducing a section on the management of royal funds, it depicts a king surrounded by his financial officers, who include a knight, several clerics, and, at the left perimeter, a well-dressed, bearded figure whose pointed hat and money bag suggest that he is a Jew (fig. 31). If so, the image represents an embellishment of the original legal language, which does not refer to Jews at all, by acknowledging the new centrality of Jewish courtiers in the running of the royal fisc.[103]

While the *Corpus iuris civilis* presents the Jewish lender relatively benignly as a cog in the fiscal workings of the realm, other manuscripts present a more critical view. Characteristically incisive is the lavishly illuminated vernacular manuscript of the *Vidal mayor,* or *Feudal Customs of Aragon,* produced in Navarre in the

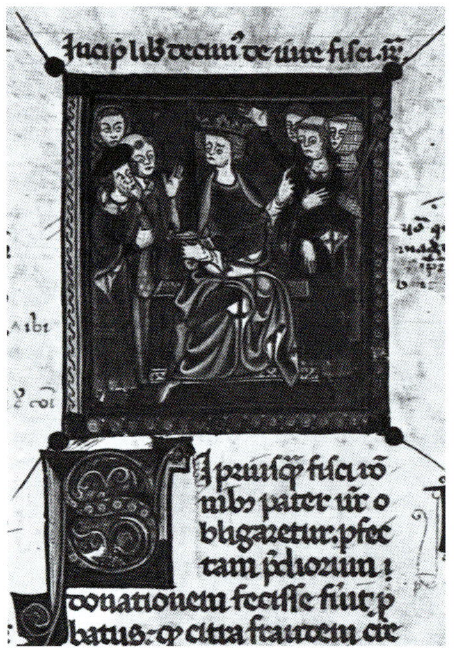

FIG. 31
A king and his administrators. *Corpus iuris civilis.* BnF, Paris, MS lat. 8936, fol. 89r. Bibliothèque nationale de France, by permission.

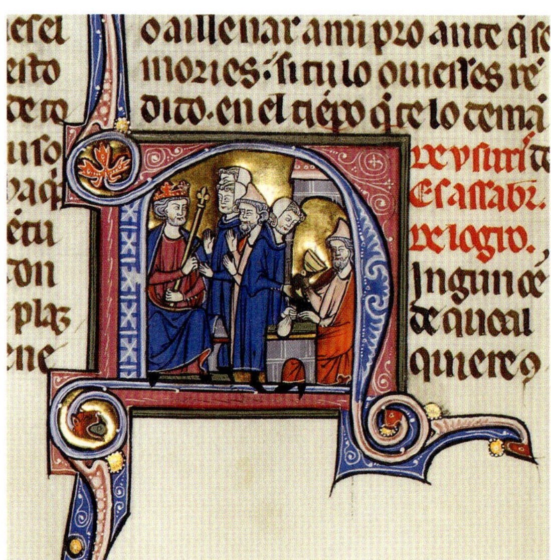

FIG. 32
Initial N depicting a Jew and Christian before their king (detail). Tempera and gold leaf on parchment, leaf dimensions 36.5 x 24 cm. *Vidal mayor,* ca. 1290–1310. The J. Paul Getty Museum, Los Angeles, MS Ludwig XIV 6, fol. 175v.

late thirteenth century and now in the Getty Museum (MS Ludwig XIV 6, 83.MQ.165).[104] First compiled in Latin in 1247, the *Vidal mayor* represents the effort of Vidal de Canellas, then bishop of Huesca, to bring together and systematize all the feudal laws of Aragon for his patron, James I. The Getty manuscript contains a Navarro-Aragonese translation of this text, the illumination of which includes large historiated initials at the opening of each book and smaller initials and marginalia at most section headings.[105]

One such illumination is the initial N preceding a chapter entitled "On Usury" (*De logro;* fol. 175v). It contains two related scenes: at left, a Christian and a Jew, the latter in a pointed hat, appeal to a king for judgment, while at right appears a scene of their original conflict, depicting the Christian handing a chalice to the Jew in exchange for a bag of money (fig. 32).[106] Its content relates most closely not to the short chapter that immediately follows it, which prohibits usury among Christians, but to the next one, on the facing page, which sets limits on the interest rates permitted to Jewish lenders. Since the initial I that begins this chapter is too narrow to allow elaborate decoration, the relevant image seems to have been relocated to the nearest preceding initial—although it is also possible that, as in the *Bibles moralisées,* a Jewish figure here served synecdochically for the subject of usury more generally.[107]

The text of the chapter on interest rates is concerned specifically with the problem of

Jewish moneylenders, whose "avarice and cupidity" are no longer restrained by Christian competition: "Therefore it is the case that the custom of the Christians is not to practice usury, and the avarice and cupidity of the Jews began to grow so that it could not be borne, so that of those Christians who receive loans from them they ask usuries upon usuries without any moderation and against what we had already established."[108] Like its caustic text, which next catalogues the restrictions to be imposed upon Jewish moneylenders, this image speaks to a growing dismay at the social and economic disruptions caused by the sudden removal of Christian lenders from the field. Along with other, thematically similar initials within the same manuscript that will be discussed below, it attests to a strengthening link between usury and Jews that would be promoted in Iberian imagery.

In many cases, this linkage was effected not in the planned elements of manuscript or sculptural decoration, but in informal or marginal zones that fostered a freer approach to such associative imagery.[109] Many, unlike the planned illuminations of deluxe manuscripts like the *Vidal mayor,* take the form of more informal scribal drawings akin to the countinghouse scene at the end of the Norwich exchequer's roll. A number of such doodles are found in the distinctively Catalan notarial records known as *libri iudeorum,* inexpensive paper manuscripts in which were recorded economic transactions of all kinds between Christians and Jews of a given community.[110]

An unforgettable image graces the vellum binding of one such work, which records financial exchanges made between 1334 and 1340 in the Catalan city of Vic (Vic, Archivo Curia Fumada). Sketched boldly but sloppily in brown pen, it portrays a hunched figure whose profile displays to great advantage an enormously sloping nose, unkempt beard, and enlarged eyes (one now partially erased) placed askew on a bulbous forehead beneath a tall, elaborate hat (fig. 33).[111] An adjacent inscription reading "Salamó Vidal," identifies this figure as a prominent Jewish citizen and moneylender in Vic who, along with his brothers Juçef and Astruch, dominated the financial markets of the city from the 1330s until his death in 1349, presumably from the plague.[112] Salamó's personal share of this business was enormous: Irene Llop i Jordana's study of moneylenders in the *libri iudeorum* for the period 1341–54 lists him as a creditor for 126 different loans totaling 35,240 sueldos, nearly 55 percent of the money lent in Vic during this period. More than one of these loans appears to have prompted convoluted legal disputes in which Salamó also showed himself to be a more than competent negotiator.[113]

Adorning the very binding of the instrument in which many of these loans were recorded, Salamó's monstrous face recalls the more complex scribal drawing on the Norwich tallage roll, not just in its deployment of widely used negative signifiers such as outlandish dress and bizarre physiognomy, but in its focus on a specific individual. This aspect distinguishes it from the more generic and often more gratuitously violent drawings found in other *libri iudeorum,* several of which will be examined below. Yet, whether individualized or generic, these impulsive scribal additions attest that the *topos* of the predatory Jewish usurer, if still rare in more formal visual contexts, enjoyed pervasive

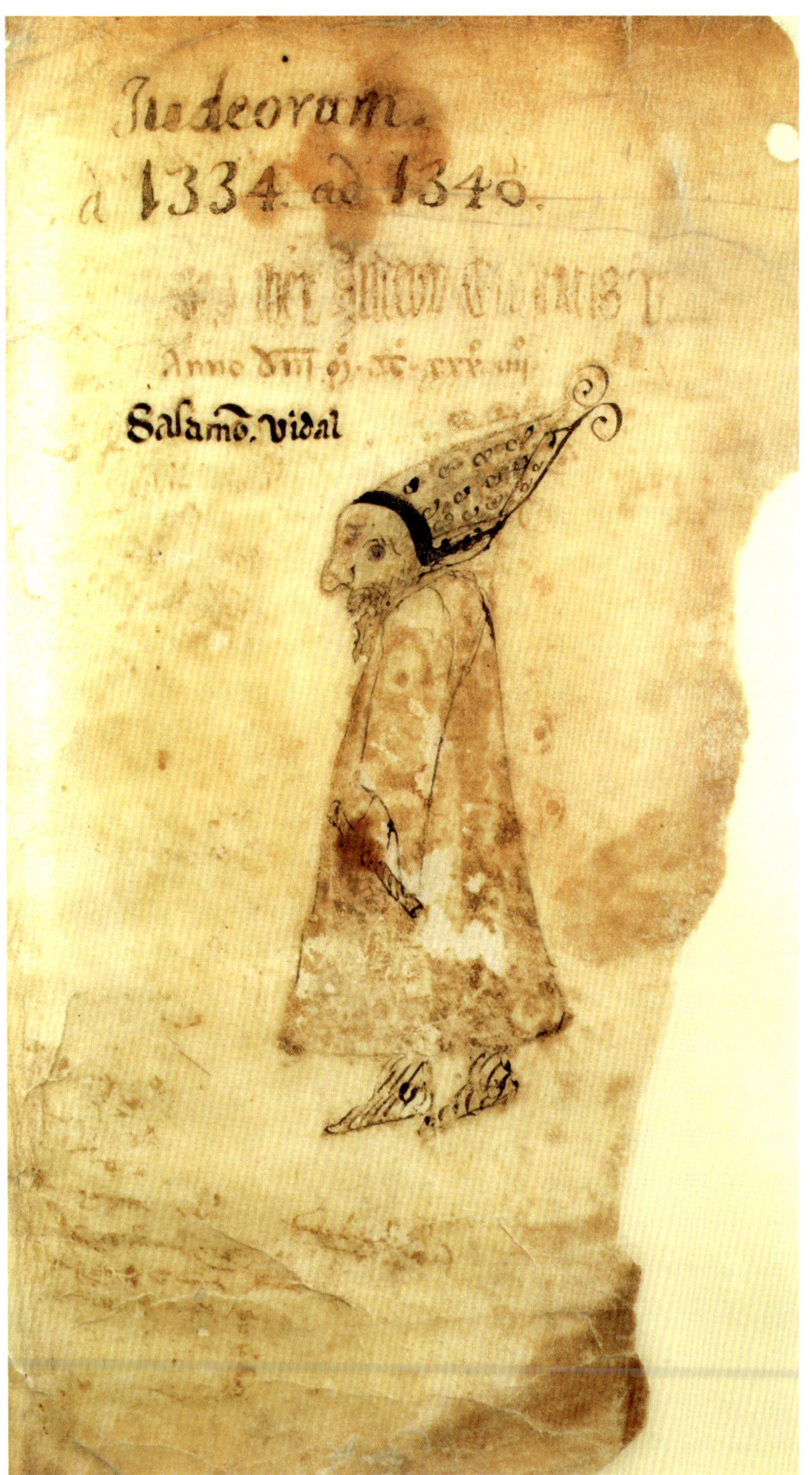

FIG. 33
Scribal doodle of Salamó Vidal. Cover of a *liber iudeorum* from 1334–40. Arxiu i Biblioteca Episcopal de Vic, Arxiu de la Cúria Fumada, núm. 4603. Arxiu i Biblioteca Episcopal de Vic, by permission.

success in the minds of fourteenth-century Catalan debtors and their scribes.

Closely related to the usurer stereotype was that of the deceptive Jew, bent on duping innocent Christians out of property, goods, or money. This stereotype was nurtured by the collections of exempla and miracle stories brought into Spain during the thirteenth century as a side effect of its engagement with northern European culture.[114] Unlike biblical narratives and religious allegories, such stories provided an unusually flexible context for imaginings about Jews and their place in a Christian society. Since such visions, paradoxically, could be both more immediate and more fantastical than reality, they were ideal for articulating contemporaneous social anxieties, whether individual or communal. One characteristic exemplum is incorporated into the *Vidal mayor* as part of a chapter entitled *De engaynno* (On trickery), which follows closely on the section discussing usury (fol. 180r). This recounts how a Christian lender is deceived by a Jew who has presented a cup of false silver as collateral for a loan. Recognizing his own deception, the Christian returns the trick by pretending to have been robbed, then restoring to the gleeful Jew not the more valuable chalice that he then expected, but the same false goods.[115]

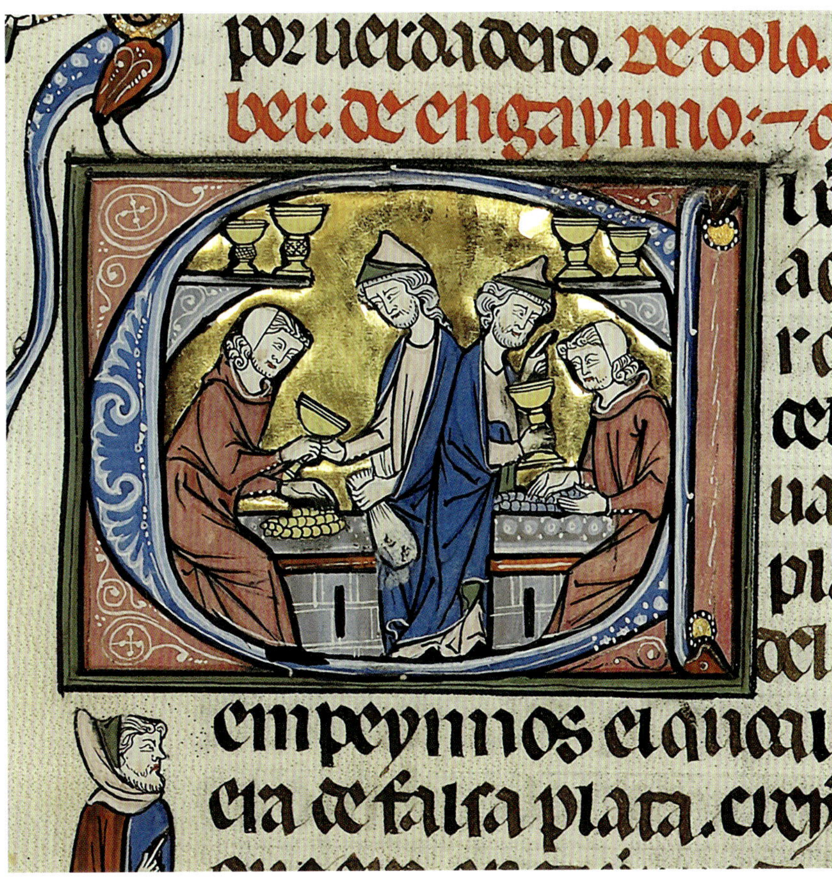

FIG. 34
Initial E depicting a Christian double-crossing a Jew (detail). Tempera and gold leaf on parchment, leaf dimensions 36.5 x 24 cm. *Vidal mayor*, ca. 1290–1310. The J. Paul Getty Museum, Los Angeles, MS Ludwig XIV 6, fol. 180r.

The miniature inhabiting the tale's initial E hews closely to the textual account, depicting it in two episodes (fig. 34). At left, a Jew in a pointed hat grasps a bag of money as he relinquishes a cup to a Christian seated in his shop; at right, the Jew raises his finger defensively as the Christian returns the worthless vessel. Both text and image draw force from the fact that the usurer is a Christian and the borrower a Jew, a reversal of the expected dynamic that emphasizes all the more powerfully the Jew's persistent deceptiveness in his dependent situation. His duplicity is alluded to in the margin as well, where a somber, hooded Jew is shown pointing reproachfully at the words "era de falsa plata" (it was of fake silver), which appear in the text column. Such mutual hostility is echoed in marginalia elsewhere on the page, one of which depicts a crowned figure battling a gryllus with a "Jewish" profile.

Resistance to Stereotypes

At least as significant as the stereotypes that found a receptive audience in Iberian art are those that did not. Whereas the majority of the Jewish *topoi* developed in high and late medieval Europe did eventually reach Iberia in some form, several themes that had become very widespread north of the Pyrenees found little footing in Spain during the period considered here. This apparent rejection of, or even active resistance to, certain themes pertaining to the Jewish-Christian relationship reveals the singularity of the Iberian Christian view of Jews and the lack of resonance that many European stereotypes held for specifically Iberian audiences.

One such theme was that of ritual murder, the claim that Jews periodically captured and ritually killed Christian children, often by crucifixion. This charge was sometimes intensified by the claim that the killers then made ritual or medicinal use of their victim's blood. The first recorded claim of this kind was leveled in the English city of Norwich following the death in 1144 of a little boy named William, although, as Gavin Langmuir has argued, its composition probably occurred years after the child's death.[116] Similar charges soon proliferated across Europe, reaching France, Germany, and Bohemia by the end of the twelfth century and—despite a papal interdict in 1247—tripling in number by the thirteenth.[117]

In Iberia, ritual murder charges developed more slowly, and they seem to have met with significant skepticism. Although legend attributes one ritual murder, that of a boy named Dominguito de Val, to mid-thirteenth-century Zaragoza, there is substantial evidence that this narrative was a sixteenth-century invention.[118] The first documented ritual murder charges did not appear until 1294 in Zaragoza and Biel, and only a handful of others followed before Iberia's most famous case, that of the Niño de La Guardia, in Castile, in 1491.[119] Iberian authorities generally handled such charges with caution: James II of Aragon roundly chastised the municipal authorities of Zaragoza for accusing Jews of an attack that later showed itself to have been false, while Alfonso X expressed a characteristically ambivalent view of the problem in the great law code known as the *Siete partidas:*

> And because we heard that in some places the Jews reenacted derisively—and continue to do so—on Good Friday the Passion of Our Lord Jesus Christ, stealing children and putting

them on a cross, or forming waxen images and crucifying them when children are unavailable, we order that if we discover from this time forward that such a thing has occurred in any part of our kingdom, and if it can be determined, then all those involved shall be seized, arrested, and brought before the king. And as soon as he has determined the truth of the matter, he shall order the guilty parties to be mercilessly put to death.[120]

The king's hesitation to accept the validity of such charges is suggested by such conditional phrases as "if we discover," "if it can be determined," and "as soon as he has determined the truth of the matter," as well as by the king's insistence that he himself should determine the authenticity of the claim. This measured attitude suggests the rarity with which this accusation was made in at all in medieval Iberia, while it also renders less surprising the virtual absence of related images in Iberian visual culture of this period.

Similarly slow to gain acceptance in Spain was a claim that often followed in the wake of the ritual murder charge: that certain Jews took steps to steal and then attack the consecrated host. This narrative was first formally documented at Paris in 1290, when, according to a variety of Christian sources, a Jew persuaded a poor Christian woman to bring him a consecrated host from Easter communion. Upon receiving it, he subjected the wafer to a series of torments meant to test whether it was truly the body of Christ: stabbing it with a knife, striking it with a hammer and nails, burning it, and hoisting it on a lance before finally dropping it into a boiling cauldron. The host remained impervious to these attacks until it was placed in the boiling water, at which it turned the water red and the wafer transformed into an image of the crucified Christ that hovered above the cauldron, demonstrating its true nature.[121] As Miri Rubin has shown, in its various forms this narrative merged a growing anxiety about Jews with Christian doubts about the validity of transubstantiation and a new focus on the Eucharist in Catholic doctrine and devotion.[122] Its focus on Jews, who rejected the whole question of Christ's embodiment on earth, is thus logical but in some cases subsidiary. This indeed seems to have been the case in Iberia, where images of host desecrations performed by Jews emerged most often, when they did at all, within a broader eucharistic context.[123]

Like the chargers of ritual murder, the earliest recorded accusations of Jewish host desecration in Spain emerged in the latter half of the fourteenth century and were limited for the most part to Aragonese centers such as Barcelona, Huesca, and Lléida.[124] The earliest example is a series of images included in a retable-frontal ensemble made for the Catalan monastery of Vallbona des Monges, possibly just after 1348, now in the Museu Nacional d'Art de Catalunya (fig. 35). The central panel of the retable reflects its double dedication to the Trinity and the Eucharist; its image of an enthroned Trinity above a sacramental wafer is flanked by a series of eucharistic events and miracles, many drawn from medieval collections of *exempla* such as the *Dialogus miraculorum* (Dialogue on miracles) of Caesarius of Heisterbach.[125] Two panels at the lower right of the retable depict two Jews first stabbing the host and then raising it on a spear, episodes identifiable as belonging to the Paris narrative and its variants. The narrative continues on the accompanying altar frontal dedicated to the Virgin Mary, where three scenes at the upper right depict a Jewish man and a woman boiling the host in a cauldron, the woman rescuing the host, and the rescued wafer hovering over an altar. As an ensemble, the images constitute, in significantly expanded form, the same essential narrative found in the predellas of several other retables made in Catalunya in the late fourteenth and early fifteenth centuries, such

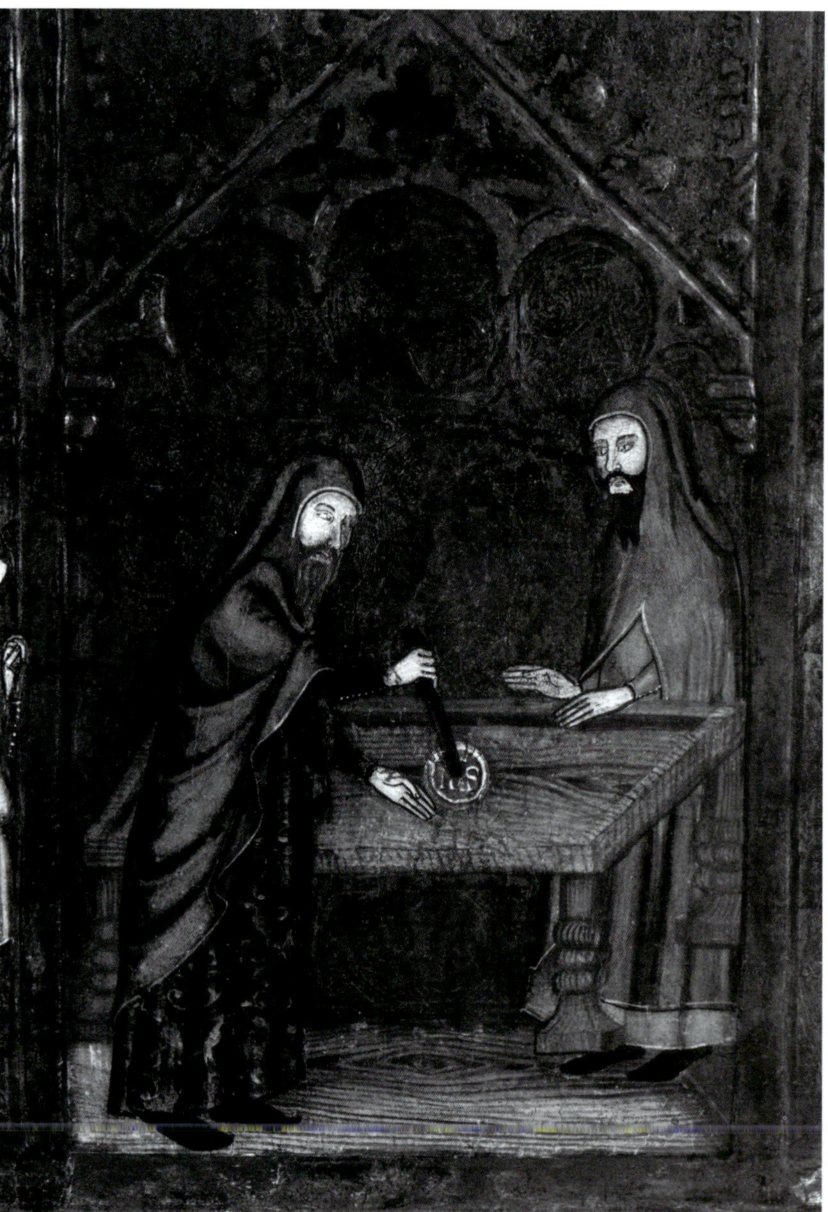

FIG. 35
Jews attacking the host. Detail of a retable from Vallbona des Monges. Museu Nacional d'Art de Catalunya, Barcelona. © MNAC. Photo: Calveras/Mérida/Sagristà.

as the retable of the Virgin from Sixena (Museo Nacional d'Art de Catalunya) and the retable of Corpus Christi from Vilafermosa (Castelló de la Plana, Valencia).[126]

The focus of the Vallbona des Monges ensemble is not exclusively on Jews, for it also portrays several eucharistic narratives in which Jews play no role, such as the tale of the heretic whose donkey refused to budge after seeing Saint Dominic holding the holy wafer. Thus, although the emergence of the anti-Jewish images here has often been presented as a direct reflection of growing hostility toward Jews within Iberia after the mid-fourteenth century, it may be more accurate to attribute such imagery to an increased appetite for eucharistic imagery and narratives more generally. As Rubin has argued, they might well have served more as a means of evaluating the nature of the Eucharist, or perhaps of testing the Jewish policies of King Pere III, than out of widespread fears concerning either host desecration or the involvement of Jews in such activities.[127]

When Jewish stereotypes did find expression in Iberian visual culture, it was, above all, on Iberian terms. Certain formulae, such as those that presented Jews as deicides or usurers, were adopted relatively readily in many areas of Iberia, especially the Crown of Aragon. Others, such as the symbolic figure of Synagoga, appear to have met with more hesitation, while some, such as the stereotype of the Jewish child murderer, found no real traction in the years under discussion here. Such *topoi* as did reach Iberian soil nearly always were adapted to suit more flexibly the preoccupations of an Iberian audience, even a specific Iberian locale, the ideals and circumstances of which often differed significantly from those of their non-Iberian source.

These differences are not to be taken lightly. The most violently anti-Jewish stereotypes to emerge in England and France flourished most fully after Jews became largely or completely absent there. In Iberia, by contrast, various kinds and degrees of social interaction with Jews as well as Muslims remained a normal aspect of Christian experience in much of Iberia throughout the late Middle Ages. The more outlandish stereotypes accepted in some parts of Europe may have stood little chance in the face of Iberian realities that repeatedly failed to bear them out. The wider variety of social and economic roles played by Jews in Iberia must also have worked against the formation of the more exaggerated forms of anti-Judaism. Moreover, as will be argued below, centuries of preoccupation with Muslims both within and outside of Iberian society may have reduced the intensity of those stereotypes that did emerge, if only by diverting the attention of those who might otherwise have focused their hostility on the newly perceived Jewish threat.

3

SHAPING THE JEWISH BODY IN MEDIEVAL IBERIA

Physiognomic and physical deformations stand among most enduring of all the visual mechanisms employed to represent Jews, both in the Middle Ages and the modern period. The commonly deployed Jewish "caricature" of modern anti-Semitic imagery, with its large or hooked noses, staring eyes, wild, curling beards, grimacing lips, and profile orientation, is fundamentally that of the Middle Ages, continuing traditions initiated in the visual culture of twelfth- and thirteenth-century Europe.[1] These traditions, as has been shown, drew in turn upon classical theories that equated the shape, size, color, and perfection of physical features, particularly physiognomic ones, with specific moral qualities.[2] The implication of this system, that mental or moral character could be read in physical appearance, deeply colored medieval depictions of Jews, contributing to the negative connotations of such images as the cabal of hook-nosed Jews that gathers beside the Crucifixion on the portable altar from Westphalia (fig. 5) or the deformed profiles of the tax collectors on the Norwich tallage roll (fig. 29).

Dysmorphic images such as these may have been related to medieval concepts of the Jewish body as actually deformed or diseased, ideas already nascent in twelfth-century religious polemics that accused Jews of carnality and bestiality.[3] Both medieval literary tradition and some scientific sources associated Jewishness with more specific bodily markers as well, including skin diseases, a foul stench, or an unnatural bloody discharge.[4] While it is difficult to draw a direct line between the somatic irregularities described in textual sources and the more conventionalized physiognomic features attached to Jews in medieval imagery, the two traditions shared a crucial foundation in the idea that the difference between Jews and Christians was something that could in fact be manifested physically, and they must have been mutually reinforcing.[5]

Several aspects of the visual tradition are especially salient here. First and most obvious is the fact that visual stereotypes of Jews—almost invariably male—were highly artificial, based less on the perceived appearance of actual Jews than on the desire to craft a recognizable and meaningful image.[6] Whereas they sometimes did incorporate features historically associated with real Jews, such as the long beards often customary for adult Jewish men, these images also included more fantastical elements, such as hooked noses and staring eyes, that in medieval visual culture were associated with specific mental or moral deficiencies. According to medieval physiognomic theory, hooked noses could be associated with vices such as excessive appetite and arrogance, and a large nose with covetousness, all characteristics often assigned to Jews in the medieval Christian imagination.[7] The often wildly distorted images that resulted, as Debra Strickland has observed, "tell us next to nothing about medieval Jews, but they reveal a great deal about medieval Christians."[8] As has been observed, the most virulent images of Jews very often developed at times and in places when interaction with actual Jews was reduced or absent; in such cases, they clearly served less as ethnic likenesses than as ciphers for a fantastic Other whose existence remained central to defining Christian self- and cultural identity in the social vacuum that remained.[9]

Such negative stereotypes were by no means passive: like the other Jewish signs discussed in chapter 2, they played an active part in disseminating Christian ideas about, and shaping Christian behavior toward, both real and imaginary Jews. It bears remembering that while many such images appeared in manuscripts and other private contexts, others emerged in works, such as portals and frescoes, that were easily accessible to a viewing public whose views could be reinforced or altered by what they saw. Such public examples could be especially influential: as Jacqueline Jung has shown in her analysis of Jews in the Passion on the Naumburg west choir screen, the physiognomic features displayed by key figures in the narrative were sometimes modified to achieve effects that were closely calibrated to both the viewers' experience and the designers' or patrons' intent.[10] While such public images certainly drew upon preexistent traditions about Jews and their place in Christian society, they simultaneously framed and endorsed such ideology for the viewer and his or her larger society.

As was the case for other signs used for Jews, the physiognomic and other physical features applied to Jews did not automatically carry with them a negative charge. Although by nature physiognomic markers were more apt to serve a negative function than were elements of costume or other attributes, exceptions certainly existed throughout Latin Europe, as well as in Iberia: biblical patriarchs and other figures seen as forerunners of Christ, such as Moses, Isaac, and David, are among those whose "Jewish" physiognomy lacks a clearly pejorative sense.[11] Indeed, as the association of certain facial features with Jews in particular became more consistent in the Latin West, they began to take on a life of their own as a conventionalized cluster of features that could effectively denote a Jew without automatically connoting a negative reading. It would be misleading to describe these as Jewish stereotypes in any absolute sense: although they generally included certain well-known elements, such as a large nose or long beard, that were traditional to such stereotypes, they display unusual variety with regard to other elements, such as hair color, eye shape, facial expression, and other bodily features.[12] Identifying and interpreting a medieval image of a Jew thus becomes a two-stage process, in which the recognition of a figure as a Jew per se is distinct from the analysis of its positive or negative connotations. An admittedly subjective enterprise, it inevitably encompasses issues of context, function, and reception as well as the agenda of patron and artist. While this might be claimed for nearly any part of the Latin West, it is nowhere more true than in the complex cultural patchwork formed by high and late medieval Iberia.

The depiction of Jews with stereotyped features was relatively slow to catch on in Spain's Christian kingdoms, reaching a form clearly comparable with those elsewhere in Europe only toward the last quarter of the thirteenth century. That this was considerably later than in many areas of Europe is significant in itself, for it signals the differing receptivity of Iberian artists to these and many other Jewish signs that became increasingly available to them during this period. The present chapter will examine how Iberian artists and viewers came to grapple with this particularly powerful means of articulating Jewish difference, focusing on their efforts to reconcile what were basically foreign visual motifs with decidedly local experiences and expectations. Given the much longer history of Jewish communities in much of Christian Iberia and the more extensive interaction with Christians there than in European lands where Jews were scarce or absent, one must ask how such imaginatively constructed visual images would have functioned for Christians whose daily contact with Jews challenged the claims on which such images drew.

In examining this question, this chapter will pursue several lines of inquiry. First, it will investigate how the physiognomic and physical distortions that played such a powerful role in formulating notions of the Jew elsewhere in medieval Europe were adapted to accommodate cultural and theological differences between Iberia and its neighbors. The study of both "high art" examples like royal and ecclesiastical manuscripts and "low" ones like the scribal drawings on late medieval notarial documents reveals the wide range of roles that such forms could play as their context and viewership varied. A subsequent section will examine briefly the handling of Jewish physiognomy in the historical, scientific, and musical manuscripts produced for the Castilian king Alfonso X (r. 1252–84). Unlike the other, highly diverse works discussed in this chapter's first section, those in Alfonso's extraordinary scriptorium were produced within sharply circumscribed social circumstances that demand closely individualized analysis. We shall find, nonetheless, that Alfonsine depictions of the Jewish body demonstrate both less consistency and greater multivalency than might be expected from the products of a single patron's court.

Analysis of the works in this chapter suggest that the so-called Jewish caricature so often sought in medieval imagery never enjoyed the consistent popularity in Iberia that it did in other areas of Europe, perhaps because it remained too abstract for many Iberian viewers, for whom, until relatively late in the Middle Ages, Jews may simply have been too real a presence to be seen from such an artificial perspective. That eventual accommodation, however, gives rise to a further question that will occupy the remainder of the chapter. Was the gradual acceptance of corporeal distortion as a way of representing Jews in Spain connected in any way with the changing late medieval perception of both Jews and Muslims as literally different races, and through this to the rising Christian anxieties about conversion and miscegenation that characterized the fifteenth century? Although the answer to this question lies partly beyond the scope of the present book, framing it here may help to clarify the role that images played in the formation of identity as Iberian history wore on.

Physiognomy and Enmity

Whereas various forms of distinctive costume, such as the hooded cloak, emerged as Jewish markers in Iberia by the turn of the thirteenth century, physiognomic distortions were slower to enter the mix of signs associated with Jews there. When they did so, they retained a characteristically Iberian pliancy. In the early thirteenth-century Isidoran manuscripts discussed in the previous chapter, the heretics Helvidius and Iovinian shared with Judaeus not just such attributes as pseudo-Hebrew text, but also the pointed nose and long beard that would come to be seen in Iberia, as elsewhere, as traditional Jewish identifiers. Clearly in this case, as elsewhere in Europe, such features could be deployed more for their reference to the deficiencies of unbelief or character than for any specific association with Jews.

The last quarter of the thirteenth century, however, ushered in more consistent, and more consistently negative, handling of Jewish physiognomy in the Christian kingdoms of Iberia. Although such traditions, as we shall see, also made their appearance in the kingdom of Castile, their emergence was more forceful in Navarre and the Crown of Aragon, where economic and social tensions had been intensified by new Jewish emigration and the formation of royal policies influenced by those in France.

One of the earliest contexts for such stereotypes would be provided by images related to current Jewish-Christian dialectics, such as those in the Vic Bible of 1273, introduced in the last chapter. Here, a number of initials inspired by the Dominican order and the religious disputations sponsored by them are intensified by the physiognomic distortion of the Jews who debate with mild-featured Christian clerics (fig. 21), while in several Old Testament initials the large eyes, menacingly lowered brows, and exaggeratedly hook-nosed profiles of the Israelites signal their recalcitrance and hostility to the leadership of Christian prototypes Moses and Joshua (fig. 20).

This distinction between these idealized prophets and their flawed Israelite followers shares much with French traditions of biblical decoration, as seen in the Psalter produced for Blanche of Castile between 1220 and 1226 (Paris, Bib. de l'Arsenal, MS 1186). In one of the full-page biblical miniatures gathered prior to the Psalms text (fol. 14r), a roundel portraying a handsome, horned Moses receiving the tablets of the Law from God is paired with one in which a party of fearful Israelites, identified by pointed hats and enlarged noses, have relapsed into worshipping idols (fig. 36). This image, like those in the Vic Bible, suggests a desire to distinguish such Old Testament exemplars as Moses and Joshua, who were described in Christian exegesis as forerunners of Christ and faithful followers of the Lord, from the disobedient biblical Israelites just as medieval Christians distinguished themselves from contemporary Jews, who were perceived as continuing to reject God's new Law.[13] Disseminated through sermons as well as through the preaching and disputations that occurred throughout the region in the second half of the century, such ideas surely were well-known in Vic's religious houses.

Another richly layered illumination in the Vic Bible extends this notion further. In an unexpected divergence from traditional decorative practices, the initial D preceding Psalm 26 has replaced the standard image of King David with a profile view of a paunchy figure with the long, slanted eyes, lowered brow, and hooked nose displayed by the Israelites in other initials of the same book (fol. 202v, fig. 37).[14] The blank scroll that he proffers likewise evokes those biblical models, while his hooded Aragonese mantle offers an obvious reference to the contemporary Jews of Vic. Even more striking are his red hair and beard, features sometimes displayed in medieval images of Jews to signal their traditional association with the treacherous Cain, who was also sometimes depicted as red-headed.[15]

Although this last association is subtle, it may offer an explanation for this figure's replacement of King David at the opening of Psalm 26. Cain's murder of his innocent brother had long been interpreted by Christian exegetes as an antetype of the murder of Christ by the Jews.[16] An extension of this reading may be intended in this initial, which suggests a link between Jewish enmity toward Christ and a text whose broad theme is confidence in divine protection from enemies: "Our Lord is the protector of my life, of whom shall I be afraid? While the harmful approach upon me, to eat my flesh. Mine enemies that trouble me, themselves are weakened and are fallen."[17] Invoking the familiar trope of Jew as Christian enemy, this reference subtly echoes other initials in the same Bible, such as those of Moses and his followers, which play upon the disbelief and implied hostility of contemporary Jews.

The deployment of physiognomic distortions to express Jewish enmity, whether toward Christ himself or toward his surrogates, found many

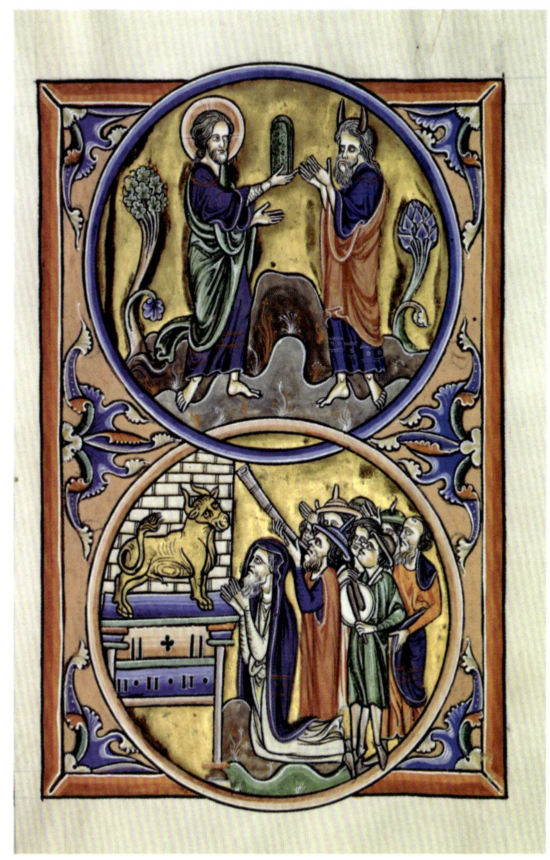

FIG. 36

Moses receiving the law and Aaron and the Israelites before the Golden Calf. Psalter of Blanche of Castile and Louis IX. Bibliothèque de l'Arsenal, Paris, MS 1186, fol. 14r. Bibliothèque nationale de France, by permission.

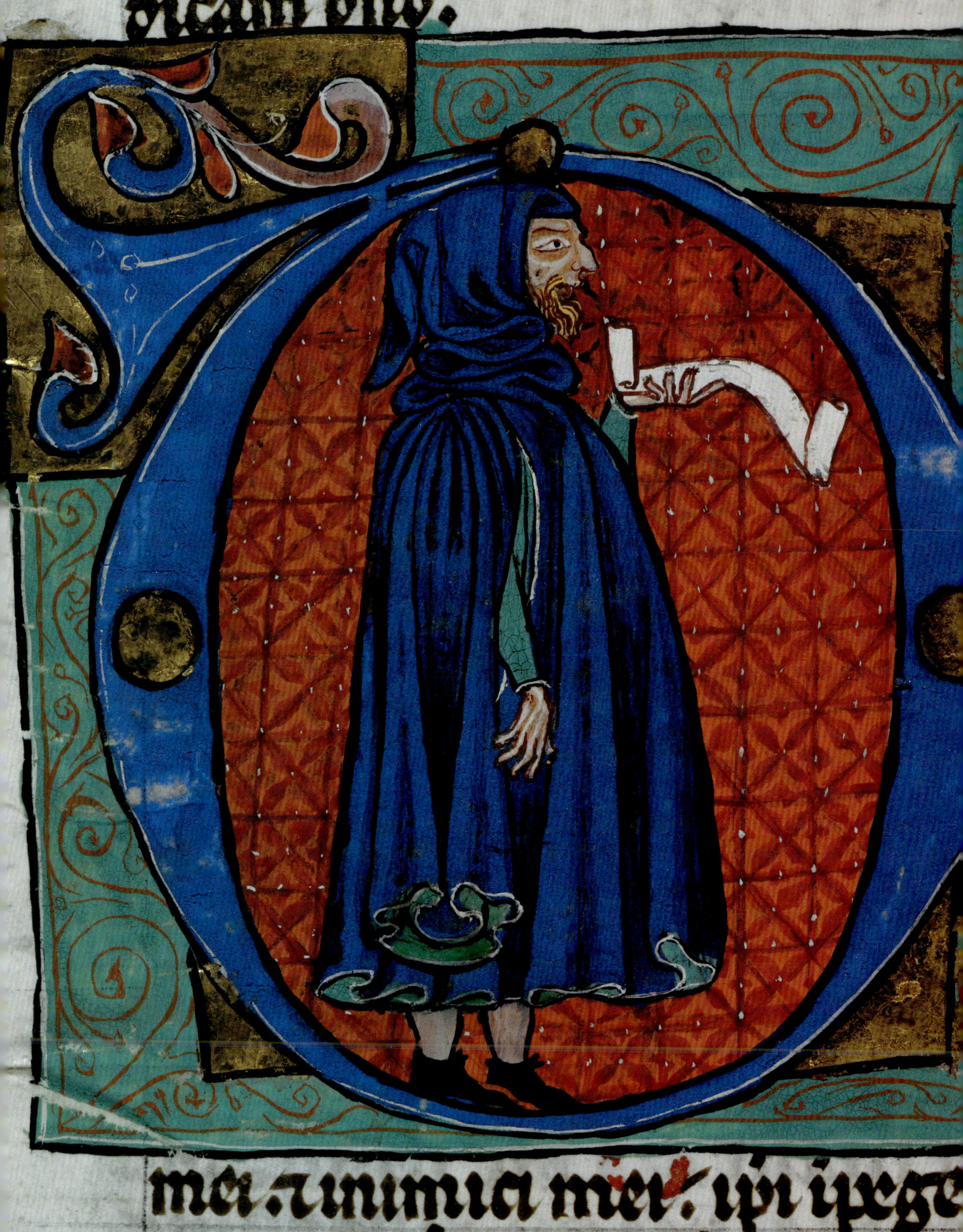
dicam dno.
mei. ⁊ inimici mei. ipsi ipege

FIG. 37
Initial D (Psalm 26) depicting a Jew. Vic Bible of 1273. British Library, Add. 50.003, fol. 202v. © The British Library Board.

related forms. One of these is the illuminated initial L that introduces the Exaltation of the Holy Cross in an early fourteenth-century Catalan manuscript of Jacobus de Voragine's *Legenda aurea,* now in the Bibliothèque nationale in Paris (MS esp. 44, fol. 199r). Here, a Jew whose enormous head, hooked nose, and grimly pursed lips protrude from a red Jew's cloak aims a now-tarnished silver sword at a figure of the Crucified Christ (fig. 38). The illumination illustrates a minor passage within this section, the main focus of which is the Emperor Heraclius's recovery of the True Cross from the Persian king Chosroes; as often in Jacobus's work, this account is followed by a list of somewhat tangentially related miracles. The relevant story is brief; it recounts how a Jew in Constantinople entered the Church of Hagia Sophia and encountered an image of Christ, which he attacked with his sword, striking it in the throat. The image began to bleed copiously, staining his attacker's face and head. Knocking the image to the floor, the Jew fled into the street, where a Christian saw him covered with blood and accused him of murder. In an effort to defend himself, the Jew led the way back to the church, where the two discovered the fallen cross and reinstalled it on its altar; recognizing the miraculous turn of events, the Jew converted to Christianity.[18]

In the illuminated initial, the protagonist is shown in the midst of his attack. Although his pose is static, his oversized head displays to advantage the long beard and enlarged nose common to many images of Jews, while his wide eyes and demented expression convey the violence of his attack with consummate economy. These exaggerations distinguish him from several other initials in the same manuscript in which the artist has forgone the opportunity to handle other Jewish figures in a similar manner. Even in a sanguineous vignette of the circumcision of Christ (fol. 30v), a subject that in later centuries would afford a popular venue for pejorative Jewish images, the Temple priests have been endowed with the same mild, three-quarter features that grace the manuscript's Christian figures.

Unlike the many miracle tales about Jews that thrived, as we shall see, in medieval Iberian visual culture, the legend that this initial illustrates was not widely disseminated in Spain beyond the *Legenda aurea* itself. What was it, then, about this story in particular that encouraged such strong visual embellishment? One aspect that must have struck a chord was the opportunity to render so succinctly the anti-Christian violence of which Jews were increasingly imagined to be capable. While more popular north of the Pyrenees, Christian imaginings about Jewish violence against Christ and his faithful had by the fourteenth century just begun to filter into the Crown of Aragon, where they would soon find expression in rumors that Jews symbolically attacked the body of Christ through acts of host desecration and, eventually, the ritual murder of young boys.[19] Given the manuscript's relatively early date and the lack of comparable imagery, this particular initial is probably best considered a rare and individualized response to a notion that had not, as yet, earned the consistent concern of most Iberians.

Fear of Jewish violence likely underlies another phenomenon known in much of Latin Europe but rare in Iberian art during this period, the extension of stereotypically Jewish features to non-Jewish figures shown attacking Christ in the context of the Passion.[20] Such a figure appears, for example, in the Crucifixion miniature added in the fourteenth century to a twelfth-century manuscript of the *Fuero de Estella* now in Salamanca (Bib. gen. de la Universidad, MS 2652, fol. 1v).[21] The inclusion of a Crucifixion image in *Fuero* manuscripts of this period was not at all uncommon, owing to the function of such books as a foundation for the swearing of oaths; however, the puzzlingly hybrid figure at the right edge of the scene is quite unusual

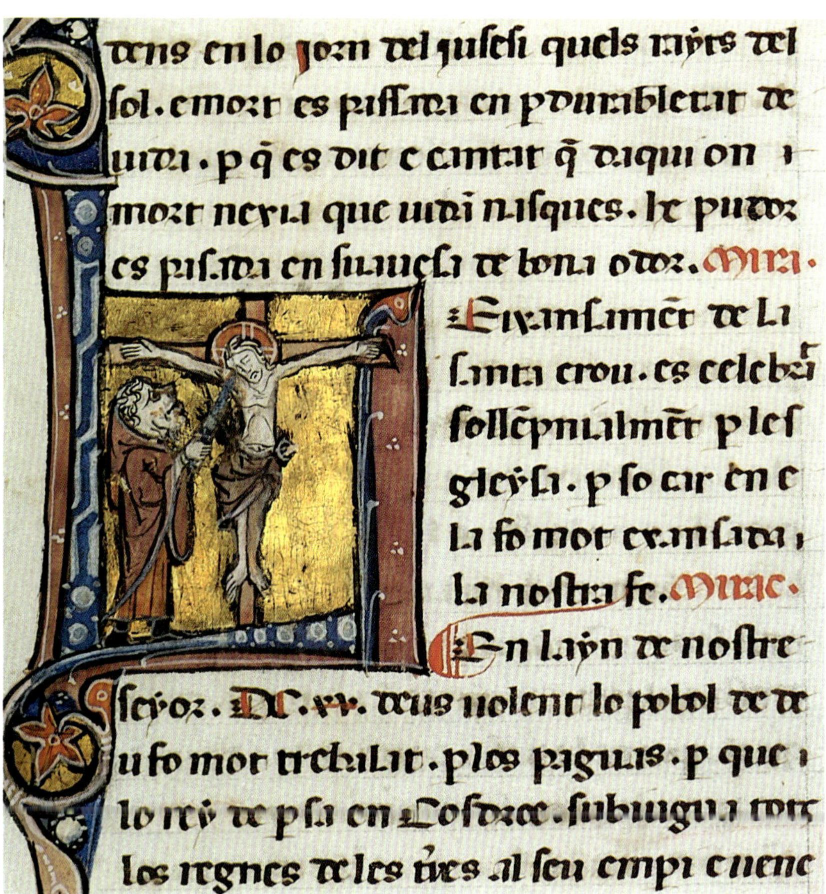

FIG. 38
Initial L depicting a Jew attacking an image of Christ. *Legenda aurea*. BnF, Paris, MS esp. 44, fol. 199r. Bibliothèque nationale de France, by permission.

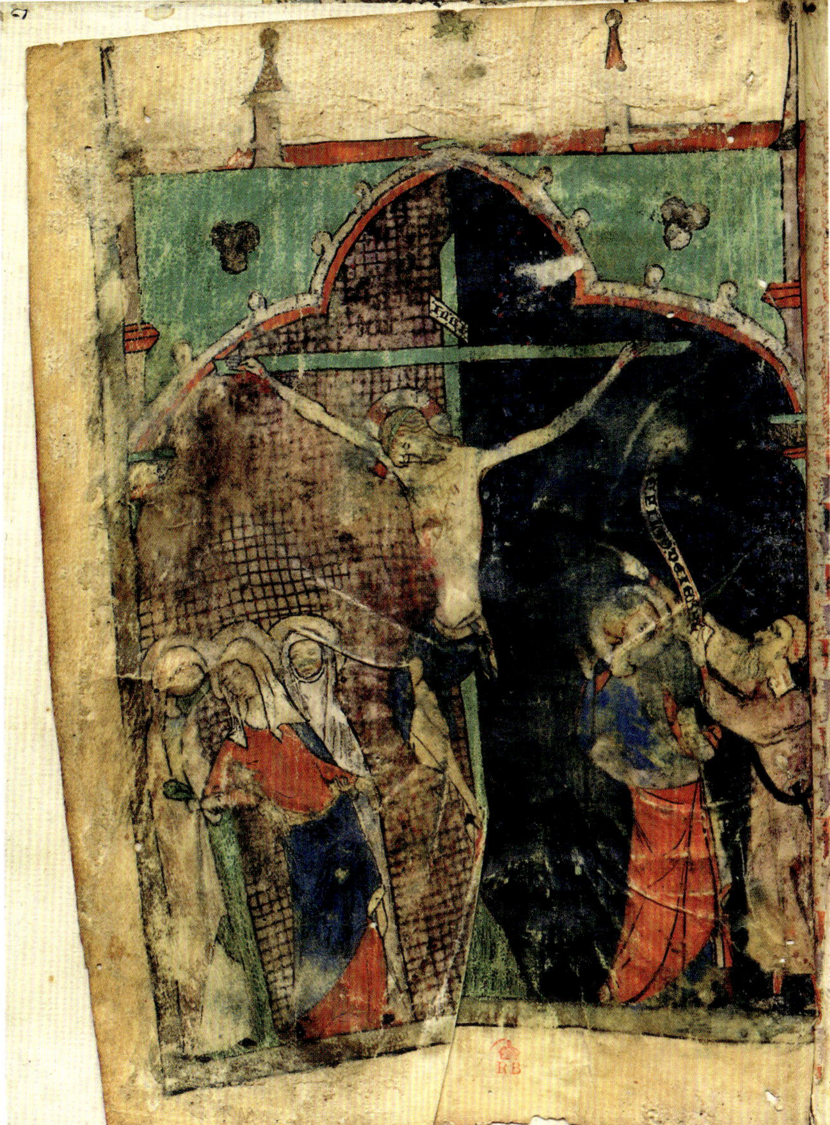

FIG. 39
Crucifixion. *Fuero* of Estella. Universidad de Salamanca, BGH, MS 2652, fol. 1v. Universidad de Salamanca (España), by permission.

(fig. 39). His helmetlike headgear and barely visible sword pommel, along with the banderole bearing the traditional inscription VERE FILIUS DEI ERAT ISTE, identify him as Longinus, the blind Roman centurion who pierced Christ's side with his lance and was converted when blood falling from the wound healed his sight. At the same time, his sharply pointed nose, abundant beard, and yellow clothing could easily be mistaken for those of a Jewish figure. In this guise, Longinus combines the violent potential associated with the Roman centurion with stereotypical Jewish features in a manner that plays upon not just the threat, but also the appealing conversionary potential of this witness to Christ's sacrifice. For thoughtful Christian viewers, the figure of Longinus might also have evoked other Jewish *topoi:* his blindness to Christ's true nature readily compared with the spiritual blindness ascribed to Jews in innumerable polemics, while his conversion after contact with Christ's blood is reminiscent of the *Legenda aurea*'s account of the Jew who attacked the image of Christ.

The Face of Deception

Physiognomic distortion played an even more powerful role in images concerned with issues that might have cut closer to home for many Iberian viewers, such as Jewish deceptiveness and control of money. Perhaps because so many images of this kind took the form of marginalia or scribal doodles, they are often highly expressive. Perhaps the most vituperative appear in the *libri iudeorum,* which, as we have seen, offered an ideal forum for the expression of fears about Jews and money. For medieval Christians, money already raised a host of bodily associations. Although inanimate, it could be provoked to reproduce as animate creatures did; moreover, it was unclean, repeatedly associated by Christian writers with bodily pollutants like blood and excrement.[22] Jewish involvement in the money trade therefore could be understood by medieval Christians as a logical outgrowth of the Jews' fundamental materiality, their inability to abandon the world of the senses and the body for the spiritual truths open only to Christ's followers. From this perspective, it was only logical that Jews' apparent preoccupation with the material, and especially their greed for lucre, should be reflected in depictions of Jewish bodies whose visible deficiencies reflected these flaws.

The emergence of visual imagery related to these concerns coincided with the rising prominence of Jews as moneylenders in the Aragonese Crown during the late thirteenth and early fourteenth centuries, and in particular with the economic growth of Barcelona as a result of participation in Mediterranean trade. While Jews in Barcelona, Vic, and elsewhere continued to participate in a variety of trades during this period, many were encouraged into financial business by the high demand for loans and, at least in the thirteenth century, largely favorable policies toward Jewish lenders on the part of Aragonese rulers eager for their own share of the profits.[23]

As has been noted, popular resentment of the increased Jewish control over moneylending grew along with this trend. Repeated complaints in the documents of the Catalan Corts, beginning as early as the mid-thirteenth century and intensifying in the fourteenth, soon prompted increased restrictions on the terms of Jewish loans and, under James II, repeated deferrals of debts owed to Jews. The continuing Christian appetite for Jewish credit, exacerbated by episodes of economic weakness in individual communities as well as self-interested royal meddling, added to the heightened social tensions that gave rise to the distorted figure of the Jewish usurer Salamó Vidal of Vic, introduced in the last chapter (fig. 33). Salamó's bulging forehead, monstrously displaced eyes, and long-lipped sneer reflect the hostility of a Christian community that clearly viewed itself as victimized by his domination of their city's moneylending trade.

Scribal doodles from the notarial books of other Catalan cities employed a similar visual language. A *liber judeorum* produced in Cervera for the period 1352–53 (Archivo Histórico Comarcal) depicts a crudely drawn figure with a hood and pointed nose; he holds a fish in his right hand and another, it seems, in his teeth (fig. 40).[24] Although the fish in this context have been interpreted as a reference to Levitical dietary laws, their presence here might also play upon the medieval tradition of offering fish in feudal obligation to one's lord.[25] The depiction of such offerings in the possession of a Jew, who as the literal property of a secular lord was sometimes also empowered to collect taxes in addition to lending money, embodies the contradictions inherent in this role, implying that the Jew has seized tithes not properly due him, or even that he is aping feudal status. Another dimension not likely to have been lost on the medieval viewer would have been the recognition of the fish as a long-standing symbol of Christ. Images of Judas stealing a fish at the Last Supper, derived from local Passion plays, still survive in the frescoes and sculptures of a number of Iberian churches in the region.[26]

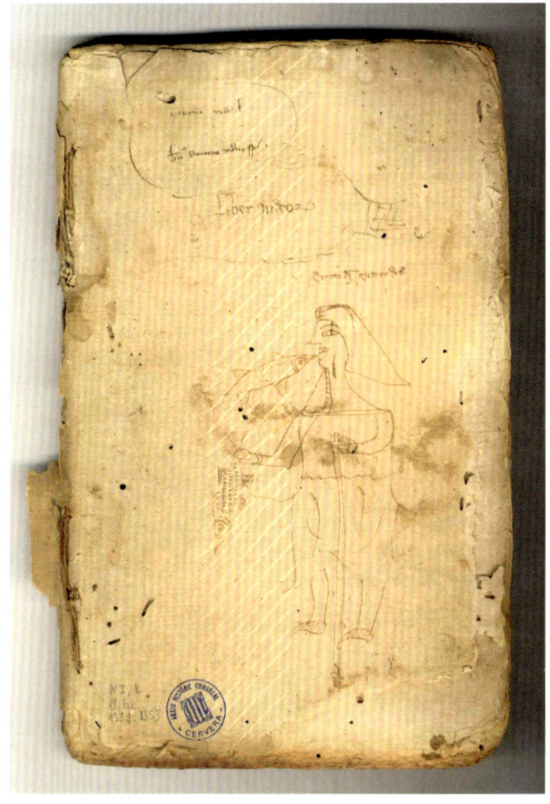

FIG. 40
Scribal doodle of a Jew. Cover of a *liber iudeorum*. Arxiú Comarcal de la Segarra, Fons del Districte Notarial de Cervera, notari Ramon Rama, 1350–53. Arxiú Comarcal de la Segarra, by permission.

A scribal drawing on the cover of a fifteenth-century account book from Cardona (Barcelona, Bib. de Catalunya, Archivo de la Bailía de Cardona, B-VI-3) illustrates the role of physiognomic distortion in evoking another association that was sometimes linked to their pecuniary stereotype: the association of Jews with the devil (fig. 41).[27] In this crude yet curiously intricate sketch, two Jews are suspended from a pole and carried off over the shoulder of a demon, who drags a third Jew by the headdress. The demon's sharply pointed nose and staring eye mirror those of his victims, especially the knifelike nose and jagged grimace of the Jew who hangs at the farthest end of his pole. Although clearly victims of the devil (as well as, presumably, their own avarice), the trio also seem to be his kin.

At the foundation of the perceived association of Jews with the devil was a simple equation: if Christ represents good and Satan is his opponent, then the Jews, who also opposed Jesus, must be on Satan's side.[28] This reasoning is reflected in innumerable texts and images that attribute the Jews' purported responsibility for the murder of Christ, and many related misdeeds, to the devil's influence. Already discussed in this light is the fourteenth-century Yates Thompson manuscript of the *Breviari d'amor,* in which demons physically prevent Jews from receiving the truths of their own scripture by covering their eyes and ears (fig. 2). However, the concept of a Jewish association with Satan could also escape its traditional theological frame to impinge upon medieval secular culture, best exemplified by the many moralizing tales in which Jews served as intermediaries for weak-

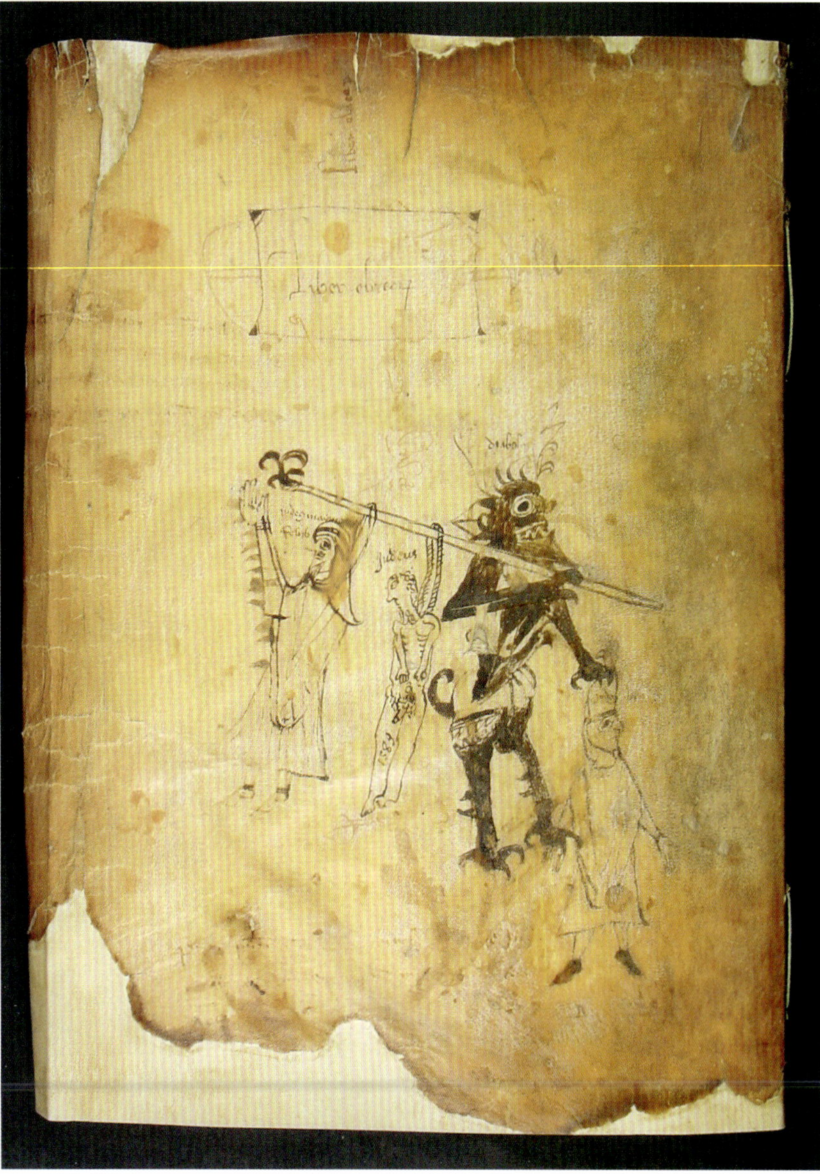

FIG. 41
Scribal doodle of the devil carrying off several Jews. *Liber iudeorum* from Cardona. Biblioteca de Catalunya, Barcelona, Archivo de la Bailía de Cardona, B-VI-3. Biblioteca de Catalunya, by permission.

willed Christian victims seeking consort with the devil. A particularly vivid account appears in the early twelfth-century autobiography of Guibert of Nogent, who describes a Jewish doctor who was called upon to cure a monk, but instead led his patient into the study of black magic and thence into a debased worship of the devil.[29] A similar relationship is formed in the story of Theophilus, a proto-Faustian tale with deep Byzantine roots, in which a vicar desirous of earthly power sells his soul to the devil with the aid of a Jewish magician, only to be rescued by the Virgin. The Theophilus tale in particular was widely disseminated in literary and dramatic form, as well as in works of art, reaching Iberia by the thirteenth century, where it was included in the *Milagros de Nuestra Señora* of Gonzalo de Berceo and as Cantiga 3 in the *Cantigas de Santa María,* among others.[30]

In the *cantiga* illustration, the tale is told in six panels, the initial two of which focus on his dealings with the Jew and the devil (Escorial, T.I.1, fol. 8r). In the first, Theophilus consults the magician; in the second, he is led by the Jew to the tent of Satan, to whom he kneels and offers fealty as the Jew, standing behind him, waves a letter in which the vicar's pact has been sealed (fig. 42). Behind the Jew appears a small legion of demons whose faces echo his hook-nosed profile and parlaying pose of his hands, emphasizing his collusive role. As we shall see, this is only one of a number of divergences from the *cantiga* text that emphasize the Jew's nefarious role in the narrative.[31] For the present, it suffices to demonstrate that Iberian artists, like those elsewhere in Europe, readily grasped the potential of physiognomy to underscore such demonic relationships.[32]

Cataloguing Jewish Difference at the Court of Alfonso X

The Jewish stereotypes discussed thus far have varied in keeping with their wide diversity of function and audience. However, a more homogeneous milieu was provided by the itinerant court of that most prolific of Iberian patrons, Alfonso X of Castile. Even before his accession to the throne in 1252, Alfonso had initiated what would become an enormous cultural enterprise including scientific, legal, historical, and literary projects, among other endeavors.[33] The often luxuriously illustrated manuscripts in which this work was preserved, and from which many of the images discussed here are drawn, were produced by a scriptorium whose organization and activities remain incompletely understood. Most probably, it comprised an informal association of scribes and artists who traveled with the king as his court moved, as was customary, among the major cities of his realm. The great number and lavish scale of the manuscripts surviving from his reign would have required the production of multiple projects simultaneously, so that several different artists, or groups of artists, might have been at work on different manuscripts at the same time.[34]

Both the lavishness and the variety of the manuscripts produced at Alfonso's court are remarkable. Their subjects range from history, geology, and astronomy to Mariolatry, hunting, and games, and they draw upon an even wider range of Eastern and Western models. They also present sufficient differences of scale, format, and decoration to result in illuminations that varied widely in quantity, style, and character. The function and expected viewer of each

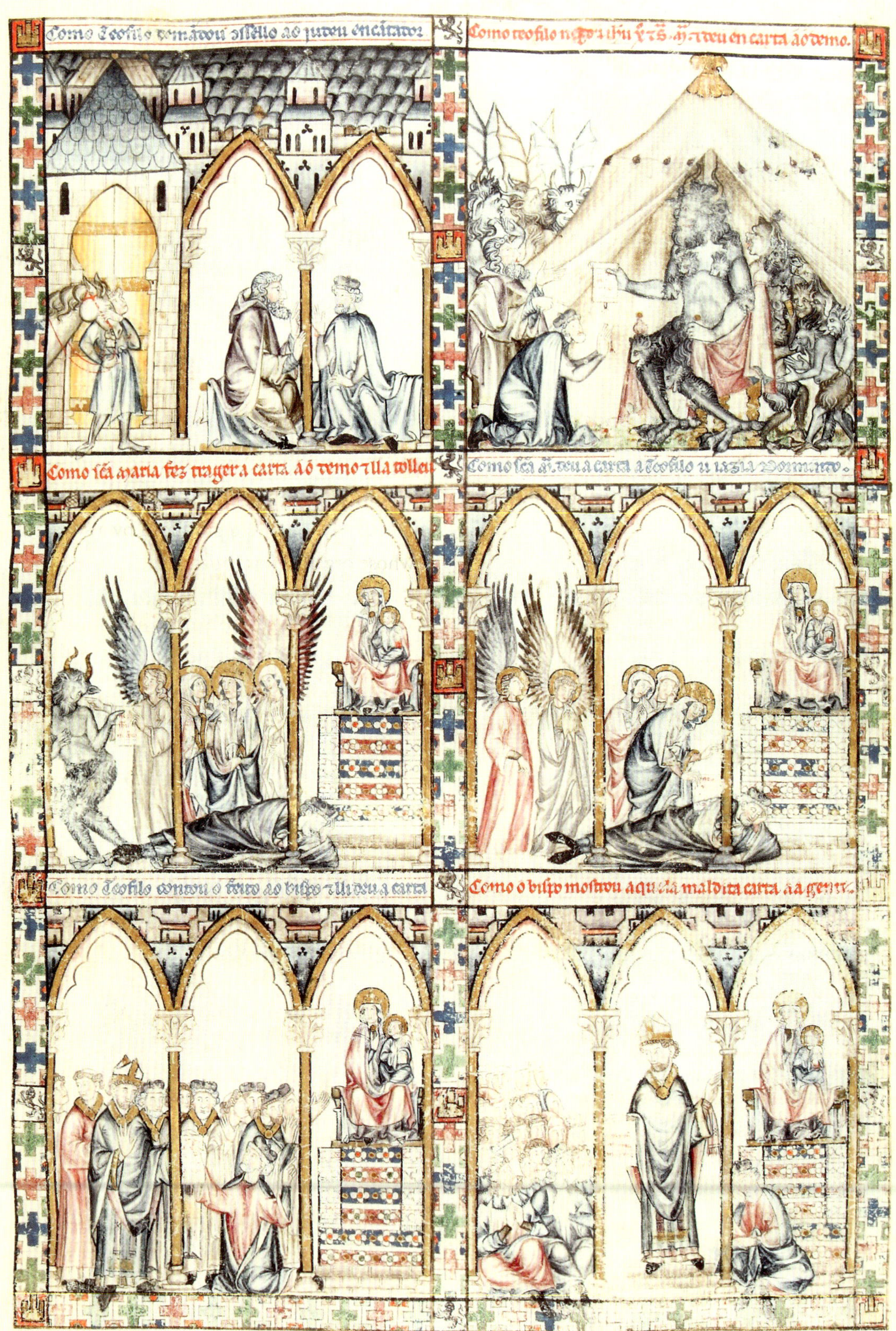
Como sca maria fez trager a carta aó demo i lla tollet
Como o bispo mostrou aquela maldita carta aa gente.

FIG. 42
The Story of Theophilus (Cantiga 3), *Cantigas de Santa María*. Real Biblioteca de El Escorial, Madrid, MS T.I.1, fol. 8r. © Patrimonio Nacional.

manuscript, of course, also would have shaped the character of its illustration. Whereas the more luxurious of these codices probably were intended for the king's personal collection, and thus for a highly limited viewership, others may well have been produced for occasional display, or even as gifts for others.

An additional factor that must have shaped the manuscripts produced by Alfonso's artists was the peculiar multiculturalism of the Castilian court. The king's hunger to surround himself with experts in the broad range of intellectual endeavors that were undertaken on his behalf, many of which drew upon reservoirs of knowledge preserved in Islamic Spain, opened his circle to a wide variety of Muslim and Jewish courtiers, including Jewish physicians, scientists, and administrators, who enjoyed high status and comfortable circumstances as members of the royal court.[35] The situation of Jews in Alfonso's Castile was thus dichotomous: while the king's formal Jewish policies, such as those regarding moneylending or the endorsement of distinctive dress, theoretically resembled those of his peers in Iberia and in Europe generally, the upper-class Jews attached to the court often were accorded a great deal more freedom. This unusual situation, and its discordancy with the realities of Jewish existence and experience in wider Castile, form a recurrent theme in the products of the royal scriptorium.

The diversity of imagery related to Jews in the manuscripts produced at Alfonso's court is very much in keeping with the diversity of the king's broad cultural pursuits and the deep intertwinement among the religious cultures at his court. In some works, renderings of Jews remain relatively uncomplicated, with physical features aimed primarily at a denotative treatment. In a codex containing a partial text of the *General Estoria* (Escorial, MS I.I.2), Jews are identified primarily by elements of costume, such as the brightly decorated peaked hats, some resembling episcopal miters, that are worn by the priests who dispute with the young Christ in the Temple (fol. 191v; fig. 43).[36] This approach is consistent with the conservative character of the manuscript as a whole, and it is also in keeping with the work's function and structure: as a vernacular retelling of the Bible, its dedication to a "historical" presentation of the narrative had little need for an overtly polemical treatment.

Greater effort to signal Jewish difference through physiognomic and somatic features can be observed in other manuscripts produced at Alfonso's court. However, such difference is not always indicated in the same way, nor for the same apparent purpose, from manuscript to manuscript. The illustrations of the *Lapidario* (Escorial, MS H.I.15), a book on the properties of minerals that was produced at Alfonso's instigation in 1253, takes a quasi-ethnographic

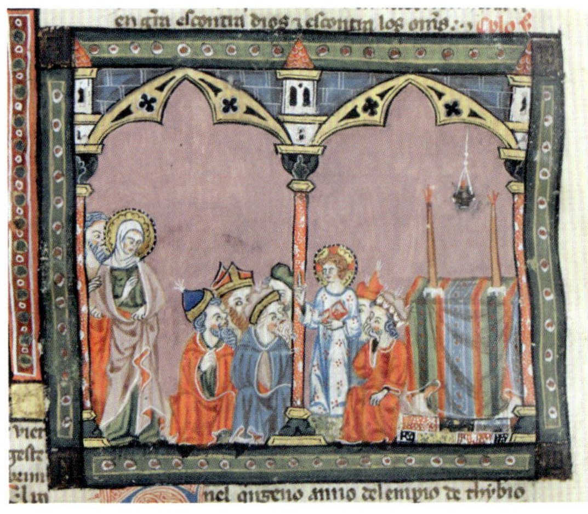

FIG. 43
Christ Among the Doctors. Detail from the *General Estoria*, Real Biblioteca de El Escorial, Madrid, MS I.I.2, 191v. © Patrimonio Nacional.

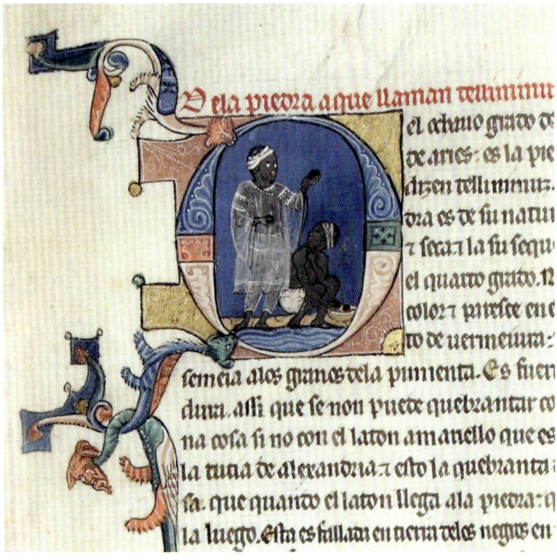

FIG. 44
Initial D depicting Africans holding *tellinimuz*. *Lapidario*. Real Biblioteca de El Escorial, Madrid, MS H.I.15, fol. 4r. © Patrimonio Nacional.

approach to rendering not only Jews but figures from all parts of the king's known world.[37] The goal of the text, written in Castilian but heavily based on Arabic sources, was to catalogue the properties and uses of various stones and minerals, presented in an order corresponding to their correlation with the signs of the zodiac. Each entry introduces the origins of each stone, lists the locations where it can be found, and describes its appearance and features before expanding upon its history, geography, and scientific and medicinal uses.

Each of the *Lapidario*'s entries is headed by a miniature illustrating the discovery of the stone in question. These vignettes often reflect the textual descriptions of the setting in which each stone is found, such as oceans, brooks, and caverns, including specific geographical locations both actual and fantastical. They sometimes also endow the discoverers of the stones with physical features inspired by their ethnic or geographical origin, so that stones are held aloft by a diverse range of figures, from Asians and Arabs in turbans and long beards to Africans with dark gray-brown skin and curly hair (fig. 44), as well as smooth-haired, fair-skinned Europeans.[38]

Nearly hidden among this panoply of types is one that seems clearly to represent a Jewish figure (fig. 45). It appears at the head of an entry on a mysterious substance identified only as *zamoricaz,* or "the hermit's stone" (fol. 14r). The adjacent passage describes the stone as translucent, yellow, and chestnut-shaped and as particularly effective in suppressing the sex drive. It is found after storms on the banks of the Red Sea, "through which Moses [and] the children of Israel passed."[39] The miniature depicting the discovery of the stone appears to have been inspired by this description: it shows the small yellow stone held aloft by a blue-robed man who wears a pink, tightly pointed cap and a long, wavy gray beard beneath a sharply profiled nose. Across the sea, a small cityscape must represent "Bocaliz," the city near which *zamoricaz* purportedly was found.

This figure's subtly modulated physiognomy must have relied partly on its geographical context for recognition. Appearing as he does beside the very waters where Moses and the children of Israel walked, he surely would have been recognized as a Jewish figure. Yet while his general appearance resembles images of Jews found in more evidently negative contexts, in this setting the figure must have been aimed primarily at illustrating the stone's geographical origin, as were the numerous images of Africans and Asians in similar vignettes within the same manuscript.

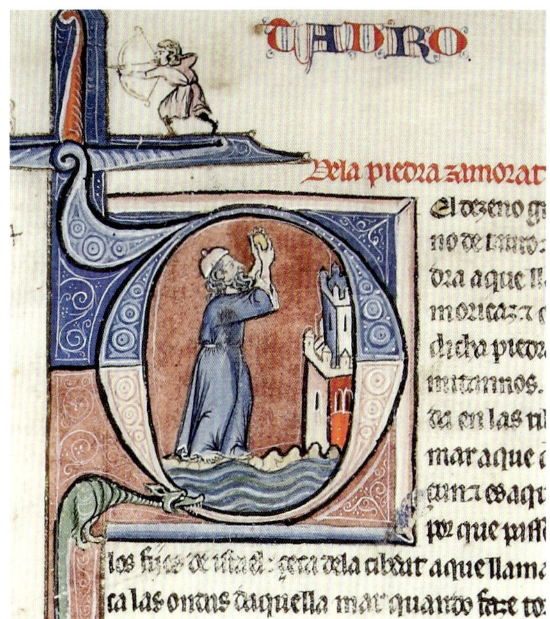

FIG. 45
Initial D depicting a Jew holding *zamoricaz. Lapidario.* Real Biblioteca de El Escorial, Madrid, MS H.I.15, fol. 14r. © Patrimonio Nacional.

Despite its moral neutrality, the Jew's depiction in the *Lapidario* marks a relatively early exemplar of the cluster of physiognomic features that would later become more inflexibly associated with Jews in both Castile and Aragon. As such, it presents a contrast to the fluid and nearly interchangeable features of the Jews and heretics in the Isidoran manuscripts produced some fifty years earlier. That Castile should be the locus in which formulaic images of this kind should make a relatively early appearance may seem surprising in light of the greater frequency and intensity with which such images would flourish in the Aragonese Crown only a few decades later. However, in both this and other cases, its motivations appear to have been quite different. Whereas the images from Aragon emerged in a climate of deep Christian anxiety about changing economic and social relationships with a rapidly growing Jewish population, the Alfonsine images seem related instead to the king's more detached desire to understand and order the world and its inhabitants.

A characteristic reflection of this desire appears in the illustrations of the *Libro de ajedrez, dados y tablas* (Escorial, MS T.I.6), produced in 1283, three decades later than the *Lapidario.*[40] The *Libro de ajedrez* expounds upon the origins, rules, and variations of chess and a variety of other board games for those who wish to learn them as an avenue of leisure. In the Escorial manuscript, each chess problem or game variation is prefaced by a large, framed miniature depicting a small group of figures playing at the game in question. Its decoration was produced by a distinctive group of artists whose saturated hues, large figures, and comparatively loose handling demarcate them from the more sophisticated team that was concurrently at work on the *Cantigas de Santa María* in the late 1270s and early 1280s. What these images lack in technical finesse is compensated by their strikingly experimental treatment of complex spatial settings and dynamic, unconventional postures, such as that of the oddly twisted figures throwing dice (fols. 76v and 77r) or the craftsman who turns his back to the viewer as he bows a lathe with his right hand and steadies the apparatus with his left foot (fol. 3r).

Equally distinctive in this manuscript is the portraitlike vividness of the individuals shown engaged in the illustrated games. Richly garbed

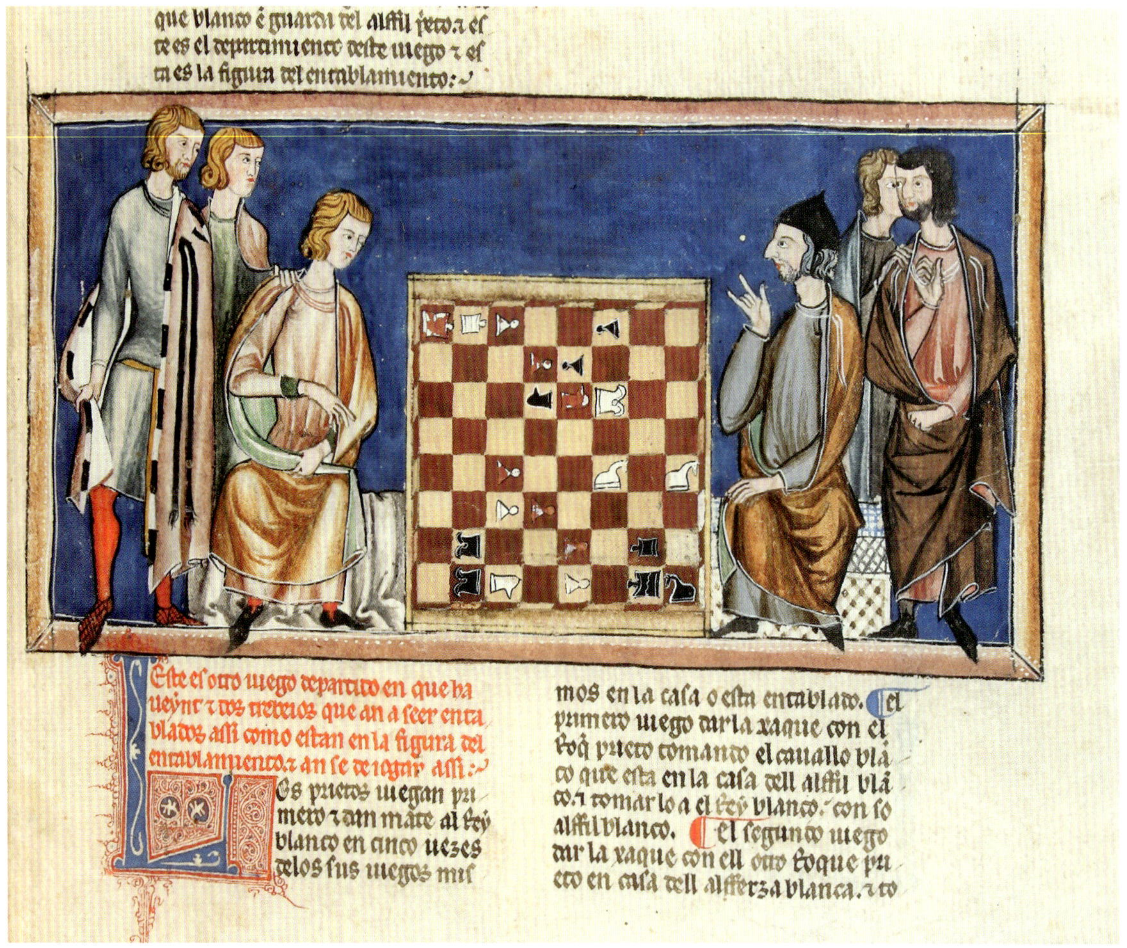

FIG. 46

A Jew playing chess with a Christian. *Libro de ajedrez, dados y tablas*. Real Biblioteca de El Escorial, Madrid, MS T.I.6, 20r.

Gothic kings, dark-skinned Africans, wispy-mustached Arabs, Indians in turbans, aristocratic youths and ladies, wrinkled old women, balding men, scantily dressed servants, seminude youths, and even small children are all evoked with unprecedented naturalism. Their participation in their games is similarly lifelike: as has been shown, each game illustrated corresponds to its description in the text, with the positions of pieces often reflecting the moves or strategies elaborated in each problem.[41] While the artists also made liberal use of their imagination, as in the case of the fantastically garbed Indian sages with which the codex begins, their approach suggests an interest in the observable world that seems to represent a later stage of the *Lapidario*'s attentive handling of ethnic and geographical subtleties.

The *Libro de ajedrez* portrays a number of Jewish players. Most wear either a hooded cloak or a tightly fitting black cap with a slight ogival peak. Nearly all are shown in profile, with an enlarged or pointed nose and long beard, in keeping with common conventions. Within these parameters, however, they display a surprising individuality, marked by variations in facial expression, hair color, and beard length, as well as by differences in costume. The stereotyped features of the Jewish backgammon player discussed in chapter 1 (fol. 75r) are mitigated by lean, pale cheeks, unusually wispy facial hair, and an intent, almost quizzical expression (fig. 1), while a Jew shown playing chess with a Christian on folio 20r sports wavy gray hair and a hooked nose that contrast jarringly with the Christian youth's slicked-down blond coiffure and regular features (fig. 46). Such individualization, suggestive of authentic portraiture, coexists with what Constable has characterized as generic "professional portraits" of Alfonsine courtiers and servants.[42]

The deployment of Jewish physiognomy in such images contributes in important ways to their underlying social dynamics. In one chess matchup (fol. 37v), a Jew whose gray hood falls back slightly to reveal abundant reddish-brown hair and a short beard smiles slightly, his heavy brows lifted above a hawkish nose, as he gestures toward his balding, gray-haired opponent (fig. 47). The latter's social difference from the Jew is suggested not only by his unexaggerated physiognomy and three-quarter positioning, but also by his elevated location: he sits on a low wall covered by a cloth, while the Jew sits cross-legged on the ground. In another image (fol. 71v), a nearly full-page illustration of a dice game, a Christian youth, accompanied by a gaily dressed trio of colleagues, faces off against a young Jew and his companions (fig. 48). The Jews' beardlessness and cropped hair suggests an effort to ape the courtly habits of the Christians, but their pointed coifs and prominent noses undermine any chance they might have had at "passing." The discordancy between courtly hairstyle and stereotyped Jewish profile seems to contribute to the vulnerable facial expression of the foremost Jewish figure, whose brows rise in concern at his opponent's aggressive gesture, apparently provoked by a winning throw.[43]

The individualization of Jewish figures in the *Libro de ajedrez,* like the equally broad variety displayed by many other types of figures in the manuscript, may represent one way of illustrating the king's stated intent to present games that were beneficial to a wide variety of people.[44] Throughout, they maintain a precarious tension between the use of traditional

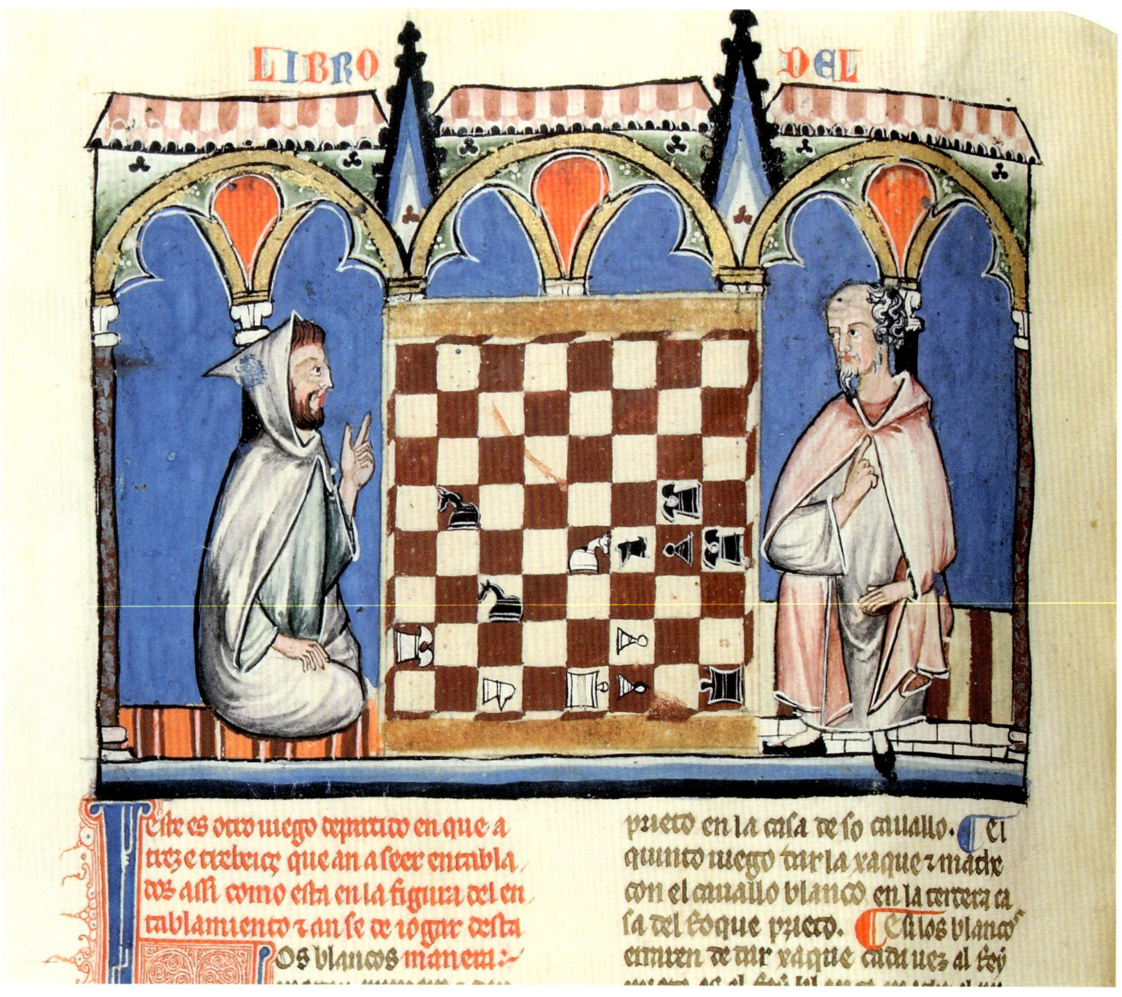

FIG. 47

A Jew playing chess with a Christian. *Libro de ajedrez, dados y tablas.* Real Biblioteca de El Escorial, Madrid, MS T.I.6, 37v. © Patrimonio Nacional.

visual formulae that facilitate recognition of certain types or cultural groups—hooked noses for Jews, or brown skin and tightly kinked hair for Africans—and the variations of hair color, face shape, beard, or skin tone that begin to convert these stereotypes into individuals. It is tempting, if not entirely fair, to compare this dichotomy with the similarly dichotomous approach taken by Alfonso toward his Jewish subjects. On the one hand, the manuscript seems to speak of the deep degree of integration achieved by upper-class Jews at the Castilian court. On the other, it preserves the sense of distance suggested by broader Alfonsine laws, such as those in the still-unenforced laws of the *Siete partidas*, which demanded the sharp social and visual segregation of Jews from Christians.[45]

A contrasting approach to Jewish physiognomy is taken in the best-known products of Alfonso's scriptorium, the two illustrated manuscripts of the *Cantigas de Santa María,* which were produced toward the end of the king's reign, about 1278–83 (Escorial, MS T.I.1 and Florence, Bib. Naz., MS Banco Rari 20). Conceived, although not entirely completed, as a complementary pair of volumes in which four hundred miracle songs compiled over two decades of the king's long reign were embellished by full-page narrative illustrations, these luxurious manuscripts present an idealized vision of Castilian society in which Jews, along other moral and religious opponents, cast into relief the Virgin's benevolent protection of her faithful. The specific content, character, and mechanics of these codices' richly layered textual and visual narratives, as well as the role of Jewish figures within them, will be discussed at length

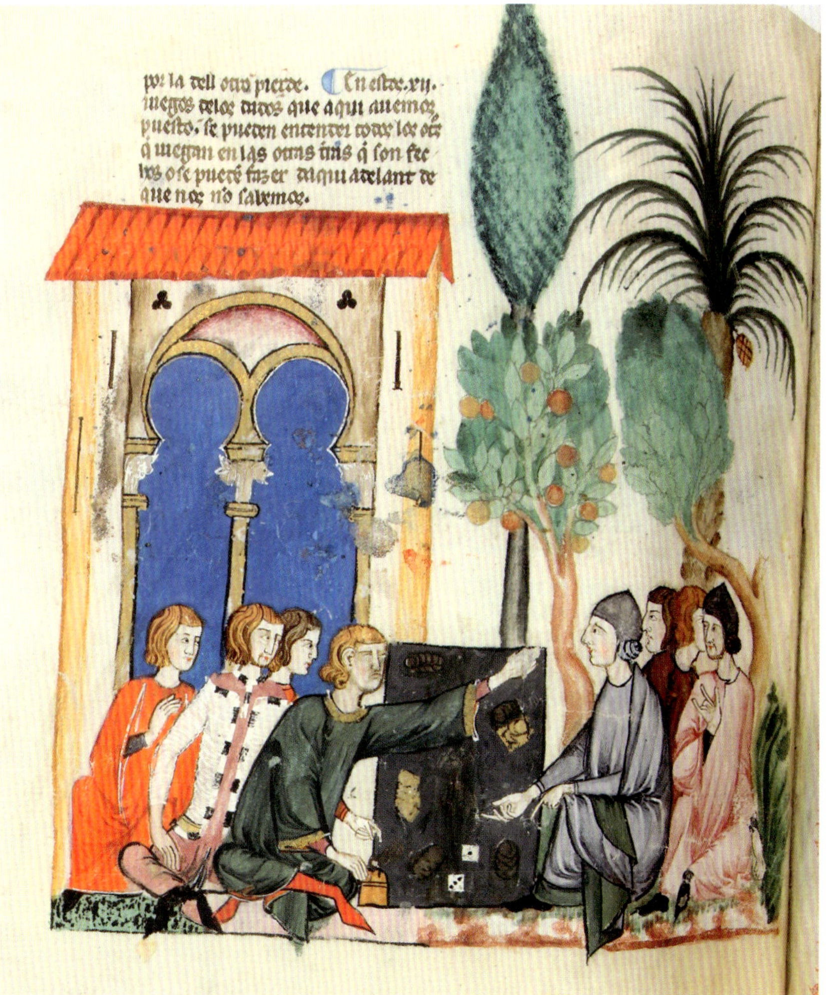

FIG. 48
Jews playing dice with Christians. *Libro de ajedrez, dados y tablas.* Real Biblioteca de El Escorial, Madrid, MS T.I.6, 71v. © Patrimonio Nacional.

FIG. 49
The Story of the Jew Who Stole an Image of the Virgin (Cantiga 34), *Cantigas de Santa María*. Real Biblioteca de El Escorial, Madrid, MS T.I.1, fol. 50r. © Patrimonio Nacional.

in chapter 5. However, the strategic handling of Jewish physiognomy in these works is so distinctive from that in the other Alfonsine manuscripts as to warrant a separate discussion here.

Whereas the physiognomic distortions employed for Jews in the *Lapidario* remained fundamentally taxonomic and those of the *Libro de ajedrez* unusually individualized, the Jewish figures presented in the *Cantigas de Santa María* adhere to a visual stereotype as fully articulated as the foreign literary models on which nearly all of their narratives were based. This quality is in keeping with the nature of the whole *Cantigas* enterprise, which was founded on the collection and retelling of largely preexistent tales that were highly formulaic in themselves. Jewish figures in the *Cantigas de Santa María* rarely vary in appearance. The common formula is exemplified by the protagonist of Cantiga 34 (Escorial, MS T.I.1, fol. 50r), a Jew whose theft of an icon of the Virgin will be discussed in a subsequent chapter. His sharp-edged profile, with its enormous nose, enlarged eyes, and abundant beard, resembles those in other Alfonsine manuscripts, but his leering expression and disjointed gestures reveal a hardening and exaggeration of those forms that embroiders upon the harsher visual traditions of northern Europe (fig. 49). This stereotype is repeated with little variation throughout both manuscripts, regardless of context or of the alternation among the several individual artists whose hands can be distinguished in these pages. As displayed by the gaggle of grimacing Jews who reenact the Crucifixion with a waxen image in the illustration of Cantiga 12 (Escorial, MS T.I.1, fol. 20v, fig. 50), the Jew who leads Theophilus in Cantiga 3 (Escorial, MS T.I.1, fol. 8r, fig. 42), and the Jews who attack Christ himself in Cantiga 50 (Escorial, MS T.I.1, fol. 74v, fig. 18), the fluid stereotype of the *Libro de ajedrez* is reduced here to a cipher and deployed whenever the character of "Jew" is required.

This visual rigidity permits the Jewish stereotypes of the *Cantigas de Santa María* to convey more negative implications than did the denotative or descriptive images of Jews in other Alfonsine manuscripts. In many tales, the physiognomic stereotype intensifies the negative qualities of a character already clearly hostile to the tale's Christian protagonist, as is the case in the illustration for Cantiga 6 in the Escorial manuscript (MS T.I.1, fol. 13v). As do most illustrations in both the Escorial and Florence codices, this one takes the form of a full-page, six-panel pictorial summary of its text, in this case the widely disseminated story of a boy who was killed by the Jews for singing praises to the Virgin Mary (fig. 51). The *cantiga* recounts that

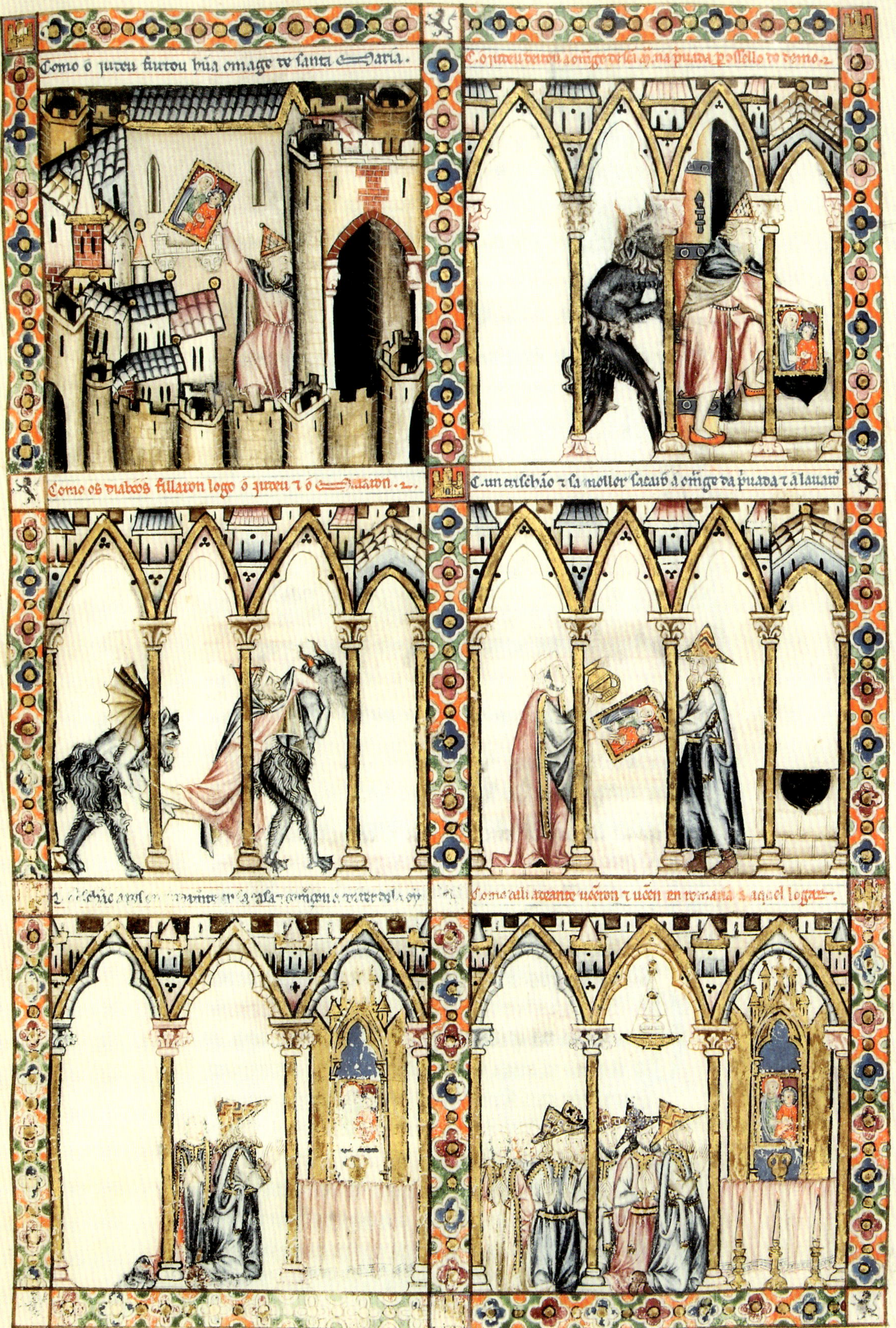
LXXIIII
Como o judeu furtou hũa omage de santa Maria.
C. o judeu deitou a omage de sca M. na pudada possello do demo.
Como os diabos fillaron logo o judeu e o mataron.
C. un crischão e sa moller sacaró a omage da pudada e a lavaró
Como ali aveante uéeron e uéen en romaria a aquel logar.

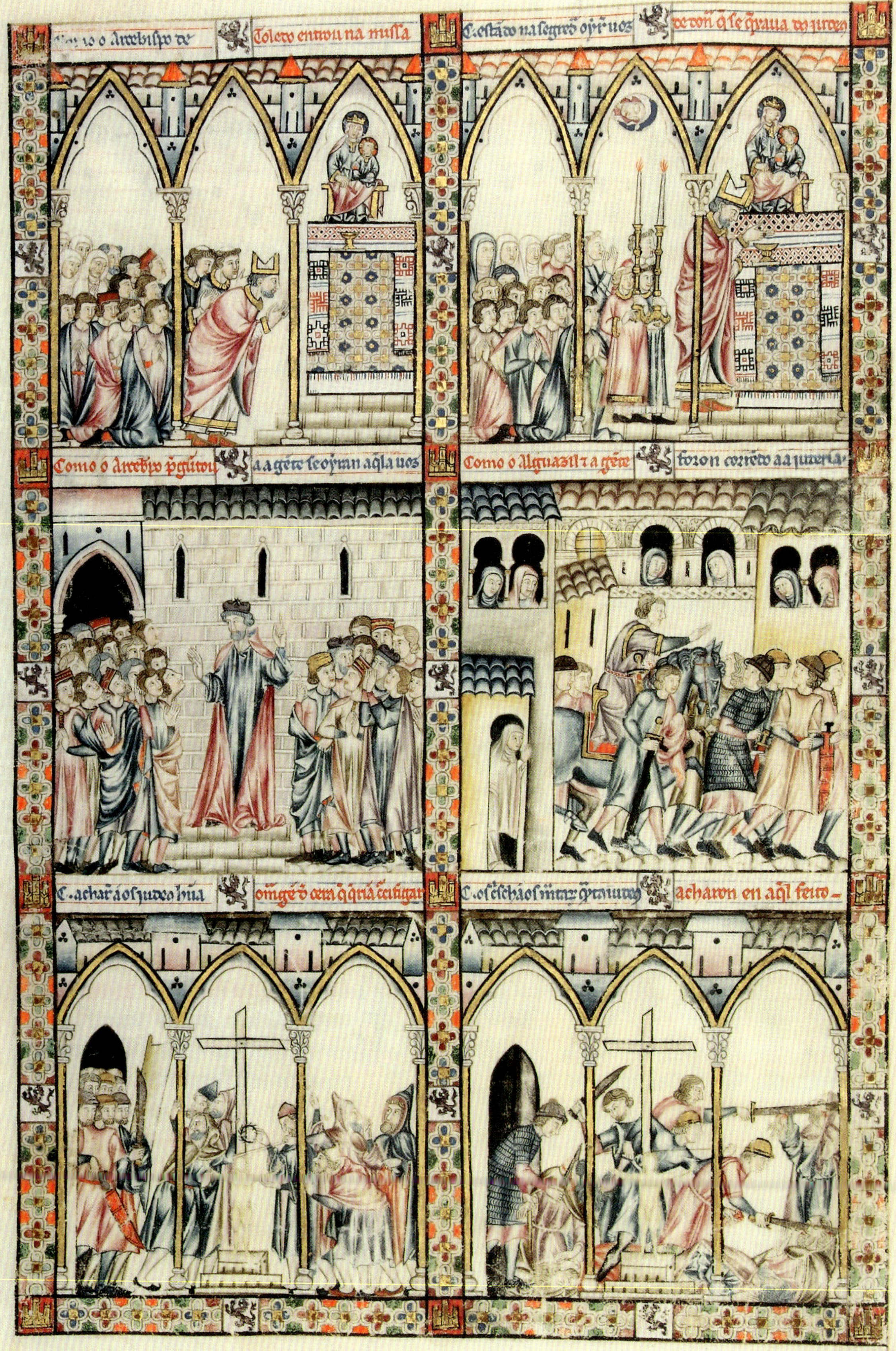

FIG. 50
The Story of the Jews of Toledo (Cantiga 12), *Cantigas de Santa María*. Real Biblioteca de El Escorial, Madrid, MS T.I.1, fol. 20v.

the boy, who had been offered to the Virgin by his mother after his father's death, had a beautiful voice, excelling especially in the singing of the hymn "Gaude Virgo Maria." On one feast day, when a number of Jews and Christians were gathered together in a public square, he sang his favorite hymn, offending a listening Jew. The Jew kidnapped the boy, killed him, and hid the body in his wine cellar, but after his grieving mother called upon the Virgin, the boy miraculously began to sing again and was discovered, fully revived. Hearing of this miracle, the song continues, the boy's hearers massacred the city's Jews.[46]

The illustration first depicts the mother offering the boy to the Virgin in her church. The next panel depicts him singing in a public square, surrounded by a crowd that includes one Jew, conspicuous for his exaggerated features and brown, hooded robe. In the next two panels, he is joined by several other Jews, who dispatch the boy with an ax and bury the body in a wine cellar. The final two panels depict the boy's recovery and the burning of the Jews, their bodies barely visible as they writhe in translucent red flames. The deployment of stereotyped features functions especially powerfully in the two scenes of the boy's murder and disposal in the cellar: the murderer's staring eyes, furrowed brows, and disordered hair underscore the violence of the scene. The inhumanity of the Jews' distorted profiles heightens the monstrous nature of their acts.

In other cases, variations in physiognomy and gesture perform a more specialized semiotic function. It should not be surprising, perhaps, that this dynamic is especially evident in those *cantigas* concerned with Jewish conversion, a process concerned above all with the transformation of the individual as he is absorbed into the body of the Christian faithful. In some *cantigas,* the facial stereotype acts as a barometer of this transformation, emerging, receding, and in extreme cases disappearing altogether as individual Jews achieve enlightenment or experience baptism.[47] As such, it functions simultaneously as a sign of the figure's Jewishness and a measure of the spiritual deficiency that conversion will correct, while its visual approximation to first "Jewish" and then "Christian" physiognomy illustrates the relative distance of such converts from their former coreligionists.

Such is the case in the illustration following Cantiga 4, the widely known tale of the little Jewish boy who took communion with his Christian friends and then was thrown into an oven by his father, Gonzalo de Berceo's version of which was introduced in chapter 1.[48] In the Alfonsine version (Escorial, MS T.I.1, fol. 9v), the boy (here named suggestively "Abel") is easily

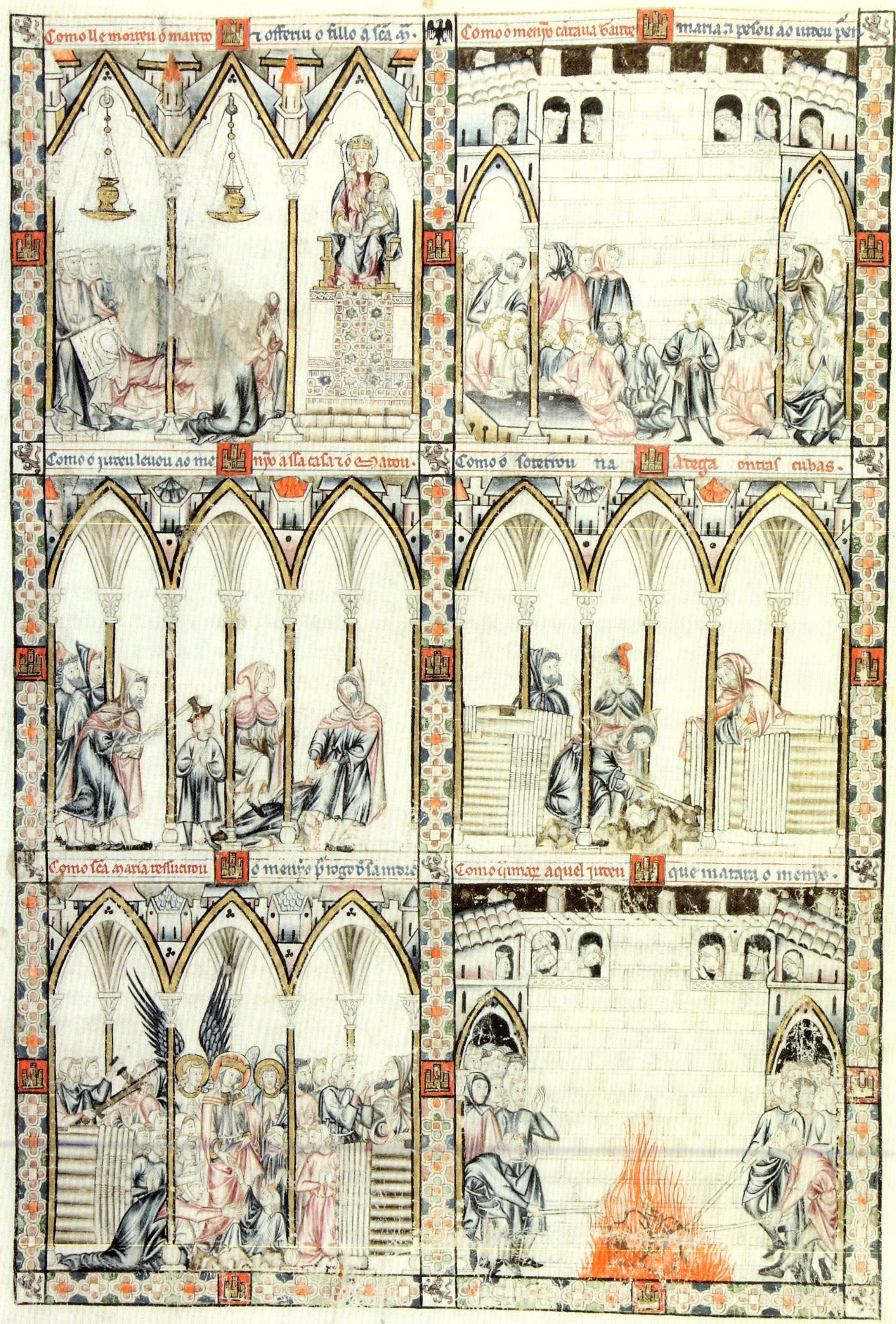
Como lle moireu o marido
⁊ offereu o fillo a sca. M.
Como o meniño cataua Sainte
maria ⁊ pesou ao iudeu
Como o iudeu leuou ao me
niño a ssa casa ⁊ o matou.
Como o soterrou na
adega ontras cubas.
Como sca. maria resuscitou
o meniño p rogo d sa madre
Como queimar aquel iudeu
que matara o meniño.

FIG. 51
The Story of the Boy Who Sang *Gaude* (Cantiga 6), *Cantigas de Santa María*. Real Biblioteca de El Escorial, Madrid, MS T.I.1, fol. 13v. © Patrimonio Nacional.

distinguished from his peers in the first scene by his hooded Jewish mantle and an oversized, beaky nose, a miniature version of his father's (fig. 52). This feature, in both differentiating the boy from his Christian classmates and asserting his Jewish identity, represents an innovation, for neither in Iberian imagery nor in that of northern Europe was it common for depictions of children to include stereotyped facial features of this kind. More innovative still is the suddenness with which this feature recedes once the boy has taken communion: as he returns home and is confronted by his father in the illustration's third panel, his nose instantly appears smaller and straighter. It is possible that this change relates to other versions of the tale, like that of Gautier de Coincy, in which the father learns of the boy's conversion when he notices a change in his face.[49] Even so, the change functions powerfully as a sign of the transformative potential of the Eucharist—an element of the Christian faith soundly rejected by the Jews—in effecting spiritual salvation and, as the *cantiga* itself recounts, the conversion of unbelievers.[50]

Facial and physical deformation plays a still more vivid role in Cantiga 108 (Escorial, MS T.I.1, fol. 155v). This song recounts how the magician Merlin, here cast as a defender of the Christian cause, becomes frustrated in a debate with a Jewish sage who refuses to accept the Incarnation, countering, "God could never enter into such a place, it stands to reason, for how could He Who contains so many things be contained?"[51] This response echoes the Jewish position in a number of contemporary polemics, for which the Incarnation consistently represented one of the most troubling points of disagreement.[52] The angry Merlin chooses a revenge peculiarly suited to the Jew's stubborn disbelief, asking the Virgin Mary to cause the baby expected by the Jew's wife to be born with its head facing backward. When the father attempts to kill the deformed infant, Merlin rescues it, eventually employing it, as the *cantiga* recounts, "to convert the Jews in order to lead them from their erroneous beliefs."[53]

The illustration of this *cantiga* plays heavily on the baby's physical deformation (fig. 53). The helpless, almost comical reversal of the infant's head, which peers out bemusedly over tiny buttocks as Merlin snatches the child from the Jew in the fourth panel, fully embodies the perversion of the Jewish father. It is augmented further still in the next to last panel, where adolescence has added a monstrous nose to the lad's reversed profile. The implications of both tale and illustration are very rich indeed. Although Merlin's choice of punishment is not explored in the *cantiga* text, it plays heavily on

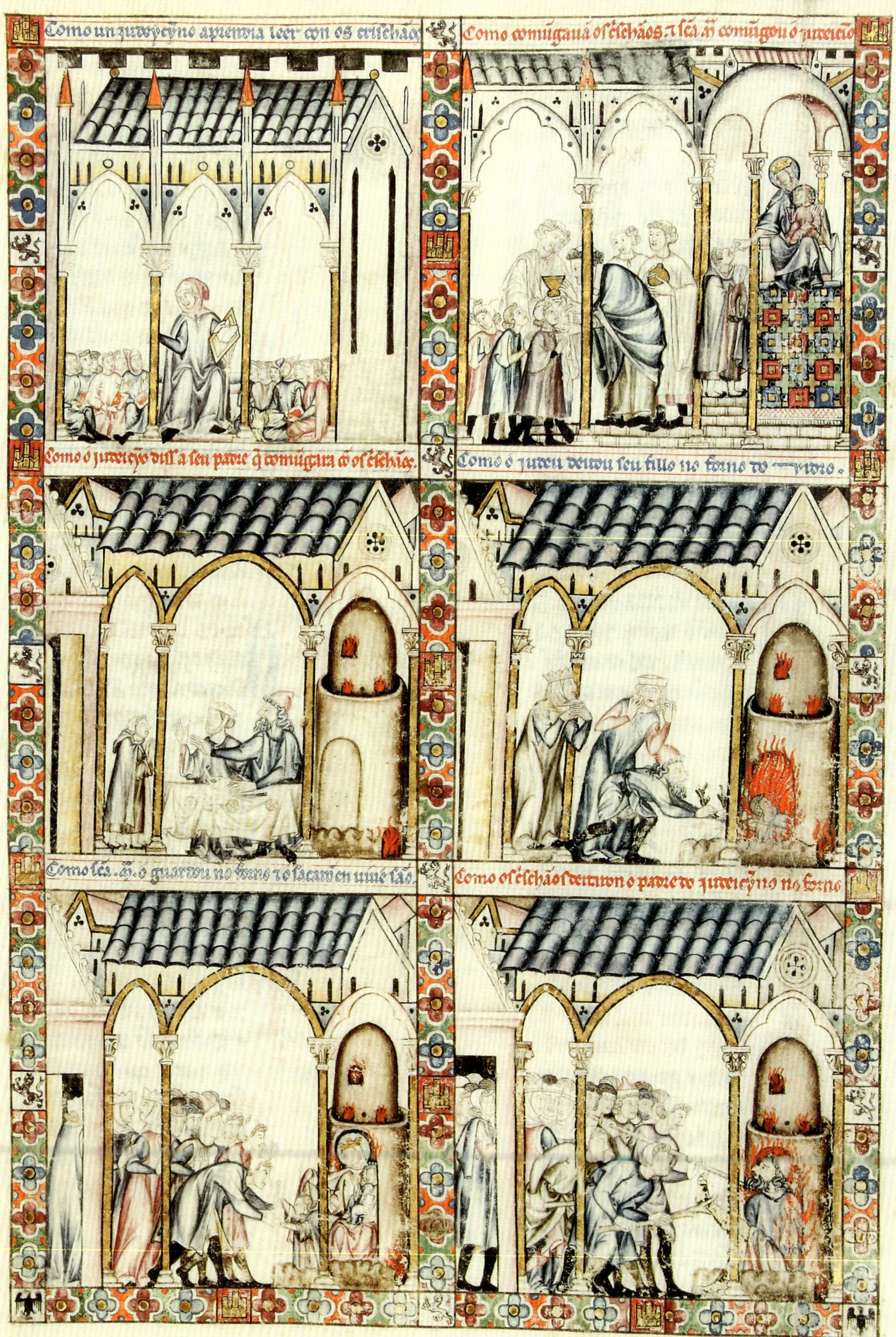

deste ninno todo al pueblo menaron lo en
e morio e qmado por la muerte cruel

FIG. 52
The Story of the Little Jewish Boy (Cantiga 4), *Cantigas de Santa María*. Real Biblioteca de El Escorial, Madrid, MS T.I.1, fol. 9v.

the trope of the Jew as stubborn unbeliever, a figure who balks at seeing the truth although it is set out plainly before him.[54] His refusal to countenance Christian doctrine is embodied in his son's reversed head, which the Virgin rather pettily elects not to restore to normalcy even after the child's adoption into Christian culture. The innocent boy's face thus becomes a walking exemplum of his father's sin, a disbelief so unyielding that neither Christian reason nor divine evidence can move it.

In these examples, the distortion of Jewish faces and bodies is both powerful and multifarious. On one level, the formulaic, almost standardized character of the facial stereotype serves to demarcate and identify Jewish characters within intricate, multiepisodic visual narratives, the clarity of which was crucial to their function within the manuscript. Like the captions inscribed above each panel, they offered signposts for a viewer seeking to correlate the narrative carried out in pictures with a heard or read one. On another level, to be explored further in chapter 5, the often negative connotations of this stereotype concur with the pejorative construction of Jews that was already inherent in the foreign textual and visual narratives upon which these manuscripts drew.

These foreign models help to account for the difference between the highly charged facial stereotypes of the *Cantigas de Santa María* and the more neutral imagery of the *Lapidario* or the portraitlike images of the *Libro de ajedrez.* In the *Lapidario,* the chief aim of which was identification and classification of minerals, Jewish, African, and Asian figures served accordingly, signaling the location and culture to which individual stones were ascribed without playing significantly into the analysis of the minerals themselves. In the *Libro de ajedrez,* Jews feature as accepted members of the courtly circle, a class of individuals who often seem likely to have been known personally to Alfonso and other viewers of the manuscript. Such familiarity must have fostered the individualized quality of the imagery at the same time that it discouraged more abstract stereotypes such as those in the *Cantigas de Santa María.* Although the "Jewish profile" did eventually become a fixture in the works of Alfonso's scriptorium, its character and meaning remained extraordinarily pliant, in keeping with the variety of perspectives possible within the king's newly expanded Castilian world.

Comparatively few manuscripts from the period following Alfonso's death in 1284 remain to testify to the fate or impact of this rich arsenal of images in the centuries that followed. Nonetheless, the variably nuanced images examined here pose an evident contrast to the

FIG. 53
The Story of the Baby Born with His Head Backwards (Cantiga 108), *Cantigas de Santa María*. Real Biblioteca de El Escorial, Madrid, MS T.I.1, fol. 155v. © Patrimonio Nacional.

aggressively distorted faces and bodies of the Jews in many Aragonese works. There are many likely reasons for this difference, beginning with Aragon's strong cultural orientation toward France and the other parts of Europe from whose visual traditions Iberian Christian artists borrowed so liberally during the centuries of greatest southward expansion. A second powerful factor resulted from the strengthening court and dynastic ties between southern France and Aragon, which had fostered other forms of cultural exchange as well, particularly in the realm of literature.[55] This geographic proximity, and the political ties and cultural exchange that it fostered, must have offered easy access to visual *topoi* that had been more fully developed north of the Pyrenees.

Another and yet more influential factor was the contrasting political and social status of Jews in Castile versus those in the Aragonese Crown, and especially in Old Catalunya. Whereas the long-Christianized cities of this region struggled mightily to adjust to the growing numbers and economic prominence of recently settled Jewish communities, such as the one in Vic, those in the newly conquered regions of Castile still seem to have perceived Jews as a vital cog in the establishment of frontier Christian communities.[56] This variation may help to explain the contrast in the ways in which Jewish bodies were represented by Iberian artists at different times and places.

Physiognomic and physiological distortions were employed less often overall in Iberian representations of Jews than in many parts of Europe, such as England and France. However, when they were used, it was with a noteworthy deliberateness and imaginative capacity. Rarely were such motifs adopted slavishly, in mere imitation of forms already in use in the visual traditions on which they drew in other ways. Instead, they were judiciously appropriated and deftly manipulated, suggesting a deliberate vision of how such forms would play within a larger visual and social context.

Evolving Notions of Jewish Difference

This chapter opened by exploring the argument that the bodily distortions developed to represent Jews in European imagery were tied to a desire to visualize differences between Christians and Jews that were predominantly moral, rather than physiological. Yet examples from both Castile and Aragon suggest that such efforts sometimes expanded beyond the bounds of mere abstraction. It surely is no coincidence that the language and images describing Jews as fantastically deformed, diseased, and malodorous, so widely diffused throughout Europe in the twelfth century, very shortly were

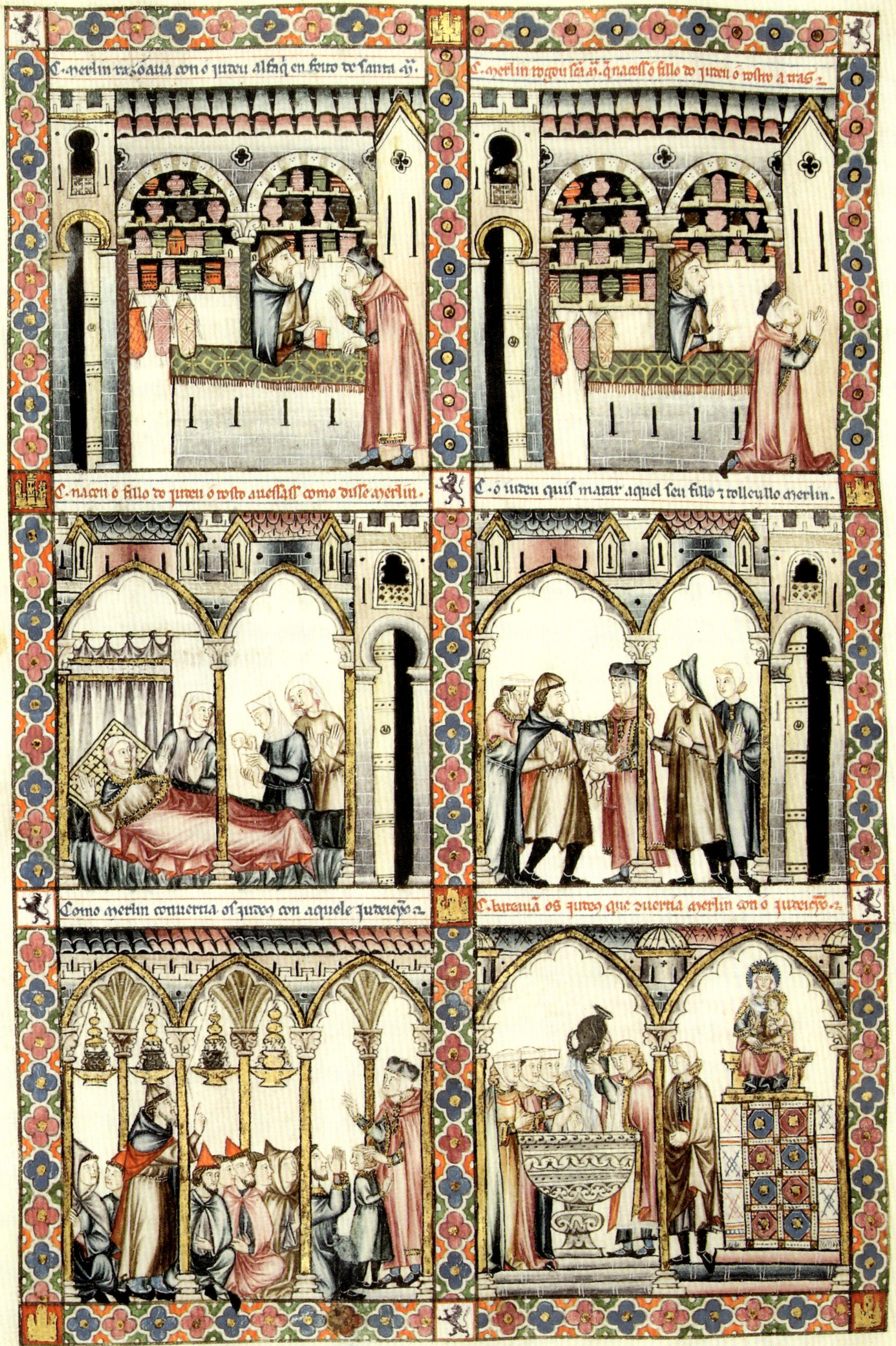
C. merlin razõaua con o judeu alfaq̃ en feito de santa M.
C. merlin rogou sca M. q̃ nacesse o fillo do judeu o rostro a tras.
C. naceu o fillo do judeu o rosto auessas como disse merlin.
C. o judeu quis matar aquel seu fillo e tolleullo merlin.
Como merlin conuertia os judeus con aquele judeiçño.
C. bateauã os judeus que cõuertia merlin con o judeiçño.

followed by signs that Christians had begun to think of Jews as different from themselves in a more concrete biological sense. Such a possibility begs the question of whether differences among faith groups were by this era coming to be understood as fixed biological characteristics or as accidental features that developed in connection with location, climate, language, and social practice and thus remained to some extent alterable.[57]

Recorded Christian perceptions of Jews in the central Middle Ages certainly reveal this flexible sense of what constituted Jewishness. Nonetheless, throughout Latin Europe in this period, evidence also emerges to suggest that Jewish difference had begun to be thought of at least to some extent in biological terms. Some scholars have perceived the roots of this tendency in the quickness of the twelfth-century rationalists to link Jews with carnality (both literal and metaphorical), sensuality, and corruption of the body, tendencies attested abundantly in the Iberian images we have seen.[58] That such tendencies had begun to be seen as permanent enough to be handed down to unsuspecting, if not undeserving, future generations is traceable in responses such as Bernard of Clairvaux's disapproval of the papal pretender Anacletus, whose great-grandfather had been Jewish, as unfit for rule because of his "Jewish lineage."[59]

Additional evidence that Jewishness was coming to be thought, at least by some, to reside in physiology is suggested by a *quodlibetum* written around 1300 concerning the bloody flux that, according to a peculiar Christian rumor, was suffered by Jewish men. This malady is described by the text as a combined result of inborn factors characteristic of Jews, such as a melancholic makeup, and environmental ones, such as the eating of "gross and salted food."[60] This text, which rests on conceptual foundations traceable to the late twelfth century, bolsters what had begun as a fundamentally folkloric belief about Jews with a scientific explanation that rests implicitly on the idea that Jews as a people shared a specific set of biological characteristics.[61]

Despite the physiological emphasis of this and similar texts, a wide gap still remained between the medieval sense of such shared biological characteristics and the strictly racial sense of Jewish difference that emerged in the modern era. Even those differences described by medieval writers as natural or biological do not seem to have been viewed as permanent, but as qualities whose formation by social and physical factors, such as the influence of parents and neighbors, might allow them to change again under the right conditions. As Robert Bartlett and others have shown, the Latin term *gens* and the concept underlying it still had less to do with a biological sense of "race" than with a sense of common collective origin or history more analogous to the modern phrase "ethnic identity."[62] While some who have studied medieval Spain in particular have been tempted by the notion that late medieval concepts of a biologically or genealogically grounded Jewishness might be connected fundamentally to the emergence of more modern anti-Semitism, recent scholarship has shown this question to be less easily resolved than it might at first seem.[63]

Another domain in which the question of Jewish physicality persisted was in religious conversion. Although in theory any effective conversion of a Jew to Christianity should have eliminated any ambiguities of religious and cultural identity, from at least the thirteenth century onward both official and popular attitudes toward new converts from Judaism throughout Latin Europe reveal a growing suspicion regarding the permanence of their new state. On the official side, the persistence of labels such as *conversus* or *quondam judaeus* for Jews who had long ago been converted to the new faith reveal a desire, at some level, to emphasize the importance of this personal history. On the popular side, legends and rumors sprouted about newly converted Christians who seemed unable to shed "Jewish" weaknesses such as doubt over the doctrine of transubstantiation. These tales, like that of the convert whose doubtfulness about the host led him to test the wafer by removing it from his mouth during communion, only to discover that it had transformed into a miniature Christ child, certainly imply a concern over the lingering Jewishness of such individuals.[64] To what extent the incompleteness of these Jews' spiritual transformation was believed to result from their physical makeup, rather than from a failing of upbringing or culture, remains unclear.

In Iberia, such ideas are less clearly attested before the fifteenth century, when a sharp decline in the Jewish population and a corresponding increase in converts to Christianity began seriously to challenge prevailing ideas about Jewish identity. By the late fourteenth century, repeated fluctuations in royal policy toward Jews in both Castile and Aragon, continuing ecclesiastical pressure, and the popular hostility resulting from both economic crises and calamities like the Black Plague had intensified sharply. They climaxed in June, July, and August of 1391, when the instability following the death of John I of Castile sparked a series of anti-Jewish pogroms that spread from Seville to the other major Jewish centers of Spain.[65] In 1412–15, a combination of newly repressive legislation and the dynamic missionary campaign of Vicente Ferrer prompted a fresh wave of conversions. The number of "New Christians" whose conversions followed these efforts, whether as a result of coercion or the simple desire to escape the increasingly fettered existence to which practicing Jews were now restricted, has been estimated by some to have been in the tens of thousands.[66]

An intriguing facet of this phenomenon is the interest in the biological or at least hereditary aspects of Jewishness that becomes traceable at just the time when the Jewish population had begun to be dramatically reduced. Rather than eliminating concerns about the presence of Jews in Christian society, the absorption of former nonbelievers into the majority culture seems instead to have heightened them. As David Nirenberg has argued, the disappearance of visible signs and behaviors by which Jewishness previously was measured led "Old Christians" in the fifteenth century to turn instead to less easily measurable questions of personal history and genealogy as a means of identifying and preserving difference.[67] By such measures, the genuineness and permanence of conversion, and hence the Christianness of a given individual, could be questioned merely on the basis of the circumstances and recentness of baptism or even, eventually, on the existence of Jewish ancestors. The climax of this line of thinking was the creation of laws concerning *limpieza de sangre,*

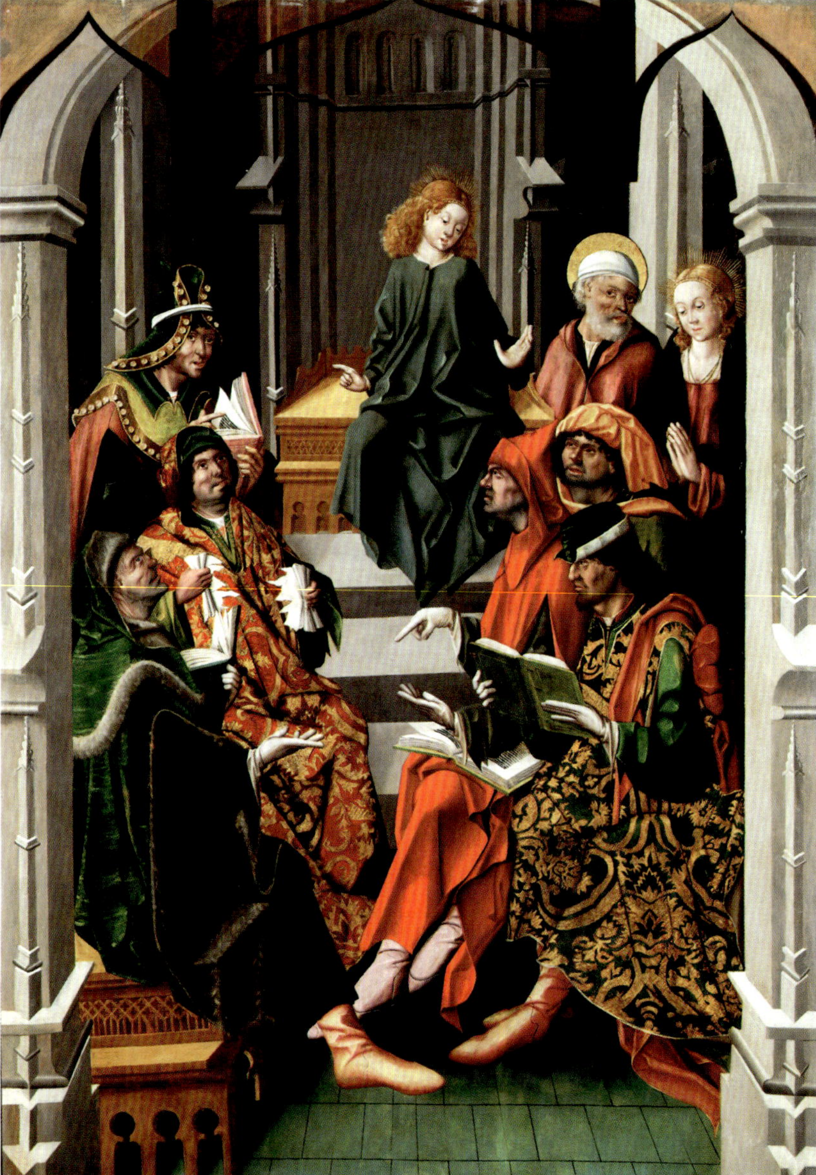

FIG. 54
Master Bartolomé, *Christ Among the Doctors.* The Collection of the University of Arizona Museum of Art and Archive of Visual Arts, Tucson, by permission.

purity of blood, which allowed the vetting of individuals for various social and economic opportunities to rest at least in part on the presence of Jewish or Muslim ancestry.[68]

The first recorded regulation of this kind was promulgated in 1449 by the mayor of Toledo, Pedro Sarmiento, following civil unrest sparked by a tax imposed by the Castilian constable Álvaro de Luna to fund the war between Castile and Aragon. The edict accused the city's *conversos* not only of secretly relapsing to Judaism, but—in an echo of legislation aimed at Jews themselves—of preying financially upon the city's Old Christians with an eye toward the ruination of the city. It ended by barring New Christians from holding any public office that enjoyed authority over Old Christians, from working as notaries, and from serving as legal witnesses.[69] Although the Castilian King John II revoked this decree shortly afterward, it was followed by similar blood purity regulations, first on the part of the monastic orders and eventually on that of Ferdinand and Isabella, who in 1501 approved such regulations for those selected to hold government offices. Such statutes continued to assert that their main goal was to obviate the religious backsliding to which New Christians were thought to be prone; however, a second and powerful motivation was the competition posed by the entry of New Christians into social and economic fields once closed to them as Jews.[70]

Although most of these historical developments lie beyond the chronological parameters of this study, the conception of Jewish difference that they reflect—one that rests on an immutable difference of blood, not a changeable one of belief—seems akin to the physiognomic and other bodily distortions by which Jews were distinguished in visual images of a somewhat earlier period. But is this a viable link? It is difficult to verify, since the development of blood purity laws in Spain was not accompanied by significant changes in the depiction of Jewish bodies, which even by the fifteenth century tended to preserve, if in stylistically updated form, the visual formulae that had been established two hundred years earlier. The vividly realized Temple priests of the late fifteenth-century panel of *Christ Among the Doctors* from the main altarpiece of Ciudad Rodrigo (Tucson, University of Arizona Museum), with their dark, sneering faces, oversized noses, and preposterous headgear, represent just such a preservation of established Iberian iconographic traditions, leavened somewhat by the naturalism of the northern European painters who provided such works' primary formal models (fig. 54).[71]

Despite this new tangibility, the physiognomic formulae used for Jews in late medieval Iberian imagery essentially continued and extended previous efforts to represent in visible form what were in fact largely abstract ideas about the moral and religious qualities of the Jews as a group. As such, they offer less a prefiguration than an outright reversal of the premise behind the Iberian blood laws. Whereas Iberian imagery of Jews came to treat Jewishness as a quality that was above all visible, the blood laws tacitly admitted its invisibility by seeking its traces in the equally invisible domains of personal history and family lineage. Moreover, while blood purity laws claimed a moral component in their concern over possible judaizing among recent converts, they may have been still more strongly motivated by pragmatic fears about social and economic competition, a theme which continued to take a back seat to the fundamentally theological framework from which the anti-Jewish imagery of this period had sprung.

4

JEWS AND MUSLIMS IN THE IBERIAN CHRISTIAN IMAGINATION

Local factors played a powerful role in the Iberian images of Jews examined so far in this study. The replacement of the European Jew's hat with the Iberian hooded cloak, the manipulation of traditional symbols such as Ecclesia and Synagoga, and the recalibration of northern physiognomic stereotypes of Jews reveal the efforts made by Iberian artists to adapt these essentially foreign traditions to the concerns and expectations of viewers whose cultural experience differed fundamentally from that of Christians north of the Pyrenees. However, nowhere do these efforts reach more unorthodox heights than in a genre of imagery even more firmly accommodated to its specifically Iberian context: depictions of Jews that are shaded by visual references to Muslims and Islam.

Exemplary of this tradition is a painted pine beam, produced in the early thirteenth century in north-central Spain, in which a scaled-down series of traditional Passion scenes has been infiltrated by dark, peculiar figures with features evocative of Muslims (figs. 55, 56). Rendered in profile, with deep gray-brown skin, enlarged eyes, lips, and noses, and white-tasseled head scarves, they engage actively in the most violent moments of the Passion: the Flagellation, the Road to Calvary, and the Crucifixion. As we shall see, their physiognomy, skin color, and costume suggest that their northern Christian viewers would have understood them as Muslims, yet the roles that they play in the Passion are those traditionally assigned to Christ's biblical enemies, the Jews. Parsing the mechanics and message of this work, and of other images that similarly conflate "Jewish" and "Muslim" signs, will be the goal of the present chapter.

The emergence of these complex and often anachronistic images coincides with the multiplication of Christian victories in Al-Andalus in the twelfth and thirteenth centuries, which brought vast new zones of Islamic Spain within the Christian purview. Two aspects of this

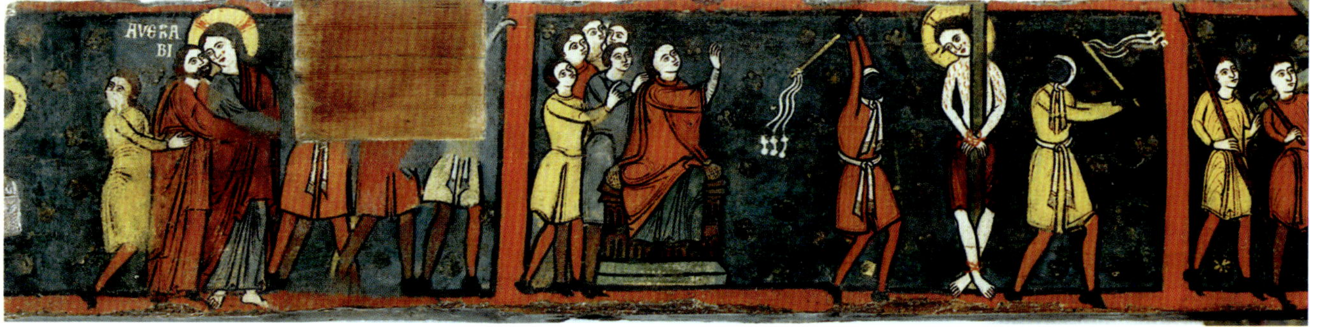

FIG. 55
The Arrest and Flagellation of Christ, from a wooden beam painted with Passion scenes. Museu Nacional d'Art de Catalunya, Barcelona. © MNAC. Photo: Calveras/Mérida/Sagristà.

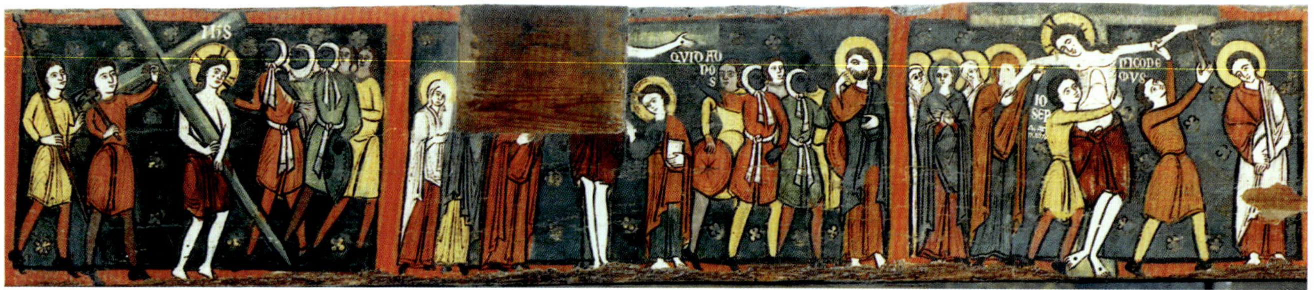

FIG. 56
Christ Bearing the Cross, the Crucifixion, and the Deposition, from a wooden beam painted with Passion scenes. Museu Nacional d'Art de Catalunya, Barcelona. © MNAC. Photo: Calveras/Mérida/Sagristà.

trend merit special attention. First, in their astonishing diversity of medium, function, and social frame—from manuscripts, frescoes, and sculpture to ceramics and painting on wood and from royal to monastic to the secular and quotidian—such images suggest the depth to which new ideas about Jews as related to other faith groups had penetrated Iberian society. Second, their discerning handling of visual forms associated with Andalusi culture, by contrast to the often fantastical images of Muslims produced in northern Europe, speaks to both the originality of their production and the singularity of their message.

The continuing presence of Muslims in high medieval Iberia, both as rulers of a shrinking Islamic polity in the south and as an often populous minority in the expanding Christian north, necessarily and powerfully affected how both Christians and Jews on the peninsula constructed their own cultural identities. The best-known artistic outgrowth of this is the phenomenon today labeled *mudéjar,* most simply defined as the adoption of originally Islamic visual forms and materials into the visual traditions of non-Islamic Iberian cultures, both in architecture and in smaller-scale works.[1] It is exemplified in such classic *mudéjar* monuments as the early fourteenth-century church towers of Teruel (fig. 57), in which the unorthodox admixture of ornamental brickwork, interlaced arches, and brightly colored *azulejos* with ponderous Gothic forms reveals a decisive absorption of Islamic materials and motifs into a framework that has been seen by some as a self-conscious expression of indigenous Christian culture.[2] In Jewish *mudéjar* structures, the best-known of which is the mid-fourteenth-century synagogue of Samuel Ha-Levi ("El Tránsito") in Toledo (fig. 58), the assimilation of Islamic forms is so extensive that it has sometimes been interpreted as an expression of Iberian Jewish resistance to the recently imposed Christian majority.[3] While such resistance is difficult to substantiate in the few monuments that survive today, it does seem clear that in both Christian and Jewish contexts, the choice of *mudéjar* forms over traditional Romanesque or Gothic ones represented an active preference on the part of artists and/or patrons, one closely tied to their self-perceptions and agenda.

Beyond, and perhaps because of, their utility in such cultural self-fashioning, Islamic visual traditions could also function as lenses through which Iberian Christians understood and represented others, especially the Jews with whose existence they continued to grapple for centuries as they forged their own place on the Iberian Peninsula. As this chapter will show, the resultant images often combined or exchanged visual forms that modern viewers might associate exclusively with either Muslim or Jewish culture alone.

This imprecision initially may seem perplexing, given the obviously contrasting roles played by each group with respect to Christian society. For most thirteenth-century Christians in Spain, Muslims represented either an external military threat or a recently and uncertainly repressed minority. In both senses, their oppositional relationship to the body of the Christian faithful remained implicit, as trenchantly expressed by Ferdinand III's legendary exclamation, "Christ, God, and Man, is on our side; on that of the Moors, the infidel

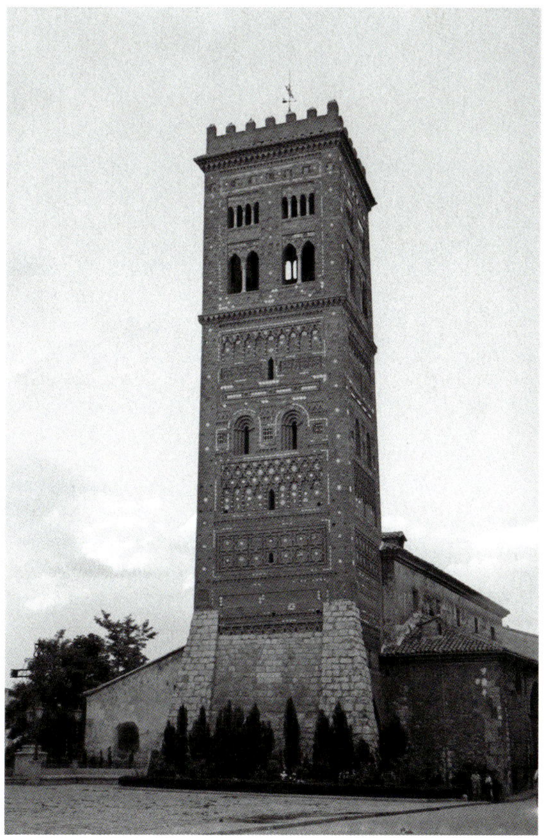

FIG. 57

Teruel, San Martín. © Fundació Institut Amatller d'Art Hispànic. Arxiu Mas.

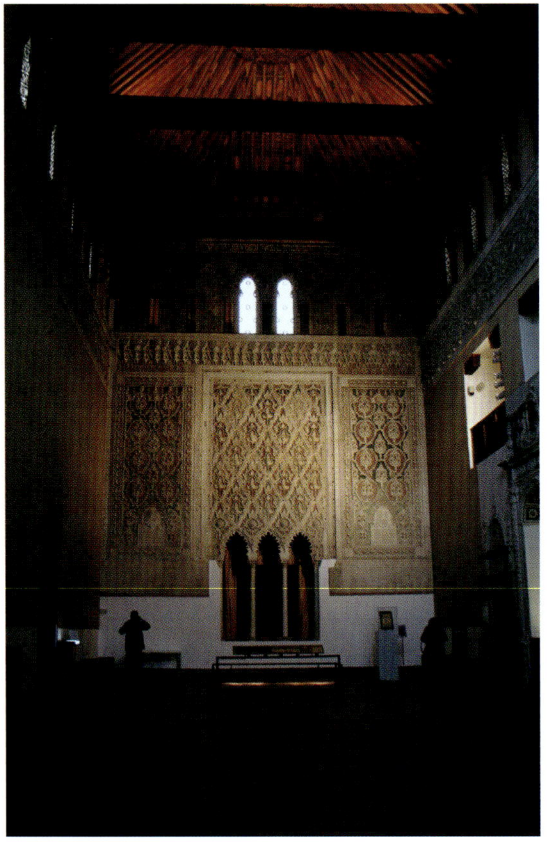

FIG. 58
Toledo, Synagogue of Samuel Ha-Levi Abulafia.
© Pamela A. Patton.

and damned apostate, Muhammad. What is to be done?"[4] By contrast, Spain's Jews, whose centuries-old subjugation to Christian rule had remained unquestioned, instead posed a challenge that was primarily ideological, based in their refusal to acknowledge the validity of Christianity despite the two faiths' closely shared roots. Nonetheless, as the works analyzed in this chapter will show, such distinctions seem to have faded from the late twelfth century onward as Iberian Christians attempted sporadically to articulate a perceived kinship between Jews and Muslims, forged on the basis of their parallel opposition to a newly dominant Christian majority.

This phenomenon was not exclusively Iberian, but drew upon a widespread and surprisingly persistent tendency among Christians in Europe to compare, ally, or even elide Jews and Muslims, along with other outgroups, as opponents of a "normative" Christian culture. Throughout Latin Christendom from the twelfth century onward, this tendency strongly shaped the Western worldview about how such minorities fit into both a social and soteriological frame, as well as about how their existence shaped the self-image of a flourishing Christian majority. As explicated with particular clarity by scholars like R. I. Moore and Jeremy Cohen, Christian thinkers increasingly came to see the practitioners of Judaism and Islam as parallel religious Others, a view intensified by the hostile confrontation of western Christendom with Muslims and Islam in the course of the Crusades.[5] Thus, both groups came to be defined as much in relation to each other as in opposition to Christianity, and the abstraction once famously labeled by Cohen as "hermeneutical Jew" was reconceptualized in tandem with an equally hermeneutical Muslim.[6]

Links drawn between Jews and Muslims in the mentality of medieval Christendom ranged from the empirical to the fantastical, with an emphasis on the latter. Christians recognized that adherents to the two faiths shared certain practices, like circumcision and the avoidance of pork, as well as key points of theology, including the rejection of doctrinal points like the Trinity and the Incarnation. However, they also were quick to apply more wild-eyed claims, such as blasphemy, idolatry, and satanic affiliation, to members of both communities. The perception that both faith groups shared such susceptibilities facilitated their tandem placement in new kinds of Christian polemic that attacked Jews and Muslims as parallel categories of unbeliever, as suggested by Peter the Venerable in his frequently cited exhortation to Louis VII of France: "Why should we pursue the enemies of the Christian faith in far and distant lands while vile blasphemers worse than any Saracens, namely the Jews, who are not far away from us, but who live in our midst, blaspheme, abuse, and trample on Christ and the Christian sacraments so freely and with impunity?"[7]

Peter's concern with Christendom's religious opponents extended beyond wartime rhetoric; he composed multiple tracts that mined translations of both the Talmud and the Qur'an for evidence that would discredit their parent traditions conclusively in the eyes of his flock.[8] His approach was distilled more purposefully by thirteenth-century churchmen like the Franciscan Nicholas of Lyra (ca. 1270–1349), in whose view Jewish and Muslim error was literally of a kind: "it is obvious that the Jews have fallen into the error of the Saracens, who define the beatitude of the future life as the corporeal delights of food and sex, which is deemed absurd not only among the Catholics, but also among the Gentile philosophers who view the beatitude of man in the works of his rational faculty."[9]

The pursuit of this "Muslim Connection," as Jeremy Cohen has described it,[10] finds some visual parallels in northern European art of the same era. Especially memorable is the tiny figural group on a late thirteenth-century *mappa mundi* in Hereford, a grandly scaled late medieval diagram of the then-known world that includes among its landmarks representations of its multiple peoples in relevant locations.[11] Near the center of the map, in a zone adjacent to the Red Sea, a group of hook-nosed, bearded figures labeled "judei" kneels before a squatting, bovine idol labeled "Mahū," from the anus of which issues a row of coins (fig. 59). This common medieval corruption of the name "Muhammad," the idol's visual evocation of the Golden Calf worshiped by the biblical Israelites, and the impure coinage it produces all draw upon stereotypes that medieval Christians imputed to practitioners of both faiths: to Muslims, an improperly worshipful adherence to Muhammad; to Jews, the avariciousness and uncleanness associated with money; and to both, idolatrous practices that defied God's commandments. In this, the Hereford image both confuses and dismisses the boundaries between the two religious groups and positions them both at the margins of faithful Christian society.[12]

The "Muslim Connection" in Medieval Iberia

The tendency to conflate Jews and Muslims gained traction in Iberia's northern kingdoms too in the twelfth and thirteenth centuries. As in northern Europe, signs of this trend can be found earliest in theological and polemical texts, although in Iberia it would be in visual form that such ideas flourished most imaginatively.[13] In such works, the decisiveness with which the features of Muslim and Jew have been blurred suggests the strength of the Iberian Christian drive to rethink the relationship with both faith groups as the northern kingdoms' power expanded—to create and enforce a new conceptual distance between themselves and the two minority communities, whose long-standing familiarity threatened to erode the new self-identity that they had worked so hard to fashion.

This dynamic calls to mind Stephen Greenblatt's characterization of self-fashioning as relying on precisely this kind of hostile differentiation of Self from Other, succeeding when it is accomplished "in relation to something perceived as alien, strange, or hostile . . . [which] must be discovered or invented in order to be attacked and destroyed."[14] While Greenblatt had in mind a specific and self-conscious process that by definition took place at the individual level, and one that he argued was peculiar to the Renaissance, it is possible to argue

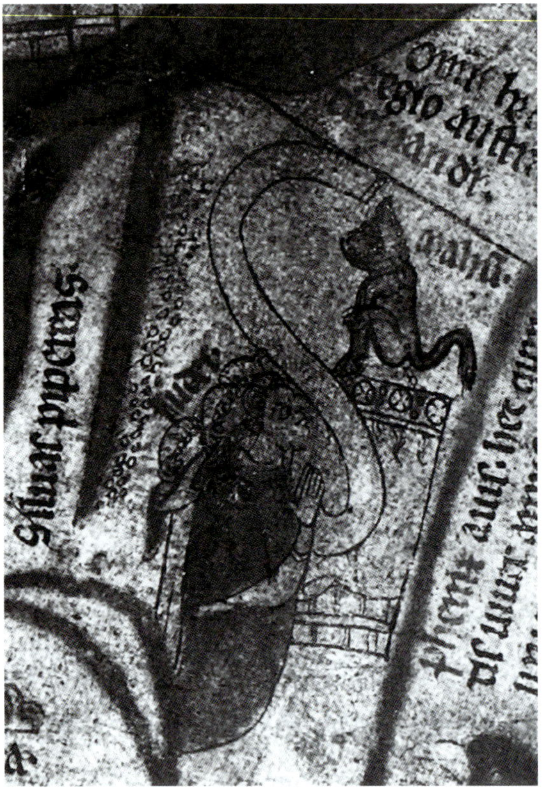

FIG. 59
Jews worshiping an idol (detail). Hereford World Map. Hereford Cathedral. © The Dean and Chapter of Hereford Cathedral and the Hereford Mappa Mundi Trust.

that a similar process obtained here. In effect, the Spanish kingdoms' new orientation toward the culture, language, dynasties, and social structures of mainstream Europe in the course of the Reconquest might be said to have prompted their own "discovery" of Jewish and Muslim differences from Christianity, one that overlooked the fine distinctions between the two groups in order to gather them into a broad collectivization of what Christians were not.

This is a complex claim, since Spain was one of the few places in western Europe where the average Christian might be expected to have firmly grasped the difference between a Muslim and a Jew to begin with. Although the religious and cultural differences between Jews and Muslims in the central Middle Ages must have been fairly clear to the Christians with whom they shared the Iberian Peninsula, such differences would have seemed far less concrete to many of their brethren in the West, whose relatively limited exposure to individuals of either religious culture and new sense of the wide range of cultural and religious Others who existed beyond the bounds of an expanding Europe seem to have increased their readiness to compare or elide them.

Iberian efforts to trace out a perceived alliance between Muslims and Jews can be found as early as the turn of the twelfth century, in the work of the Christian convert Petrus Alfonsi (1062[?]–after 1121). Petrus had begun life in Al-Andalus as a Jew named Moses but converted to Christianity in Huesca in 1106, a move he employed shortly afterward as the pretext for his rationalistic *Dialogus contra iudaeos* (Dialogue Against the Jews).[15] This text, conceived as the Christian Petrus's imaginary theological debate with his former Jewish self, broke the mold typical of such dialogic works by including within its extensive critique of Judaism a lively and knowledgeable section attacking Islam, the first such polemic in the Latin West since it predates that of Peter the Venerable by several decades.[16] Petrus's decision to consider the two faiths in tandem may represent primarily a logical response to the fact that a disillusioned Jew in Spain had not one, but two viable religious alternatives close at hand, and one of them had to be discredited. Yet his calculated pairing created a structure in which the two faith systems could be understood as parallel alternatives to his own new religion.

While Alfonsi's *Dialogus* circulated primarily in northern Europe, where he himself relocated shortly after its completion, it had echoes in Iberian theological and polemical texts produced later in the century. One such work is the oft-cited but rarely analyzed "Letter of Toledo," an anonymous missive purportedly addressed by astrologers in Toledo to Pope Clement III around 1185.[17] Based on astrological signs of an apocalypse in the following year, it foretold the arrival of an Age of Peace that involved not just the conversion of the world's Jews, as was relatively common in apocalyptic literature, but also the conquest or conversion of its Muslims.[18] Dominican missionaries arriving in Spain in the second quarter of the thirteenth century likewise seem to have viewed Jews and Muslims as tandem targets for conversion. Although it is true that Dominican interest in the conversion of non-Christians in Spain sometimes has been exaggerated, the order's desire to identify and confront what they clearly saw as opponent faiths can be sensed in such adaptations as the foundation of *studia* in which the brothers could learn Hebrew and Arabic for more direct access to Jewish and Muslim texts. The writings of Catalan friars such as Ramon Martí also make it clear that the two faith groups had now become part of the bloc of nonbelievers with whom these preachers would have to cope. In his *Capistrum iudaeorum* (Muzzle of the Jews) Martí presents the Jews as trumping even Muhammad in their potential to damage Christendom:

> If Muhammad, for instance, who at the outset was so all alone, entirely uneducated, utterly impoverished, hated by his own kinsmen and foreigners alike, so far removed from our borders, and so obvious in his falsehood, could introduce so much corruption into the world on behalf of the devil—what do you think the devil can accomplish through the Jews, who are so numerous, almost all educated and most adept at trickery, so well endowed from the good life and the usuries allowed them by Christians, so loved by our princes on account of the services they provide and the flatteries they spew forth, so scattered and dispersed throughout the world, so secretive in their deceptions that they display a remarkable appearance of being truthful?![19]

Judaism and Islam are also paired in the rhetoric of Reconquest, which by this period had evolved into an international military effort tantamount to a crusade.[20] Growing papal and European interest in the Christian victories in Al-Andalus surely fostered the tendency of local armies and chroniclers to view their attacks upon Muslims as part of a wider confrontation with the nonbeliever, and circumstances on the ground encouraged this view. The capture of any Muslim city by Christian forces naturally necessitated engagement not only with its Islamic community, but also with its Jews, who in many cases were deeply acculturated to Islamic ways and language and must have seemed, in some ways, remarkably like them.

Spain's Christian kings evidently recognized the value of their new Jewish subjects' conversancy with an existing Islamic infrastructure in their newly conquered lands, and this could and sometimes did result in friendlier treatment of the entire *aljama.* This indeed occurred in Tudela following its conquest in 1119, when the victorious King Alfonso I offered the Jews who had fled the formerly Muslim city in advance an array of protections to entice their return.[21] In many cases, however, the confrontation with not one, but two non-Christian communities in the course of a city's conquest appears to have bred a certain cultural confusion, or at the very least a surprising lack of precision. In the mid-twelfth century, the author of the *Chronica Adefonsi imperatoris* recorded how in the course of his campaign of 1118 the young Alfonso, future Alfonso VII of León-Castilla, destroyed Muslim "synagogues" and burned copies of the Qur'an (*et synagogas eorum destruxerunt et libros legis Mahometi combusserunt igne*).[22] This odd misusage is not new: the description of Muslim places of worship as "synagogues" echoes terminology current elsewhere in Europe.[23] The adoption of similar language in Iberia, where the difference between a mosque and a synagogue surely was clear to most Christians, suggests that semantic accuracy was trumped in such cases by the impulse to draw clear distinctions between all such structures and their Christian counterparts.

The semideliberate confusion of the two non-Christian faiths in Spain sometimes took the form of actual violence against Jews, often by bands of soldiers temporarily diverted from their official campaign against Muslims. In 1063, French and Spanish forces sent by Pope Alexander II to battle Muslims in Aragon inexplicably extended their attack to Jewish communities there;[24] similar attacks occurred in 1108 in Toledo after the battle of Uclés and in 1212, when an international gathering of soldiers assembling for the battle of Las Navas de Tolosa attacked the city's Jewish quarter.[25] Often these attacks appear to have been instigated by the non-Iberian troops, for whom violence against Jewish communities had been a side effect of the crusading mentality since the serial attacks of Crusaders against Jewish communities in Speyer, Mainz, Worms, and other cities in 1096, and Spanish soldiers are in at least one case recorded as having come to the defense of the Jews.[26] Nonetheless, such episodes suggest the degree to which that underlying mentality had begun gradually to infiltrate the Iberian sphere.

Legislation that guided the settlement of newly conquered cities in this period likewise treated Muslims and Jews with some degree of parallelism. The *fueros,* or town charters, that were offered the inhabitants of newly conquered towns traditionally had lumped Jewish and Muslim communities together, and this practice was preserved as royal legislation expanded in the thirteenth century: in 1286, Alfonso III simultaneously denied both faith groups the exemption from tolls and taxes offered the Christian community of Játiva, while in 1300,

James II passed an edict compelling both groups to kneel when a priest bearing a consecrated wafer passed in public procession.[27]

The richest evidence for the conceptual linkage of Jews and Muslims in Iberia, however, is not textual but visual. It emerges in images that conflate or compare Jews and Muslims in a manner intriguingly similar to the theological, polemical, and legal works in which such connections are more often sought. Such images freely combine or confuse the two groups' respective cultural trappings in a manner that stands at odds with the presumed familiarity of both Jews and Muslims to Iberian Christians. Yet one might argue that it was this very familiarity that facilitated the precision and effectiveness with which Christian artists deployed these cultural markers. In examining these works, my goal is to understand more clearly why, in a context within which many practical and cultural differences between Jews and Muslims must have been perfectly clear to both artists and their viewers, such elisions still were made, and what they meant to these same constituencies.

In examining such works, it will remain important to recognize the multiple interpretive possibilities afforded by their varying contexts and viewership, as well as the pitfalls inherent in the modern temptation to label such forms as concretely "Jewish" or "Muslim." Both the complexity and the porousness of Iberian medieval culture militate against such firmly bounded classifications; what matters is not whether the modern viewer may think a form looks "Jewish" or "Islamic," but whether it was perceived as such by the medieval artists and viewers in question. It is equally important to recognize that using forms derived from the work of another group may reflect not a conscious desire to shape one group's identity so much as how fully the other group's cultural practices have become naturalized to it.

Jews as Muslims, Muslims as Jews

A subtle Muslim-Jewish conflation appears in the narrative cloister of Santa María la Mayor in Tudela, introduced in chapter 2. The image in question appears on a capital depicting the conspiracy of the Temple priests and Pharisees in the house of the high priest Caiaphas to plot the arrest and execution of Jesus (fig. 14).[28] As has been noted, the prominent location of this capital near the northeast entrance to the cloister also places it at the midpoint of a Passion narrative that proceeds sequentially along the cloister's north and east ranges, according the episode unusual narrative centrality.

Easily visible in this scene is the book held by the priest in the center of the capital, who proffers it toward the viewer as the rest of the men turn expectantly toward the seated Caiaphas. Its protected location on the inner face of the pier has left this tiny sculpted codex in good condition, and its assiduously rendered details are easily read. Held frontally, with its spine to the viewer's right, it displays a pentagonal flap, its peak decorated by a minute eight-pointed star, which wraps around the book's fore-edge to overlap the front cover. These features distinguish it decisively from the straight-edged, clasped codices held by Christian figures in the same cloister.[29]

The pentagonal flap identifies this as an Islamic envelope-flap binding, an originally Coptic form that emerged in Islamic Egypt in the late eleventh century.[30] Opening on the left, as consistent with the right-to-left progression of written Arabic, such bindings often were made of pasteboard rather than wood and featured a pentagonal extension of the book's lower cover, which folded over the fore-edge to point back toward the spine and protected the outer edges of the leaves. In many bindings of this type, the flap seems to have been designed to tuck inside the upper cover and rest on the leaf block; however, Islamic depictions of such bindings often show the flap resting outside the cover instead, perhaps in an effort to render it more recognizable.[31] The flap of the Tudela capital, with its radial star at the peak, closely resembles the few actual Islamic exemplars of this period that survive.[32]

Envelope-flap bindings of this kind seem to have been unknown in western Islamic lands until the final decades of the twelfth century, when documents, though not actual exemplars, suggest their use in Almohad Morocco.[33] The earliest actual bindings to survive from the region do not appear until the mid-thirteenth century, and none survive from Spain before the late Middle Ages.[34] The acutely observed bookbinding on the Tudela capital thus represents the only surviving visual evidence that this technique had been introduced into Iberia at all by the end of the twelfth century. To a monastic viewer accustomed only to straight-edged board bindings that closed with clasps, it must have seemed both strikingly modern and extremely foreign.

The book's atypical format lends several potential valences to the image of the Conspiracy. First, because it takes the form of a modern codex, rather than the generically scriptural scroll that was more traditional in the Conspiracy scene, it had the potential to invoke other, less venerable Jewish books, of which the best known to Christians was the Talmud. This postbiblical compendium had become the target of controversy since gaining the serious attention of Christian churchmen in the twelfth century. The discovery that Jews acknowledged an authoritative work outside the confines of the Bible provoked a series of church offensives that culminated in the papal investigation, trial, and burning of the Talmud at Paris in 1240–42.[35] Such concerns were not unfamiliar within Iberia, where Muslim polemicists such as Ibn Hazm of Córdoba (d. 1064) and the converted Jew Petrus Alfonsi already had undertaken critiques of the Talmud that would echo distantly in the Barcelona disputation of 1263.[36]

While the codical format of the Tudela book implied its controversial content, its foreign style and structure placed it firmly beyond the cultural boundaries of Latin Christendom. Although there is no surviving evidence that Jews themselves used envelope-flap bindings in Iberia at this date,[37] it is unlikely that this question had much saliency for the cloister's monastic inhabitants, who are likely to have seen it above all as non-Christian. Whether or not they recognized the bookbinding's specifically Islamic roots, they would have grasped the cultural distance, and with this the suspect nature, of the book it protected as well as of the treacherous figures in whose hands it rests.

Tudela's monastic community would have been primed for such a reading. As Augustinian regular canons who were actively engaged in resettling a formerly Muslim city with a flourishing Jewish population,[38] they were well aware of the challenges that these Others might present to the stabilization of their city. As literate religious, they might even have recognized the cloister's envelope-flap binding as specifically Islamic. If so, they might also have been provoked to consider the conflation that it implied between the biblical Jews who had betrayed Christ and the medieval Muslims whose rise to power in the course of the early Middle Ages had made them Europe's most concretely feared opponent. Anachronistic though it was, this conceptual connection provided a vivid parallel to the texts discussed above, which reinforced the perception of Jews and Muslims as common enemies to the Christian cause. The embedding of this image within a narrative of Christ's Passion, one in which Jews with "Muslim" attributes figure prominently in the attack upon Christ, can only have strengthened this notion.

The Passion narrative also offers a framework for the linkage of Jews and Muslims in Spain in the painted pine beam with which this chapter opened (figs. 55, 56). Today in the National Museum of Catalan Art, the work was for some time believed to have originated in the Crown of Aragon, although recent scholarship has linked it instead with early thirteenth-century Castile on the basis of stylistic comparisons with manuscripts such as the *Liber feudorum maior,* the closely related *Liber feudorum Ceritaniae* (Barcelona, ACA, Real Cancillería, Reg. 1 and Reg. 4), and the Las Huelgas Beatus (New York, Pierpont Morgan Lib., MS M. 429).[39] Although usually described as a fragment of a baldacchino, the beam in its current state measures nearly seven and a half feet long, and incomplete imagery at both ends indicates that it once was longer. Thus, it more likely derived from a larger architectural structure such as a wooden ceiling or choir screen.[40]

Painted in tempera on the face of the beam are seven Passion episodes, which proceed chronologically from left to right: the Arrest of Christ, the Flagellation, Christ Bearing the Cross, the Crucifixion, the Deposition, the Entombment, and the Holy Women at the Tomb. The presence of a fragmentary figure to the left of this series suggests that the beam was once longer by at least one episode. The imagery is interrupted also by three large rectilinear losses, possibly related to a reuse of the beam, which were subsequently filled in by unpainted pine that obscures several figures in the scenes of the Arrest, Crucifixion, and the Holy Women. Smaller losses throughout the beam are now filled in with passages of *tratteggio.*

The most striking feature of this Passion series is the physical appearance of the figures who most actively attack Christ in its climactic episodes: the Flagellation, the Bearing of the Cross, and the Crucifixion. Their dark skin, exaggerated lips and noses, and white head scarves and sashes set them sharply apart from the pale, lank-haired figures that surround them. In the Flagellation (fig. 55), two such figures, dressed in short red or yellow tunics with fringed white sashes, lash at Jesus with cats-o'-nine-tails; three more, one holding a round shield, point and open their mouths to harass him as he carries the cross. At the Crucifixion, three additional figures, one with his head uncovered to reveal tightly curled black hair, turn to the side to confront Judas, who gestures, peculiarly, toward his own mouth (fig. 56). The foremost two lean intently toward the fallen disciple as their companion points back toward the cross and the prominent inscription "QUID AD NOS" (What is that to us?). Several similar figures probably also appeared to the right of Christ in the now-damaged scene of the Arrest, where the lower parts of their tunics reveal the same white-tasseled sashes worn by other dark-skinned figures.

The appearance and meaning of these carefully differentiated figures have long eluded explication, and for good reason. Their dark skin, large eyes, enlarged lips, and curled hair conform to medieval stereotypes of Africans, such as those discussed in chapter 3; their scarves and sashes suggest that they are Muslim; and they appear in a biblical narrative in which neither group holds a historical place. Each of these layers must be considered in turn.

By the twelfth century, figures with African features certainly formed part of the Ibero-Christian visual lexicon, where they generally play subordinate or inimical roles, such as those of servants and soldiers, consistent with those assigned black figures elsewhere in medieval Western imagery.[41] The cross-legged African musician with tightly curled hair found on a cloister capital in Santa María in Tudela and the soldier with African features and curly hair who impales a child on his sword, both there and in a late twelfth-century image of the Massacre of the Innocents at San Miguel de Estella, exemplify such usage.[42] By the thirteenth century, however, black or African figures could hold a more expansive range of meanings for Iberian viewers. In Alfonso X's *Lapidario,* as was shown, black men seem to have represented actual peoples from Africa, just one category among the many exotic foreigners shown mining the various stones catalogued in that manuscript. One such illustration is associated with the mineral called *tellinimuz;* it depicts a small stone held by one of two black men while the adjacent text describes it as deriving from the *tierra de los negros,* or "Land of the Blacks," presumably the Castilian equivalent of the Arabic phrase *bilād al-sudān,* referring to sub-Saharan Africa (fol. 4r; fig. 44). A similar illustration accompanies the discussion of *muruquid* on a subsequent folio (73v).[43]

In other manuscripts associated with Alfonso, such as the *Libro de ajedrez* and the *Cantigas de Santa María,* black figures play a wider variety of roles. Both male and female blacks appear among the court retainers and slaves at play in the *Libro de ajedrez,* while still others represent soldiers, servants, and other "Moors" in the illustrations of the king's beloved miracle tales.[44] Whereas this juxtaposition may in some cases reflect the actual diversity of peoples in Alfonso's Spain, where black Africans lived in significant numbers among ethnically Arab Muslims,[45] it also echoes established conventions used to depict master-servant relationships in western Islamic manuscripts, a genre also certainly known to Alfonso and his artists. In either case, such figures reveal an intersection with the actual visual and social experience of the king and his artists that is lacking in the more formulaic black figures of northern European art.

More powerful still must have been such figures' identification with Islam, an association made frequently outside of Iberia as well. In its broadest sense, this connection seems to have been rooted less in medieval ideas about ethnicity than in classical and earlier medieval racial theories, in which blackness came to be linked with such figures' geographical remoteness or character deficiencies, both readily associated by western Christians with a Muslim enemy.[46] The *Chanson de Roland*'s several references to the black skin of the Muslim king Marsile and his followers play actively upon this heritage, as does the more complex elaboration upon the black skin and beard of the Saracen who is cooked and served to Richard I in the late medieval romance *Richard Coeur de Lyon.*[47]

Geraldine Heng has argued that by the thirteenth century, such mechanisms can be read as part of a broadly developing "racializing discourse" that was aimed at reading both racial and religious difference in terms of skin color and other bodily features.[48] Such might indeed have been the case in medieval Iberia, where, to a greater extent than in many parts of Europe, the Christian understanding of dark skin as a Muslim feature may have been bolstered by the actual ethnic situation. There were, after all, many Africans in Spain, and many of these were also Muslim. The perceived correlation between skin color and religion that resulted was strong enough in early fourteenth-century Aragon that in at least one recorded case a black Christian mistakenly sold as a slave found it difficult to convince his captors that he was not Muslim, and that he was therefore ineligible to be sold.[49] Religious identity and skin color are similarly imbricated in historiographic and legal writing of the same period: in the *Estoria de España,* composed under Alfonso X in the third quarter of the thirteenth century, the Muslim invaders of Spain are repeatedly described as "black as pitch" or "black as a kettle," while in the *Siete partidas,* the common Castilian name for the descendants of those putatively dark-complexioned invaders, *moro,* is offered as the standard vernacular translation of the Latin *sarracenus* (Saracen).[50]

The word functions similarly in the bilingual section headings of the thirteenth-century *Vidal mayor,* a work introduced in chapter 2. Several of these treat *moro* and *sarracenus* as virtual equivalents: "Of Jews and Saracens. That is, of Jews and Moors."[51] The equation is underscored visually in the historiated initials accompanying such passages, which sometimes include Muslim figures with dark brown skin, curly black hair, red lips, and white teeth and nails. One such initial (fol. 242v), opening a section of laws about the voluntary baptism of Muslims and Jews, depicts a nude black figure kneeling in a font to be baptized by a cleric while a white Christian man and woman, presumably his sponsors, reach toward him (fig. 60). Another initial (fol. 244r), which lays out royal policies regarding runaway slaves, depicts two black men with similar features and simple white tunics, who are presented to the king by two soldiers. The distinction between these figures and their pale-skinned captors is heightened by their unusually rich brown skin tone, created by a subtle mix of pigments that in this manuscript appears to have been reserved for Muslim figures alone.[52]

The illustrated manuscripts of the *Cantigas de Santa María* also associate dark skin with Islam. In the Escorial illustration of Cantiga 186 (Escorial T.I.1, fol. 244r), the story of a "Moor" who was sent by his Christian mistress to get into bed with her daughter-in-law so that the latter would be accused of infidelity, a black, curly-haired servant climbs obediently under the young woman's covers (fig. 61). His extremely dark complexion is consistent with the *cantiga*'s claim that he is "black as pitch," and this must have heightened its shock value for a medieval viewer attuned to the tale's implication that the pair's alleged adultery was compounded by

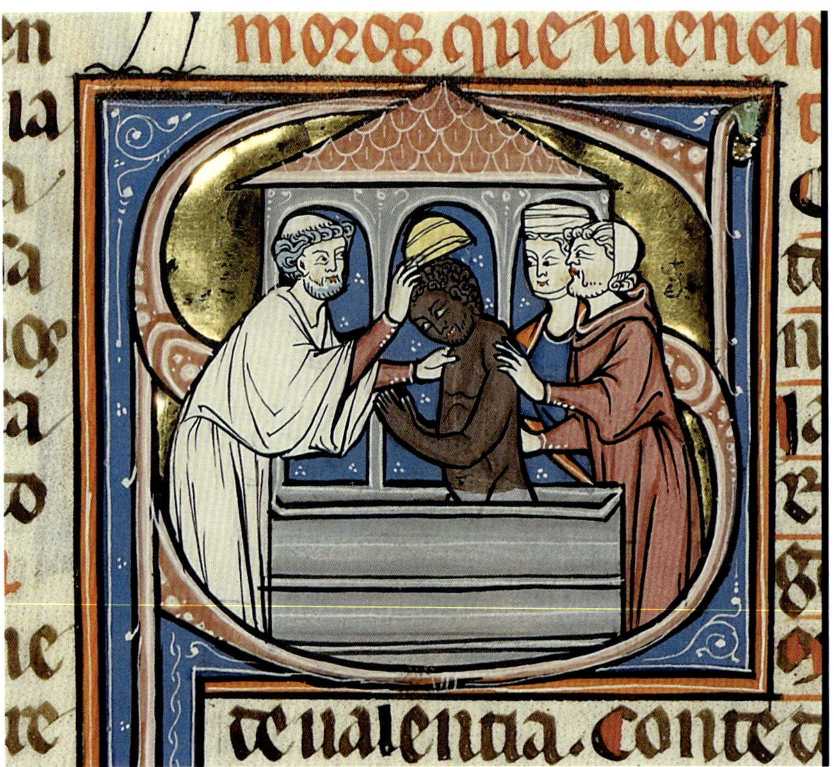

FIG. 60
Initial S depicting the baptism of a Muslim (detail). Tempera and gold leaf on parchment, leaf dimensions 36.5 x 24 cm. *Vidal mayor,* ca. 1290–1310. The J. Paul Getty Museum, Los Angeles, MS Ludwig XIV 6, fol. 242v.

miscegenation, a crime in its own right under both Castilian and canon law.[53]

Such associations were far from fixed. As has been noted, the illustrators of the *Cantigas de Santa María* deployed a wide range of ethnic types in illustrating stories about Muslims and occasionally even disregarded textual cues regarding skin color: while Cantiga 185 describes how Christians threw "three Moors, blacker than Satan," over the wall of a castle, the Escorial illustration depicts two fair-complexioned Muslims with beards and turbans in the act of being tossed over the ramparts (Escorial T.I.1, fol. 247r; fig. 62).[54] The discrepancy seems here to derive from the traditional association of light skin color with higher rank, so that the role of antagonist in the tale could be undertaken by lighter-skinned, and thus implicitly higher-ranking, Arab soldiers. It remains impossible to know how the artists might have handled similar references in tales for which illustrations today are lacking, such as Cantiga 406, in which the author requests that Mary confound all the Moors, "including those who are fair complexioned," and Cantiga 325, which describes Muslims going out to work in a vineyard, "some of them fair complexioned."[55] In such cases, the desire to indicate the existence of fair-skinned Muslims as a category at all implies an exceptionality that must reflect how strongly Islam and dark skin had become linked.

The depiction of military conflicts offered an especially attractive field on which to articulate these connections, tied as they were to already extant European stereotypes of the black soldier-enemy. In the panoramic, if now fragmentary, frescoes of the battles of Portopí and Mallorca, painted in the Palau d'Aguilar in Barcelona between 1285 and 1290 and now in the Museu Nacional d'Art de Catalunya, a combination of dark- and light-skinned soldiers peer out from the crenellations of the Muslim strongholds, while others enter into hand-to-hand combat with Christians (fig. 28).[56] Scalloped banners bearing hexagrams or the *ḥamsa,* motifs to be discussed more extensively below, reinforce their outsider status. Unlike the exaggerated physiognomy of the Muslims depicted in the *Vidal mayor,* the facial features of these figures are unexceptional in shape: shown in three-quarter view, they are small and regular like those of the Christian soldiers they oppose. Skin color thus provides the chief sign of their physical and hence religious difference from their adversaries.

Such examples lend sharpened significance to the black figures of the Barcelona beam. Whereas dark-skinned or African tormentors, especially dark-skinned soldiers, do sometimes appear in northern European Passion imagery, in such cases their appearance seems to derive primarily from the traditional association between dark skin and evil or demonic behavior, and there is little evidence that they also would have been associated with Islam, a faith that would not exist for six hundred years following the Passion.[57] What differentiates the black figures of the Passion scenes in Barcelona is their specific addition to the European formula of attributes, from their brown skin and African features to their turbanlike scarves, that a thirteenth-century Iberian surely would have read specifically as Muslim.

But were the Barcelona figures then understood literally *as* Muslims? This seems unlikely, given their viewers' awareness of other Iberian contexts in which black figures represented distinctly varied categories of people and the slippages of meaning that this made possible. A short poem on the lamentations of the Virgin by Gonzalo de Berceo suggests just how deeply such multivalency would have inflected any reading of these figures. Berceo's poem, which offers a first-person account of the Passion as told by the Virgin Mary, refers to those who enacted the Crucifixion alternately as both *moros* and *paganos,* a "dark company" *(compaña negriella)* that is nonetheless distinguished from the *judíos* who were unwilling to accept responsibility for Christ's death. Such usage suggests that for Berceo and his audience, whatever distinctions between "Muslims" and "pagans" might have been perceived in daily life had lost their relevance in the context of the Passion story.[58]

The collapse of all these categories is completed in the Passion beam, where several dark-skinned figures perform actions ascribed by both convention and Scripture specifically to Jews. The three who turn away from the crucified Christ to confront the recoiling Judas represent an episode concurrent with the Crucifixion, which is recounted in Matthew 27:4. After Jesus's arrest, the suddenly repentant Judas attempted to return the thirty silver pieces with which the Temple priests had bribed him to betray his master, saying, "I have sinned in betraying innocent blood." The priests refused the money, and their dismissive response, "What is that to us?" (QUID AD NOS), appears in bold white letters to the left of the Barcelona

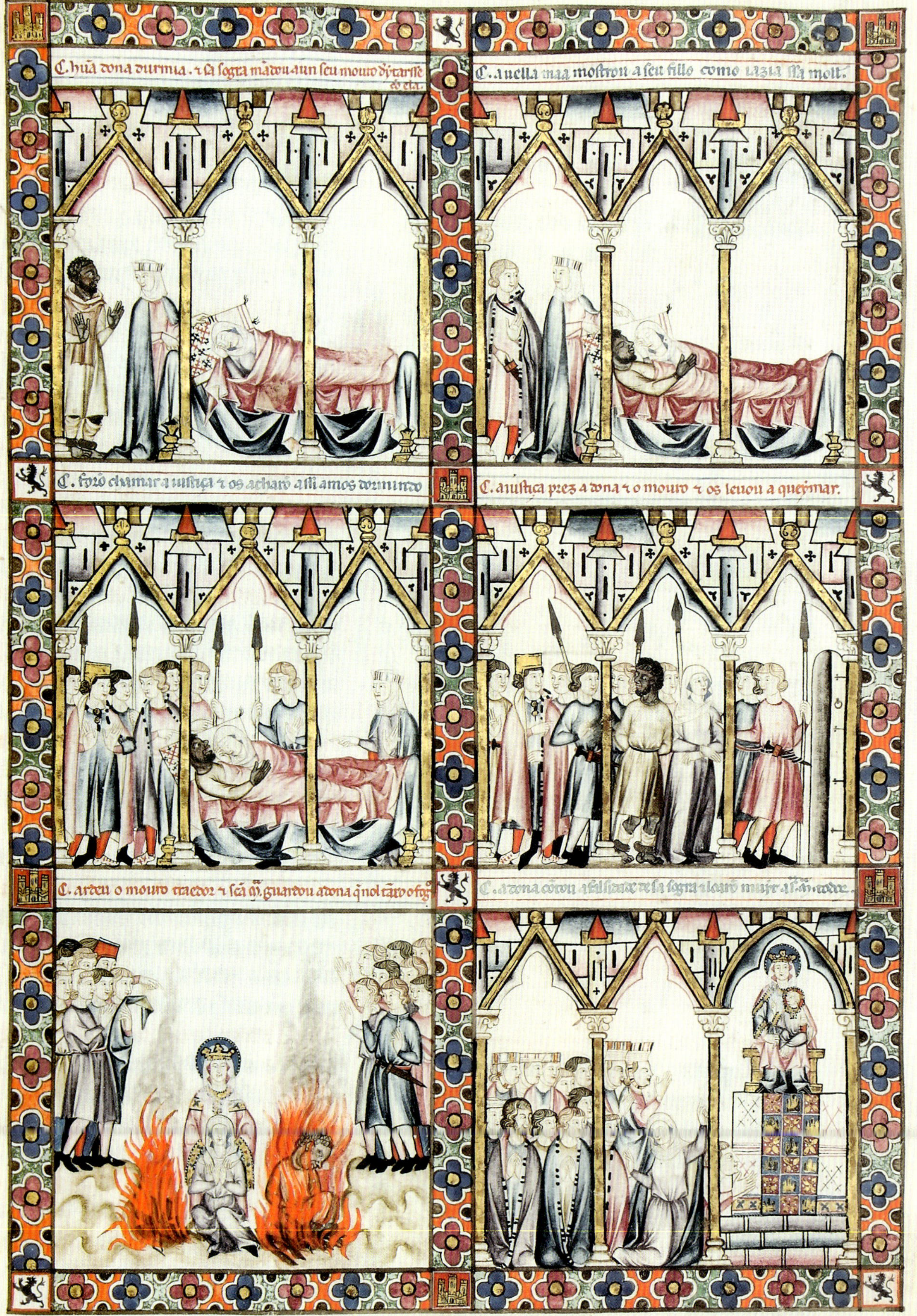
C. hũa dona durmia. ⁊ sa sogra mãdou a un seu mouro d'ytarsse cõ ela.
C. a uella maa mostrou a seu fillo como iazia ssa moll.
C. forõ chamar a iustiça ⁊ os acharõ assi amos dormindo
C. a iustiça prez a dona ⁊ o mouro ⁊ os leuou a queymar.
C. ardeu o mouro traedor ⁊ scã M. guardou a dona q̃ nol tãyo o fog.
C. a dona cõtou a falsidade de sa sogra ⁊ loarõ muyt a s. M. todos.

FIG. 61
The Story of the Woman Accused of Adultery with a Muslim (Cantiga 186), *Cantigas de Santa María*. Real Biblioteca de El Escorial, Madrid, T.I.1, fol. 244r.

trio, the third of whom points back to their words in possessive emphasis. In this form, the three figures can be read neither as soldier stereotypes nor as Muslims pure and simple; they are universal Others who have also become the Temple priests, collapsing the theological and historical divide among Jews and Muslims to lay the blame for Christ's murder at the feet of all opponent faiths.

The Passion beam attests decisively to a shift in attitude toward non-Christian faith groups in high medieval Iberia. Here, the presence of a familiar Islamic culture, so unlike the quasi-mythical enemy constructed by Europeans north of the Pyrenees, provided Iberian Christian artists with a potent and distinctive means to create distance from a Jewish culture that was equally if not even more familiar. Both in its perceptive specificity and in its stubborn refusal to recognize the differing positions of Jews and Muslims within salvation history, it crafts a new place for both in the temporal world as well, arraying them side by side as imaginary enemies of a single triumphant religion.

Ornament, Symbol, and Identity

Not all Jewish-Muslim conflations in Iberian visual culture display such self-consciousness. Others are more subtle, relying on the association with both faith groups of a common vocabulary of ornamental and abstract motifs that include Arabic writing, pseudo-Arabic, and other abstract forms, such as the hexagram, which seem to have served both ornamental and symbolic functions. The efficacy of these signs seems to have lain not in their specific association with one or the other religion, but in their dissociation from Christian culture, in their non-Christianness. While some of the motifs to be discussed here have today earned a more limited religio-cultural association—the hexagram, for example, is now seen in the West as virtually synonymous with Judaism—it remains clear that in the Middle Ages, and especially in Iberia, they displayed far greater cultural fluidity.

This fluidity had logical roots. After centuries of living as Muslim subjects, Jews in Islamic centers such as Córdoba, Seville, Zaragoza, and Valencia had become deeply acculturated to the practices and material legacy of their hosts by the time that Christian troops arrived in the twelfth and thirteenth centuries. Jewish *mudéjar* architecture and manuscripts aptly illustrate this engagement. In the Toledan synagogue of Samuel Ha-Levi Abulafia, for example, Islamic building style, materials, and ornamental vocabulary created a monument much in keeping with Nasrid structures of the same era, even to the inclusion of lozenges with fluid

Arabic inscriptions within the carved stucco decoration of the interior (fig. 58). Acculturation had its limits: although these inscriptions were in the past mistaken for quotations from the Qur'an and thus misread as everything from uniquely interreligious expressions of faith in God to surreptitious Islamic propaganda, they are in fact largely illegible forms that should be understood primarily as emulating prevailing court traditions.[59] Similarly, the ornamental forms in some Castilian Hebrew Bibles that resemble *sūrah* markings in illuminated Qur'ans can be attributed to a process of cultural adaptation that may have had little to do with religious ideology.[60] Whether their presence can be linked with the presence of actual Muslim craftsmen or simply because of the relative ease with which Iberian Jews absorbed many aspects of this particular host culture over the centuries, one might argue that such forms had by now become just as Jewish as they were Islamic.

The medieval Christian understanding of such motifs was a different matter. While Iberian Christians also eventually absorbed originally Islamic forms into their own architecture and other media, for at least a limited time in the thirteenth and early fourteenth centuries, they seem to have retained a greater self-consciousness about such elements' foreign origins.[61] At the same time, it is not always easy to know when a

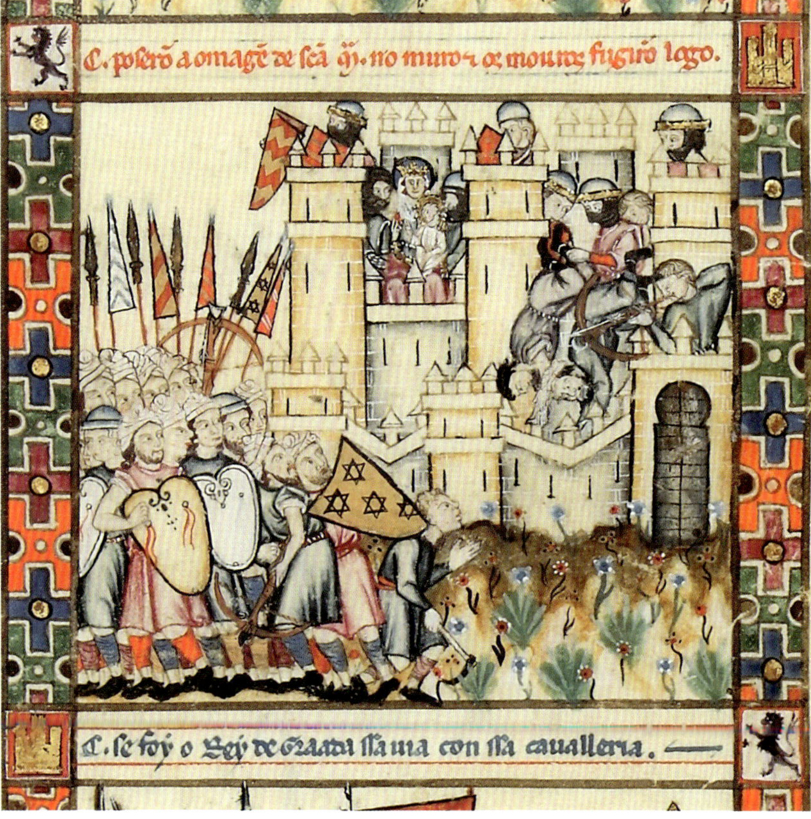

FIG. 62
Muslim warriors at the Battle of Chincolla. Detail from The Story of the Battle of Chincolla (Cantiga 185), *Cantigas de Santa María*. Real Biblioteca de El Escorial, Madrid, MS T.I.1, fol. 247r. © Patrimonio Nacional.

Christian artist or viewer understood a certain element to be specifically Islamic or Jewish, or even if such a question would have been considered of any relevance. Far clearer is the effect that such blurring boundaries could have had in heightening the perceived distance between Jewish and Muslim cultures and that of the majority community.

The illustrations of the *Cantigas de Santa María* are rich with such motifs, often combining them with relatively culture-specific Jewish signifiers like the pointed hat or hooded cape. One such element is the black, low-vamped slipper, often with a curled and pointed toe, that is worn both my many male Jews in the narrative illustrations and by Muslims in Alfonsine imagery. Resembling a form also found in Islamic manuscript painting of the same period, they may reflect traditional Ibero-Islamic footwear of the twelfth and thirteenth centuries.[62] Whether in the *Cantigas de Santa María* they were meant to represent actual Jewish dress or were assigned to such figures for other, visually strategic purposes, their contrast to the ornate shoes and short boots worn by Christians in the same manuscript underlines Jewish cultural distance from this norm.

More visually forceful are the depictions of various hanging textiles, suggestive of luxurious silks, that appear in the interior spaces of many *cantiga* illustrations, often over a bed or the seat of an authoritative figure such as a king or lord. These hangings appear in Christian, Muslim, and Jewish settings alike, where they are best understood as reflecting the status associated with such luxury textiles among the elites of all three medieval Iberian cultures.[63] In other images, however, the design of such textiles specifically correlates to the demarcation of religious identity. With a few notable exceptions to be discussed below, textiles associated with Christians tend to display entirely abstract ornamental forms, such as foliate patterns or repeated geometric elements. By contrast, those found in Jewish or Muslim settings often bear panels of pseudo-Arabic script. Such a textile appears in the illustration to Cantiga 25 (Escorial, T.I.1, fol. 39r), in which a rectangular panel containing spidery pseudo-Arabic writing, as well as a pair of hexagrams, appears on a textile above the bed under which a Jewish moneylender hides a chest of money (fig. 63). With the exception of the hexagrams, which will be considered below, this inscribed textile markedly resembles one that hangs over an alcove in the Muslim household that is the setting for Cantiga 46 (Escorial, T.I.1., fol. 68v), where it encloses a Muslim woman and her child while her husband is at prayer (fig. 64).

The prominence of Arabic or Arabic-like writing in such illustrations suggests the consistency with which such inscriptions must have come to be linked with both Muslims and Jews in thirteenth-century Castile. Whereas a few Christian communities, such as the Mozarabs of Toledo, preserved Arabic as their language into the centuries following Christian conquest of Muslim territories, by the thirteenth century Castilian and Latin had emerged as the predominant languages of administration, commerce, and culture.[64] Many Jews, by contrast, maintained their facility in Arabic, for which they were valued as translators and cultural intermediaries on the part of both Christian and Jewish communities.[65] It is no surprise, then, that in this period Arabic

FIG. 63
Jew hiding money under his bed. Detail from The Story of a Christian Who Borrowed Money from a Jew, right half of opening (Cantiga 25), *Cantigas de Santa María.* Real Biblioteca de El Escorial, Madrid, MS T.I.1, fol. 39r. © Patrimonio Nacional.

language and writing might have been seen by Castilian Christians as both a Muslim and a Jewish attribute.

In the rare cases where Arabic and pseudo-Arabic inscriptions appear in Christian contexts within the *Cantigas de Santa María,* it is particularly in ceremonious settings to which such silks' costliness, beauty, and exotic character would have been seen as especially well suited. Often the context is funerary, as when inscribed textiles drape the deathbed of an especially distinguished individual, but sometimes it is sacred, as in the case of the brilliantly floral exemplar draping the Virgin's altar in the illustration to Cantiga 56 (Escorial MS T.I.1, fol. 83r; fig. 65).[66] This cloth is bisected by a broad golden band with red and blue Arabic letters that appear to form a debased imitation of an Arabic epigram, perhaps *al-mulk lillah* (the kingdom is God's), a phrase found on a diversity of Islamic textiles and luxury objects throughout the Mediterranean. Within the *Cantigas de Santa María,* such epigrams seem to have served as stock motifs for Alfonso's Castilian artists, who deployed them in a wide variety of other contexts.[67]

With or without inscriptions, textiles of this kind must be understood primarily as reflective of the aristocratic Castilian taste for luxury textiles, which had become an enduring symbol of wealth and status in Christian culture. Islamic silks had been employed to enrich Christian liturgical objects and altars from the eleventh century onward, and expensive Andalusi textiles, including many with Arabic inscriptions quite unrelated to their new function, are known to have been reused as burial shrouds for royal and noble Castilians.[68] The exoticism of such textiles might well have heightened their desirability: as spolia of a sophisticated foreign culture that was simultaneously feared and admired, they implied the new owner's wealth and authority, perhaps tinged with a desire to display the spoils of a triumphant Christian culture. The importation of such textiles into similar contexts within the *Cantigas de Santa María* must have struck the medieval viewer as only fitting.

Textiles depicted in Jewish contexts must have suggested somewhat different connotations. Those that appear in the room of the money-lender in Cantiga 25 (fig. 63) attest to the Jew's wealth and high social status, already implied by his claim of friendship with the Christian merchant to whom he lent money: he is clearly able to surround himself with luxury items identical to those used by upper-class Christians. However, his use of such textiles in his bedroom,

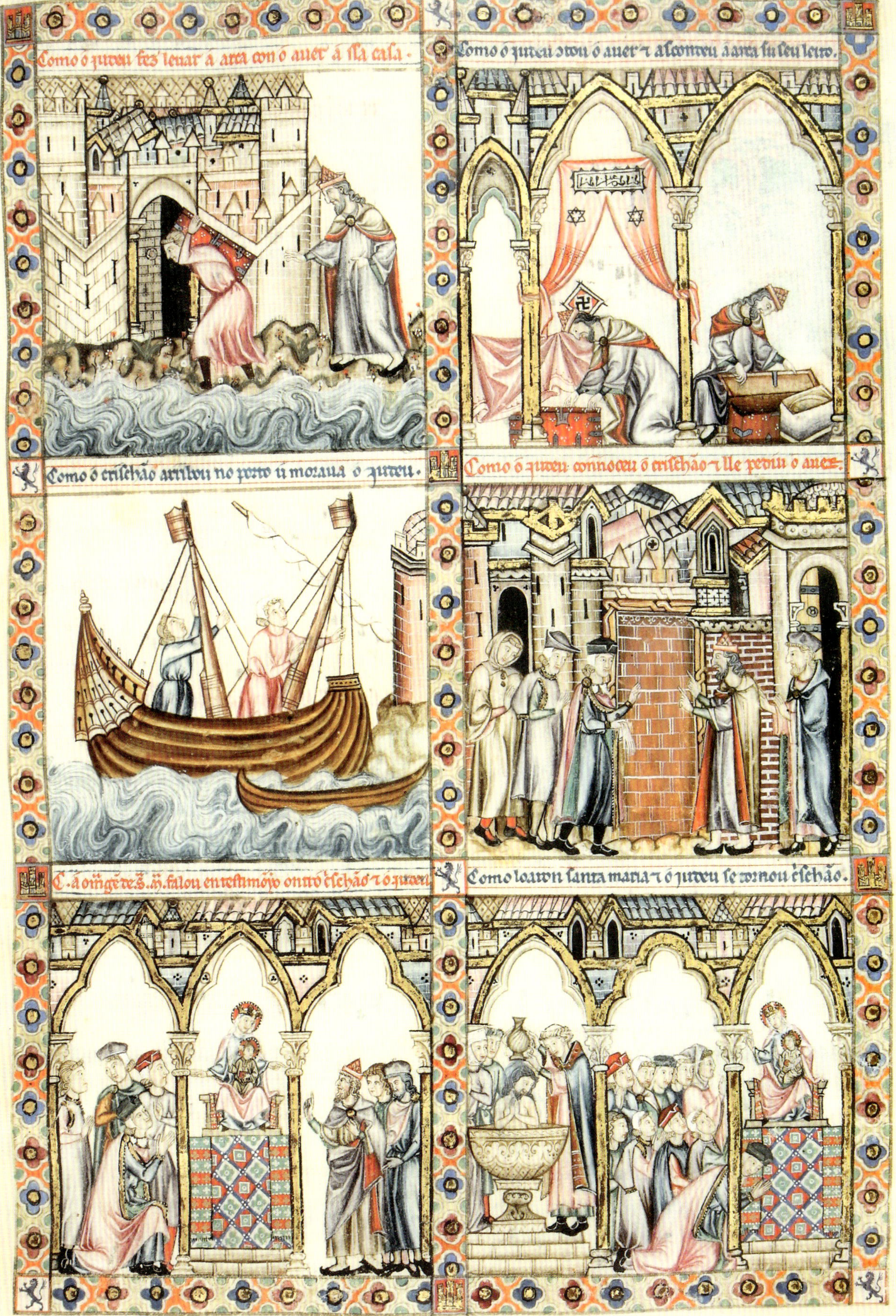

Como o iudeu fez leuar a arca con o auer a ssa casa ·
Como o iudeu uiu o auer e asconteu a arca su seu leito.
Como o crischão arribou no porto u morava o iudeu ·
Como o iudeu connoceu o crischão e lle pediu o auer ·
C. a omagen de S. M. falou en testemoyo ontr' o crischão e o iudeu
Como loaron santa maria e o iudeu se tornou crischão ·

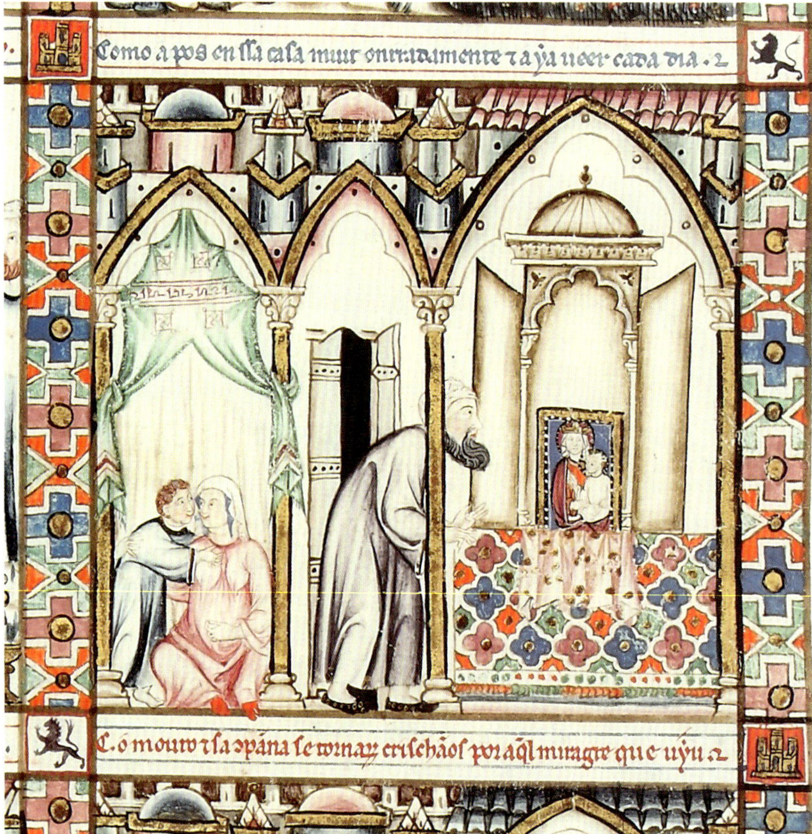

FIG. 64
Muslim admiring an image of the Virgin Mary. Detail from The Story of the Muslim Converted by an Image of the Virgin (Cantiga 46), *Cantigas de Santa María*. Real Biblioteca de El Escorial, Madrid, MS T.I.1, fol. 68v. © Patrimonio Nacional.

rather than in a more ceremonious location such as an altar or tomb, simultaneously comments on his materialistic disregard for these practices. Its presence in this image thus offers one more outlet for the impulse to draw distinctions between a waxing Christian majority and the non-Christian populations whom they now ruled.

Outside of their depiction in textiles, Arabic and pseudo-Arabic inscriptions are associated nearly exclusively with Muslim figures in Alfonsine manuscripts. A clear contrast exists in the *Libro de ajedrez* between depictions of the king's scribes writing illegibly (but presumably in Castilian) in their manuscripts while Muslim game players examine convincingly legible Arabic writing in the books that they hold, as on fol. 14r (fig. 66).[69] While these examples may also reflect the fact that the chess manuals on which Alfonso's manuscript was based were written in Arabic, they suggest the semiotic linkage of this language to non-Christians at Alfonso's court.[70]

Mudéjar architectural forms represented yet another means of signaling Jewish difference in Castilian imagery of this period, although here a consistent pattern is more difficult to identify. In the *Libro de ajedrez,* fantastical *mudéjar* architecture sets the stage not just for Muslims and Jews, but for exotic figures of all kinds as they pursue their sports. Two scenes of ancient sages bringing games to the Persian king (fols. 2r

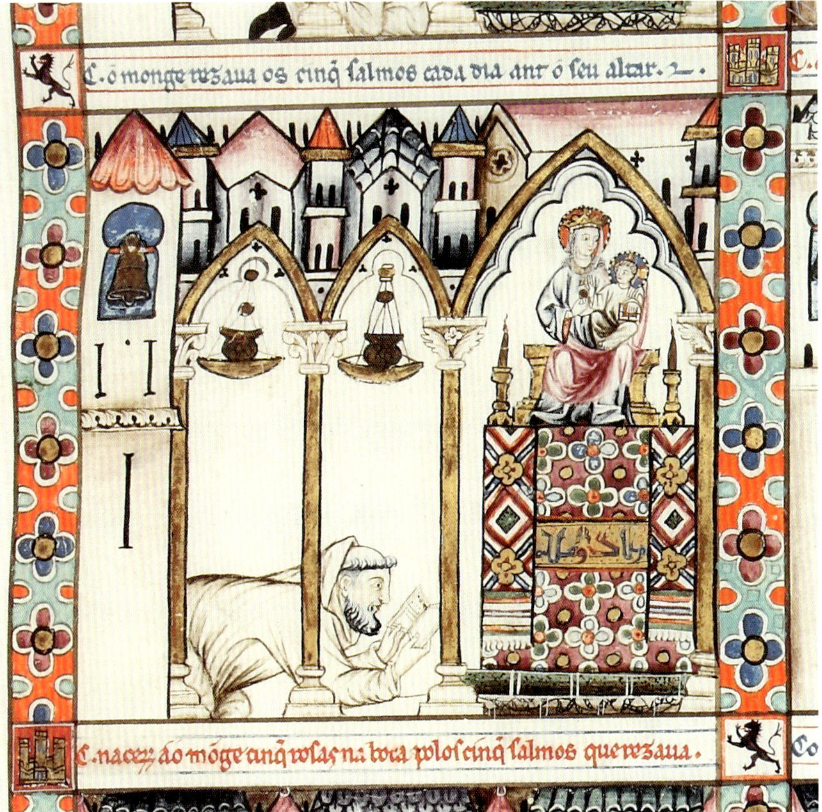

FIG. 65
Monk before the Virgin's altar. Detail from The Story of the Five Roses (Cantiga 56), *Cantigas de Santa María.* Real Biblioteca de El Escorial, Madrid, MS T.I.1, fol. 83r. © Patrimonio Nacional.

and 2v) are set within a complex confection of domes above multilobed and horseshoe arches; another image (fol. 12r) features a pair of Muslims playing chess before a tile-roofed building with a cusped ornament on an ogival doorway (fig. 67). The dice game between Jewish and Christian youths on fol. 75r, discussed above, occurs in a similar setting (fig. 48). While Christian figures too might occasionally inhabit *mudéjar* settings, the most traditional Gothic architecture is more selectively deployed, being reserved nearly exclusively for scenes of the king with his Christian courtiers.

Such correlations are less consistent in the *Cantigas de Santa María,* where the involvement of a greater number of artists blurs any pattern observable. Nonetheless, architecture does at times aid in defining the cultural spaces within which some tales play out. Spaces associated with Jewish presence, such as the Jewish quarter through which soldiers ride to dispatch a group of Jews accused of abusing a wax figure of Christ (Escorial, T.I.1, fol. 20v), tend more heavily than Christian settings toward the brick architecture, horseshoe arches, and alternating voussoirs of the *mudéjar* (fig. 50); the synagogue whose ownership is at issue in Cantiga 27 (Escorial, T.I.1, fol. 41v), a tale discussed further below, is distinguished from the more generic structures surrounding it by the small arched windows high

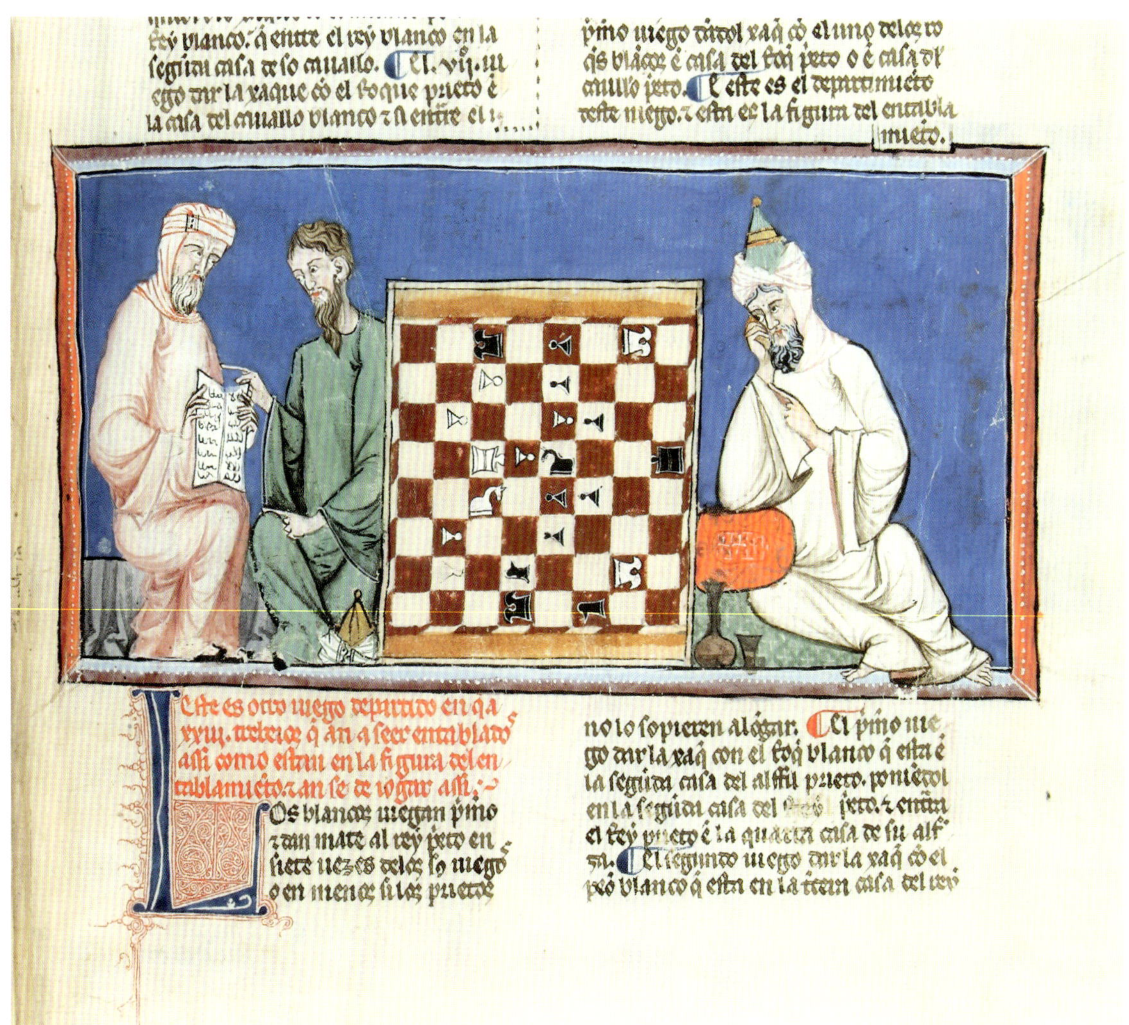

FIG. 66

Muslims playing chess. *Libro de ajedrez, dados y tablas.* Real Biblioteca de El Escorial, Madrid, MS T.I.6, fol. 14r. © Patrimonio Nacional.

up near the roof, similar to the reduced windows found in surviving Iberian synagogues.

Although not a perfect correlation, this pattern suggests that at least in the context of Alfonso's court, representations of Gothic architecture were seen as the province of Christians in particular, while the more culturally flexible *mudéjar* was often associated with multiple groups outside the Christian norm. This pattern is confirmed in the examination of Alfonso's actual architectural patronage, which included such structures as his unapologetically Gothic additions to the Islamic Alcázar in Seville in 1248, his foundation of numerous Gothic parish churches in the region, and his more distant sponsorship of Rayonnant

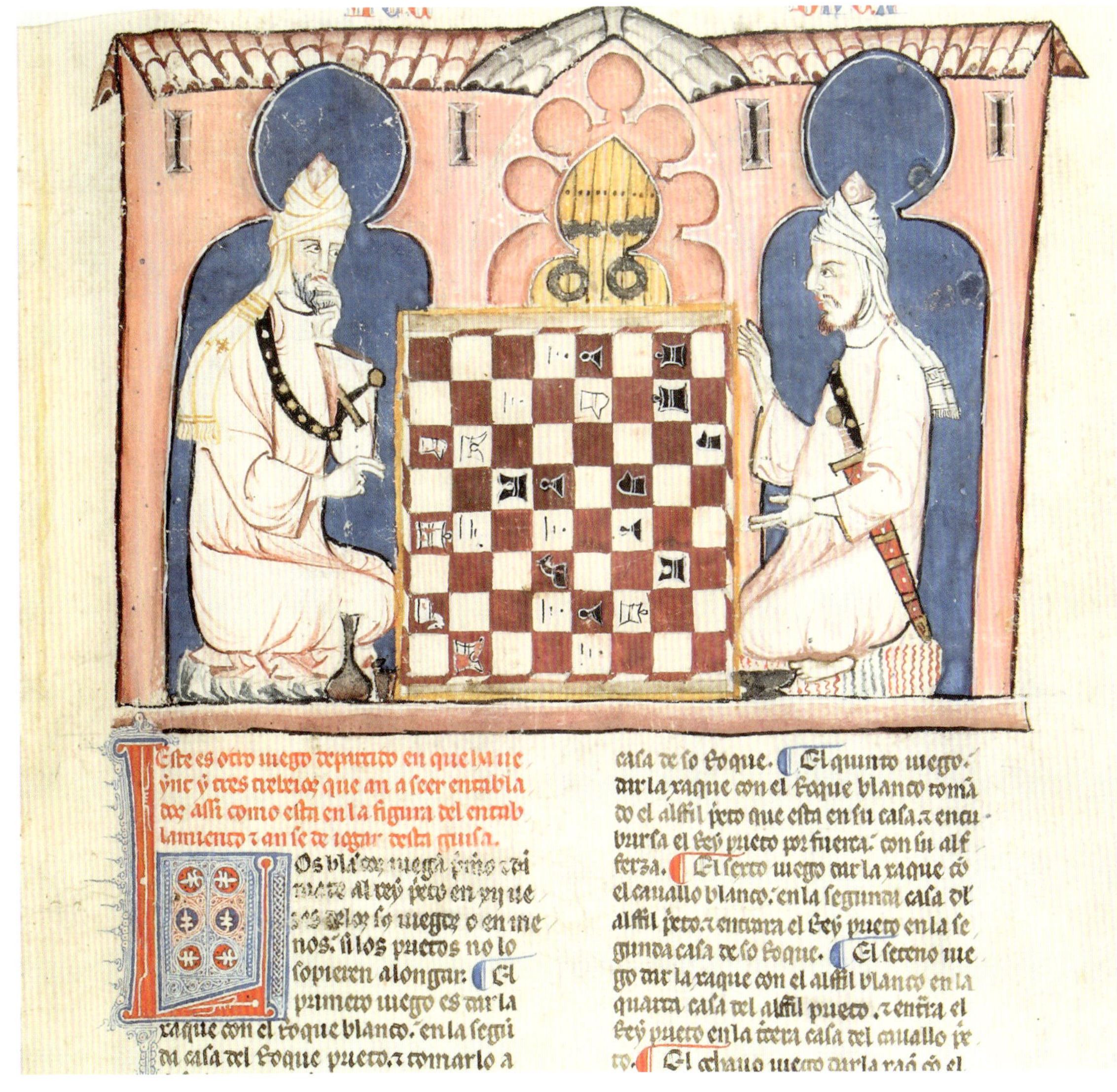

FIG. 67

Muslims playing chess. *Libro de ajedrez, dados y tablas.* Real Biblioteca de El Escorial, Madrid, MS T.I.6, fol. 12r. © Patrimonio Nacional.

Cathedral of León, founded in 1255 and arguably the most "Gothic" cathedral in Spain.[71]

Such conclusions perhaps could only be drawn about manuscripts made in Alfonso's Castile, where Iberia's three faiths were still deep in the process of working out their cultural affiliations in the wake of recent Christian victories at cities like Córdoba and Seville. As these relationships stabilized during the fourteenth century, the semiotic specificity of such Islamic visual language would gradually lose its force as it was embraced by the cultured Christian elite in the construction of fully hybrid *mudéjar* monuments such as Pedro I's Alcázar and the churches of Teruel.

The Hexagram as Symbolic Form

For modern Western viewers, analysis of the hexagram, or six-pointed star, is obfuscated by its nearly exclusive association with Judaism from the eighteenth and nineteenth centuries onward. In the Middle Ages, however, the hexagram preserved far more semiotic fluidity as it passed among a variety of cultural and religious contexts. Already an ornamental motif in Phoenician and Assyrian monuments, it also appeared in such late antique Jewish structures as the second-century synagogue of Capernaum.[72] From the sixth century onward, the motif sometimes came to be associated with the "Seal of Solomon" or "Shield of David," described in extrabiblical literature as possessing magical, especially apotropaic, properties that persisted into the medieval occult literature of Jews, Christians, and Muslims alike.[73] Although throughout the Middle Ages the hexagram was employed occasionally in Jewish contexts, at no point before its adoption by Enlightenment Jews of the eighteenth and nineteenth centuries does it seem to have been seen as exclusively connected with Jews or Judaism.[74]

The hexagram also enjoyed a parallel development as an abstract ornamental form in Islamic art from the tenth century onward.[75] In Iberia, it emerged in this capacity especially during in the Almohad period, when, along with the eight-pointed star, it came to serve as one of the fundamental elements in the repeated geometric fields used in mosaic, carved stucco, bookbindings, and other media. From here, it also found its way into the *mudéjar* vocabulary of first Jewish, and eventually also Christian architectural and decorative traditions. In the late twelfth-century Toledan synagogue now known as Santa María la Blanca, the hexagram appears among a wide variety of other motifs within the carved stucco ornament of the central aisle (fig. 68). In the neighboring synagogue of Samuel Ha-Levi Abulafia, six-sided *cuerda seca* floor tiles containing nested hexagrams are believed to have been added in the fifteenth century.[76] During the same span, the form also

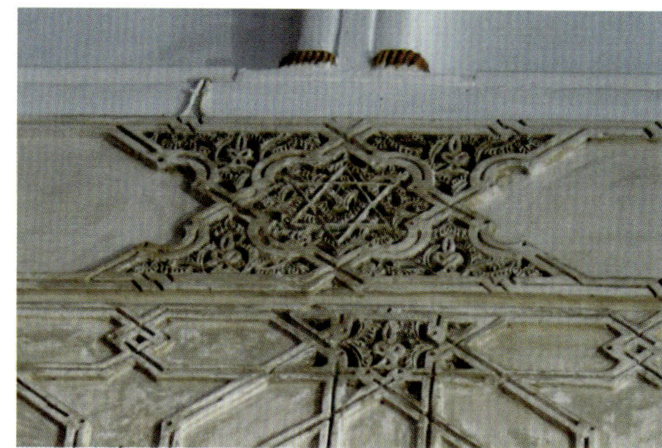

FIG. 68
Carved stucco hexagram. Santa María la Blanca, Toledo. © Pamela A. Patton.

had found its way onto small utilitarian objects used by Jews, such as belt clasps and bridles.[77]

Within Christian culture, the hexagram form emerged somewhat later, during the fourteenth century. A hexagrammatic tile pavement of this period, recently discovered in the Christian church of Santa María la Blanca in Parque de Castillo (Burgos), represents one of the earliest examples.[78] Hexagrams also appear, along with rosettes and five- and eight-pointed stars, as enframing devices for fourteenth-century Christian seals, both royal and private, in the kingdom of Navarre.[79] In both these and the Jewish examples, the function of the motif might well have been, to adopt Oleg Grabar's term, primarily "calliphoric": possessing minimal symbolic value, but aimed instead at bringing beauty to that which it adorns.[80]

Only in a few Iberian examples does a more specific symbolic association seem to lie behind the selection of the hexagram as a decorative motif. One of these is a fourteenth-century lusterware dish, probably a salt or spice container, from the Valencian town of Paterna. Its bowl contains a loosely sketched hexagram enclosed within an outline of an open hand, or *ḥamsa,* a form sometimes known in Muslim tradition as the "hand of Fatima" (fig. 69).[81] Like the hexagram, the *ḥamsa* enjoyed wide cross-cultural use in Iberia, where it often played an apotropaic role similar to its modern one. Paintings of stylized hands appear in the recesses of a fifteenth-century seder plate made in Teruel, and stamped hands probably intended to protect the baptizand flank the monogram of Christ on a ceramic baptismal font made in Toledo around 1400.[82] The pairing of the *ḥamsa* with the hexagram on the Paterna dish perhaps resulted from a similar desire to invoke the combined potential of multiple magical symbols rather than a specific religious affiliation.

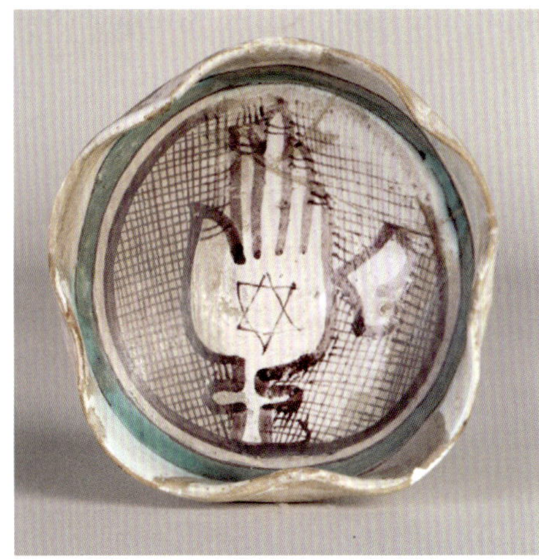

FIG. 69
Lusterware dish with a hexagram enclosed in a *ḥamsa.* Colección Cerámica Municipal, on deposit at the Museo Nacional de Cerámica "González Martí," no. inv. 59. Ajuntament de Valencia, Sección de Arqueología, by permission.

Rather than in Islamic or Jewish culture, then, it was in the hands of thirteenth- and early fourteenth-century Christian artists that the hexagram's potential as a religious symbol was most powerfully exploited. For these artists, the motif's comparative scarcity in Christian contexts must have rendered it an effective sign by which to distinguish both Jews and Muslims from Christians as a body. Its apotropaic dimensions, which fed into the common perception of both faith groups as involved in the practice of magic or in the supernatural, would have strengthened this dimension, enabling Christian artists to highlight not just these communities' differences from, but also their purported dangers to, the faithful Christians who constituted their main viewership.

The motif's predatory implications are at their most forceful in a pair of scribal drawings on the covers of two *libri iudeorum* from Puigcerdà (Archivo Histórico Comarcal, 8). One, containing accounts dated 1286–87, bears on its cover a six-pointed star drawn with double lines, its triangular arms filled in and enclosed by a twisted-rope border.[83] On the second example, dating from the fourteenth century, a similar star enframes the profile of a hooded Jew with a staring eye, long, sloping nose, protruding lips, and shaggy beard (fig. 70). The dates at which these drawings were added to the manuscripts are uncertain; their similarities of format suggest that they might have been produced at the same time, perhaps during the early fourteenth century. Whereas in both examples the star serves to identify the books and their contents as the domain of those beyond the Christian faithful, this message is enhanced in the later book by the inclusion of the stereotyped head and its references to the stereotype of the unscrupulous Jewish lender so often caricatured in books of this kind. In this case, the hexagram is not the symbolic element that drives the meaning of this image; it is in fact the more forceful Jewish "portrait" that lends meaning to the hexagram.

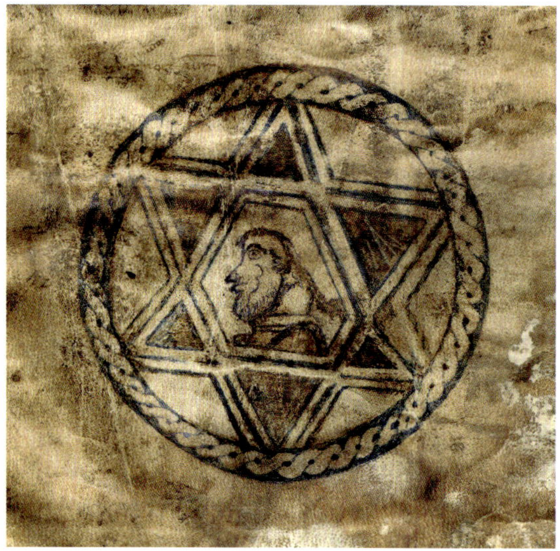

FIG. 70
Head of a Jew in a hexagram. Cover of a *liber iudeorum* of 1286–87, from Puigcerdà. Arxiu Comarcal de Cerdanya, Arxiu Històric Comarcal, 8, by permission.

Christians frequently also deployed the hexagram as an Islamic sign during this period. Six-pointed stars appear twice in the thirteenth-century frescoes commemorating the conquest of Mallorca, in both cases on the banners displayed by Muslim troops. One is today barely visible on one of the tabbed standards carried by Muslim soldiers in the battle of Portopí; a second features vividly on a banner flying from a city tower, accompanied by one white and one black Muslim soldier, in the battle for the capital (fig. 28).[84] In this setting, the stars represent only one of a number of alien ornamental motifs, which also include the *ḥamsa,* that adorn the shields and banners of the island's Muslim defenders and distinguish these Others from the Christian troops, easily identified by their Western coats of arms and the frequent appearance of the distinctive red and yellow stripes of the Crown of Aragon.

Hexagrams are likewise linked with Muslim armies in the illustrations of the *Cantigas de Santa María.* In the illustration to Cantiga 185, discussed above, groups of six-pointed stars appear on the shields of several Muslim soldiers as they attack Chincolla (fig. 62). In both the frescoes and the illumination, the stars effectively heighten the alterity of the Muslim troops, while their status as magical emblems stands in counterpoint to the divine intervention that will be lent to the Christians by the Virgin Mary by the end of the battle. It is certainly no coincidence that victorious Christian armies in Spain often were described as bearing an image of the Virgin in exactly the same location, on the banners of the charging army.[85] Such examples demonstrate the ease with which the hexagram could be linked simultaneously with Islamic and Jewish culture, a fluidity that probably facilitated the use of the form, along with other "foreign" motifs of Islamic origin, such as Arabic script and *mudéjar* architecture, in a manner that positioned Jews and Muslims side by side in opposition to the Christian faith.

The frequency with which six-pointed stars functioned as a Muslim signifier in the *Cantigas de Santa María* illustrations helps deepen their significance in Jewish settings, as when they appear on the silk bed-curtains of the Jewish moneylender of Cantiga 25, discussed above (fig. 63). Although the star's modern-day transformation into the exclusively Jewish *magen David* has tended to favor its interpretation as a simple reference to the figure's religious identity, its thirteenth-century multivalency permits a more textured reading. Found in a manuscript where hexagrams also are linked with Muslim soldiers, these stars become a more flexible, even generic, sign of alterity, one applicable to multiple faith groups outside the Christian majority. In this particular image, moreover, the stars may lend an added layer of meaning through their implication of the Jew's potential adeptness at magic, a possibility reinforced by the adjacent and equally magical swastika that hovers over the moneylender's head.[86] Although in the *cantiga* text the Jew's power over the Christian is gained through wealth rather than by magic, the implication that he might also have drawn his strength from the occult surely would not have been a difficult cognitive leap for most Iberian Christian viewers.

The key to all these images is the consistency with which the hexagram was applied to all of Spain's non-Christian Others. In all the works examined here, as so often in the thousands of illustrations produced for the *Cantigas de Santa María,* the six-pointed star remains associated consistently with non-Christian rather than Christian figures. Its significance derives in large part from this selectivity, which aids in expressing the distinction between such figures and the Christian protagonists against whom their acts are perpetually contrasted. In the *Cantigas de Santa María,* specifically, it also helps preserve the negative implications of this difference, since it most often appears in association with Muslims and Jews who display active hostility toward Christian protagonists. Like the Arabic and pseudo-Arabic inscriptions discussed above, the hexagram's identifying and polemical function is intensified by the polarities it helps forge between Christianity and its two most important religious antagonists.

The immediate presence of a familiar Islamic culture provided Iberian Christian artists with some of their most powerful visual language. As we have seen, they deployed this with great originality in constructing images of Jews that, through comparison with the more numerous and more materially threatening Muslims, intensified the perceived Jewish threat to a normative Christian culture. This strategy must have proved particularly powerful for thirteenth- and fourteenth-century Iberians, for whom the daily presence of flesh-and-blood religious Others in both long-held and newly conquered lands brought such conflations an immediacy unparalleled in most of the Latin West.

Visual culture of this era offers compelling testimony of a growing Christian desire to conflate the features of Iberia's non-Christian faiths. This effort would intensify after the mid-fourteenth century as the Christian kingdoms' reach across the peninsula extended and their concerns about religious orthodoxy found new and still more creative means of expression. Although this subsequent development lies beyond the scope of the present study, a glimpse into it is offered by the fifteenth-century polemic known as the *Fortalitium fidei contra iudaeos, sarracenos, alioso christianae fidei inimicos,* composed ca. 1460 by the Franciscan Alonso de Espina (active 1450–65), confessor to King Enrique IV of Castile and a key supporter of the introduction of the Inquisition into Spain.[87] In 1460, less than a generation before the defeat of Muslim Granada and the expulsion of Iberian Jews, Alonso composed his "Fortress of Faith" as a blanket indictment of all the outgroups, real and imaginary, by which he perceived Christian society to be threatened—as he pithily put it: "The enemy is the heretic, the enemy is the Jew, the enemy is the Saracen, the enemy is the devil."[88] That the printed editions of this enormously popular work came to be illustrated with an array of deeply anti-Jewish imagery based not on Spanish but on northern European models merely illustrates the centrality of this notion to the process by which Iberian Christians continued to pursue their cultural union with the rest of Latin Europe.[89] For Alonso de Espina, as for so many Iberian Christians at this pivotal historical moment, all ideological enemies had begun to seem one and the same.

5

THE *CANTIGAS DE SANTA MARÍA* AND THE JEWS OF CASTILE

Earlier chapters have touched on how the illustrated manuscripts of the *Cantigas de Santa María* (Escorial, MS T.I.1 and Florence, Bib. Naz., MS Banco Rari 20) articulated certain aspects of Jewish difference, such as the manipulation of the face and body and the deployment of motifs linking Iberian Jews and Muslims. However, as a visual, textual, and musical ensemble, the illustrated codices of the *Cantigas de Santa María* have much more to disclose about the process by which Iberian Christians began to reframe the Jewish-Christian relationship after the Reconquest had peaked. The present chapter will differ from previous ones in its close focus on these two manuscripts and their precocious portrayals of Jews, both as key actors in their own tales and as ancillary players in others. It will consider in particular how the Alfonsine workshop's production methods, context, and apparent openness to contemporaneous imagery and narratives helped to shape the final character of the illustrations.

Despite what might be perceived as the *sui generis* nature of the *Cantigas de Santa María* illustrations—they neither trace back clearly to earlier visual traditions nor were widely enough exposed beyond Alfonso X's intimate circle to inspire significant imitations—the representation of Jews in these manuscripts bears strong relevance to the broad questions set out in this study as a whole. As has been suggested in previous chapters and will be explored further here, the collection's ready absorption of themes that in the late thirteenth century still remained little known within Iberia offers key evidence of when and how such ideas first began to penetrate there, while the process of their adoption helps to identify the kinds of conceptual and visual accommodations that helped to naturalize them to the visual lexicon of artists throughout the peninsula. The conclusions permitted by the study of this process offer an appropriate capstone to the larger inquiry undertaken here.

The collection of miracle songs known as the *Cantigas de Santa María* was a characteristically ambitious endeavor for the "Learned King" Alfonso X of Castile, at whose initiative scores of well-known miracle narratives were compiled, revised, and combined with other newly invented tales into a collection that eventually would number over four hundred. Modeled on the great *mariales* of such ultra-Pyrenean authors as Gautier de Coincy and Vincent of Beauvais, but written in Galician-Portuguese and set to music that drew liberally on both Christian and Muslim traditions, the songs combine narratives of miracles enacted by the Virgin on behalf of her faithful with *loores,* or songs of praise, that laud her purity, maternity, and intercessory powers. The compilation and composition of the songs was an extensive process, probably under way by 1260 and extending until the king's death in 1284, to culminate in the production of the four luxury manuscripts in which they are preserved today.[1]

Two of these manuscripts, MS 10069 of the Biblioteca Nacional de España and MS B.I.2 of the Escorial, lack extensive illustrations. The former is a collection of 127 songs that is thought to reflect the earliest redaction of the collection, made in the 1260s or early 1270s; the second contains just over 400 songs and thus serves as the most complete record of the collection as a whole.[2] The other two manuscripts, Escorial T.I.1 and Florence, Biblioteca Nazionale B.R. 20, were designed to include narrative illustrations of the tales. The two codices resemble each other closely in both dimensions and design and were apparently intended as a pair, which in the end was to contain at least 400 songs, including musical notation, text, and single or double full-page, six-panel illustrations. Escorial T.I.1, often referred to in scholarship as the Códice Rico to distinguish it from Escorial B.I.2 (nicknamed the Códice de los Músicos for its forty vignettes of musicians at play), still preserves 193 of a presumed original 200 songs with music and illustrations. The Florence codex presumably was intended to include the same number of narratives but remained unfinished at Alfonso's death; today, it contains the texts of only 133 songs, 48 of which are accompanied by complete or partial illustrations, and it lacks musical notation entirely.[3]

The quirky, poignant, often humorous pictorial narratives of the two illustrated *Cantigas* manuscripts have been admired as much for their vivid evocations of human crisis and spiritual faith as for their convincingly detailed treatment of the costumes, setting, and daily habits of thirteenth-century Iberian life. Nonetheless, with some notable exceptions, it is only since the 1990s that art historians have begun to join scholars from other disciplines, particularly literature, in serious engagement with this imagery. This scholarship has focused especially on questions surrounding the illustrations' stylistic and iconographic sources and their relationship to contemporary religion, music, and political ideology, as well as their depiction of women and religious minorities, and it has begun to provide much-needed context for the manuscripts within the broader history of medieval Iberian and European visual culture.[4]

Scholarship on the *Cantigas*' depiction of Jews has followed a similar trajectory: although the topic has elicited widespread interest among medievalists generally, literary specialists and historians were until recently predominant among those who addressed it directly. Such work traditionally has tended to focus more closely on the evidence provided by the songs' texts than on their illustrations, and it has centered especially on how these examples shed light on the attitudes and policies of Alfonso X, their putative author.[5] Recent scholarship by art historians has opened the way to a more nuanced view of the problem, whether by exploring the complexity and frequent ambiguity of images whose reading has in the past been oversimplified,[6] or by arguing for the unique potential of the *cantiga* illustrations to illuminate aspects of individual and community identity that were key to the formation of Alfonso's Castile.[7] Yet even this literature often fails to break away from the understandable impulse simply to categorize the tales in accordance with major themes in European anti-Jewish thought, or to privilege their relevance to the king's personal views over other, broader aspects of their significance to medieval Iberian culture.

The present chapter aims to extend and complement such work by exploring the broader dimensions of the manuscripts' production: the visual and verbal models that often lay behind their illustrations of the stories concerning Jews; the social trends and intellectual impulses that motivated their more inventive details; and the deeply creative processes by which the artists of Alfonso's unique scriptorium brought these often foreign tales to life in a manner both coherent and meaningful within an Iberian context.

Such work necessitates the confrontation of several conceptual pitfalls that have discouraged a more nuanced understanding of the illustrated *Cantigas de Santa María* manuscripts. One is an inclination to view the miniatures, like their corresponding verbal texts, as reflective above all of the personality and values of the king who commissioned them. Whereas most scholars now concur that Alfonso's personal involvement in the composition of the songs, not to mention the production of the manuscripts, was likely less direct than once was believed, many continue to interpret the *Cantigas* texts and images as strongly correlated to the king's personal views and policies.[8] Without dismissing Alfonso's unusually active interest in the cultural enterprises of his court, I seek to balance this tendency with the recognition that not every product of his scriptorium, especially those produced during the period of illness and political tension that marked the last years of his reign, can have enjoyed his engagement to the same degree as those produced in his relatively carefree youth. As will be suggested below, while Alfonso surely was active in the conception, motivation, and approval of the *Cantigas de Santa María,* many innovative aspects of the manuscripts and their imagery should be credited not to the king, but to the compilers, musicians, and especially artists of the royal atelier.

Also limiting has been the perception, most prevalent in older literature, that the *Cantigas de Santa María* miniatures represent an authentic historical record of how people actually looked and behaved in thirteenth-century Castile. Judiciously pursued, this "archaeological" approach to the miniatures, as José Guerrero Lovillo has called it, can offer useful information regarding the appearance and function of clothing, furniture, and everyday objects proper to Alfonso's Spain.[9] However, it can quickly become misleading if it fails to take sufficient account of the constructed nature of the pictorial narratives, especially those concerning religious minorities. Since these tales in particular derive from verbal and visual traditions far distant from thirteenth-century Castile, the artists' awareness of and respect for these traditions had the potential to shape the appearance of their narratives at least as much as did their observation of the world around them. The naturalism so enthusiastically associated by some with Gothic artists was still a fragile concept in the thirteenth century, not only in Castile, but throughout western Europe. While an interest in live observation can be sensed in everything from Villard de Honnecourt's sketchbook to Marco Polo's journal, artists' choices still were heavily governed by the *auctoritas* of prevailing tradition and what might be called an "editorial" approach to image making.[10] The *Cantigas de Santa María* illustrations thus are best understood not as snapshots of their day, but as the inventive marriage between a new interest in the observable world and a respect for authoritative visual models that would retain their centrality to image making for centuries to come.

A final question to be considered here concerns the degree to which the visual narratives of the *Cantigas de Santa María* depended upon their texts. Past scholarship often has assumed that the illustrations were produced as ancillary to, if not directly dependent upon, the verbal versions of the tales that they accompany. Thus, any changes or additions made in the pictorial narrative had necessarily to be understood as the result of intervention by the authors of that text, whether this is understood to mean the king himself or his surrogates.[11] While this conclusion may seem natural given the sequence in which the songs and images were created, it does not take sufficient account of the chronological, conceptual, and possibly sociocultural gap between these two creative phases. The likelihood that the composition of some of the texts in question occurred fifteen or even twenty years before the first illustrations were begun renders it impossible to assume that either the composers of the songs or their advisors determined the ultimate form of the visual narratives that would later take shape to accompany them. Instead, as we shall see, the artists of the *Cantigas de Santa María* seem to have enjoyed a surprising degree of independence from the language of the texts that it was their task to illustrate, and this enabled them to call upon familiar variants of the tales, as well as on their own imaginative powers, to craft pictorial versions that sometimes differ strikingly from their purported models.

The present chapter will take these trends into account as it examines the fourteen *cantiga* illustrations in which Jews play a substantial narrative role. My goal is to reach beyond both the broad categorization of themes and the question of the king's individual patronage to scrutinize how the illuminators of the manuscripts adapted what by the thirteenth century had become stock Jewish *topoi* and narratives elsewhere in Europe. Acknowledging the independence of the manuscripts' visual narratives as discourses that were conceived and executed separately, though not entirely independently, from the texts will permit them to be understood in terms not of what they reveal about the views of Alfonso or of the prominent church authors to whose work historians so often turn, but of the artists' collective encounter with the diverse oral and visual models, narratives, and ideals available to them in their mutable Iberian context.

The Making of the Illustrated Codices

Central to any study of the *Cantigas de Santa María* illustrations is an understanding of the circumstances and chronology of their production, and especially of the important but often overlooked lacuna between the initiation of the collection circa 1260 and the production of illustrated manuscripts into which they would be gathered toward the end of the king's life.[12] Most scholarship dates the collection of the initial one hundred *cantigas,* which included most of the tales with which this study is concerned, to the first decade of Alfonso's reign, possibly as early as 1257 and certainly before the early 1260s. The project of producing illustrated manuscripts containing an expanded collection of songs seems to have been initiated in the late 1270s: Escorial T.I.1, the earlier work, likely was completed circa 1280, while the Florence codex was probably begun just as production of the Escorial manuscript drew to a close, but then was left incomplete at the time of the king's death in 1284. The Florence manuscript was further altered by an inept fourteenth-century attempt to complete some of the unfinished illustrations and a haphazard rebinding that left its folios badly disordered.[13]

With the exception of the easily distinguished late medieval additions, the miniatures of the Florence codex resemble those of Escorial T.I.1 strongly enough to associate it with the same small group of illustrators, which probably consisted of several closely affiliated artists who worked sequentially on first one codex and then the other. The illustrations of the two manuscripts are consistent not only in measurements and layout, but also in the selection and application of pigments; the scale and proportions of figures, architectural forms, and framing elements; and the precise, delicate handling of the medium. Their facture is easily differentiated from the freer and at times more experimental miniatures of contemporaneous works such as the *Libro de ajedrez,* and thus they seem likely to have been produced by a cadre of artists occupied more or less exclusively with the *Cantigas* project. Such a conclusion is consistent with Victoria Chico's characterization of the extremely productive Alfonsine scriptorium as "an ensemble of successive and varied working groups" which, although often engaged in discrete projects, drew together around the figure of the king.[14]

Both *Cantigas* manuscripts also share an organizational scheme in which each song's lyrics and musical notation are followed by full-page illustrations of either six or twelve panels each.[15] While most of the songs offer narrative accounts of miracles performed by the Virgin Mary, every tenth song is a nonnarrative *loor,* or song of praise. This predictable structural pattern is complemented by a syncopating pattern of illustrations, in which each song ending in the number five is followed by two facing pages of pictorial narrative, rather than the single page found elsewhere. The systematism of this design necessarily would have demanded a well-organized production process, in which work carried out by several artists, as was customary for works of this scale, were overseen by a closely attentive supervisor.

Who this supervisor might have been remains unknown. Both manuscripts lack the final leaves on which a colophon with such information might have appeared, and no firm connection can be made with the individuals occasionally named in connection with other works of the Alfonsine scriptorium: the "Juan González" on the final folio of Escorial B.I.2, or " Martín Pérez de Maqueda," the self-described "scribe of the books of the most noble king Alfonso" in the *General estoria* (Vatican, MS Urb. lat. 539).[16] Nor can the scant internal evidence offered by the manuscripts, such as the inscription of the name "D. Andrés" on a scroll held by a cleric in the illustration to Cantiga 156 or the manuscript painter "Pedro Lorenzo" who is referred to in the text of Cantiga 377, be linked conclusively with the codices' actual artists.[17] Only the consistency of format and execution with which both manuscripts were carried out attests to the presence of such a figure.

As has been noted, the *Cantigas de Santa María* as a literary work closely emulated earlier Latin and vernacular collections of Marian miracle tales that had been disseminated throughout Europe by figures such as John of Garland, Vincent of Beauvais, and Gautier de Coincy.[18] This Mariale tradition had enjoyed wide appeal in northern Europe since the early twelfth century, and its penetration into Iberia by the middle of the thirteenth is attested not only by the *Cantigas de Santa María,* but by two other significant Iberian collections that emerged nearly simultaneously with it. The first, composed by Gonzalo de Berceo in the mid-thirteenth century, was the widely circulated vernacular *Milagros de Nuestra Señora,* all of which would eventually come to be included in the *Cantigas de Santa María.*[19] The second, produced in the last quarter of the same century, was the Latin prose *Liber Maríae* of Juan Gil de Zamora (d. 1318), a Franciscan friar who became affiliated with Alfonso's court around 1278 and is thought to have collaborated in the production of the king's collection.[20] Standing at either end of the period during which the *Cantigas de Santa María* was composed, and intended for an audience that was not merely courtly but also clerical and, in Berceo's case, probably popular, both works provide important context for the Alfonsine collection and its illustrations.[21]

Some visual *comparanda* for the illustrated *Cantigas* exist as well, and these also derive from northern Europe. While individual depictions of a few very popular tales, such as the story of Theophilus (Cantiga 3) or the tale of the Jewish boy (Cantiga 4), were produced in many media in the twelfth and thirteenth centuries,[22] illustrated miracle collections as a genre are more scarce. Most closely comparable are the illustrated manuscripts of Gautier de Coincy's *Miracles de Nostre Dame,* which had been circulating in France since about 1260, some of which feature historiated initials or modest narrative vignettes at the opening of each tale.[23] On the basis of significant parallels between Coincy's textual narratives and those in the *Cantigas,* it has been hypothesized that such a manuscript might in fact have been known by the composers of the Alfonsine songs. The occasional iconographic correspondences between the illustrations of certain Alfonsine narratives and those of known illustrated Coincy manuscripts support this possibility.[24] Nonetheless, since illustrations of surviving Coincy manuscripts are far less extensive than those of the *Cantigas de Santa María,* their usefulness as a visual source surely remains limited.

Less direct inspiration for the *Cantigas de Santa María* illustrations may have derived from the extraordinary luxury manuscripts produced during the mid-thirteenth century at the court of the French king Louis IX. This extraordinary royal output included not only the Psalter and Moralized Bibles referred to in previous chapters, but also the famous illuminated Psalter of Saint Louis, probably produced for the king following his return from crusade in 1254 (Paris, Bib. Nat., MS lat. 10525), as well as a lavish picture Bible now in the Morgan Library (New York, Morgan MS M. 638).[25] Both individually and as an ensemble, such royal manuscripts represented an achievement that Louis's contemporaries justifiably admired and that the more ambitious among them, including Alfonso, must have aspired to emulate. As the French king's second cousin and peer, Alfonso was well aware of doings at the Parisian court: he had sojourned there in the 1240s while still crown prince and later betrothed two of his children to Louis's offspring.[26] This awareness could only have been heightened by Louis's gift to his Castilian cousin, possibly in relation to one of these betrothals, of a three-volume Moralized Bible that is now preserved in Toledo Cathedral (Toledo, Tesoro de la Catedral).[27] Although the biblical and exegetical illustrations of this complex work would have provided few specific iconographic sources for the *Cantigas* illustrations, its opulent yet systematic design, featuring page after page of glittering narrative roundels packed tightly within a rectangular frame, must have provided a strongly appealing model for a king already inclined to emulate the cultural achievements of his French peers.[28]

The conception and general format of the *Cantigas de Santa María* might be compared with Louis's manuscripts, but few would call their style Parisian. They have more often been compared with south Italian works of the thirteenth century, such as King Manfred's copy of his father Frederick II's hunting manuscript, *De arte venandi cum avibus* (Bibliotheca Vaticana, Pal. lat. 1071) and a thirteenth-century copy of Peter of Eboli's *De balneis puteolanis* (Rome, Bib. Angelica MS 1474).[29] Alfonso's engagement in Sicilian affairs was less friendly than that in France, since both Manfred and his successor Charles of Anjou posed obstacles to Castilian interests in this part of the Mediterranean, but his involvement in the region certainly was sufficient to have brought south Italian artistic trends within reach of his own artists.[30] More rarely acknowledged is the resemblance of the *Cantigas* miniatures to those of illustrated Islamic manuscripts of the same period, which present potential models for the handling of battle scenes, the distinctive treatment of different ethnic groups such as Africans and Arabs, and the use of a bare vellum background.[31] Despite the scarcity of such western Islamic examples today, such works must have been well known at Alfonso's deeply multicultural court, where artists and images from Europe and the Islamic world mingled as easily as did the Christian clerics and Jewish and Muslim scientists with whom the king surrounded himself.[32]

To what extent King Alfonso himself shaped the distinctive character of his manuscripts remains debatable. Although convincing arguments have been made to position the king as a kind of "general editor" of the songs, especially during the earliest phase of their compilation,[33] very little evidence exists regarding his engagement in the production of the illustrated codices during the last six years of his life. During the final decade of his reign, Alfonso traveled frequently as he struggled to cope with a string of political and personal crises: increasing unrest among his nobles in the face of an uncertain economy; the invasion of southern Iberia by the Marinids of North Africa in 1275 and 1277; and the succession dispute that followed the death of Crown Prince Fernando de la Cerda in the first of those conflicts, culminating in the efforts of the king's younger son Sancho to replace his father on the throne in 1282. These external conflicts were compounded by the king's personal struggle with his own progressive illness, possibly caused by a brain tumor, during the same period.[34] That these calamities would have permitted Alfonso sustained personal involvement in the design of his manuscripts seems unlikely.

At the same time, it seems certain that the king remained the manuscripts' most important and frequent viewer. Quite possibly he might have been its only consistent one, since occasions to display the manuscripts to other viewers are likely to have been rare. In the thirteenth century, songs of the kind represented in the *Cantigas de Santa María* were generally sung from memory;[35] even were written music needed for performance, this more likely would have taken the form of inexpensive scrolls rather than massively scaled, intricately illustrated codices such as Alfonso's. The modern condition of the manuscripts attests to this: Escorial T.I.1, the manuscript completed during the king's lifetime and thus the most likely candidate for such use, lacks the rubbing, darkening, flaking, and other signs of wear that would be expected from a heavily handled book. It is more likely that the two illustrated *Cantigas* manuscripts, like those in Louis IX's collection and the other luxury manuscripts that had come into vogue for aristocratic bibliophiles of the period, were produced for private and limited use, so that they are best understood as a sort of "library copy" intended primarily for the king's perusal during his leisure hours and for display only to his close intimates.[36] This conclusion accords with what is known of Alfonso's determination to emulate prevailing aristocratic practices generally, as well as with his personal desire to honor the Virgin Mary as her self-described troubadour.[37]

Recognizing the exclusivity of the manuscripts' viewership also permits an adjustment of our assumptions regarding the purpose and reception of their illustrations. Rather than serving to teach or reinforce specific social values either to those at the Alfonsine court or to a larger audience, as is sometimes assumed, the books presented a discourse destined mainly for the king's own eye, a decidedly hermetic arrangement that might have fostered, more than did any other factor, the independence of their artists.

Jews in the Illustrations of the *Cantigas de Santa María*

The fourteen illustrations of the *Cantigas de Santa María* in which Jews play a significant narrative role resemble virtually nothing else produced in Spain before this period. Their rigidified facial stereotypes, with their sharply profiled noses, furrowed brows, and wildly curling beards, strongly echo the exaggerations of northern European manuscripts. In their masklike consistency, they offer a marked contrast to the cropped blond hair and tidy beards traditionally assigned to the manuscripts' Christian figures, as well as to the considerably more varied range of facial types and skin colors given to Muslims in the same manuscripts. The seemingly haphazard physiognomic signs that ebbed and flowed in earlier Iberian works such as the Toledan Ildefonsus manuscripts and the Vic Bible of 1273 have here coalesced into a formula that would remain nearly immutable throughout the massive Alfonsine work.

Equally distinctive, at least in an Iberian context, are the roles played by Jewish figures in their fourteen *cantigas,* all but one of which appear in the illustrated Escorial manuscript. These *cantigas* are by no means the only ones to mention Jews, who in several other cases play peripheral or symbolic roles in the text alone, as when Cantiga 5 describes the passengers of a ship as "all good folk with no Moors nor Jews among them."[38] More rarely, Jewish figures emerge unbidden in the illustration to a text that does not mention them directly, as in the illustration to Cantiga 88, the tale of a successful Christian physician who gives up the practice of medicine to become a monk whose scientific renown is emphasized by the presence of Jewish figures within his rapt multicultural audience (Escorial, T.I.1, fol. 129v; fig. 71).[39] Independent visual and textual references such as these constitute evidence in their own right regarding Christian attitudes toward religious minorities in Alfonso's Castile, but they will not feature centrally in this chapter, the main goal of which is to examine how the *cantiga* illustrations worked both with and against their corresponding texts to craft a persuasive new model of the Jewish-Christian relationship, tailored to Iberian ends.

Like their usually foreign models, the illustrations of these *cantigas* frequently present Jewish figures as inimical, deceptive characters whose moral failings or hostile acts earn either Marian retribution or, more rarely, an opportunity for conversion. They include the following:[40]

Cantiga 2. "how Holy Mary appeared to Saint Ildefonso in Toledo and gave him an alb which She brought from Paradise which he should wear to say mass" (Esc. T.I.1, fol. 7r).

Cantiga 3. "how Holy Mary made Theophilus recover the letter which he had signed with the devil, promising to become his vassal" (Esc. T.I.1, fol. 8r).

Cantiga 4. "how Holy Mary saved from burning the son of the Jew, whose father had thrown him into the furnace" (Esc. T.I.1, fol. 9v).

Cantiga 6. "how Holy Mary revived the little boy whom the Jews had killed because he sang 'Gaude Virgo Maria'" (Esc. T.I.1, fol. 13v).

Cantiga 12. "how Holy Mary lamented in Toledo on the day of Her feast in August, because the Jews crucified a waxen image of Her Son" (Esc. T.I.1, fol. 20v).

Cantiga 25. "how the statue of Holy Mary served as witness between the Christian and the Jew" (Esc. T.I.1, fols. 38v–39r).

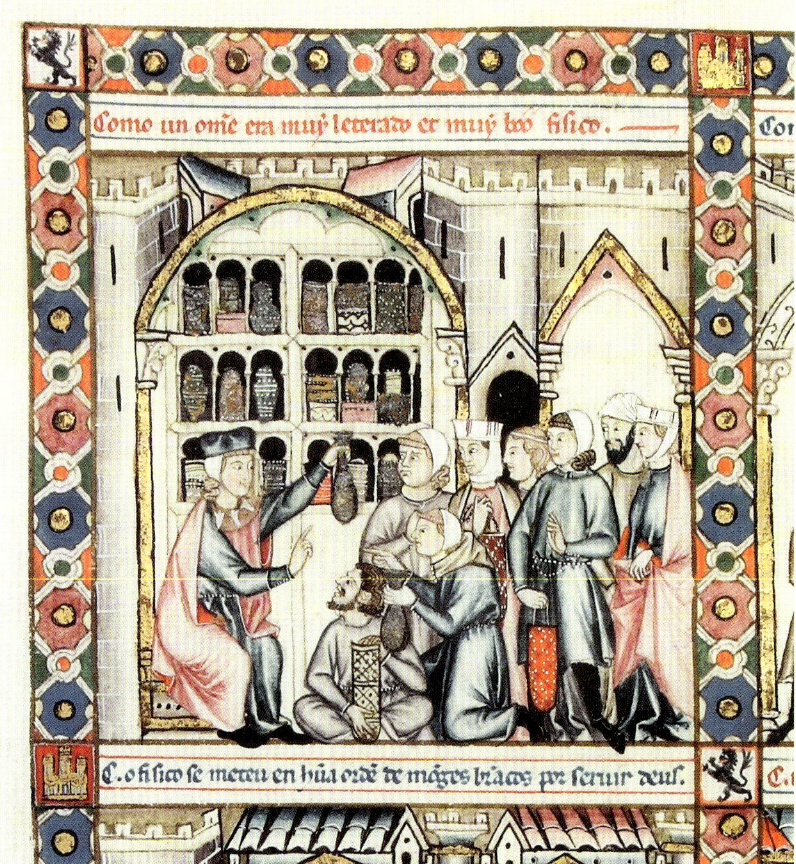

FIG. 71
A physician lecturing. Detail from The Story of a Physician Who Became a Monk (Cantiga 88), *Cantigas de Santa María*. Real Biblioteca de El Escorial, Madrid, MS T.I.1, fol. 129v. © Patrimonio Nacional.

Cantiga 27. "how Holy Mary took the synagogue from the Jews and made a church out of it" (Esc. T.I.1, fol. 41v).

Cantiga 34. "how Holy Mary got even with the Jew for the dishonor he did Her image" (Esc. T.I.1, fol. 50r).

Cantiga 85. "how Holy Mary delivered from death a Jew whom some thieves had taken prisoner. She freed him from the prison and made him become a Christian" (Esc. T.I.1, fols. 125v–126r).

Cantiga 89. "how a Jewess was near death in childbirth and called on Holy Mary and was delivered at that moment" (Esc. T.I.1, fol. 131r).

Cantiga 107. "how Holy Mary saved from death the Jewess who was thrown over a cliff in Segovia. Because she commended herself to Holy Mary, she did not die or suffer harm" (Esc. T.I.1, fol. 154r).

Cantiga 108. "how Holy Mary caused the son of the Jew to be born with his head on backward, as Merlin had asked of her" (Esc. T.I.1, fol. 155v).

Cantiga 109. "how Holy Mary Jew freed a man from five devils who tried to carry him off and kill him" (Esc. T.I.1, fol. 156v).

Cantiga 286. "how the portico fell down on two Jews who were ridiculing a good man" (Flor. B.R. 20, fol. 5r).

One of the most important characteristics of this group is its early emergence within the collection as a whole. Nine of the songs also appear in the first collection of one hundred songs today preserved in the so-called Toledo Codex in Madrid (BNE, MS 10069), a late thirteenth-century manuscript that is believed to reflect the initial collection of one hundred *cantigas* that was compiled around 1260. Four of the remaining five *cantigas* were likely added to this group soon afterward, since they appear at the beginning of the second hundred songs.[41] The entrance of these narratives into the Alfonsine collection thus probably predated, by a considerable remove, the production of any illustrations for the tales.

Another feature shared by the Jewish narratives is their almost exclusively foreign extraction. Some, like the stories of Theophilus (Cantiga 3) and the Jewish boy (Cantiga 4), can be traced to prototypes in sixth-century Byzantium prior to their ninth-century emergence in the Latin miracle tradition and thence into the Mariales of the West.[42] Eight other narratives (Cantigas 2, 6, 12, 25, 27, 34, 85, and 89) had also become part of the European miracle repertoire by the early thirteenth century, appearing in the collections of such well-disseminated authors as John of Garland, Vincent of Beauvais, and Gautier de Coincy before their inclusion in Alfonso's collection. Of the remaining four tales, Cantiga 108 has been linked convincingly with a legend originating in British Isles, and Cantiga 107 is known to have derived from a preexisting Iberian narrative; only Cantigas 109 and 286 remain without a firmly identified source.[43] Regardless of origin, nearly all of these narratives seem to have been relatively new within Iberia when they were adopted into the Alfonsine collection. Only five of them (2, 3, 12, 25, and 89) appear in Gonzalo de Berceo's *Milagros de Nuestra Señora,* and only six are found in the late thirteenth-century *Liber Mariae* of Juan Gil de Zamora (2, 3, 4, 12, 27, and 34).[44]

Both the newness and the foreignness of these *cantigas* bear important implications for their ability to reshape the conception of Jews and Judaism for Iberian Christians. First, since their roots lay primarily beyond the borders of Alfonso's court, they can hardly be taken as unfiltered expressions of the king's or his subjects' attitudes toward Jews.[45] Whereas the decision to include these tales in the *Cantigas de Santa María* surely connotes a certain degree of approval on the part of the king, exactly what this says about his views or those of others can only be understood after examining how the tales were adapted to an Iberian context: which elements of the tale were preserved, which rejected, and which modified.

Making the Miracles at Home

Even cursory study of the illustrated narratives of the *Cantigas de Santa María* reveals the freedom

FIG. 72
The Story of Marisaltos (Cantiga 107), *Cantigas de Santa María*. Real Biblioteca de El Escorial, Madrid, MS T.I.1, 154r. © Patrimonio Nacional.

and inventiveness with which they were adapted to an Iberian viewership. Like many other works discussed here, these adaptations succeeded in equipping what were essentially foreign formulae with a more familiar local cast. A common strategy, used both in *cantigas* concerning Jews and in other tales with foreign settings, involved the reenvisioning of the tales using buildings, furnishings, and even urban settings appropriate to the their adoptive Iberian home. Just as stories set explicitly in Iberian locales such as Elche or Segovia lovingly reproduce those cities' most characteristic visual elements—Elche's famous palms in the illustration for Cantiga 126 (Escorial, T.I.1, fol. 179r) and Segovia's Roman aqueduct, re-envisioned with horseshoe arches, in that for Cantiga 107 (fig. 72)[46]—tales described as taking place in more far-flung locations like Constantinople and Syria are transformed into Iberian cityscapes by the addition of *mudéjar* towers, brick architecture, and horseshoe arches with alternating voussoirs. In Cantigas 111 and 134, even Paris acquires a distinct *mudéjar* cast as the Seine is traversed by magnificent brick horseshoe arcades (Escorial, T.I.1, fols. 158v and 189r, fig. 73).

The telescopic effect of such adjustments, which propel actions set in distant, near-mythical places like "Jerusalem" and "Paris" into a familiar, even homely cultural sphere, is particularly forceful in the *cantigas* concerning Jews, many of which are set in especially far-flung times and places. One such site is the ancient city, identified in certain other versions of this tale as Lydda or Dispolis, near Jerusalem, in which Cantiga 27 is set. This tale recounts how the city's Jews sold a synagogue to the Apostles for conversion into a church; when the Jews then contested the sale, they and the Apostles were instructed by the emperor to close the building for forty days to test the validity of each side's claim. At the end of the waiting period, the Apostles' claim was confirmed by the appearance of an image of the Virgin. Although the story is set in the first century of the Common Era, its illustrators went to some lengths to provide it with a viable Iberian context (fig. 74). The sale itself takes place just outside the city, the tile roofs, crenellations, and pointed arches of which could represent nearly any Iberian townscape. The synagogue itself, shown with its portal sealed during the ownership dispute, offers additional local resonance, with its *mudéjar* tower and high, small windows, the latter evoking the restricted apertures required of synagogue architecture in the legislation of most reconquered cities.[47]

This setting is not merely local; to thirteenth-century eyes it must also have looked distinctly contemporary. This transformation of the

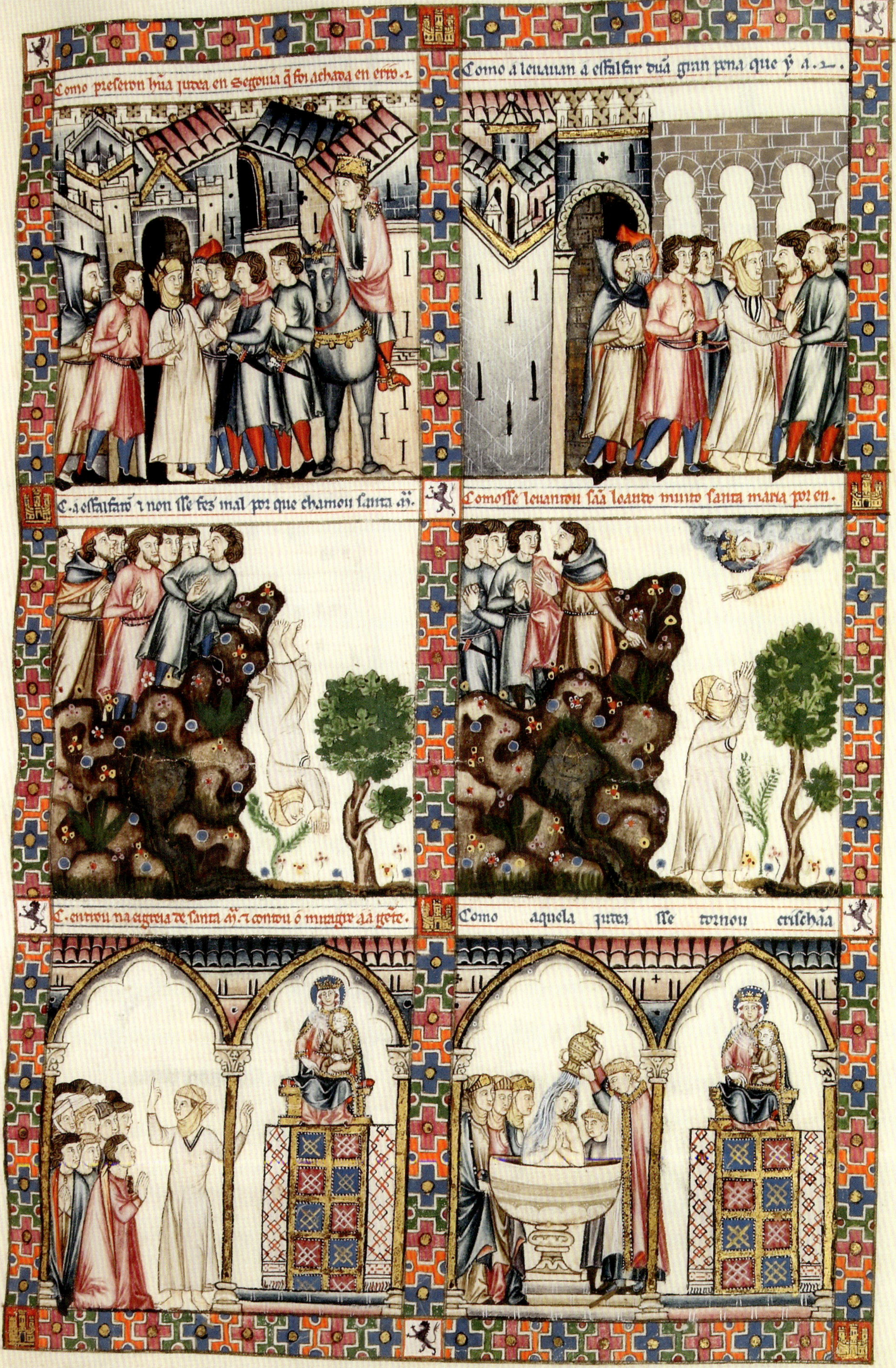
Como preseron hũa judea en Segouia q̃ foi achada en erro. ⁊
Como a leuauan a espeñar dũa gran pena que y a. ⁊
E a espeñaron ⁊ non lle fez mal por que chamou santa M.
Comosse leuantou sãa loando muito santa maria por en.
E entrou na eigreia de santa M. ⁊ contou o miragre aa gente.
Como aquela judea sse tornou crischãa

Apostles' ancient city, possibly Jerusalem itself, into a medieval Castilian town, and the representation of the synagogue as a familiar *mudéjar* structure offer a setting entirely in keeping with contemporaneous tensions over the ownership and appropriation of religious houses during the most active years of Christian conquest in Al-Andalus. The administration of both mosques and synagogues in the newly conquered cities customarily fell to the Christian ruler, who decided which buildings would be left to their respective communities and which would be appropriated to new uses, and these often included conversion to a church.[48] While more mosques than synagogues are recorded as having been converted during this period, the contemporary appearance of the Apostles' captured building would have evoked and perhaps justified this practice in its medieval form.

Imagining Jewish Enemies

The artists of Alfonso's scriptorium faced a deeper challenge in confronting the anti-Jewish stereotypes that lay at the heart of many imported *cantigas.* A number of these, as we have seen, had already found a lively reception in

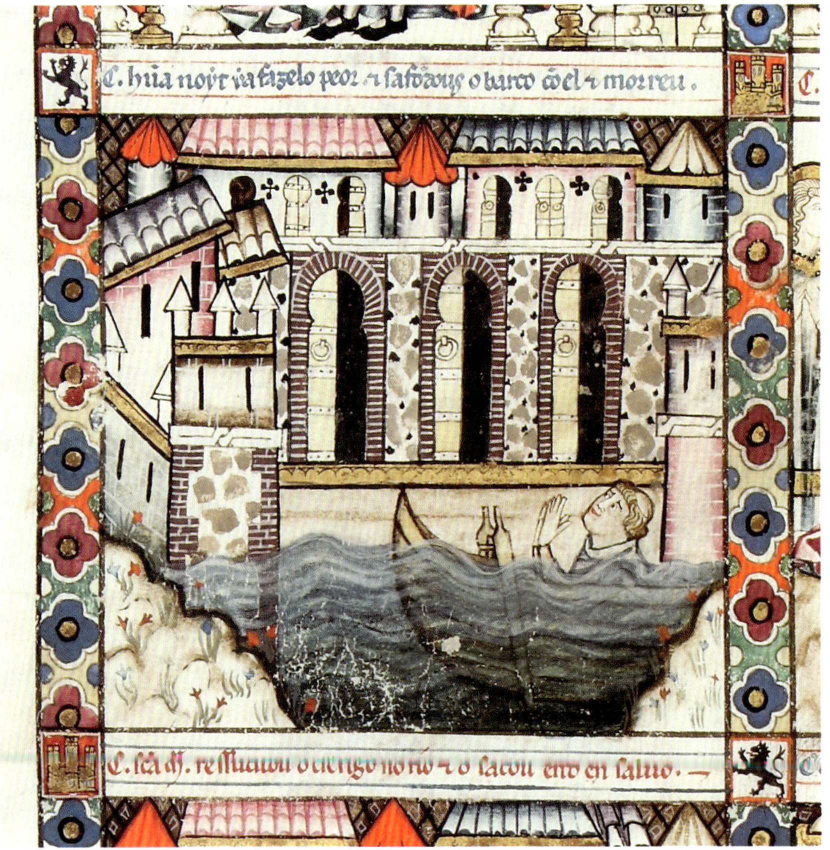

FIG. 73
The sacristan falls into the Seine. Detail from The Story of the Drowned Sacristan (Cantiga 111), *Cantigas de Santa María.* Real Biblioteca de El Escorial, Madrid, MS T.I.1, fol. 158v. © Patrimonio Nacional.

medieval Iberian imagery, while others had met with resistance or rejection. As a class, Marian miracles represented a desirable devotional medium that had earned the king's special sanction, yet the phenomenon of Marian devotion was itself still new to Iberia, and the often unfamiliar themes of its most traditional narratives, including those concerning Jews, must at times have seemed outlandish to the artists charged with their illustration.

Some themes were familiar enough to be readily accommodated. One was the trope of Jews as enemies of Christ, the substantial Iberian variations upon which were explored in chapter 2. The ease with which this theme was adapted in the *Cantigas de Santa María* is illustrated by the seemingly gratuitous insertion of malicious-looking Jews into the crowd that torments a patiently suffering Christ in the illustration to Cantiga 50 (Escorial T.I.1, fol. 74v; fig. 18). As was suggested above, these figures surely responded to the *cantiga*'s thematic juxtaposition of Christ's incarnation with his murder, since both themes raised the specter of Jewish hostility toward Christ. A similar association likely shaped the Crucifixion scene illustrating Cantiga 140 (Escorial T.I.1, fol. 196r), in which two clusters of Jews, some holding implements of the Passion, flank the crucified Christ, one turning toward his companions as he points to the Virgin Mary, who kneels at the foot of the cross (fig. 75).[49] No specific textual prompt appears to have inspired the addition of Jews in this case: the *cantiga* itself is a very brief *loor* that praises the Virgin's virtues and asks her assistance "in the weary battle of this world."[50] The addition of Jewish tormentors instead has the character of an improvised contribution, one that recognizes the power of Jewish presence to intensify the song's emotional charge, as well as its glorification of the Virgin.

Cantiga 12 elaborates upon the deicide charge. A widely known Marian narrative, it tells how the archbishop of Toledo was interrupted at mass one Assumption Day by the voice of the Virgin Mary, who claimed that the Jews were "again" killing her son. When the archbishop announced this apparition to the townspeople, they rushed to the Jewish quarter to find a group of Jews engaged in beating and spitting on an image of Jesus, preparatory to crucifying it. They then killed all the Jews.[51]

Although this narrative is set explicitly in Toledo, it did not originate in Spain, but in the Marian miracle collections of England and France. There, after the middle of the twelfth century, its rise in popularity paralleled closely related accusations that Jews also ritually crucified young boys. The illustrated *cantiga* has sometimes been considered through that same lens, as evidence that fears of Jewish predation upon young boys had by this date reached Castile as well.[52] However, since such claims remained unfamiliar throughout Spain generally in the late thirteenth century, a Castilian viewer seems unlikely to have connected it readily with that still-distant controversy.[53] Much stronger resonance for a Castilian viewer may have been found in its repeated reference to the participation of Jews in the death of Christ and the possibility that they continued to nurture hostility toward him. This claim pervades the *cantiga* text, and its first expression issues from the mouth of the Virgin herself:

> The voice, as though weeping, said: "Oh, God, oh, God, how great and manifest is the

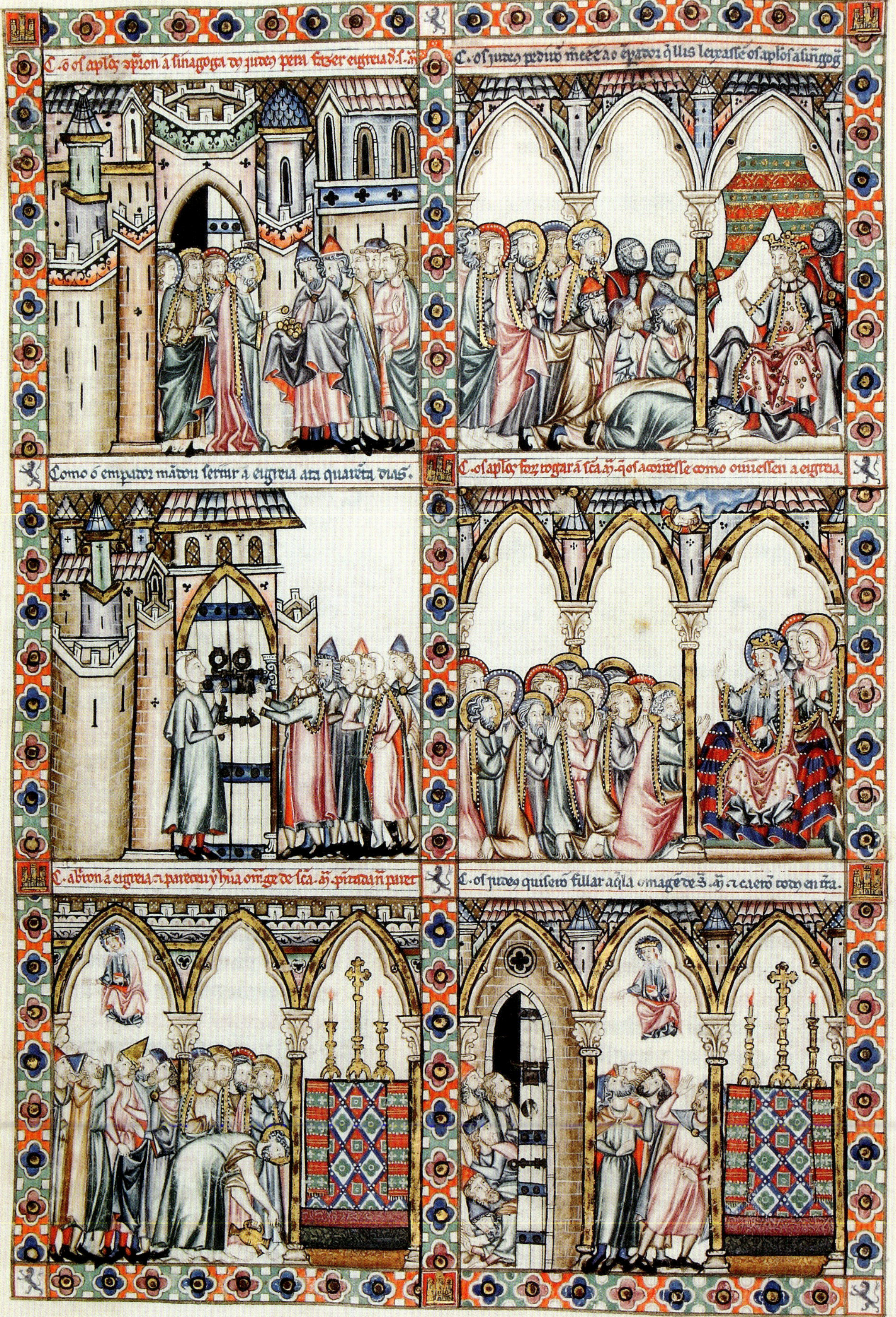

FIG. 74
The Story of the Apostles' Conversion of a Synagogue (Cantiga 27), *Cantigas de Santa María*. Real Biblioteca de El Escorial, Madrid, MS T.I.1, fol. 41v. © Patrimonio Nacional.

> perfidy of the Jews, who killed my Son, though they were his own people, and even now they wish no peace with Him."
>
> After the mass was sung, the archbishop went out of the church and told everyone what he had heard the voice say, and the people replied: "The evil Jewish people did this deed."
>
> Then they all hastily set out for the Jewish quarter and found, it is no lie, an image of Jesus Christ, which the Jews were striking and spitting upon.
>
> And furthermore, the Jews had made a cross upon which they intended to hang the image. For this deed they were all to die, and their pleasure was turned to grief.[54]

Rather than dwelling on the details of the reenacted Crucifixion, the text draws attention instead to the parallels between the historical crucifixion of Jesus and the Jews' ritualistic reenactment of the crime: the Virgin's accusation that the Jews had killed her son is echoed by that of the townspeople as they confront the prospect of new violence by "the evil Jewish people." The illustration reinforces this, depicting the townsmen bursting through the door of a house to catch a group of grimacing Jews holding a lance and a crown of thorns as they abuse a pale, featureless figurine held before a cross (fig. 50). The scene strongly resembles the Crucifixion panels of Cantigas 50 and 140, not just in the obvious elements of Christ-figure and cross but also in the disjointed gestures and leering faces of the Jews who participate in the crime and in the weapons and crown of thorns, clear references to the Passion. Their crime is nothing less than a pseudo-Crucifixion, which exceeds the baldness of the *cantiga* text by evoking its biblical model.

These elaborations were not entirely the artists' innovation. Several elements echo another version of the same narrative that is likely to have been well known to them, since it was preserved in the *Milagros de Nuestra Señora* of Gonzalo de Berceo. The central stanzas of this poem offer close parallels to both the structure and the details of the *cantiga* illustration. Here, the Virgin's call to the people is not an anguished cry for help, but five stanzas of anti-Jewish invective that foregrounds the symbolic attack by harping on Jewish agency in the actual Crucifixion:

> A voice from Heaven spoke, pained and angry:
> it said, "Hear, Christians, a remarkable thing!
> The Jewish people, deaf and blind,
> have never been so wicked to Lord Jesus!

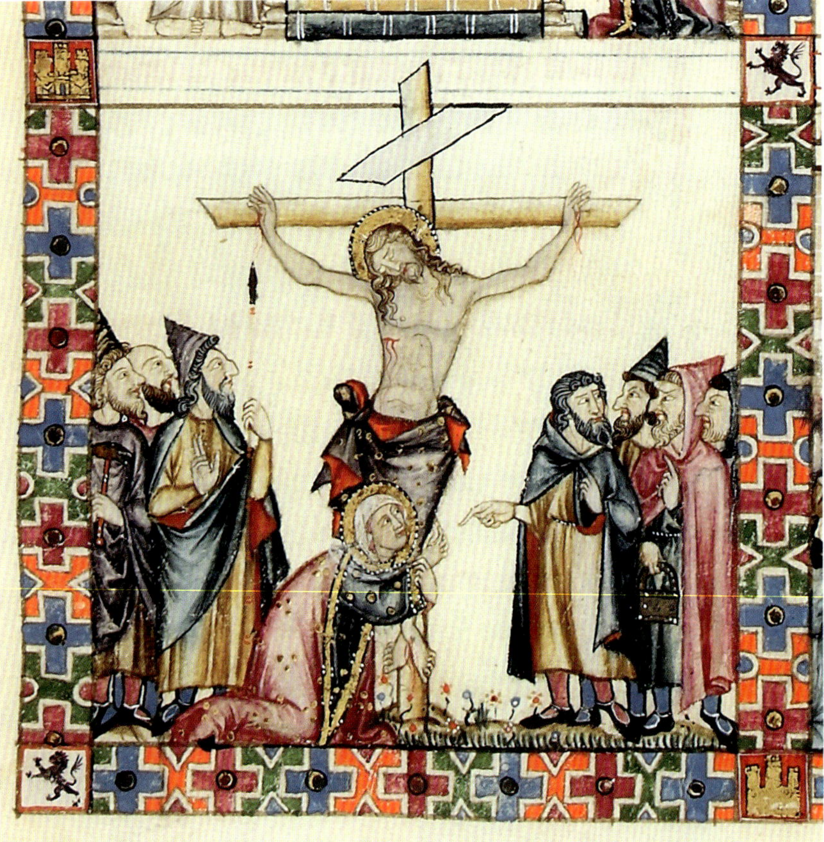

FIG. 75
Crucifixion. Detail from Cantiga 140 (*loor*), *Cantigas de Santa María*, Real Biblioteca de El Escorial, Madrid, MS T.I.1, fol. 196r. © Patrimonio Nacional.

. . . .
They are again crucifying My dear Son.
Nobody could know how great is My pain!
A bitter vine sprout is growing in Toledo—
never was one so wicked nurtured on this
  earth!"[55]

The account of the attack itself hammers home this comparison by emphasizing those elements of the attack that repeat the ones visited on Christ himself, even to the figurine's wounds:

They found in the house of the most
  honorable rabbi
a large body of wax shaped like a man.
It was like Jesus Christ; it was crucified,
held with large nails, and had a great wound
  in its side.[56]

The likelihood that the *Cantigas de Santa María* artists were aware of Berceo's text, or at least of an oral version like it, is very strong. The *Milagros de Nuestra Señora,* although often assumed to have been composed for a monastic audience, have been shown to display signs of composition with a broader audience in mind, including the pilgrims who might have passed through San Millán de la Cogolla, the foundation with which Berceo remained affiliated for most of his life.[57] The yellow, waxy color of the figurine and theatrical brutality of the Jews' attack, which echoes the composition of traditional Crucifixion scenes even to the inclusion of a crown of thorns, reinforce its resemblance to Berceo's account.

Other themes that found ready reception in the *Cantigas de Santa María* echoed doctrinal disputes that had their own substantial foundation in Iberian polemics. One such theme emerges in the legend of the Visigothic saint Ildefonsus, who was rewarded with a golden chasuble for his dedication to the Virgin. Ildefonsus's role as a devotee of the Virgin had been reinforced especially in Iberia, as we have seen, by the incorporation of his *Virginitate perpetua sanctae Mariae adversus tres infideles* into the liturgy associated with the Feast of the Annunciation, as well as by the wide dissemination of this text as an independent book between the tenth and thirteenth centuries.[58] Such preparation may have bred a special receptiveness to the legend of the chasuble, which, like the tale of mock crucifixion in Toledo, had been a stock element in the Marian collections of France and Britain despite its putative Iberian setting.

The endowment of the chasuble itself does not appear to have interested the Alfonsine artists as strongly as did the opportunity to emphasize Ildefonsus's confrontation with nonbelievers, the same heretics and Jews with whom the saint is shown disputing in the thirteenth-century Ildefonsus manuscripts discussed earlier in this study (fig. 19). While this theme earns reference in only one line toward the beginning of the *cantiga* text—indeed, the main body of text is occupied primarily with other, miraculous aspects of the saint's tale, such as his own vision of Saint Leocadia and his visitation by the Virgin[59]—the illustration gives pride of place to his role as a defender of the doctrines central to his cause, the Incarnation and the Virgin birth (Escorial MS T.I.1, fol. 7r; fig. 76). In its first panel, Ildefonsus is shown writing busily at a desk before a cabinet of jumbled books, presumably composing the "excellent writings" with which the *cantiga* describes him as armed; in the second, he engages in disputation with a highly animated crowd of heretics and Jews. The latter image recalls the imagery of the Ildefonsus manuscripts in the saint's confrontational stance and the outlandish features of his combatants, although here the three individual disputations portrayed in the earlier manuscripts have been telescoped into a single event in which all the disputants appear together. The negative signs earlier distributed as if at random among Iovinian, Helvidius, and the Jew are now concentrated among the Jewish figures alone, whose large noses and abundant beards and the aggressive gestures with which they count off their points with their fingers stand in sharp contrast to the mild-featured heretics who quiescently ponder the saint's words.

This transformation suggests the artist's awareness of the newly prominent place held by Jews in the polemics and disputations that had increased throughout Iberia during the great territorial expansions of the thirteenth century, as well as of the involvement of the preaching orders in these. Although, as we have seen, these missionaries' best-known activity during the late thirteenth century occurred in the Crown of Aragon, their Castilian impact can be traced in the foundation of new Franciscan and Dominican houses throughout the realm and in the prominence of the friars both at court and in the ecclesiastical hierarchy: the Marian author and Alfonsine courtier Juan Gil de Zamora himself was a Franciscan, and Dominicans held the Castilian bishoprics of Seville, Badajoz, Cádiz, and Cartagena during this same period.[60] The late thirteenth century also witnessed the emergence in Castile of new polemical treatises against the Jews written by local authors, such as the *Tractatus contra caecitatem iudeorum,* composed by the Augustinian Bernardo Oliver in 1317.[61]

As was shown in an earlier chapter, reference to anti-Jewish polemics of this kind had already found its way into other narratives in the *Cantigas de Santa María,* as in Cantiga 108, in which the doctrine of the Incarnation provided the sticking point between Merlin and the Jew whom the Virgin punished through the deformation of his child (fig. 53). A second

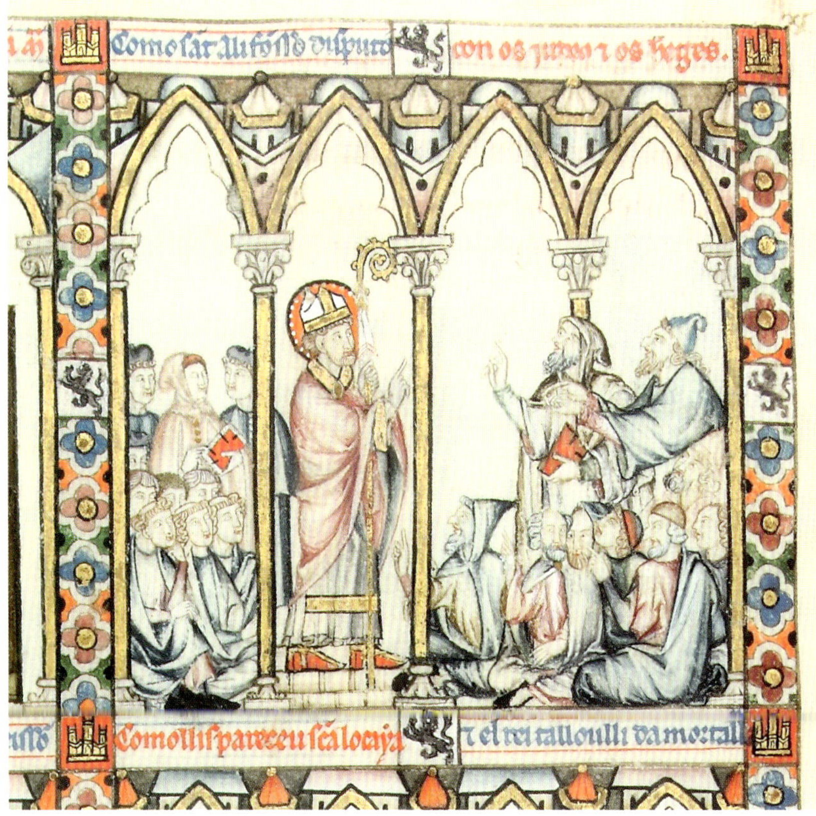

FIG. 76
Ildefonsus preaching to heretics and Jews. Detail from The Story of Ildefonsus (Cantiga 2), *Cantigas de Santa María*. Real Biblioteca de El Escorial, Madrid, MS T.I.1, fol. 7r. © Patrimonio Nacional.

doctrinal controversy to find expression in the *Cantigas* concerned the validity of the Eucharist, an issue alluded to in Cantiga 4, the tale of the Jewish boy (fig. 52).[62] In this tale, the father's near-demented violence may be understood as prompted less by his son's error than by his fear that the child had been permanently altered because he ate eucharistic bread. While consumption of the Eucharist was believed by most thirteenth-century churchmen to have no effect on nonbelievers, the same thinkers seem to have assumed that Jews would nonetheless be fearful of its effects. Such is suggested, for example, by Pope Innocent III's oft-cited accusation that Jews forced their Christian wet nurses to express their milk into a latrine after taking communion so that Jewish babies would not accidentally ingest the body of Christ.[63] Understood as a projection of Christian anxiety about the transformative power of the Eucharist, the Jewish boy's changeable profile echoes his own awareness of the nature of the bread he has just eaten, reflected also in his explanation to his father that he had "taken communion" (*me comingóu*).

Not all religious conflicts in the *Cantigas de Santa María* were so sophisticated: in the illustration for Cantiga 286, found in the Florence codex, the Jewish-Christian debate has devolved into a puerile exchange of insults. The song recounts how a particularly devoted Christian man, who used to lie prostrate in prayer before the portico of a church, was one day interrupted when a passing dog disturbed him—either by biting him, as the illustration suggests (fig. 77), or by urinating on him, as implied by the text preserved in the most comprehensive thirteenth-century manuscript of the songs (Escorial, MS J.B.2). When two passing Jews laughed at his misfortune, the man called upon the Virgin to punish them: "Oh, My Lady, please take vengeance for me on these Jews, for they are enemies of yours who killed your Son, who was man and God, and they ridicule me on your account, as you see."[64] The Virgin caused the portico under which the Jews had been standing to crush and kill them, to the delight of the Christian onlookers.

The source of this simple narrative remains unknown, and its late appearance in the collection, along with many other tales known to have been composed at Alfonso's court, suggests that it might have been invented for this setting. Its gratuitous hostility and scanty doctrinal foundation offer a reminder that the conflict among Spain's religious minorities was not always conceived or conducted on a lofty plane.

More nuance emerges in the numerous *cantigas* that express socially founded anxieties about Jews. Whereas many of these fears—especially those concerning Jewish violence against Christians and control over money—evoke the spectrum of anti-Jewish concerns that had permeated much of Europe by the second half of the thirteenth century, they did not always carry the same force in Iberia, nor were they always articulated there in the same way. As a work whose narrative sources were deeply rooted in northern European traditions, the *Cantigas de Santa María* offers an instructive illustration of how such concerns could be adapted to a specifically Castilian context.

Exemplary of this adaptation are those tales that feature Jewish violence against Christians and particularly against young boys, whose special dedication to their faith could allow them

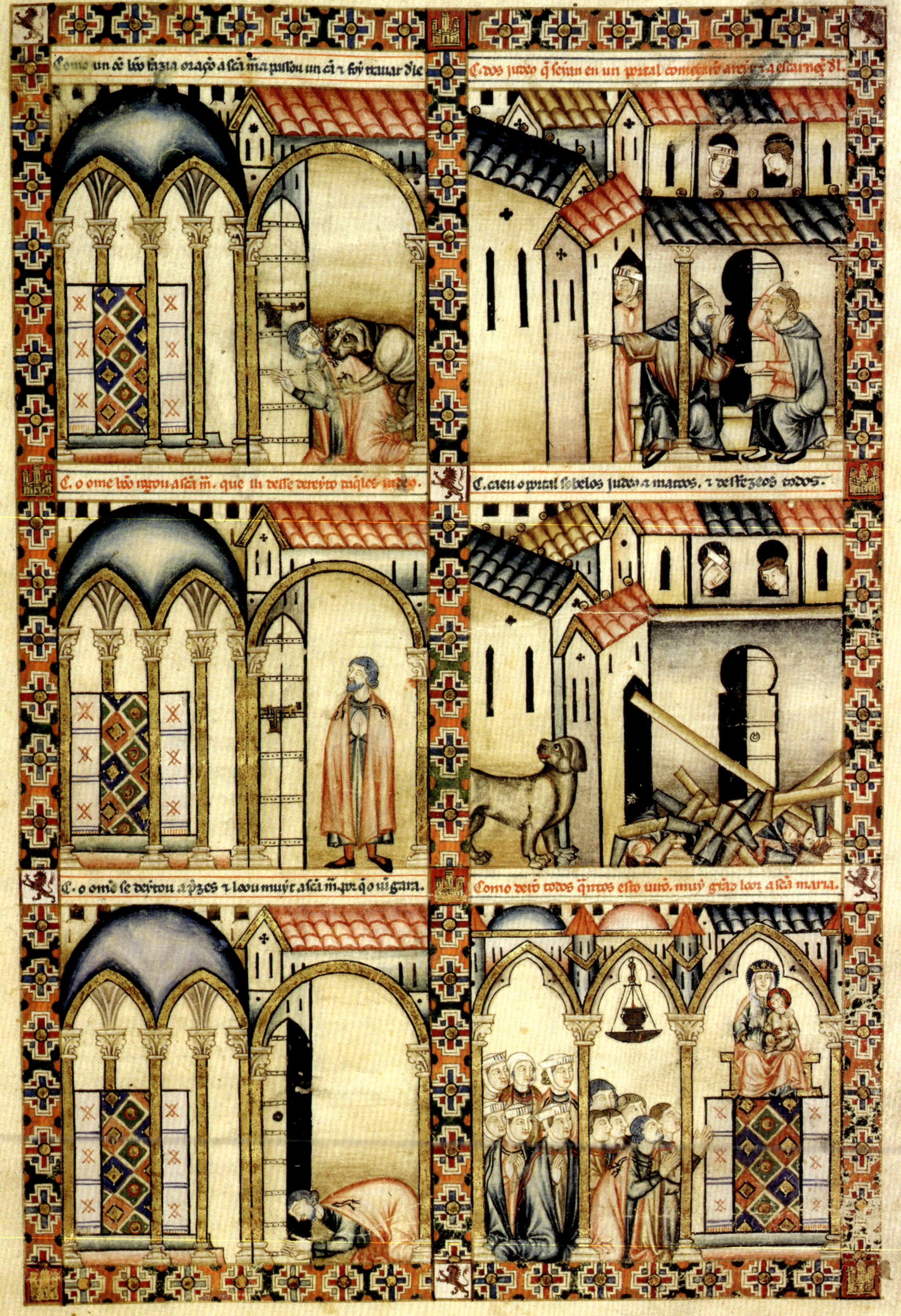
Como un ome bõo fazia oraçõ a scã ma pusou un cã e foy travar dle
C. dos judeos q̃ seian en un spital começarõ a rijr e a escarnecẽ dl.
C. o ome bõo rogou a scã m. que lli desse dereyto daqles judeos.
C. caeu o spital sobelos judeos e matoos. e desfezeos todos.
C. o ome se deytou a prezes e loou muyt a scã m. por q̃ o uĩgara.
Como derõ todos q̃ntos esto uirõ. muy grã loor a scã maria.

FIG. 77
The Story of Two Jews Who Laughed at a Devout Man (Cantiga 286), *Cantigas de Santa María.* Biblioteca Nazionale, Florence, B.R. 20, fol. 5r. Reproduced by kind permission of the Ministero per i Beni e le Attività Culturali, Italy / Biblioteca Nazionale Centrale.

to be viewed as virtual substitutes for Christ.[65] As we have seen, this notion lies at the heart of both Cantiga 4 and Cantiga 6, particularly the latter. Recounting the murder of a boy who sang praises to the Virgin Mary, this *cantiga* actively develops the boy's role as innocent Christ-surrogate in a manner similar to the famous version of the same narrative that was immortalized by Chaucer in "The Prioress's Tale." As in Chaucer's story, the *cantiga* recounts that the fatherless boy, dedicated to the Virgin by his mother, was beloved for his beautiful singing and especially for his performance, as the *cantiga* recounts, of "the song which says '*Gaude Virgo Maria*' and then berates the Jew, who takes great exception to it." The narrative continues: "Then, on a feast day, when many Jews and Christians were gathered together and were playing dice, the boy sang. All were very pleased, except a Jew, who hated him for it."[66] The hymn that so angers the Jew is "Gaude Maria Virgo," in which praise of the Virgin's purity as the vessel of the Incarnation is set in counterpoint to Jewish disbelief: "erubescat judaeus infelix, qui dicit Christum Joseph semine esse natum" (Let the miserable Jew be ashamed, who says that Christ was born of the seed of Joseph).[67] Following the boy's murder and miraculous reanimation and rediscovery through the agency of the Virgin, the townspeople respond by killing not just the Jewish murderer, but all the town's Jews: "When the boy said that, all who were there went at once to the Jews and killed them all. The one who had struck the boy they burned in the fire, saying, 'He who commits such a deed reaps such a reward.'"[68]

In the context of the *Cantigas de Santa María,* the slaughter of many Jews for a crime perpetrated by only one seems excessive, a mass killing of a kind practiced in parts of medieval Europe but still largely unfamiliar to Castilian experience. It seems a relic of a northern European literary tradition in which such exaggerated responses to fictitious Jewish violence were more common; indeed, in the version of the tale told by Gautier de Coincy, the massacre extends to all the Jews in the city who were not inspired to convert in response to the miracle.[69] In the illustration, Alfonso's artists might have felt compelled to rationalize this violent conclusion by casting not one but several Jews in the crime almost from the beginning of

FIG. 78
The Story of the Man Possessed by Demons (Cantiga 109), *Cantigas de Santa María*. Real Biblioteca de El Escorial, Madrid, MS T.I.1, fol. 156v. © Patrimonio Nacional.

the tale (fig. 51).[70] After the opening panel showing the boy's dedication as a baby, the second depicts him singing among a gathering, at the right of which is an offended-looking Jew in a brown hooded cloak. In the middle two panels, this figure is joined by several companions, who look on with lively interest as he cleaves the boy's head with an ax, drags the body off, and buries it. After the mother's recovery of the boy, which is attended by the Virgin Mary and a pair of angels, the murderous Jew is burned in the same square where the boy had sung his song. This resumption of focus on a single culprit perhaps represents an artistic device in which the murderer's execution serves metonymically for the community massacre to come, but it also may reflect the artists' discomfort with the group attack demanded by the text.

A foreign trope even more variably adapted into the *Cantigas de Santa María* was the association between Jews and the devil, a theme that enjoyed a long life on the Iberian Peninsula despite its often ambivalent handling there.[71] In the Theophilus tale, as we have seen, the relationship is at its deepest: the Jew's quasi-collegial gestures reveal his familiar relationship with Satan while his physiognomic similarity to the surrounding demons underscores his affiliation (fig. 42). In other instances, Alfonso's artists responded more diffidently to the opportunity to develop this link. Such a case is Cantiga 109, in which a Christian man possessed by five demons is rescued by the Virgin Mary. As the victim is brought into a church to be exorcised, a Jew who has observed the goings-on asks one of the demons why they did not attack his own people, and he responds, "Because you already belong to me and serve me. Therefore, we do not harm you for you are already ours."[72] Thus informed, the Jew flees, paralleling the departure of the demons from their victim.

The illustration does little to expand upon this near-tangential textual exchange (fig. 78). The Jew appears only once, in the fifth panel, where he hovers on the periphery of the exorcism scene, peering in at the church portal as the demons flutter upward from their vomiting victim. Only one demon, a beak-faced gray creature with ass's ears, seems sufficiently concerned with the Jew's question to react to it; he twists his head around casually to speak without interrupting his upward trajectory. The Christian's possession and salvation by the Virgin instead remain the primary focus of both verbal and visual narrative.

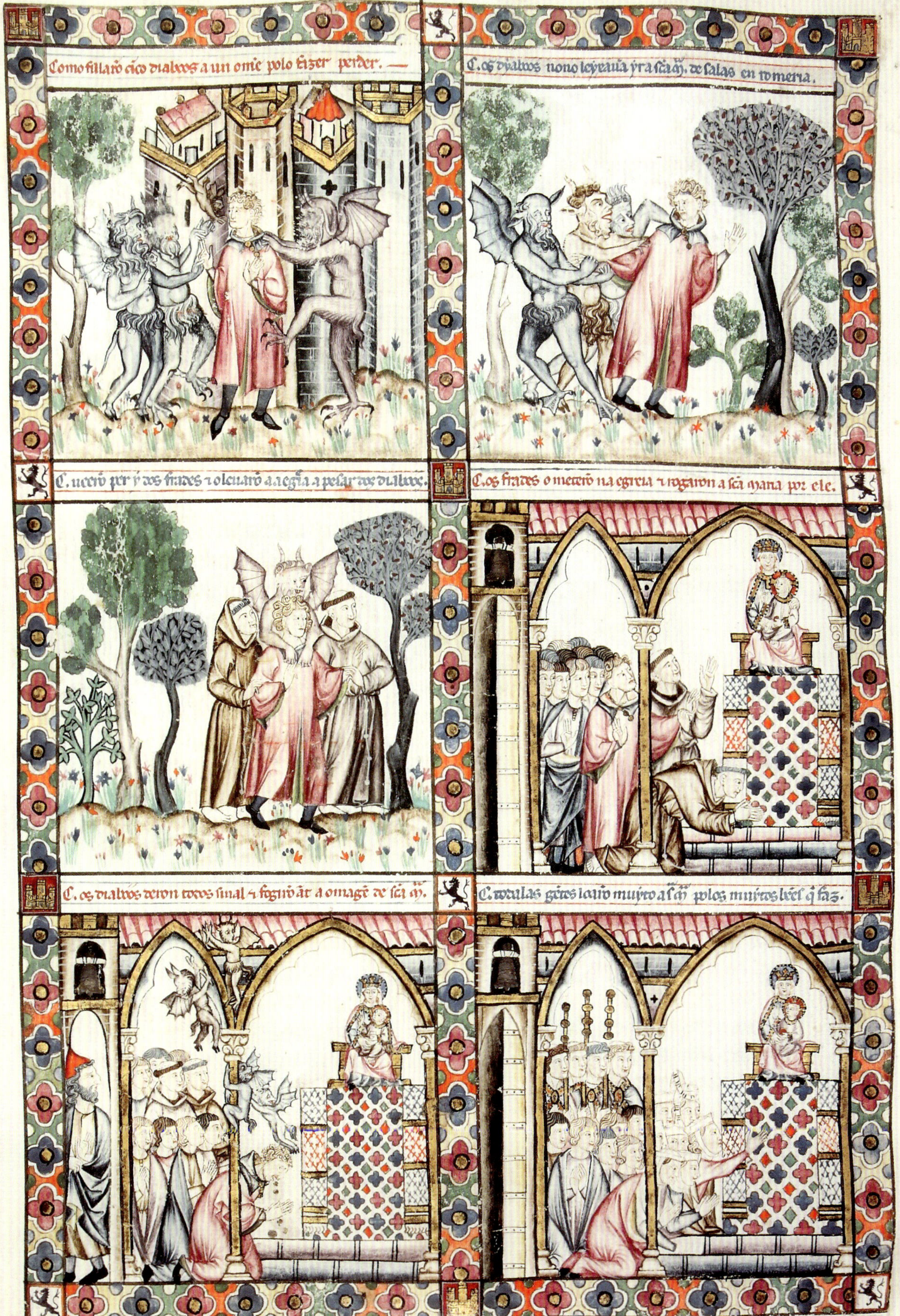
Como fillarō cīco diaboos a un omē polo fazer perder.
C. os dyaboos nono leyxauã yr a scã m. de salas en romeria.
C. ueeron per y dos frades e o leuarō a egia a pesar dos diaboos.
C. os frades o meterō na egreia e rogaron a scã maria por ele.
C. os diaboos deron todos sinal e fogirō ant a omagē de scã m.
C. todalas gētes loarō muyto a scã m. polos muytos bēes q̄ faz.

FIG. 79
The Story of the Jew Converted in Prison, left half of opening (Cantiga 85), *Cantigas de Santa María.* Real Biblioteca de El Escorial, Madrid, MS T.I.1, fol. 125v. © Patrimonio Nacional.

The illustrations to other tales that play on Jewish affiliation with the devil often display a similar detachment. Cantiga 85 tells the story of a Jew who is taken prisoner by thieves and converted by the Virgin while in captivity. Appearing to him in prison, Mary shows him a vision of his fate should he continue in his native religion: a pit in which sinners are tormented by devils and dragons. She then proffers a vision of Christ in heaven, promising the Jew that he will be with them "if you believe in Him and eat suckling pig and stop cutting the throats of goats."[73] The Jew goes immediately to a monastery and is baptized. Striking here is the absence of Jewish stereotypes among the sinners in the hell scene (Escorial, MS T.I.1, fols. 125v–126r). Although the text describes these victims as the souls of Jews and describes the flames as "singeing their beards and moustaches,"[74] the men and women crowded into two large cauldrons within the flames are generic, light-haired, and beardless, lacking any recognizable Jewish sign (fig. 79). While their unstereotyped appearance has been interpreted as approximating the "infantile" quality often given to souls after death in medieval imagery,[75] their lack of specifically Jewish markers tends to undermine the Virgin's admonitory message, breaking the visual link between the generic figures already damned and the obviously Jewish protagonist, who, despite his own lack of beard, preserves the other traditional identifiers of hood, dark coloring, and enlarged nose.

A less ambivalent image appears in Cantiga 34, where the Jew who throws an image of the Virgin into a latrine is killed by the devil for his crime. The text offers little motivation for the actions of the Jew, whose own agency is suggested by the illustration's dynamic first panel, in which the oversized thief scuttles along the fortifications of his snug, circular town like a predator from a horror movie. In the second panel, a demon follows the Jew as he disposes of the image, and the caption above reads, "How the Jew put the image of Holy Mary in the privy on the advice of the Devil,"[76] while in the third, two demons dispassionately cart off the body of the Jew, now dead (fig. 49). Although this tale has at times been interpreted as expressing Iberian Christians' fears of the hostility of Jews toward images of Christ—a preoccupation known in Spain by the fourteenth century, but fairly rare before this—there is little evidence that this would have occurred to the compilers of the *Cantigas de Santa María,* who passed up the opportunity to include several other well-

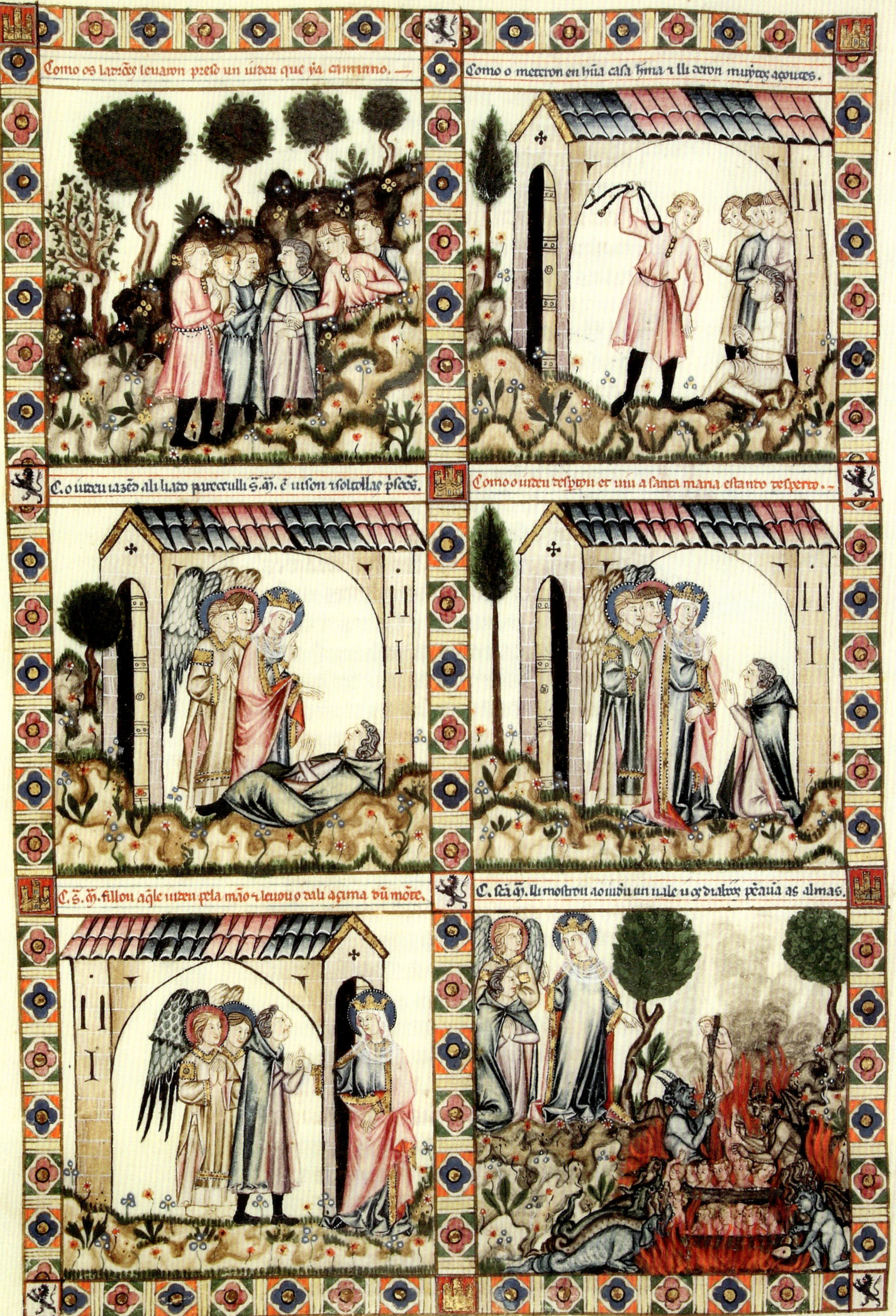
Como os ladrões leuaron preso un iudeu que ya caminno.
Como o meteron en hũa casa hma e lli deron muytos açoutes.
C. o iudeu iazẽdo ali liado pareceulli S. M. e uison e soltoulle as presões.
Como o iudeu despertou et uiu a santa maria estando desperto.
C. S. M. fillou aqle iudeu pela mão e leuou o dali acima dũ mõte.
C. scã M. lli mostrou ao iudeu un uale u os diaboos pẽauã as almas.

known narratives on this theme.[77] Instead, its driving significance is its emphasis on the Jew's devilish inspiration.

Perhaps the most ambivalent of all the *cantiga* illustrations are those concerning moneylenders. Although the vicissitudes of the money trade figure repeatedly throughout the *Cantigas de Santa María,* only one of the lenders involved in these stories is clearly identified as a Jew. This is the moneylender of Cantiga 25, a venerable Marian tale that also figured in Berceo's *Milagros de Nuestra Señora.*[78] It tells of a Christian merchant who asked a Jew for a loan; lacking the customary security, he requested that the Jew accept the Virgin and Christ as his guarantors. The Jew agreed on the grounds that, as he put it, "I know that She was a saintly woman and He a saintly man and a prophet."[79] When the time came for repayment, the Christian was still far from his home in Byzantium, so he placed the money in a chest, entrusting it to the sea and God's guidance. Although the chest found its way to the Jew, he then hid the money under his bed, claiming that the Christian had defaulted on his loan. When the latter appealed to the Virgin, she confirmed

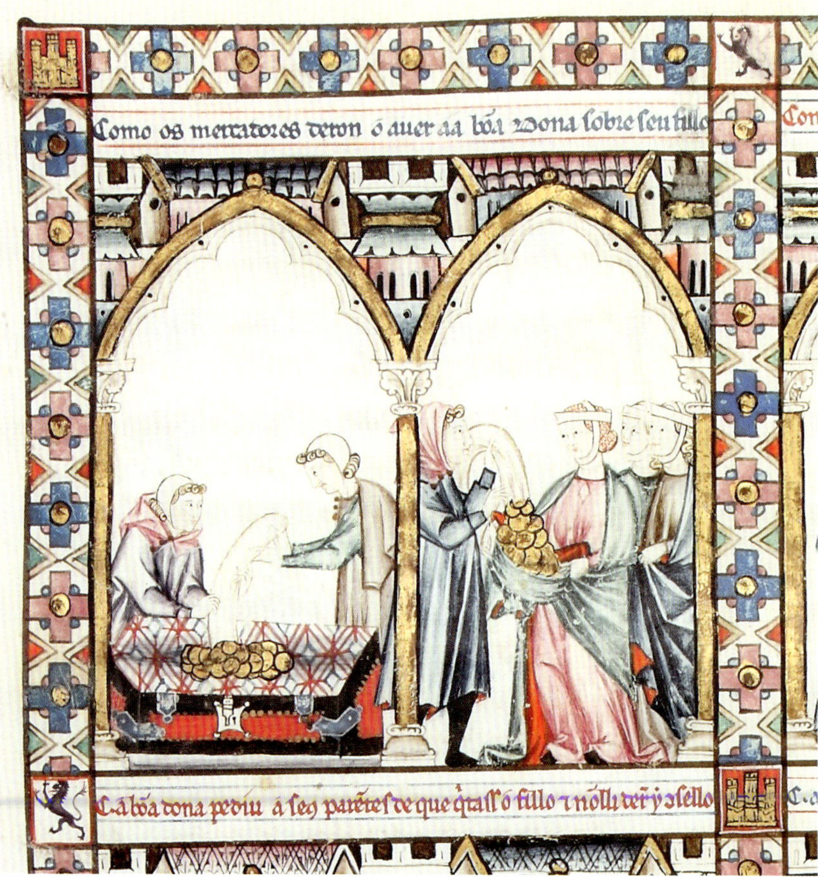

FIG. 80
A woman at a moneylender's house. Detail from The Story of a Woman Who Put up Her Son as Collateral (Cantiga 62), *Cantigas de Santa María*. Real Biblioteca de El Escorial, Madrid, MS T.I.1, fol. 90v. © Patrimonio Nacional.

that the debt had been repaid and chastised the Jew for his deceptiveness, prompting his conversion.

Because this tale was one of those assigned a number ending in five, its illustration comprises two facing pages of the Escorial manuscript, including twelve panels in all (fig. 63). Although this format offers ample space to elaborate a potentially complex theme, the illustration recounts the tale with comparative literality. Apart from his stereotyped features and pointed hat, the Jew's figure displays few other signs of the deceptiveness and greed implicit in the narrative.[80] His gestures and expressions are restrained, and his transaction with the Christian is businesslike; when he kneels in the font to accept baptism, even his stereotyped profile seems to be mitigated by its newly three-quarter orientation. Only in the scene where he hides his money under his bed does the presence of magical hexagrams and swastika hint at his potential to manipulate the honest Christian.

Other *cantigas* entirely forgo prime opportunities to develop the Jewish moneylender *topos.* Cantiga 62 tells the story of a woman of noble lineage who lost her property in doing good works and was forced to put up her son as surety on her debts. The Virgin answered her appeal for help by instructing her to return to her creditors and causing them to release her son without objection. Like earlier and contemporaneous variants of the tale, the text does not identify her creditors specifically as Jews, but describes them using the more neutral term *devedores.*[81] The illustration follows suit, portraying the lenders as conventional Christian figures: beardless and small-featured, with short, light hair (Escorial, T.I.1, fol. 90v, fig. 80). The moneylender in Cantiga 305 (Florence, B.R. 20, fols. 43r–44v), who fails in his attempt to dupe a poor woman by offering to lend her only the weight of the certificate of absolution that she has offered as collateral, is handled in a similar manner. Failing a known source for this story, one might imagine that both author and artist would be free to imagine a Jewish lender here—the text, in fact, may hint at this by reporting that he "tore his beard" in frustration when the Virgin caused the certificate miraculously to increase in weight.[82] The artist, however, passed entirely on the opportunity to render the figure as a Jew, instead depicting both the lender and his assistants as blond, clean-shaven, and wearing traditional Christian dress.

The artists' lack of responsiveness to the moneylender *topos* was not for lack of controversy surrounding the actual role of Jews in Castilian moneylending. By the late thirteenth century in Castile, just as in Aragon, Jews had become sufficiently engaged in moneylending as to prompt a fairly vigorous Christian response. The combined pressures of a declining economy and the new influx of Castilian Jews into the money trade drew the resentment of Christian debtors, many of them nobles already burdened by increasing taxes and devaluations of the coinage. Their discontent is discernible in repeated demands at the Cortes of Castile that Alfonso reduce the level of interest that Jewish lenders were permitted to charge, a controversy that was complicated by the involvement of Jews in collecting the heavy taxes with which the king hoped to keep his kingdom afloat.[83] Resentment among the minor nobility sometimes found expression in direct attacks upon wealthy Jews, as when Alfonso's rebellious nobles attempted to claim the property of several Jewish courtiers, even kidnapping and holding at ransom the king's Jewish astronomer.[84] It may be that such conflicts had not yet become frequent enough to have inspired the same degree of concern here as they evidently did in the Crown of Aragon, where the vivid visual stereotypes of Jewish lenders in the *Vidal mayor* and the *libri iudeorum* attest to a well-established visual tradition. It is here, perhaps, that the relative insularity of the Alfonsine scriptorium retained some effect.

The Alfonsine artists seem to have offered even stronger resistance to the notion of Jewish attacks on the Eucharist, a theme that as we have seen was slow to penetrate elsewhere in Iberia as well. Three *cantigas* directly treat the theme of eucharistic desecration; they are loosely based on tales recounted in the *Dialogus Miraculorum* of Caesarius of Heisterbach.[85] Cantiga 104 recounts how a woman hoping to win her lover away from his new bride hid a consecrated host in her headdress so as to use it in a love charm, as suggested by some neighbor women (Escorial, T.I.1, fol. 150r, fig. 81). Her crime revealed when blood from the hidden wafer began to run from her headdress, the woman confessed her wrongdoing and immediately entered a convent. The closely related narratives of Cantiga 128 and 208 (Escorial, T.I.1, fol. 182r, and Florence B.R. 20, fol. 118v) both tell how a beekeeper put a consecrated wafer in his hive in hopes of increasing his yield of honey. One tale ends with the apparition of the Virgin and Child within the hive, the other with the miraculous discovery that the bees had built a miniature chapel with a statue of those holy figures.[86] As in the European prototypes, all three protagonists here are Christian, although the beekeeper in Cantiga 208 is identified as a heretic from Toulouse, "where there used to be heretics of many kinds who would not believe either in God nor his mother."[87] This slightly unorthodox turn is the only thread that might connect the crime with doctrinal concerns. In the *Cantigas de Santa María,* then, as elsewhere in Iberia until the mid-fourteenth century, crimes against the Eucharist are presented as the province of misguided Christians rather than Jews.[88]

Conversion Tales

More readily adapted to an Iberian context were those *cantigas* that concerned the conversion of religious minorities, both Muslims and Jews. One significant difference between these two types of conversion tale is that nearly all of those involving Jews derive from preexisting foreign sources, whereas those involving Muslims are more varied in origin and sometimes seem to have been invented ad hoc for the Alfonsine collection. The illustrations attached to narratives about Jewish conversion nonetheless display considerable effort to adapt them to an Iberian context. Although set in England, Cantiga 85 is hispanicized by the handsome *mudéjar* portal, with its large horseshoe arch and red-and-white voussoirs that the Jew approaches after being persuaded to convert (fig. 79). Cantiga 108, also set in the British Isles, is likewise reconceived in Iberian terms: the apothecary's shop owned by the tale's contentious Jewish sage, "who had no equal in learning in all of Scotland," resembles an airy Mediterranean portico, its arches tricked out in red-and-white carved stucco and its shelves filled with colorfully painted lusterware jars (fig 53).[89] Even more specific is the fantastical synagogue in which the sorcerer later lectures to the Jews, its cusped arches, hypostyle design, and Islamic-style hanging lamps a sharp contrast to the spacious Gothic church in the succeeding panel, where his converts go to be baptized after they are persuaded by Merlin's preaching.

Not just his architectural backdrop but also the actions of the triumphant Merlin must have rung true for a thirteenth-century Iberian viewer accustomed to the increasing reality of Christian sermonizing in synagogues. Such sermons had already been permitted to a limited extent by James I of Aragon following the 1263 Barcelona disputation; while Alfonso's own legislation did not overtly permit such incursions, his theoretical openness to missionary preaching in the realm is suggested by the *Siete partidas*' approval of the use of persuasion to convert those of other faiths.[90] One wonders if Merlin's sermon might have constituted a discrete, Iberian addition to the tale, since nothing comparable to it appears in the thirteenth-century Old French text that Carpenter has identified as the most immediate source of this narrative.[91]

Although some of the *cantigas* related to conversion concern adult male Jews or Muslims, women and children play a special role in many such stories. The Jewish boy who converts after

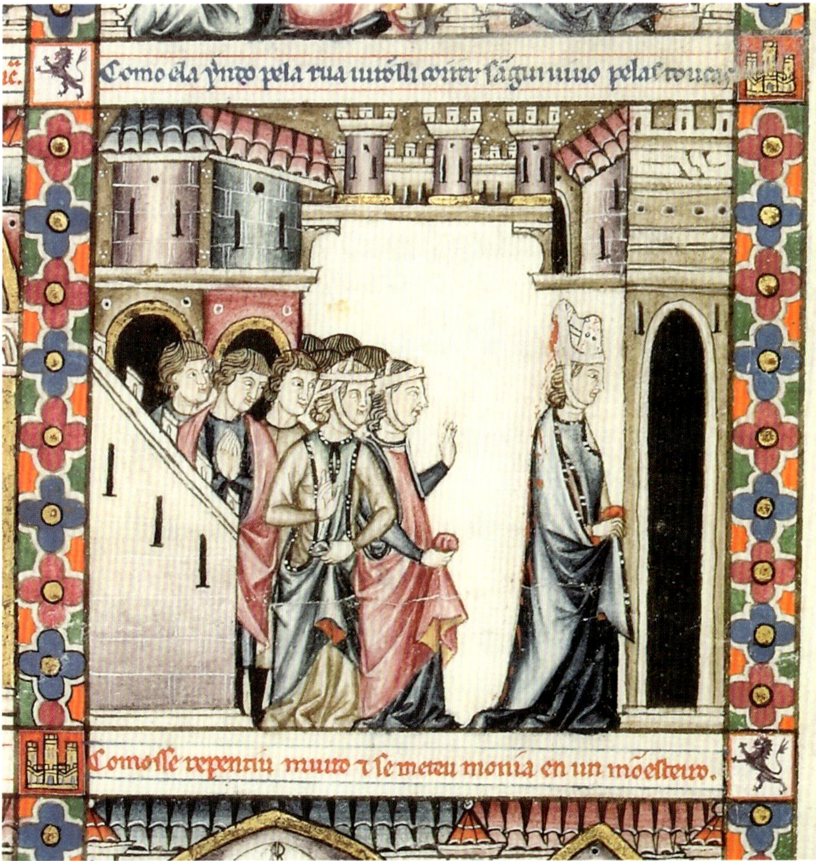

FIG. 81
The woman who stole the host is discovered. Detail of The Story of the Woman Who Stole the Host (Cantiga 104), *Cantigas de Santa María*. Real Biblioteca de El Escorial, Madrid, MS T.I.1, fol. 150r. © Patrimonio Nacional.

FIG. 82
The Story of a Jewish Woman Converted in Childbirth (Cantiga 89), *Cantigas de Santa María*. Real Biblioteca de El Escorial, Madrid, MS T.I.1, fol. 131r. © Patrimonio Nacional.

taking communion in Cantiga 4 is the most widely known of these, perhaps because of the self-awareness with which the child accepts communion and its implicit connection with the conversion reported in some versions of the narrative. This adultlike understanding of his actions poses a contrast, as Harriet Goldberg has observed, to the greater ingenuousness of the Jewish boy in other versions of the tale.[92] In other *cantigas,* both Jewish and Muslim child conversions often occur in tandem with the conversion of a parent, usually the mother, as would have been considered natural for children who had not yet reached the age of reason. It is thus mothers, and women in general, who stand at the center of most conversion tales.

Jewish women convert in two illustrated *cantigas.* Cantiga 89, a narrative drawn from the miracles of Vincent of Beauvais, tells how a Jewish woman near death in childbirth called on the Virgin in desperation and immediately produced a healthy child.[93] Her horrified midwives upbraided her as a heretic and *christchaã tornada*—literally, a "person turned Christian"—and abandoned her. After her thirty-day purification, the Jewess went promptly to church to be baptized, bringing with her both the son she had just borne and a young daughter mentioned at the beginning of the tale. Both children take a prominent role in the *cantiga*'s illustration (fig. 82): the daughter appears in the opening two panels, first standing lovingly near her mother, then attending her with concern during her labor; she is shown once again in the font with her mother, who also holds her baby son as they are baptized.

The tale's emphasis on the children's conversion underscores a factor that counted significantly in the actual conversion of medieval Iberian minorities: the expectation that the mother's conversion to Christianity would bring with it that of her actual and future children. Whether this was fueled by Christian awareness of the rabbinic tradition of matrilineal descent in Judaism is unclear, since Christian law codes such as the *Fuero Real* routinely treated as Christian the children of mixed parentage in which either parent was of that faith.[94] Each convert to Christianity, of course, added stability to a recently expanded kingdom much in need of new Christian subjects. Especially in Castile, where King Alfonso presided over the vastly enlarged territories captured by his father, Fernando III, the successful, if fictitious, conversion of the Jewess and her children—the contribution of not

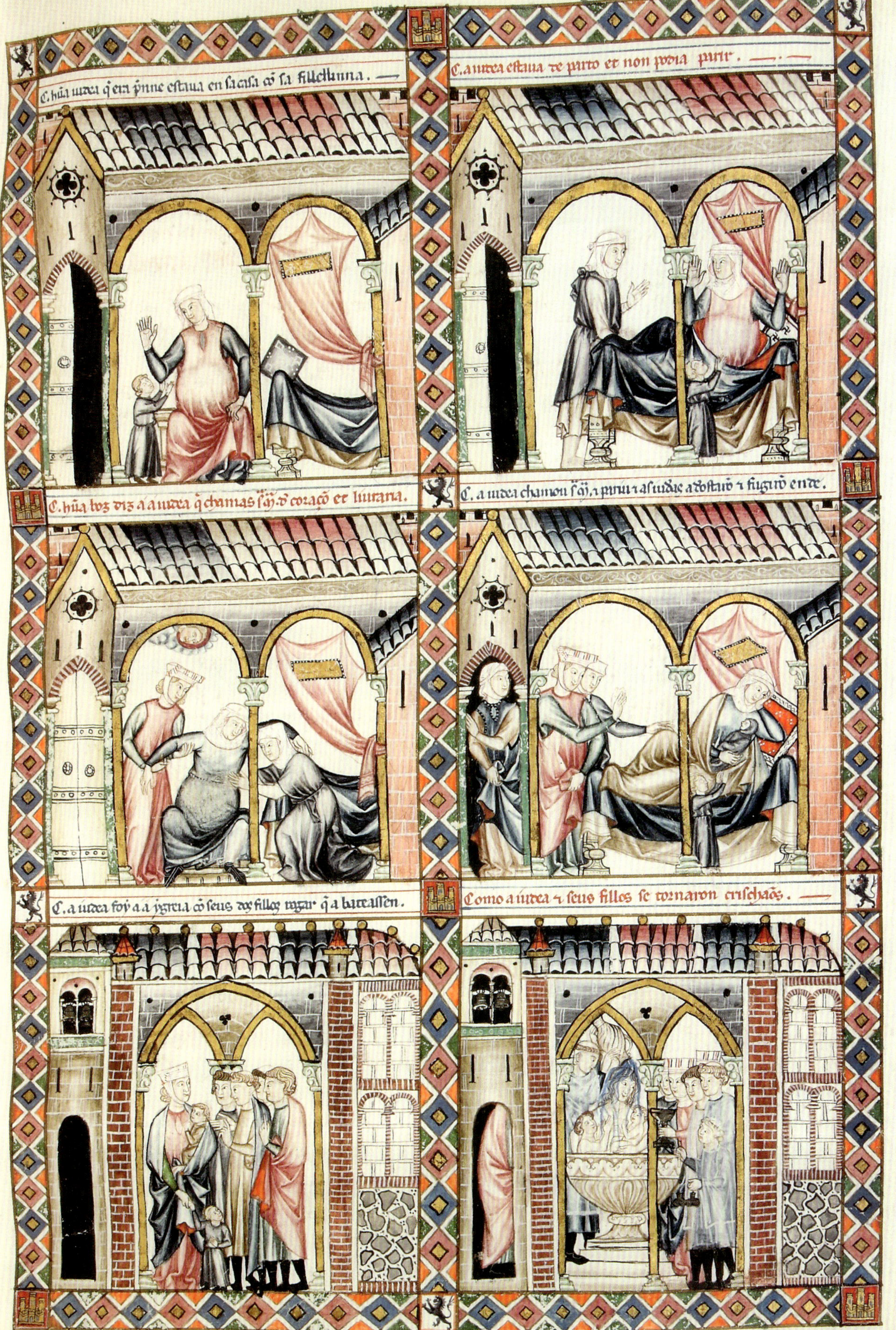
C. hũa iudea q̃ era prenne estaua en sa casa cõ sa filhelinna.
C. a iudea estaua de parto et non podia parir.
C. hũa voz diz a a iudea q̃ chamas S. M. de coraçõ et liuraria.
C. a iudea chamou S. M. e pariu e as iudias a dostarõ e fugirõ ende.
C. a iudea foy a a ygreia cõ seus dos fillos rogar q̃ a bateassen.
Como a iudea e seus fillos se tornaron crischaõs.

one but three souls to the body of Christendom in a single act of conversion—must have seemed a signal victory.[95]

The same implications permeate a second tale of a female Jewish convert, Cantiga 107, which is also the only *cantiga* with a Jewish protagonist to possess demonstrable Iberian roots.[96] Its protagonist, a Jewish woman of Segovia, is described by the *cantiga* as having been "caught in a crime" and sentenced to death by being thrown off a cliff.[97] While the nature of her crime is never made clear, related versions of the tale imply that it might have involved adultery. Once thrown from the cliff, the woman called on the Virgin for salvation and was brought down unharmed at its foot; she immediately presented herself at church to be baptized. The tale's local origin is confirmed by the survival of a related thirteenth-century account of the event, composed by the Dominican friar Rodrigo de Cerrato, which nicknames the woman "Marisaltos" (Leaping Mary) in reference to the nature of the miracle.[98] This text, although not precisely dated, places the miracle in the year 1237, lending weight to the supposition that the narrative must have been well-established locally by the time it was incorporated into the *Cantigas de Santa María.* The quaintly horseshoe-arched likeness of the Segovian aqueduct that frames her arrest plays on the tale's local pedigree (fig. 72).

As in Cantiga 89, the conversion of Marisaltos is presented as a highly positive event, in keeping with its place within a specifically Iberian economy of conversion. It is small wonder that the Virgin shows no hesitation in halting this Jew's fall to her death. A youthful, presumably fertile woman and a potential, if not actual, mother, she would have represented a coveted prize for Iberian Christians seeking to solidify an expanding Castilian population, a convert who embodied the kind of success that Christian Iberians could only hope others would emulate.

At its heart, the process of illustrating the *Cantigas de Santa María* was far more than a matter of turning text into pictures. It required the generation, based on knowledge of an often laconic verbal narrative or the shadowy memory of an oral one, of a fully fleshed-out pictorial narrative that could expand meaningfully upon the expanse of vellum allotted it by Alfonso's commission. The *cantiga* illustrations examined here offer a vivid sense of the freedom with which the king's artists approached this process, diverging whenever needed from the details and structure of texts that may have been unfamiliar to them in order to develop pictorial versions of the tales reflective of their own visual and ideological frame. Such divergences testify not only to the inventiveness demanded of Alfonso's artists, but also to the vast matrix of texts, images, and ideas that were available to them as they worked.

In certain cases, such as the straightening of the Jewish boy's nose in Cantiga 4, these divergences can be attributed to the artists' awareness of specific variants of the tales offered by authors like Gautier de Coincy, Gonzalo de Berceo, and other authors in whose hands the stories had circulated over the course of the twelfth and thirteenth centuries. In other cases, such as the expanded role of the Jew in the Theophilus tale, such discrepancies may reflect an awareness of other visual variants of these same stories. Most often, however, the artists' unique alterations of their source narratives suggest a more deeply creative response, a desire to resolve the discrepancies between the cultural frame within which most of their source tales originated and the context within which they had now to be developed.

The artists' flexible handling of the tales also attests to a degree of creative freedom that they might not have enjoyed had the king been able to supervise the production of the illustrated manuscripts with the same close attention that he apparently could give the composition of the songs. Working at least a few years, and often a decade or more, after the relevant *cantigas* were composed and without evident direction from the king, both the artists and their advisors made full use of their artistic license. Their efforts to enhance the narrative in ways that, in their own eyes, would have lent local relevance to their narratives help to minimize for modern scholars the dominating question of what Alfonso thought about Jews, instead permitting us to explore the broader question of what his famous *Cantigas de Santa María* reveal about the worldview shared by his subjects during the most active phase of the Castilian Reconquest.

As both literary and artistic constructs, these manuscripts matter less for their direct reflection of the social realities of thirteenth-century Castile than for their power to signal the sea change in Christian thinking about Jews as the transformations of the thirteenth century wore on. Like Cohen's "hermeneutical Jew," they are of value as indicators not simply of what medieval Iberians did, but of what they thought, and how. As a case study, the illustrated manuscripts of the *Cantigas de Santa María* shed light on questions of cultural identity that became central not just in Castile, but in Iberia as a whole during the most active years of the Reconquest. Their ready adoption of some themes, hesitant response to others, and active manipulation of still others that bore most directly on local concerns speak to the vitality and inventiveness with which Iberian artists endeavored to articulate a newfound place for both Christians and Jews within a transformed Iberia.

EPILOGUE

This book opened with the premise that images and objects produced by Iberian Christians in the late twelfth through early fourteenth centuries, during and after the greatest expansions of the Reconquest, offer a key to understanding that newly dominant culture's altered perceptions of and relationships with the peninsula's other faith groups, and specifically with its Jews. It suggested that such works contributed to the formation of a new visual language connected with a desire on the part of Iberian Christians to distinguish themselves from these Others as they rose to newly expanded authority, as well as with an urge to identify their own culture, broadly speaking, with that of Latin Christendom outside the peninsula. This process relied on both the cultivation of affinities with Europe north of the Pyrenees and the demarcation of a "normative" Ibero-Christian culture from those of both Jews and Muslims.

One consequence of these developments, as we have seen, was an increasing exposure to cultural forms originating outside of Iberia and especially in northern Europe. The wealth of unfamiliar images, *topoi,* and patterns of thought that flooded into the northern kingdoms as its orientation shifted more decisively toward Europe north of the Pyrenees helped to shape a new visual lexicon that equipped Iberian Christians to reconceive and articulate their own relationships with the Jews of their kingdoms and local communities. This process was both selective and adaptive, and one in which both artists and patrons took an unexpectedly active role: very few of the visual or conceptual formulae that were imported from lands beyond Iberia were adopted wholesale or survived unchanged. Whereas certain types of images, especially those that evoked familiar polemical flashpoints such as the question of Jewish deicide, did gain relatively rapid acceptance into Iberian visual culture, most imagery became subject to modifications aimed at adapting them to a local context and viewership. The widespread preference for the Iberian hooded cloak as a *prima facie* Jewish sign represents one such case of local preference trumping foreign practice; others include the introduction of Andalusi textile patterns to Iberian images of Synagoga and the portraitlike softening of the Jewish stereotype in Alfonso X's *Libro de ajedrez, dados y tablas.* The most decisive expression of Iberian selectivity, however, was the total or near-total rejection of those European *topoi* for which an ideological foundation did not yet exist in Iberia during this period: the Jew as child murderer or the Jew as desecrator of the host.

Certainly not all of the visual forms deployed in Iberian depictions of Jews were imported, and those created locally display an inventiveness that shaded easily into outright idiosyncrasy. The modest Barcelona Passion beam, in which the role of the Jewish priests who bribed Judas is performed by figures with the dark skin and head scarves traditionally linked with Muslims, represents this phenomenon at its height; related blendings of Muslim and Jewish signifiers in a wide range of other Iberian objects as well as in literature and law suggest that linking the two non-Christian faiths as a practice extended among all Iberian social strata. In such cases, the endowment of Jewish figures with the costumes, textiles, and ornament more often assigned to their Muslim compatriots functioned multifariously by tying Iberia's Jews assertively, if illogically, with the Muslims who posed the Christian kingdoms' most powerful existential threat. At the same time, such figures reinforced the new dichotomy of Christian versus nonbeliever upon which the former's self-identity had come to depend.

The willingness of Iberian artists to select, modify, and reject what must have been perceived as fairly rigid European formulae attests not only to their own dynamic approach to image-making, but also to enduring differences between the Jewish-Christian relationship in Iberia and that elsewhere in western Christendom. As comparatively new arrivals to many parts of medieval Europe, especially in the north, Jews in many areas never achieved the degree of social integration that Iberian Jews had enjoyed for centuries. By the early thirteenth century, the Jews' small numbers and relative segregation in France, England, and the German states facilitated the imposition of even more isolating legal and social restrictions that, as we have seen, met with resistance in much of Iberia for a century or more. The relatively unambiguous sense of Jewish difference that such decisive segregation had made possible in the European north seems likewise to have been delayed in penetrating the Iberian kingdoms.

The social and religious preoccupations reflected in the works that this study has examined were not held universally by Christians in Iberia, for the anxieties, goals, and even visual traditions proper to Spain's multiple Christian kingdoms still could vary significantly from one region to the next. Although the phrase "Christian Iberia" has functioned expediently here as a catchall for Spain's northern Christian communities, by now it should be clear that the disunified cluster of polities encompassed by this designation was anything but a uniform cultural entity. The political, historical, ethnic, linguistic, and other lines that had separated and even mutually alienated the northern kingdoms of Spain since their emergence in the ninth and tenth centuries continued to differentiate them during the central and late Middle Ages, and this extended into visual culture as well. Aragonese concerns about the deep engagement of Jews in society and commerce, and especially in the money trade, which emerged more suddenly and more powerfully there than in neighboring Castile, found expression in the testy vignettes of the *Vidal mayor* and the outright vitriol of the scribal drawings on the *libri iudeorum.* The relatively direct exposure of the Aragonese Crown to the culture of southern France likely facilitated this, just as it facilitated the absorption there of less concretely grounded fears concerning Jewish heresy and violence.

In Castile, where the role of Jews remained more varied and also, one might argue, more critical to the economic and administrative success of the kingdom's enormously expanded territories, the depiction of Jews remained comparatively conservative, tending to emphasize theological concerns rather than social ones. Moreover, the stereotypes most common in Castile, such as the Jew who constructs the young martyrs' tomb on the Ávila cenotaph, the Jew who disputes with Ildefonsus, or the elegantly garbed Synagoga, are also those who remained implicitly susceptible to enlightenment and conversion. The significant exception to this Castilian tendency, as we have seen, is the *Cantigas de Santa María,* a far more international work which drew on anti-Jewish *topoi* that otherwise would remain absent from the larger Castilian picture for at least another half century. The exceptional products of an exceptional court, the *Cantigas de Santa María* illustrations represent a kind of complexity that would enjoy surprisingly little afterlife.

The adoption, invention, and reception of imagery that addressed the Jewish-Christian relationship were also affected by context: artistic choices made by individual patrons, makers, and viewers could be altered by any number of factors: a sudden change in a community's local cultural relationships, as occurred in late twelfth-century Tudela; the availability of iconographic models that dovetailed compellingly with current events, as in the Vic Bible; or the imposition of a forceful new cultural vocabulary, such as that afforded by Alfonso X to his prolific scriptorium. All this remained consistent with the high degree of flux in which so many Iberian communities found themselves during this period, and it reinforces the importance of giving such works the most individualized consideration possible.

The study undertaken here is intended as a beginning rather than an end, a suggestion of the rich potential of Iberian visual culture to deepen modern understanding of the religious and cultural relationships that lay behind the making of such imagery. It is also intended to argue for the value of expanding the study of such relationships to include this visual evidence. Many works that have been considered here contribute important new voices from Spain's past that could not always be clearly discerned in charters and chronicles. The xenophobic militancy of Tudela's monks, the resentment of the Catalan notaries charged with tracking the dealings of Jewish financiers, and the ambivalence of ethnic and religious dealings in Alfonso X's multicultural court resound more clearly when historians are receptive to the full panoply of evidence that medieval culture lays open to us. Such voices are bound to complement, if also to contradict, the conclusions drawn through other forms of historical study, and they promise a fresh perspective on traditionally broad historical questions.

To take full advantage of this visual evidence requires an attentive and measured approach, one that moves beyond the concern with style, patronage, and regional origin that has so strongly colored the field of medieval Iberian art history. Moreover, as a work to which the study of another traditional disciplinary method, that of iconography, remains central, this book has argued for greater delicacy in assessing and interpreting medieval imagery as it functioned within its broad and often complex cultural frame. The images studied here are not the hidebound imitation of older forms nor the mere visual translation of authoritative texts, but neither are they *ex nihilo* inventions. They are the imaginative, perceptive, unpredictable, and above all independent result of their creators' drive to adapt visual prototypes, for which they preserved unshaken respect, to the protean network of ideas, experience, and expectations—what Clifford Geertz might call the "web of significance"—that surrounded each.[1]

This recognition frees art historians, as well as scholars in other disciplines, to recognize and explore the implications of such images' constructed character, their highly varied reception, and their potential to function multivalently. Although many of the images studied here furnish important information about the workings of daily life—what tools might be used in constructing a church, or how altars were decorated—they rarely yield comparably concrete evidence of how Jews, Christians, and Muslims actually interacted in the period in question. As manipulated visions of medieval life, they reveal far more about the desires or objectives of their makers than they do about what "really" happened. Since their creation was controlled by only one of these three medieval Iberian constituencies, there is no logic in expecting otherwise. If, as Winston Churchill is said to have claimed, history is written by the victors, then it is also depicted by them, and the images examined here served to concretize the Ibero-Christian victors' idealized vision of society, one in which subordinate communities played the roles, and fulfilled the expectations, that most effectively served them.

All this can only facilitate an understanding of how the works discussed here relate to the larger story of Jewish-Christian relations in Latin Christendom as a whole. Spain's historical and cultural distinctiveness within medieval Europe has long shaped modern understanding of its past, and perhaps rightly so. The 1960s-era tourism slogan "Spain is different" succeeded precisely because it got at the heart of an idea that was crucial to that nation's history and self-understanding. Yet overemphasis of this difference easily disguises the many links that bound medieval Iberia to other parts of the medieval world—links that have emerged persistently in the chapters of this book, exposing the delicate cultural machinery by which community and religious identity were created, both within medieval Iberia and within Europe as a whole.

NOTES

Chapter 1

1. "Venié un judïezno, natural del logar, / por savor de los ninnos, por con ellos jogar; / acogiénlo los otros, no li fazién pesar, / avién con elli todos savor de deportar." Berceo, *Los milagros de Nuestra Señora,* 129. For the English, see Berceo, *Miracles of Our Lady,* 77.

2. This audience likely included both monks and lay listeners, most likely pilgrims. See Flory, *Marian Representations,* 24–46.

3. Lourie, "Cultic Dancing and Courtly Love"; see also Ray, *Sephardic Frontier.*

4. Perarnau i Espelt, "Els quatre sermons catalans de sant Vicent Ferrer." The epigram at the beginning of the chapter ("nunqua sera bon christià lo qui és vehí del juheu" in the original) appears on 232.

5. See esp. Meyerson, *Jews in an Iberian Frontier Kingdom.*

6. Nirenberg, "Enmity and Assimilation," 142–45.

7. As early as 1252, the Aragonese ecclesiastic and chancellor Vidal de Canellas characterized Christian hostility to both Jews and Muslims as so powerful that only the king's protection prevented their total massacre. See Lourie, "Anatomy of Ambivalence," 77.

8. Influential examples include Camille, *Gothic Idol;* Mellinkoff, *Outcasts;* Weber, "Di Entwicklung des Judenbildes"; Schreckenberg, *Jews in Christian Art;* Lipton, *Images of Intolerance;* Frojmovic, *Imagining the Self, Imagining the Other;* Strickland, *Saracens, Demons, and Jews;* Merback, *Beyond the Yellow Badge;* and Kessler and Nirenberg, *Judaism and Christian Art.* Sources on Iberia in particular will be discussed below.

9. García Morencos, *Libro de ajedrez, dados y tablas;* and Alfonso X, *Libro de ajedrez, dados y tablas.* For the social context of the manuscript, see Constable, "Chess and Courtly Culture."

10. Constable, "Chess and Courtly Culture," 335–41.

11. A distinction made effectively by Molina Filgueiras, "Las imágenes del judío," 374–76.

12. Constable, "Chess and Courtly Culture," 343–47. On the other hand, Constable notes that in the illustrations of games between Christians and Jews, Christians nearly always are depicted as winning, suggesting a desire to preserve social hierarchy despite the scenes' apparent egalitarianism.

13. For the text, see Ermengaud, *Le Breviari d'amor;* see also Ricketts, "Hispanic Tradition." On Jews in the *Breviari d'amor,* see Blumenkranz, "Ecriture et image"; Miranda García, "Consideraciones sobre el judío y el hereje"; Rodríguez Barral, *La imagen del judío,* 38–49.

14. Miranda García, "Consideraciones sobre el judío y el hereje"; see also Blumenkranz, "Ecriture et image"; and Rodríguez Barral, *La imagen del judío,* 38–49.

15. Peter the Venerable, *Adversus iudaeorum inveteratam duritiem,* I CCCM 58:10, quoted in Cohen, *Living Letters of the Law,* 255. Peter here echoes Augustine's use of Romans 11.8 in his *Tractatus adversus judaeos:* "God has given them a spirit of stupor; eyes that they may not see, and ears that they may not hear, until this present day." Augustine, *Treatises on Marriage,* 413.

16. As most famously explored by Trachtenberg, *Devil and the Jews;* for more, see esp. chap. 2.

17. James F. O'Callaghan offers substantial evidence that by the twelfth century at the latest, Christians in medieval Iberia perceived their efforts to conquer Muslim lands as a reconquest of lands originally their own. My use of the term throughout this book acknowledges this paradigm, which is central to the dynamics of image-making under discussion here. See O'Callaghan, *Reconquest and Crusade,* 3–22; and González Jiménez, "¿Re-Conquista?"

18. An approach exemplified by Meyerson, *Jews in an Iberian Frontier Kingdom.*

19. Nirenberg, *Communities of Violence,* 8–10.

20. Castro, *España en su historia,* esp. 206–14. On the afterlife of Castro's concept, see Glick, "Convivencia"; Ray, "Beyond Tolerance and Persecution"; and Wolf, "*Convivencia* in Medieval Spain."

21. On the importance of specific context to social relations in Iberia, see Ruiz, *Spain's Centuries of Crisis,* 139–45.

22. An especially ambitious example of such work is Robinson and Rouhi, *Under the Influence.*

23. In this, I follow James D. Herbert's definition of visual culture as including "all human products with a pronounced visual aspect—including those that do not, as a matter of social practice, carry the imprimatur of art." Herbert, "Visual Culture / Visual Studies," 452.

24. See O'Callaghan, *Reconquest and Crusade,* 50–123.

25. The classic source for the history of Jews in the Christian kingdoms is Baer, *History of the Jews in Christian Spain.* More recent and specialized literature will be cited as relevant below.

26. Ray, *Sephardic Frontier,* 15–35.

27. Blumenkranz, *Le juif medieval au miroir de l'art chrétien.*

28. Cohen, *Living Letters of the Law;* for the impact of this trend on the visual, see Lipton, "Unfeigned Witness."

29. See, for example, Dodds, *Architecture and Ideology;* Ruggles, "Representation and Identity"; Robinson, *In Praise of Song;* Ecker, "How to Administer a Conquered City"; Feliciano, "Muslim Shrouds for Christian Kings?"

30. See esp. such exhibition catalogues as Mann, Glick, and Dodds, *Convivencia;* Bango Torviso, *Memoria de Sefarad;* and Mann, *Uneasy Communion.* Like other and less wide-ranging exhibitions, these focused primarily on the potential of visual culture to document actual aspects of medieval Jewish life, with more limited attention to their relationship to Christian ideology.

31. E.g., Kogman-Appel, *Jewish Book Art;* Kogman-Appel, *Illuminated Haggadot;* and Dodds, "Mudejar Tradition and the Synagogues."

32. Such broadly framed works are to be commended nonetheless for making available previously little known material; they include Alcoy i Pedros, "Canvis i oscil·lacions"; Molina Filgueiras, "Las imágenes del judío"; Molina Filgueiras, "La imagen y su contexto"; Espí Forcén, *Recrucificando a Cristo;* and Rodríguez Barral, *La imagen del judío.*

33. Cohen, *Living Letters of the Law,* 2–3.

34. On this phenomenon in other disciplines, see esp. Bale, *Jew in the Medieval Book;* Kruger, *Spectral Jew,* esp. xvii–xxiii; and Dangler, *Making Difference in Medieval and Early Modern Iberia.*

35. Ruiz, *Spain's Centuries of Crisis,* 28–50; Nirenberg, *Communities of Violence,* 231–49.

36. The following summary is especially indebted to the account by O'Callaghan, *Reconquest and Crusade,* esp. 23–123. For a broad treatment of the later Middle Ages, see also Hillgarth, *Spanish Kingdoms, 1250–1516.*

37. Glick, *Islamic and Christian Spain,* 168–78.

38. O'Callaghan, *History of Medieval Spain,* 336.

39. On Burgos, see Sánchez Ameijeiras, "Church Reform." For arguments about the appeal of the Gothic style for Alfonso X in particular, see Cómez Ramos, *Arquitectura Alfonsí,* and Crites, "Churches Made Fit for a King."

40. Cowdrey, *Cluniacs and the Gregorian Reform,* 214–47; Williams, "Cluny and Spain"; Campo del Pozo, "El monacato de San Agustín en España"; Linaje Conde, "Vida canonical en la 'Repoblación' de la Península Ibérica?" For Cluny's impact on visual culture, see Mann, *Romanesque Architecture.*

41. As famously formulated by Porter, *Romanesque Sculpture of the Pilgrimage Roads;* for an accessible synthesis, see Moralejo Álvarez, "On the Road."

42. On the preaching orders in Spain, see Webster, *Els Menorets;* García Serrano, *Preachers of the City;* and Vose, *Dominicans, Muslims, and Jews.*

43. See Moore, *Formation of a Persecuting Society,* but note the modification of his arguments regarding Jews in the 2007 edition, 167–69. On the centrality of the Cluniac Order in the development of such thinking, see Iogna-Prat, *Order and Exclusion.*

44. Moore, *Formation of a Persecuting Society,* 6–11.

45. Nirenberg, *Communities of Violence,* rightly cautions against an overly teleological view of this phenomenon, and this caution is especially warranted in Spain. However, the significant increase in episodes of violence toward and polemics against religious minorities during the twelfth and thirteenth centuries in Spain cannot be overlooked.

46. Cohen, *Living Letters of the Law,* esp. 147–312.

47. Trends well summarized by Hsia, *Myth of Ritual Murder;* see also Rubin, *Gentile Tales.*

48. Schroeder, *Disciplinary Decrees of the General Councils,* 236–96; for Canon 68, which mandates distinguishing dress, see 290–91.

49. See, e.g., Cohen, *Friars and the Jews;* Chazan, *Daggers of Faith;* and Chazan, *Barcelona and Beyond.*

50. Baer, *History of the Jews in Christian Spain,* 2:424–43.

51. On the 1096 attacks, see Chazan, *European Jewry and the First Crusade;* on ritual murder, see Langmuir, "Historiographic Crucifixion"; and McCulloch, "Jewish Ritual Murder."

52. Trachtenberg, *Devil and the Jews;* Bonfil, "Devil and the Jews"; additional sources will be cited as relevant below.

53. Ray, *Sephardic Frontier,* 156–64.

54. Baer, *History of the Jews in Christian Spain,* 1:78–90; Ray, *Sephardic Frontier,* 36–71.

55. N. Roth, "Jewish Collaborators."

56. On the incident at Las Navas de Tolosa, see O'Callaghan, *Reconquest and Crusade,* 70; see also Flórez et al., *España sagrada,* 23:396–97.

57. Nirenberg, *Communities of Violence,* 231–49. On the impact of the plague on Jewish communities generally, see Cohn, "Black Death."

58. Ruiz, *Spain's Centuries of Crisis,* 72–85.

59. On the foreign roots of many aspects of Iberian anti-Judaism, see Monsalvo Antón, "Mentalidad antijudía en la Castilla medieval."

60. For an exemplary recent study of such issues, see Brann, *Power in the Portrayal.*

61. Solomon Alami, *Igeret Musar* (Epistle on Morality), quoted in Baer, *History of the Jews in Christian Spain,* 2:240.

Chapter 2

1. See esp. Blumenkranz, *Le juif medieval au miroir de l'art chrétien,* 15–39; Strickland, *Saracens, Demons, and Jews,* 95–155; Klein, "'Jud, dir kuckt der Spitzbub'"; and Lipton, "Jew's Face."

2. Lipton, "Jew's Face," 262.

3. As discussed especially by Lipton, *Images of Intolerance.*

4. Ibid., 20–21; Strickland, *Saracens, Demons, and Jews,* 105–7; Molina Filgueiras, "La imagen y su contexto," 76–77.

5. See Baert, "New Observations."

6. Sansy, "Chapeau juif ou chapeau pointu?" See also Yarza Luaces, "Del alfaquí sabio."

7. See, e.g., Lipton, *Images of Intolerance,* 18–19.

8. Rico Camps, "Shrine in Its Setting"; and Goldschmidt, "Sepulcro de San Vicente, en Avila."

9. Hymn V (*Passio Sancti Vincenti martyris*); see Prudentius, 2:169–203; and Ferrer García, "El santo y la serpiente," esp. 16–20.

10. Angel Fábrega Grau deduces that this episode had become attached to the saints' legend in the late seventh century, before it emerged as part of the so-called *Pasionario Hispánico* in the tenth century. See Fábrega Grau, *Pasionario Hispánico,* 1:166–67 and 2:358–63; the passage concerning the Jew appears in 2:363.

11. Ibid., 1:166; Ferrer García, "El santo y la serpiente," 41.

12. Rico Camps, "Shrine in Its Setting," 58; the implements held by the Jew are identified in Moralejo Álvarez, "Artistas, patronos y público."

13. Ferrer García, "El santo y la serpiente," 33; Rico Camps, "Shrine in Its Setting," 63.

14. See Vila da Vila, "La iconografía de San Vicente." Ferrer García reports a local legend that recounts how a rich Jew joined the saints' torturers merely because he enjoyed seeing them suffer ("El santo y la serpiente," 33–39 and 41).

15. Cohen, "Jews as Killers of Christ"; and Cohen, *Christ Killers,* esp. 73–92.

16. León Tello, *Judíos de Ávila,* 5–7.

17. Ibid.; Baer, *History of the Jews in Christian Spain,* 1:107–8, 277–81, and 292. On Abraham of Avila, see Sharot, "Jewish Millenarianism," 397.

18. Ray, *Sephardic Frontier,* 18–35.

19. A similar argument is made by Ferrer García, "El santo y la serpiente," 42–45.

20. Schroeder, *Disciplinary Decrees of the General Councils,* 290–91.

21. Kisch, "Yellow Badge in History"; Robert, "Étude historique et archéologique I" and "Étude historique et archéologique II"; and Wisch, "Vested Interest," 146–48.

22. See Ray, *Sephardic Frontier,* 157.

23. As in Tarragona in 1263; see Sánchez Real, "La judería de Tarragona," 341.

24. Assis, *Golden Age of Spanish Jewry,* 283–84.

25. Linehan, *Spain, 1157–1300,* 87; Chazan, *Church, State, and Jew,* 179–80.

26. The section of the *Siete partidas* related to Jews has been published by Carpenter, *Alfonso X and the Jews;* the passages concerned with distinguishing dress are also cited in Chazan, *Church, State, and Jew,* 195.

27. Nirenberg, "Conversion, Sex, and Segregation," 1081n54.

28. Sobrequés i Callicó, *Llibre verd de Barcelona.*

29. Yarza Luaces, "La il·lustració," 2:297–98.

30. Blasco Martínez, "Jaime I y los judíos de Aragón," 103–9; Assis, *Jewish Economy in the Medieval Crown of Aragon,* 15–27.

31. See Sánchez Real, "La judería de Tarragona," pl. 1, and Coll i Rosell, "Les pintures murals."

32. Coll i Rosell, "Les pintures murals," 254–55.

33. Sánchez Real, "La judería de Tarragona," 342, and Sánchez Real, "Los judíos de Tarragona."

34. The low-vamped shoes appear to be an approximation of Islamic footwear also worn by Jews in Spain: see Menéndez Pidal and Bernis, "Las Cantigas," esp. 150.

35. On the cloak as an actual Jewish marker in Iberia, see Assis, *Golden Age of Spanish Jewry,* 283–85; Alcoy i Pedros, "Canvis i oscil·lacions," 373; Cantera Montenegro, *Aspectos de la vida cotidiana,* 132–36; and Ray, *Sephardic Frontier,* 156–58. By 1302, the cloak was also required in Mallorca; see Delcor, "Les juifs de Puigcerdà," 21–23.

36. On the decoration of Usatges manuscripts in the fourteenth century, see Coll i Rosell, *Manuscrits juridics i il·luminació;* for the text, see Kagay, *Usatges de Barcelona.*

37. This copy is now bound together with two compilations of the Constitutions of Catalunya; the relevant folios are 67–240. On the date and general decoration, see Coll i Rosell, *Manuscrits juridics i il·luminació,* 19–43; see also Avril et al., *Manuscrits enluminés,* cat. 105, 90–91.

38. E.g., fol. 200v, in which such an image accompanies the heading "quod carta usure judeorum non habeat valorem a vi annis in antea"; see Blumenkranz, *Le juif medieval au miroir de l'art chrétien,* 31–32; and Kagay, *Usatges de Barcelona,* 81. Similar marginalia are found on 104v, 118r, 215r, 220v, 225v, and 229v.

39. Cohen, *Living Letters of the Law,* 372–75.

40. Parker, "Editing the Cloisters Cross," 149–55.

41. Tolan, *Petrus Alfonsi.*

42. Cohen, *Friars and the Jews,* 145; Cohen, "Jews as Killers of Christ," 21–27.

43. Ramon Martí, *Pugio Fidei,* cited in Cohen, *Friars and the Jews,* 143.

44. For these narratives, see Rodríguez Barral, *La imagen del judío,* 96–109.

45. Patton, "Cloister as Cultural Mirror," 319–25.

46. For a translation of the document, here dated incorrectly to 1115, see Chazan, *Church, State, and Jew,* 19–20; see also Patton, "Cloister as Cultural Mirror," 317.

47. Patton, "Cloister as Cultural Mirror," 330.

48. "Non deve null'ome desto per ren dultar que Deus ena Virgen èo carne fillar" ("No man should doubt in any way that God took on human flesh in the Virgin"). Numbering of the *cantigas* throughout the present work follows the critical edition by Walter Mettmann: Alfonso X, *Cantigas de Santa María;* for Cantiga 50, see 1:144–45, as well as the English translation in Kulp-Hill, *Songs of Holy Mary,* 66.

49. Early Jewish objections to the Incarnation appear, for example, in *The Polemic of Nestor the Priest,* which is based on a ninth-century Arabic source; see Lasker and Stroumsa, *Polemic of Nestor the Priest,* 1:57–58, secs. 30–32. The Christian response to this concern is discussed by Abulafia, "Bodies in the Jewish-Christian Debate," 123–26.

50. "[E] quis ena Virgen por nos carne prender, e leixou-[ss]' encima, demais, por nos matar." Cantiga 50, lines 23–24; Alfonso X, *Cantigas de Santa María* (ed. Mettmann), 1:144. A similar scene appears in the illustration to Cantiga 140, discussed below.

51. Moore, *Formation of a Persecuting Society;* see also Cohen, *Living Letters of the Law,* 157–59 and 317–63.

52. On the Dominican concern with Jews in general see Cohen, *Friars and the Jews,* 103–69. For Spain in the relevant centuries see García Serrano, *Preachers of the City;* and Vose, *Dominicans, Muslims, and Jews.*

53. Chazan, *Church, State, and Jew,* 38.

54. Cohen, *Friars and the Jews,* 104–8; see also Tolan, *Saracens,* 234–35. Robin Vose (*Dominicans, Muslims, and Jews*) has argued that conversion of Jews and Muslims was less significant to the broad Dominican agenda than has been thought. However, it seems equally clear that this was a goal of certain individual Dominicans influential in Spain, such as Ramon de Penyafort and Ramon Martí.

55. Summarized in Cohen, *Friars and the Jews,* 108–22; for more extensive analysis, see Chazan, *Barcelona and Beyond,* 1–79; and Maccoby, *Judaism on Trial,* 39–75.

56. Cohen, *Friars and the Jews,* 108.

57. Ibid., 118–22.

58. See Abulafia, *Christians and Jews in Dispute,* and Chazan, *Daggers of Faith.* In Iberia, private disputations seem to have offered a common alternative: see Shalom, "Between Official and Private Dispute."

59. Raizman, "Rediscovered Illuminated Manuscript"; and Blasco García, *San Ildefonso, De Virginitate Beatae Mariae,* 74–80.

60. Raizman, "Rediscovered Illuminated Manuscript," 44; and Schapiro, *Parma Ildefonsus,* esp. figs. 4–6.

61. Kupfer, ". . . lectres . . . plus vrayes"; Camille, "Devil's Writing," 356.

62. Blumenkranz, *Le juif medieval au miroir de l'art chrétien,* 30–31, figs. 20 and 21. On the manuscript itself, see Warner, *Descriptive Catalogue,* 1:262–65 and 2: pls. XCV, XCVI, XCVII; see also Watson, *Catalogue of Dated and Datable Manuscripts,* 1:no. 422 and 2:pl. 164; Domínguez Bordona, *Diccionario de iluminadores españoles,* 98; Gudiol i Cunill and Sanpere i Miquel, *La pintura mig-eval catalana,* 1:56. The colophon reads, "Mille. ducentenis, tredecim triginta bis annis. Post carnem domini sumptam de uirgine uerbi. Canonicus dictusque iohannes poncii ego. uictus hanc . . . domino bibliam prece scripsi. hinc ubi uita manet Û scriptor cum presule regnet."

63. On other products of the Vic scriptorium, see Escandell Proust, "La Biblia de 1268"; and Junyent, "Le scriptorium de la cathedrale de Vich." Another Bible apparently originating in Vic is now in the Schøyen Collection as MS 262; to my knowledge, it is not yet published. On the association of such Bibles with mendicants, see De Hamel, *The Book,* 131–39.

64. This initial, on fol. 329v, depicts a hooded figure with prominent nose standing behind a cleric in a doctor's cap, who holds up a book inscribed "Joelis prophe[tas]."

65. Abelard, *Dialogue of a Philosopher;* Petrus Alfonsi, *Dialogue Against the Jews;* for Ramon Llull's *Book of the Gentile and the Three Wise Men,* see Ramon Llull, *Doctor Illuminatus,* 73–171.

66. Baer, *History of the Jews in Christian Spain,* 1:142.

67. Llop i Jordana, "Jewish Moneylenders"; see also Ollich i Castanyer, "Aspectes economics."

68. Ollich i Castanyer, "Un nou document"; Llop i Jordana, "Aportacions"; Corbella i Llobet, *L'aljama de jueus de Vic,* 11; see also Baer, *History of the Jews in Christian Spain,* 1:422.

69. Ollich i Castanyer, "Un nou document," 267. References to a synagogue in documents from 1280 onward suggest that construction went on as planned.

70. Corbella i Llobet, *L'aljama de jueus de Vic.*

71. The initial foundation is dated 1571 by Aldea Vaquero et al., *Diccionario* 4:2752; see also Ollich i Castanyer, "Les entitats eclesiàstiques de Vic."

72. Vose, *Dominicans, Muslims, and Jews,* 71–74; Moncada, *Episcopologio de Vich,* 2:1–64.

73. Norris, "Early Gothic Illuminated Bibles at Bologna."

74. Translation from Cohen, *Living Letters of the Law,* 337; see also Shatzmiller, *La deuxième controverse de Paris,* 44.

75. Of the extensive literature on this topic, see esp. Seiferth, *Synagogue and Church in the Middle Ages;* Blumenkranz, "Géographie historique"; Jochum, *Ecclesia und Synagoga;* Lipton, "Temple Is My Body"; and Rowe, *The Jew, the Cathedral, and the Medieval City.*

76. Rowe, *The Jews, the Cathedral, and the Medieval City,* 191–237.

77. Miquel i Rosell, *Cataleg dels llibres manuscrits,* 45–47; see also Bohigas, *La ilustración y la decoración,* 2:62–66.

78. As in a missal from Houghton Library, MS Typ-120; see Parker and Little, *Cloisters Cross,* 112. Blumenkranz includes several examples from missals and pontificals ("Géographie historique," 1148). See also Leroquais, *Les sacramentaires et les missels manuscrits,* 1:xxxiii–xxxiv and xxxix.

79. The pair was in the collection of Francisco Godia; upon his death, the Synagoga figure remained in the family's private collection while Ecclesia was placed in the Godia Foundation. Also associated with the pair are figures of Joseph of Arimathea, Nicodemus, the Magdalen, the risen Christ, and two angels. See Garabito Gregorio, "Escultura castellano-leonesa en la Colección Godia," 66 and 70; Godia and Godia Guardiola, *Románico y Gótico de la colección Francisco Godia,* 84–85; and Monreal Agustí, *El Conventet II: Colección de escultura,* 177.

80. As also suggested by Rodríguez Barral, *La imagen del judío,* 23.

81. Less indigenous in character are the jamb figures of Ecclesia and Synagoga on the "Portal of the Refectory" in the cloister of Pamplona Cathedral, produced ca. 1335. Like the Godia figures, they are juxtaposed with Passion scenes, in this case the Entry into Jerusalem and the Last Supper on the tympanum. See García Gainza et al., *Catálogo monumental de Navarra,* 5:49, pls. 38–59; Ansoleaga, "Claustro de la Catedral de Pamplona," 44; and Rodríguez Barral, *La imagen del judío,* 34–35.

82. Bucher, *Pamplona Bibles,* 1:15–26.

83. Bard, *Navarra, the Durable Kingdom,* 59–69.

84. The colophon of the Amiens codex gives a completion date of 1197 and names Sancho VII as patron. The related manuscript now in Augsburg (Universitätsbibliothek, MS Cod. I.2.4°.15, formerly Oettingen-Wallerstein Collection, Harburg) is thought to have been copied directly from it shortly thereafter. Bucher, *Pamplona Bibles,* 1:9 and 38–40.

85. "YSAIAS PRECINIT SYNAGOGA MEMINIT NUMQUAM TAMEN DESINIT ESSE CECA. SYNAGOGAM MUTAT ECCLESIA." Bucher, *Pamplona Bibles,* 1:259.

86. See esp. Kisch, "Yellow Badge in History," 118–19; and Petzold, "'Of the Significance of Colors,'" 131–33.

87. Bucher, *Pamplona Bibles,* 1:259.

88. Seiferth, *Synagogue and Church in the Middle Ages,* 143–44; Blumenkranz, "Géographie historique," 1149. Bucher (*Pamplona Bibles,* 1:96), and Rodríguez Barral (*Imagen del judío,* 22–23) both suggest French comparanda, but these are substantially later in date than the Pamplona image.

89. Ricketts, "Hispanic Tradition." See also Bolduc, "Breviari d'amor"; Rodríguez Barral, *La imagen del judío,* 38–39.

90. Ten Iberian examples are known, five of which are illuminated. The only dated example is Saint Petersburg, M.E. Saltykov-Shchedrin, Gos. Bibl., ms., esp. F.v. XIV I (formerly Hermitage 5, 3, 66), produced in Lléida ca. 1320. The others are Paris, BnF MS, esp. 353, and MS, esp. 205; London, Yates Thompson MS 31; and Madrid, BNE, MS Res. 203. On the illustration cycle generally, see Laske-Fix, *Der Bildzyklus de Breviari d'amor.* If Ricketts is correct that the Catalan texts were all based on a single Provençal source, this might explain the consistency of the illustrations among the group (Ricketts, "Hispanic Tradition," 252–53).

91. In some examples, adjacent inscriptions characterize this as illustrating the simultaneous victory of Christ over the devil and of Church over Synagogue; see Ricketts, "Hispanic Tradition," 230. On the image generally, see also Rodríguez Barral, *La imagen del judío,* 39–41.

92. A similar ring is worn by several Jewish women on a continuous pier capital in the cloister of Barcelona Cathedral; see *La vida judía en Sefarad,* 60.

93. For a broad view, see Le Goff, *Your Money or Your Life,* 9–45; Little, *Religious Poverty,* 1–41.

94. Bernard of Clairvaux, Letter 363, as cited in Cohen, *Living Letters of the Law,* 236. On the role of Jews in moneylending generally during this period, see Little, *Religious Poverty,* 42–58; and Chazan, *Reassessing Jewish Life,* 112–28.

95. Felsenstein, *Anti-Semitic Stereotypes,* 27–29; Camille, *Gothic Idol,* 182–85; and C. Roth, "Portraits and Caricatures." See also the thoughtful handling of the topic by Bradbury, "Imaging and Imagining the Jew," 68–76.

96. C. Roth, "Portraits and Caricatures," 22–23; and Felsenstein, *Anti-Semitic Stereotypes,* 27–29.

97. On the link between money and idolatry, see Lipton, *Images of Intolerance,* 40–43. On the appearance and associations of Antichrist, see Emmerson, *Antichrist in the Middle Ages,* 116; and Trachtenberg, *Devil and the Jews,* 32–43.

98. For Aragon, see Assis, *Jewish Economy in the Medieval Crown of Aragon,* 15–27; for Castile, see Ruiz, *From Heaven to Earth,* 16–24.

99. Patton, *Pictorial Narrative,* 172.

100. Jacobus de Voragine, *Golden Legend,* 1:25; see also Harris, "Performative Terms," 128–29.

101. For Nicholas imagery in France, see Harris, "Performative Terms." Nicholas was a relative latecomer to Spain, but his cult at Tarragona was fostered by Alfonso II; see Liaño Martínez, "Elementos de orígen islámico," 144.

102. Assis, *Golden Age of Spanish Jewry,* 10–12.

103. Avril et al., *Manuscrits enluminés,* 86 (cat. 102). The image introduces book 10 of the Codex Justinianus (fol. 89r).

104. Lacarra Ducay, "Las miniaturas del *Vidal mayor*"; see also Kauffmann, "Ein spanisches Gesetzbuch."

105. The layout of the illuminations and their relation to other juridical manuscripts is discussed by Grautoff, "*Vidal mayor.*"

106. The illustration is frequently illustrated but rarely discussed in depth; however, see the entry on this manuscript in Mann, Glick, and Dodds, *Convivencia,* 194–95.

107. Lipton, *Images of Intolerance,* 32–34.

108. "Por end es que la devotion de los cristianos es de non fazer usuras, et començo de crescer la avaritia et la cupiditia de los judíos, que non se puede fartar, que d'aquiellos cristianos qui reciben empriesto d'eillos demandan usuras de las usuras contra todo atempramiento et contra el nuestro establimiento que ya a tiempo fizimos." Bk. V, chap. 18; see Tilander, *Vidal mayor,* 2:344 (translation mine).

109. On this phenomenon in Gothic manuscripts generally, see Camille, *Image on the Edge,* 11–55.

110. The episcopal archive at Vic contains 26 such books, still not fully published; see Llop i Jordana, "Aportacions," 144; see also Llop i Jordana, "Jewish Moneylenders"; and Ollich i Castanyer, "Aspectes economics," 4–6.

111. Bango Torviso, *Memoria de Sefarad,* 381, no. 234.

112. Llop i Jordana, "Jewish Moneylenders," 78–79.

113. Ibid., 77; Corbella i Llobet, *L'aljama de jueus de Vic,* 47–49, 65–78, and 105–18.

114. Monsalvo Antón, "Mentalidad antijudía en la Castilla medieval," esp. 40–47.

115. Bk. V, chap. 21; Tilander, *Vidal mayor,* 2:352.

116. Langmuir, "Historiographic Crucifixion"; on the ritual murder charge in the Middle Ages and for additional literature, see Hsia, *Myth of Ritual Murder,* 1–5; and Trachtenberg, *Devil and the Jews,* 124–39.

117. Langmuir, "L'absence d'accusation de meurtre rituel," 235–42; Hsia, *Myth of Ritual Murder,* 2–3.

118. The foundation of this fabrication may be the more famous story of Hugh of Lincoln, an English boy allegedly murdered in 1255, with which Dominguito's narrative shares many details. See Despina, "Las acusaciones de Crimen Ritual en España," 66–70; Sánchez Usón, "El niño-mártir Dominguito de Val"; and Espí Forcén, "El corista de 'Engraterra.'" A more credulous approach to Dominguito's documentation is offered by Rincón García, "La devoción a San Dominguito de Val."

119. Baer records the first known Iberian claims as taking place in Zaragoza and Biel in 1294 (*History of the Jews in Christian Spain,* 2:6–7); see also Langmuir, "L'absence d'accusation de meurtre rituel," 245. Evidence of Jewish concern about such charges ca. 1300 has been analyzed by Lourie, "Plot Which Failed?" A possible predecessor to the full ritual murder charge was the claim, recorded in Andalusia in 1239, that Jews were kidnapping Christian boys and selling them to Muslims; see Ray, *Sephardic Frontier,* 162.

120. Carpenter, *Alfonso X and the Jews,* 29. On image desecration, see also Trachtenberg, *Devil and the Jews,* 121, and John of Garland, *Stella Maris,* 166.

121. Rubin, *Gentile Tales,* 40–43. See also Trachtenberg, *Devil and the Jews,* 109–23, and Schefer, *L'hostie profanée.*

122. Rubin, *Gentile Tales.*

123. Ibid., 155–57. For Iberian examples, see Melero Moneo, "Eucarístia y polémica antisemita"; Favà Monllau, "El retaule eucarístic de Vilafermosa"; and Rodríguez Barral, *La imagen del judío,* 171–214.

124. Baer, *History of the Jews in Christian Spain,* 2:89–91.

125. Discussed briefly by Rubin, *Gentile Tales,* 155–57; for more extensive and somewhat contradictory treatments of the narratives, see Melero Moneo, "Eucaristía y polémica antisemita," 23–35; and Rodríguez Barral, *La imagen del judío,* 174–95.

126. See Favà Monllau, "El retaule eucarístic de Vilafermosa"; and Rodríguez Barral, *La imagen del judío,* 197–215.

127. Rubin, *Gentile Tales,* 109–15.

Chapter 3

1. The literature is richer for the early modern and modern period than for the Middle Ages. For the former, influential studies include Fuchs, *Die Juden in der Karikatur;* Kisch, "Yellow Badge in History," 89–146; Trachtenberg, *Devil and the Jews,* 44–52; and Gilman, *Jew's Body.* On the Middle Ages, see esp. Schreckenberg, *Jews in Christian Art,* 303-40; C. Roth, "Portraits and Caricatures"; Mellinkoff, *Outcasts,* 1:127–30; Strickland, *Saracens, Demons, and Jews,* 105–7; Klein, "'Jud, dir kuckt der Spitzbub'"; and Lipton, "Jew's Face."

2. Strickland, *Saracens, Demons, and Jews,* 37–41.

3. See esp. the discussion by Abulafia, "Bodies in the Jewish-Christian Debate," 129–30.

4. Trachtenberg, *Devil and the Jews,* 44–52; Kruger, "Bodies of Jews"; Marcus, "Images of the Jews"; Resnick, "Medieval Roots." See also Biller, "Views of Jews."

5. Klein, "'Jud, dir kuckt der Spitzbub,'" 45–47.

6. On the mechanics of stereotypes, both generally and with regard to Jews, see Felsenstein, *Anti-Semitic Stereotypes,* 10–26. On the rarity of female Jewish stereotypes, see Lipton, "Where Are the Gothic Jewish Women?"

7. Strickland, *Saracens, Demons, and Jews,* 77–78.

8. Ibid., 96.

9. See Tomasch, "Postcolonial Chaucer and the Virtual Jew."

10. Jung, "The Passion, the Jews, and the Crisis of the Individual."

11. As noted, e.g., by Strickland, *Saracens, Demons, and Jews,* 97, and Lipton, *Images of Intolerance,* 20–21.

12. Merback, introduction to *Beyond the Yellow Badge,* 8–12.

13. Blumenkranz, *Le juif medieval au miroir de l'art chrétien,* 30–31.

14. In some works, this figure is replaced by a symbol of unction. See Branner, *Manuscript Painting in Paris,* 180; see also the concordance of imagery in several Iberian examples published in Avril et al., *Manuscrits enluminés,* 185.

15. Mellinkoff, *Outcasts,* 2:150; and Mellinkoff, *Mark of Cain,* 92–98.

16. Augustine, *Answer to Faustus,* 130–31.

17. Ps. 26:1–2; *Holie Bible* (Douay-Rheims version, 1609–10); spellings modernized.

18. Jacobus de Voragine, *Golden Legend,* 170–71. See also Espí Forcén, *Recrucificando a Cristo,* 38–43.

19. Langmuir, "L'absence d'accusation de meurtre rituel"; see also Rubin, *Gentile Tales,* 109–15.

20. Such imagery was more common in northern Europe; see Strickland, *Saracens, Demons, and Jews,* 111–13, and Jordan, "Last Tormentor of Christ."

21. Silva y Verasteguí, *La miniatura medieval en Navarra,* cat. 229, 369.

22. See, e.g., Abulafia, *Christians and Jews in the Twelfth-Century Renaissance,* 107–22; Lipton, *Images of Intolerance,* 35–36.

23. Assis, *Jewish Economy in the Medieval Crown of Aragon,* esp. 15–48.

24. *La Cataluña Judía,* 97; *La vida judía en Sefarad,* 268, no. 58.

25. Cothren, "Iconography of Theophilus Windows," 325.

26. E.g., in a twelfth-century fresco of the Last Supper from the church of San Baudelio de Berlanga (*Art of Medieval Spain,* 223, fig. 103d), and in the cloister of San Juan de la Peña (Patton, *Pictorial Narrative,* fig. 22).

27. *Vida judía en Sefarad,* 269, no. 60; see also Molina Filgueiras, "Las imágenes del judío," 376.

28. Trachtenberg, *Devil and the Jews,* esp. 11–56; Strickland, *Saracens, Demons, and Jews,* 77–78 and 122–30.

29. Kruger, *Spectral Jew,* 41–42.

30. On the dissemination of this legend, see esp. Plenzat, *Die Theophiluslegende;* and Lazar, "Theophilus." On Theophilus imagery in the West, see Fryer, "Theophilus the Penitent"; Cothren, "Iconography of Theophilus Windows"; Patton, "Constructing the Inimical Jew," esp. 242; and Rodríguez Barral, *La imagen del judío,* 60.

31. See also Patton, "Constructing the Inimical Jew."

32. As also observed by Klein, "'Jud, dir kuckt der Spitzbub,'" 47; Rodríguez Barral, *La imagen del judío,* 61–62.

33. The literature on Alfonso's cultural achievements is extensive. Fundamental sources include Procter, *Alfonso X of Castile;* Ballesteros Beretta, *Alfonso X El Sabio;* Cómez Ramos, *Las empresas artísticas de Alfonso el Sabio;* Burns, *Emperor of Culture;* O'Callaghan, *The Learned King;* and Márquez Villanueva, *El concepto cultural alfonsí.*

34. As suggested by Chico Picaza, "El scriptorium de Alfonso X el Sabio." For further discussion of this question, see chapter 5.

35. Romano, "Los judíos y Alfonso X," esp. 212–13; see also N. Roth, "Jewish Collaborators"; and Baer, *History of the Jews in Christian Spain,* 1:120–29.

36. Bango Torviso, *Memoria de Sefarad,* cat. 188; see also Márquez Villanueva, *Concepto Cultural,* 142–52. On the occasional resemblance between Jew's hats and episcopal miters, see Yarza Luaces, "Del alfaquí sabio."

37. Alfonso X, *Lapidario;* see also Domínguez Rodriguez, *Astrología y arte.*

38. Domínguez Rodríguez, *Astrología y arte,* 191.

39. Alfonso X, *Lapidario,* 45–46.

40. García Morencos, *Libro de ajedrez, dados y tablas;* see also Wollesen, "Sub specie ludi"; and Constable, "Chess and Courtly Culture."

41. Constable, "Chess and Courtly Culture," 302–3.

42. Ibid., 335–41; these are in addition to the better-known portraits of Alfonso himself that appear in several of his manuscripts.

43. Based on the text, his throw of 1 and 3 has won the game; ibid., 344.

44. Wollesen, "Sub specie ludi," 278.

45. Carpenter, *Alfonso X and the Jews,* 34–37.

46. Kulp-Hill, *Songs of Holy Mary,* 11–12. On textual and visual permutations of this story in medieval Europe, see Rubin, *Gentile Tales,* 8–27; for a fuller discussion of the Alfonsine narrative, see chapter 5.

47. As noted by several scholars, including Bagby, "Jew in the *Cantigas,*" 683 and 687; and Rodríguez Barral, *La imagen del judío,* 65.

48. For the legend and its visual tradition, see Patton, "Little Jewish Boy."

49. "Toute sa face resclaira de la grant joie qu'il avoit." Gautier de Coincy, *Les miracles de Nostre Dame,* 2:96, line 36.

50. Patton, "Constructing the Inimical Jew," 239–40; a similar suggestion has since been made by Rodríguez Barral, *La imagen del judío en la España medieval,* 65. Klein, conversely, ascribes the momentary exaggeration of the boy's nose to the artist's desire to emphasize the boy's Judaism as he receives the host; see Klein, "Moros y judíos," 346.

51. Kulp-Hill, *Songs of Holy Mary,* 135.

52. Carpenter, "Sorcerer Defends the Virgin," 8–12.

53. Kulp-Hill, *Songs of Holy Mary,* 135.

54. Carpenter, "Sorcerer Defends the Virgin," 14; see also Lipton, "Jew's Face," 267; and Mirrer, "Jew's Body," 7–18.

55. See Kinoshita, *Medieval Boundaries.*

56. Ray, *Sephardic Frontier,* 73–97.

57. This question has been influentially analyzed by Bartlett, *Making of Europe,* 197–242; see also Cohen, "On Saracen Enjoyment," 115–16.

58. Abulafia, "Bodies in the Jewish-Christian Debate" and "Jewish Carnality in Twelfth-Century Renaissance Thought." For Peter the Venerable on Jewishness as species-specific, and for a quodlibetum regarding whether there was a natural difference between Christians and Jews, see the very good discussion, with historiographic notes, in Iogna-Prat, *Order and Exclusion,* 319–21.

59. Elukin, "From Jew to Christian?," 183; see also Stroll, *Jewish Pope,* 156–68.

60. Biller, "Views of Jews," 196; amplified in Biller, "'Scientific' View of Jews."

61. Biller, "'Scientific' View of Jews," 142–43.

62. Bartlett, "Medieval and Modern Concepts," 53–54; and Jordan, "Why 'Race'?"

63. An excellent review of the literature and pitfalls behind this question is offered by Nirenberg, "El concepto de la raza," 39–43; Nirenberg, "Race and the Middle Ages"; Friedman, "Jewish Conversion," 16–17; and Hering Torres, "'Limpieza de Sangre.'"

64. Elukin, "From Jew to Christian?," 173.

65. For an outline of these events, see Wolff, "1391 Pogrom in Spain"; and Baer, *History of the Jews in Christian Spain,* 2:95–110. For more extensive discussion by region, see Mitre Fernández, *Los judíos de Castilla en tiempo de Enrique III,* 19–31; and Riera i Sans, "Los tumultos contra las juderías."

66. Ruiz, *Spain's Centuries of Crisis,* 155–63; Domínguez Ortiz, *Los judeoconversos en la España moderna,* 11–19 and 39–43; see also Baer, *History of the Jews in Christian Spain,* 2:166–69.

67. Nirenberg, "Conversion, Sex, and Segregation," esp. 28–31; and Nirenberg, "El concepto de la raza," 44.

68. For an overview aimed at comparing this phenomenon with modern, "racial" anti-Semitism, see Yerushalmi, *Assimilation and Racial Anti-Semitism,* 10–16. For more extended discussion of the *limpieza de sangre* statutes, see Domínguez Ortiz, *Los judeoconversos en la España moderna,* 137–72, and the fundamental study by Sicroff, *Les controverses des status de "pureté de sang."*

69. Sicroff, *Les controverses des status de "pureté de sang,"* 32–36; Baer, *History of the Jews in Christian Spain,* 2: 279–82.

70. Friedman, "Jewish Conversion," 8–11.

71. Silva Maroto, "Fernando Gallego."

Chapter 4

1. On the *mudéjar,* see the classic treatments by Torres Balbás: *Arte almohade,* 237–46; and "El mudéjar como constante artística." More recent scholarship includes Grabar, "Two Paradoxes"; Dodds, "Mudejar Tradition in Architecture"; Ruggles, "Alcazar of Seville"; and the very fine essays in Feliciano, Robinson, and Rouhi, "Interrogating Iberian Frontiers."

2. Ruggles, "Representation and Identity," 99–106.

3. E.g., Dodds, "Mudejar Tradition and the Synagogues."

4. O'Callagahan, *Latin Chronicle of the Kings of Castile,* 88.

5. Moore, *Formation of a Persecuting Society;* Cohen, "Muslim Connection"; and Cohen, *Living Letters of the Law,* 160–66. See also Strickland, *Saracens, Demons, and Jews,* 174–77; and Heng, "Romance of England," 142–50. A more controversial approach to this question has been taken by Cutler and Cutler, *Jew as Ally of the Muslim.*

6. Cohen, "Muslim Connection," esp. 141–44; and Cohen, *Living Letters of the Law,* 160–65.

7. Peter the Venerable, *Letters,* 1:328.

8. Cohen, *Living Letters of the Law,* 259–69; on Peter's translation and use of the Qur'an, see Tolan, *Saracens,* 155–65.

9. Nicholas of Lyra, *Commentary on Genesis* 1:21; quoted in Cohen, *Friars and the Jews,* 179.

10. Cohen, "Muslim Connection."

11. Kupfer, "Medieval World Maps," 271.

12. Strickland, *Saracens, Demons, and Jews,* 166.

13. Some scholars, such as Cutler and Cutler (*Jew as Ally of the Muslim,* 91–93), have attempted to root this development in sporadic medieval charges of Jewish collusion with Muslim forces in their initial invasion of Iberia. Few of these examples bear out, and I believe them to be too widely scattered to relate clearly to the phenomenon analyzed here.

14. Greenblatt, *Renaissance Self-Fashioning,* 9.

15. Petrus Alfonsi, *Dialogue Against the Jews;* for Alfonsi's biography, see 10–27. See also Tolan, *Petrus Alfonsi;* and Cohen, *Living Letters of the Law,* 201–20.

16. Petrus Alfonsi, *Dialogue Against the Jews,* 146–63; see also Tolan, *Petrus Alfonsi,* 27–33; and Cohen, "Muslim Connection," 151–53.

17. This letter does not survive in original form, but its contents are attested by subsequent copies and responses. See Lerner, *The Powers of Prophecy,* 190–91; Grauert, "Meister Johann von Toledo," esp. 175–81; and Gaster, "Letter of Toledo."

18. On Jewish conversion at the End of Days, see Emmerson, *Antichrist in the Middle Ages,* 41.

19. Cohen, *Living Letters of the Law,* 348.

20. O'Callaghan argues that the indulgences offered by Popes Alexander II and Urban II in the years leading up to the First Crusade so closely resemble those offered by the latter in 1095 as to constitute an early stage of the crusading phenomenon. O'Callaghan, *Reconquest and Crusade,* esp. 19–22 and 24–32.

21. On the return of the Jews to Tudela, see Leroy, *Jews of Navarre,* 20–21; and Baer, *Die Juden im Christlichen Spanien,* 1:920, doc. 570 (here misdated to 1115). See also Patton, "Cloister as Cultural Mirror," 330.

22. O'Callagahan, *Reconquest and Crusade,* 204; see also Falque Rey, Gil, and Maya, *Chronica Hispana saeculi XII,* 212.

23. In the *Chanson de Roland,* the Christians who have conquered Zaragoza seek out the city's "synagoges and the mahumeries" and smash the idols they find there; *La Chanson de Roland,* 2:256 (lines 3661–65); see also Camille, *Gothic Idol,* 130.

24. Parkes, *Jew in the Medieval Community,* 58; Synan, *Popes and the Jews,* 68–69.

25. On the attack following Uclés, see Dodds, Menocal, and Balbale, *Arts of Intimacy,* 134; on the 1212 incident, see O'Callaghan, *Reconquest and Crusade,* 70.

26. The *Anales Toledanos* report that the knights of Toledo defended the Jewish community during the 1212 attack; see Flórez et al., *España sagrada,* 23:396–97. On attacks against Jews in connection with the Crusades, see Chazan, *European Jewry and the First Crusade.*

27. Lourie, "Anatomy of Ambivalence," 51–52, and see her references.

28. A more extensive discussion of this work appears in Patton, "Islamic Envelope-Flap Binding."

29. Ibid., 72, fig. 43.

30. Perhaps the earliest such remnant is a tenth- to eleventh-century Qur'an binding fragment in the Rainer Collection (Inv. Chart. Ar.14100b, c), published in Arnold and Grohmann, *Islamic Book,* 47; see also Déroche, "Une reliure du Xe–XIe siècle."

31. Szirmai, *Archaeology of Medieval Bookbinding,* 51–53; and Bosch, Carswell, and Petherbridge, *Islamic Bindings and Bookmaking,* 45–46 and 55–56.

32. E.g., the back cover and flap of a binding dated ca. 1182 and now in the Berlin Staatsbibliothek; see Patton, "Islamic Envelope-Flap Binding," 71–72 and fig. 44.

33. The binder Bakr al-Ishbīlī refers to the technique in his late twelfth-century treatise on bookbinding. See Gacek, "Arabic Bookmaking and Terminology."

34. See Ricard, "Reliures marocaines du XIIIe siècle"; and Ricard, "Sur un type de reliure," esp. 75; see also Marcais and Poinssot, *Objets kairouanais,* 257–59 and pl. XLVII; and Ettinghausen, "Near Eastern Book Covers," especially pl. 4.

35. Patton, "Islamic Envelope-Flap Binding," 78–81. See also Cohen, *Living Letters of the Law,* 317–63; Cohen, *Friars and the Jews,* 60–99; and Jordan, "Marian Devotion," esp. 64–66.

36. Chazan, *Barcelona and Beyond,* 89–92.

37. Patton, "Islamic Envelope-Flap Binding," 73–75.

38. On Tudela's Muslim history and culture, see Pavón Maldonado, *Tudela, ciudad medieval.*

39. Gudiol i Cunill and Sanpere i Miquel, *La pintura mig-eval catalan,* 1:389–94; Ainaud, "Viga del Baldaquino," 86–87; Sureda, *La pintura románica en Cataluña,* 370–71; Dalmases and Pitarch, *Els inicis i l'art romànic,* 2:205–7; Alcoy i Pedros, "Biga de la Passió"; Vivancos Pérez, "Biga de la Passió," 406–8; and *Arte románico de Cataluña,* 80–81.

40. Its precise dimensions are 230.5 cm long by 20.5 cm high, and it is now only a few centimeters in thickness, having been thinned along its length with a hand saw at some point following its creation. Its dimensions exceed those of baldacchinos surviving from the same era, such as that from Tóses, also in the MNAC. For a brief reference to the Passion beam in the context of painted ceilings, see Companys Farrerons and Montardit Bofarull, *Embigats gótico-mudèixars al Tarragonés,* 50; compare also the ceiling beam from Teruel cited by Rodríguez Barral, *La imagen del judío,* 113. I am grateful to the MNAC staff for deinstalling the Passion beam to permit my close study of it.

41. On the European tradition generally, see Mellinkoff, *Outcasts,* 1:126–27; Bindman and Gates, *Image of the Black in Western Art,* vol. 2, pt. 1, 64–72, with a subsequent reference to the Passion beam at 75–76.

42. See Aragonés Estella, *La imágen del mal en el románico Navarro,* 33–38, esp. figs. 12 and 13; Monteira Arías, "Los musulmanes"; and Melero Moneo, "El Diablo en la Matanza de los Inocentes," 10.

43. "Es hallada en Tierra de los Negros, en ribera de un río que pasa por aquellos lugares donde estas piedras están" (Alfonso X, *Lapidario,* 19–20). On the phrase "Land of the Blacks," see Lewis, *Race and Slavery in the Middle East,* 50. Other black figures, such as those on 94v (*sanguina*) and 97v (*almagnitaz*), seem to have astrological rather than geographical significance; see Bindman and Gates, *Image of the Black in Western Art,* vol. 2, pt. 1, 86–89, figs. 54–55.

44. The subject of Muslims in the *Cantigas de Santa María* has inspired a substantial body of scholarship, although not nearly so extensive as that on Jews. See esp. Bagby, "Moslem in the *Cantigas*"; García Arenal, "Los moros en las *Cantigas* de Alfonso X"; Klein, "Moros y judíos," 355–63; and Klein, "Der Ausdruck unterschiedlicher Konflikte in der Darstellung der Juden und Mauren."

45. A suggested by García Arenal, "Los moros en las *Cantigas* de Alfonso X," 149–51.

46. Cohen, "On Saracen Enjoyment," 119–20; Strickland, *Saracens, Demons, and Jews,* 168–69 and 173; for the classical roots of this tradition, see Verkerk, "Black Servant, Black Demon," esp. 60–64. On the complex intersections of race, color, and religion in the thirteenth century, see Heng, *Empire of Magic,* 230–37.

47. E.g., *Chanson de Roland,* 1/176 (line 1635) and 1/187 (lines 1917 and 1932–35). On *Richard Coeur de Lyon,* see Heng, "Romance of England."

48. Heng, "Romance of England," 138–39; see also the later version of this argument in Heng, *Empire of Magic,* 68–72.

49. Lourie, "Anatomy of Ambivalence," 53.

50. On the *Estoria de España,* see Tolan, *Saracens,* 188; see also *Siete partidas,* 5:1438.

51. "De judeis et sarracenus. Es saber de los judios y de los moros" (fol. 243v); see Tilander, *Vidal mayor,* 2:474 (VII.12).

52. I am indebted to Nancy Turner of the Getty's conservation department for taking photomicrographs of representative figures and sharing her analysis of their composition.

53. Kulp-Hill, *Songs of Holy Mary,* 222–23; Alfonso X, *Cantigas de Santa María* (ed. Mettmann), 2:215–17; see line 63. This *cantiga* has been discussed at some length by Bagby, "Moslem in the *Cantigas*"; and Klein, "Moros y judíos," 356.

54. Kulp-Hill, *Songs of Holy Mary,* 222; see Alfonso X, *Cantigas de Santa María* (ed. Mettmann), 2:211–14, line 82.

55. Kulp-Hill, *Songs of Holy Mary,* 395; Alfonso X, *Cantigas de Santa María,* 3:362–64 and 184–86.

56. On the murals generally, see Melero Moneo, *La pintura sobre tabla del gótico lineal,* 47–48.

57. Jordan, "Last Tormentor of Christ," 36; and Strickland, *Saracens, Demons, and Jews,* 82–83.

58. Especially lines 31–33 and 56–57, in which those to whom the Jews entrust Christ for crucifixion are referred to by both names. Berceo, "El Duelo de la Virgen," esp. 813 and 819. In a note (812), Orduna suggests that the word *moro* should be understood as "los no-judíos, romanos or agarenos"; however, Monteira Arías ("Los musulmanes," 73) suggests that Berceo's use of the phrase "compaña negriella" signals that the figures would have been understood as black.

59. Dodds, Menocal, and Balbale, *Arts of Intimacy,* 188 and 244–45. The inscriptions have been explored at length by Foster, "Writing on the Wall."

60. Kogman-Appel, *Jewish Book Art,* 35–97.

61. As suggested, perhaps, by the preservation and extension of the mosque of Bab al-Mardum in Toledo; see Dodds, Menocal, and Balbale, *Arts of Intimacy,* 120–22; Raizman, "Church of Santa Cruz," 136–38.

62. Menéndez Pidal and Bernis, "Las Cantigas," 150.

63. Feliciano, "Muslim Shrouds for Christian Kings?"

64. Gallego, "Languages of Medieval Iberia," esp. 113–14.

65. Ibid., 116–17.

66. "How Holy Mary Caused Five Roses to Grow in the Mouth of the Monk After His Death"; see Kulp-Hill, *Songs of Holy Mary,* 73; Alfonso X, *Cantigas de Santa María* (ed. Mettmann), 1:160–61.

67. A similar inscription appears on the banners of Muslim soldiers on fol. 144r. I am indebted to Ali Alibhai for his insights on this point.

68. An Andalusi silk was used to line the twelfth-century shrine of San Isidoro in León: see Astorga Redondo, *El Arca de San Isidoro,* 62–65; and Williams and Walker, "Reliquary of Saint Isidore." On the use of such textiles as shrouds, see Feliciano, "Muslim Shrouds for Christian Kings?," esp. 113–24.

69. Although in this image the players appear to be consulting the book regarding their game, the only partly legible text seems to be copied after the Profession of the Faith, perhaps the best model at hand for an artist not literate in Arabic.

70. Constable, "Chess and Courtly Culture," 305.

71. Dodds, "Mudejar Tradition in Architecture," 596; and Crites, "Churches Made Fit for a King."

72. Scholem, "Star of David," 262–81.

73. Ibid., 265–67.

74. For example, hexagrams enclose the coats of arms of León and Castile in the Second Kennicott Bible, produced probably in Soria by 1306; see *La vida Judía en Sefarad,* 256. The form may have little symbolic value here. On the adaptation of the hexagram to Jewish contexts in this period, see Scholem, "Star of David," 275–79.

75. Baer, *Islamic Ornament,* 49–50. While interlocking patterns containing six-pointed stars are most frequent, stars also appear in a variety of contexts, from coins to architectural ornament. See, e.g., Blair and Bloom, *Art and Architecture of Islam,* fig. 7.

76. Ecker, *Caliphs and Kings,* 160–61.

77. Palomera Plaza, "Bocado de caballo" and "Pieza de cinturón," 127–29, cats. 70 and 71.

78. Ortega Martínez, "Pavimento," 140, cat. 85.

79. See Menéndez Pidal de Navascués, Ramos Aguirre, and Ochoa de Olza Eguiraun, *Sellos medievales de Navarra;* by contrast, the seal for the Jewish quarter in Tudela, dated 1350, simply depicts a castle surrounded by a band with a Latin inscription (857, cat. 3/121).

80. Grabar, *Mediation of Ornament,* 26.

81. Valencia, Museo Nacional de Cerámica "González Martí," inv. 598, XIV; see Soler Ferrer, "Salero de pellizcos"; and Bango García, "Salero de pellizcos," 157, no. 124.

82. For the plate, now in Museu de Ceràmica in Barcelona, see Mann, *Art and Ceremony in Jewish Life,* 70–72, fig. 5. The font, now in the Hispanic Society of America, has been published in Ecker, *Caliphs and Kings,* 59 and 145, cat. 53.

83. Delcor, "Les juifs de Puigcerdà."

84. See Carbonell i Esteller, *Tresors medievals,* fig. 155. The paintings are also illustrated, but the hexagrams not mentioned, in Bindman and Gates, *Image of the Black in Western Art,* vol. 2, pt. 1, 78–79, figs. 43–44.

85. Remensnyder, "Christian Captives, Muslim Maidens, and Mary," 647.

86. Fields of purely ornamental swastikas, flanked by borders of six-pointed stars, appear on the portal of the Karatay Medrese in Konya (mid-thirteenth century); see Quinn, *Swastika,* 95–96 and fig. 12. They appear frequently in the *Cantigas de Santa María* as a motif on the Virgin's altar, perhaps in an attempt to suggest the textiles or faience tiles with which these might have been faced.

87. McMichael, *Was Jesus of Nazareth the Messiah?,* 1–16. See also Ginio, *La forteresse de la foi.*

88. McMichael, *Alphonso de Espina,* 10.

89. Molina Filgueiras, "Las imágenes del judío," 378; Rodríguez Barral, *La imagen del judío,* 50–53.

Chapter 5

1. The standard critical edition is by Alfonso X, *Cantigas de Santa María* (ed. Mettmann); see also the English translation by Kulp-Hill, *Songs of Holy Mary.* Secondary scholarship on the *Cantigas de Santa María* is extremely extensive; that up to the mid-1980s has been indexed in a bibliography and two articles by Joseph Snow: *Poetry of Alfonso X;* "Trends in Scholarship on Alfonsine Poetry"; and "Current Status of Cantigas

Studies." Many subsequent publications have been gathered by Cárdenas-Rotunno, "In Search of a King"; see also the extensive bibliographic index in the *Cantigas de Santa María* database, at this writing hosted by Oxford University. Scholarship on the two illustrated manuscripts on which the present chapter focuses will be cited below as relevant.

2. Madrid, Biblioteca Nacional MS 10069, was held until 1869 in Toledo Cathedral; it contains 127 *cantigas* with skeletal musical notation. Biblioteca del Escorial, MS. J.B.2. is thought to have been produced at the very end of Alfonso's life, and remains its most complete, containing 401 songs with musical notation, along with forty small panels depicting musicians in performance. See Alfonso X, *Cantigas de Santa María* (ed. Mettmann), 1:vii–xxiv.

3. Both manuscripts have been published in facsimile with a commentary volume: Alfonso X, *Las Cantigas de Santa María. Edición facsímil del códice T.I.1;* and Alfonso X et al., *Las Cantigas de Santa María. Edición facsímil del códice B.R. 20.* On the codicology of the four thirteen-century manuscripts, see Schaffer, "Los códices de las *Cantigas de Santa María*"; and Schaffer, " 'Evolution' of the *Cantigas de Santa María.*"

4. A limited account of such scholarship up to the mid-1980s is offered by Scarborough, "Summary of the Research." Art-historical literature has expanded significantly since that point, especially with the work of Ana Domínguez Rodríguez and María Victoria Chico Picaza. See esp. Domínguez Rodríguez, "Iconografía Evangélica en las *Cantigas de Santa María*"; Domínguez Rodríguez, "En torno al Árbol de Jesé"; Domínguez Rodríguez, "Texto, imagen y diseño"; Domínguez Rodríguez and Treviño Gajardo, "Tradición del texto y tradición de la imagen"; and Domínguez Rodríguez and Treviño Gajardo, *Las Cantigas de Santa María.* In addition to the articles by Chico Picaza cited above, see Chico Picaza, "Hagiografía en las *Cantigas de Santa María*"; and Chico Picaza, "La teoría medieval." Other publications by art historians have included Guerrero Lovillo, *Las Cántigas;* Kosmer and Powers, "Manuscript Illustration"; Jackson, "Shields of Faith"; and Sánchez Ameijeiras, "Imaxes e teoría." Scholarship on images of religious minorities in the *Cantigas de Santa María* will be included in the notes that follow.

5. Some authors have interpreted the imagery as evidence of strongly anti-Jewish attitudes on the part of Alfonso and his contemporaries; see, e.g., Bagby, "Jew in the *Cantigas*"; Bagby, "Figure of the Jew"; Hatton and McKay, "Anti-Semitism in the *Cantigas de Santa María*"; and Trivison, "Prayer and Prejudice in the CSM." Other scholars have perceived greater ambivalence in such depictions: see Carpenter, "Social Perception and Literary Portrayal"; Carpenter, "Portrayal of the Jew"; Teensma, "Os Judeus na Espanha do século XIII"; Montoya Martínez, "Judíos y moros en las *Cantigas de Santa María*"; Filgueira Valverde, "Os xudeos nas *Cantigas de Santa María*"; and Fidalgo Francisco, "Consideración social de los judíos."

6. E.g., Klein, "Der Ausdruck unterschiedliche Konflikte"; Klein, "Moros y judíos"; and Rodríguez Barral, *La imagen del judío,* 57–82.

7. E.g., Freire, "*CSM*"; and Prado-Vilar, "Gothic Anamorphic Gaze." Prado-Vilar's imaginative recent article "*Iudeus sacer*" appeared just as this book went to press but should be noted as well.

8. Examples include Bagby, "Jew in the *Cantigas*"; Hatton and MacKay, "Anti-Semitism in the *Cantigas de Santa María*"; Carpenter, "Portrayal of the Jew."

9. See Guerrero Lovillo, *Las Cántigas;* see also Keller, "Daily Living as Presented in the *Cantigas*"; Menéndez Pidal, "Las Cantigas"; Menéndez Pidal and Bernis, "Las Cantigas"; Keller and Cash, *Daily Life;* and Domínguez Rodríguez and Treviño Gajardo, *Las Cantigas de Santa María,* 97–109.

10. Camille, "Labouring for the Lord."

11. Divergences between the manuscripts' textual and pictorial narratives have certainly been recognized. See, among others, Keller, "Some Remarks on Visualization"; Keller, "Verbalization and Visualization"; Scarborough, "Verbalization and Visualization"; Chico Picaza, "La relación texto-imagen"; Sánchez Ameijeiras, "Imaxes e teoría"; Domínguez Rodríguez and Treviño Gajardo, "Tradición del texto y tradición de la imagen"; Gregorio Sirem, "Las lecturas de las *Cantigas de Santa María*"; and Patton, "Constructing the Inimical Jew."

12. On the chronology of the *Cantigas* texts, see esp. Procter, *Alfonso X of Castile,* 34–46; Ferreira, "Stemma of the Marian *Cantigas*"; Chico Picaza, "Cronología de la miniatura Alfonsí"; O'Callaghan, *Alfonso X and the Cantigas de Santa María,* 8–13; Wulstan, "Compilation of the *Cantigas*"; Schaffer, "'Evolution' of the *Cantigas de Santa María,*" 206–8; and Domínguez Rodríguez and Treviño Gajardo, *Las Cantigas de Santa María,* 21–25. Most scholars date the illustrated codices toward the end of Alfonso's life: e.g., Wulstan dates Escorial T.I.1 to 1276–78 and Florence B.R. 20 to 1279 at the earliest ("Compilation of the *Cantigas,*" 170–72), and similar chronologies are suggested by Chico Picaza ("Cronología de la miniatura Alfonsí," 572) and García Cuadrado (*Las Cantigas,* 29–31). Others place the illustrated manuscripts even later; e.g., Filgueira Valverde places Escorial T.I.1 after 1179 ("El texto: Introducción histórico-crítico," 44–48); Domínguez Rodríguez and Treviño Gajardo place both manuscripts in the early 1280s (*Las Cantigas de Santa María,* 21–25); and Ferreira dates Escorial T.I.1 to the early 1280s and considers the Florence volume a posthumous work ("Stemma of the Marian *Cantigas,*" 72–98).

13. The Florence manuscript contains at least one *cantiga* that refers to an event occurring in 1283, and thus is thought to have been undertaken very late in the king's lifetime. On the state of this work at Alfonso's death, see Sánchez Ameijeiras, "La fortuna sevillana"; and Santiago Luque, "Marco histórico y texto"; Chico Picaza, "Cronología de la miniatura Alfonsí," 573; and Fernández, "Historia Florentina del Códice de las *Cantigas de Santa María.*"

14. Chico Picaza, "El scriptorium de Alfonso X el Sabio," 268–69; see also Parkinson and Jackson, "Collection, Composition, and Compilation"; and Domínguez Rodríguez and Treviño Gajardo, *Las Cantigas de Santa María,* 9–14.

15. The first *cantiga* is an exception; it is followed by an eight-panel illustration, possibly in order to accommodate its theme of the Seven Joys of the Virgin. See Domínguez Rodríguez, "Texto, imagen y diseño," 316.

16. It is not clear whether Juan González was a scribe, artist, musician, or other person involved in the work, but Martín Pérez de Maqueda may well have held a supervising role in the scriptorium, since he signed the *General Estoria* with the words "Yo Martin Pérez de Maqued escrivano de los libro del muy noble Rey don Alffonsso escrivi este libro Con otros mi escrivanos que tenía por su mandado." See Alfonso X, *Cantigas de Santa María* (ed. Mettmann), 1:viii–ix; García Cuadrado, *Las Cantigas,* 57–59; and Domínguez Rodríguez and Treviño Gajardo, *Las Cantigas de Santa María,* 13.

17. The latter figure might be linked with a painter named Pedro who is mentioned in the *repartimiento* of Murcia in 1268; see García Cuadrado, *Las Cantigas,* 58.

18. On the tradition of Marian collections, see John of Garland, *Stella Maris;* Boyd, *Middle English Miracles of the Virgin;* Southern, "English Origins"; Montoya Martínez, *Las colecciones de milagros de la Virgen,* 127–72; and Bayo, "Las colecciones universales de milagros de la Virgen." On the role of Jews in miracles generally, see Blumenkranz, "Juden und Jüdisches."

19. Berceo, *Miracles of Our Lady.* For the Castilian, see Berceo, *Los milagros de Nuestra Señora.* On the collection and its audience see Gerli, "Poet and Pilgrim"; Flory, "Berceo's *Milagros*"; and Cash, "Holy Mary Intervenes for the Clergy."

20. Gil de Zamora, *De preconiis Hispaniae,* lviii–lxxxii. The miracles have been published in two articles by Fidel Fita, "Cincuenta leyendas por Juan Gil de Zamora" and "Treinta leyendas por Gil de Zamora."

21. The availability of these texts to the *Cantigas* artists has been suggested by Keller, "Verbalization and Visualization," 226; Scarborough, "Verbalization and Visualization," 138; Hatton and McKay, "Anti-Semitism in the *Cantigas de Santa María,*" 190; and Klein, "Kunst und Feudalismus," 190. However, the potential impact of Zamora's work has been neglected.

22. For the Theophilus tale, see chapter 3; for the Jewish boy, see below.

23. Butterfield, "Introduction"; Stones, "Illustrated Miracles"; and Sánchez Ameijeiras, "Imaxes e teoría," 264–68.

24. Parallels with Coincy texts have been analyzed by many authors, beginning with Dexter, "Sources of the Cantigas"; and Marullo, "Osservazioni sulle Cantigas de Alfonso e sui *Miracles* de Coincy." Sánchez Ameijeiras ("Imaxes e teoría," 264–68) discusses specific parallels with a codex now in the National Library of Russia in Saint Petersburg (MS. fr. F. XIV.9).

25. On Louis's manuscript patronage, see esp. Branner, *Manuscript Painting in Paris;* Weiss, *Art and Crusade in the Age of Saint Louis;* and Stahl, *Picturing Kingship.*

26. On evidence of Alfonso's presence in Paris, see González Jiménez, "Alfonso X, Rey de Castilla y León," 2. On the betrothals, see MacDonald, "Law and Politics," esp. 158; and Ballesteros Beretta, *Alfonso X el Sabio,* 479–89.

27. Lowden, *Making of the Bibles Moralisées,* 1:132–34; Domínguez Rodríguez and Treviño Gajardo, *Las Cantigas de Santa María,* 48.

28. As exemplified by his Gothic-style additions to the Alcázar of Seville and his patronage of León Cathedral. See Cómez Ramos, *Arquitectura Alfonsí,* and Cómez Ramos, "El Alcázar de Sevilla."

29. Kosmer and Powers, "Manuscript Illustration"; Domínguez Rodríguez, "Filiación estilística de la miniatura alfonsí"; and Sánchez Ameijeiras, "Imaxes e teoría," 256–63; see also Domínguez Rodríguez and Treviño Gajardo, *Las Cantigas de Santa María,* 161–82.

30. See O'Callaghan, *Learned King,* 207–13.

31. Sánchez Ameijeiras, "Imaxes e teoría," 260–61; Domínguez Rodríguez and Treviño Gajardo, *Las Cantigas de Santa María,* 16–19.

32. See O'Callaghan, *Learned King,* 134–35. For an illustrated Arabic manuscript likely known in Castile, see Robinson, *Three Ladies and a Lover.*

33. On the issue of Alfonso's authorship, see O'Callagahan, *Alfonso X and the Cantigas,* 6–8.

34. O'Callagahn, *Learned King,* 234–61 and 279–80; on Alfonso's illness, see also Presilla, "Image of Death and Political Ideology," 432–40, and Delgado Roig, "Examen médico-legal de unos restos históricos."

35. On the centrality of memorization to performance, see Berger, *Medieval Music,* 47–50; for examples, see Bell, *Music in Medieval Manuscripts,* 45–47.

36. As suggested by Domínguez Rodríguez, "Texto, imagen y diseño," 318; see also De Hamel, *History of Illuminated Manuscripts,* 167.

37. Snow, "Central Role of the Troubadour Persona"; Snow, "Alfonso as Troubadour"; and O'Callaghan, *Alfonso X and the Cantigas,* 14–35. For an alternative possibility, that the king might have intended the illustrated manuscripts as a gift, see Montoya Martínez, "El códice de Florenci."

38. Kulp-Hill, *Songs of Holy Mary,* 9; Alfonso X, *Cantigas de Santa María* (ed. Mettmann), 1:19. On such gratuitous references and their possible meaning, see Carpenter, "Portrayal of the Jew," 18.

39. Kulp-Hill, *Songs of Holy Mary,* 112–13, and Alfonso X, *Cantigas de Santa María* (ed. Mettmann), 1:253–56.

40. *Cantiga* headings follow Kulp-Hill, *Songs of Holy Mary.*

41. These include the *cantigas* today numbered 2, 3, 4, 6, 12, 25, 27, 34, and 108. Cantigas 85, 89, 107, 109, and 286 apparently were added at a subsequent stage. See Wulstan, "Compilation of the *Cantigas,*" 156–59; Parkinson, "First Reorganization of the CSM"; and Schaffer, "'Evolution' of the *Cantigas de Santa María,*" 189.

42. On the Jewish boy narrative, see Wolter, *Der Judenknabe;* Pelizaeus, "Beiträge zur Geschichte der Legende vom Judenknabe"; and Nissen, "Zu den ältesten Fassungen." More recent and contextually oriented studies include Hofmeister, "Das Jüdel im Kontext"; Burmeister, *Der "Judenknabe";* and Rubin, *Gentile Tales,* 7–39. The history and sources of the Theophilus tale are summarized by Boyd, *Middle English Miracles of the Virgin,* 127–129; see also Plenzat, *Die Theophiluslegende;* Lazar, "Theophilus"; and Cárdenas-Rotunno, "Theophilus Legend."

43. Analysis of the sources for the *Cantigas de Santa María* has been made by Dexter, "Sources of the Cantigas"; see also Filgueira Valverde, "El texto: Introducción histórico-crítico," 44–48. A more comprehensive treatment is made possible by the Oxford *Cantigas de Santa María* database. On Cantiga 108, see Carpenter, "Sorcerer Defends the Virgin"; on Cantiga 107, see the discussion below.

44. Filgueira Valverde, "El texto: Introducción histórico-crítico," 44–47.

45. As also suggested by Klein, "Moros y judíos," 343.

46. See Chico Picaza, "'La arquitectura desde la miniatura,'" 67–69.

47. Assis, "Synagogues in Medieval Spain," 17.

48. See Ecker, "How to Administer a Conquered City."

49. This has been interpreted as a conventionalized expression of the *compassio Mariae;* see Domínguez Rodríguez and Treviño Gajardo, "Tradición del texto y tradición de la imagen," 9–13.

50. Kulp-Hill, *Songs of Holy Mary,* 173. On this and the Crucifixion in Cantiga 50 as expressions of the *compassio Mariae,* see Domínguez Rodríguez and Treviño Gajardo, "Tradición del texto y tradición de la imagen," 9–13.

51. Kulp-Hill, *Songs of Holy Mary,* 19; Alfonso X, *Cantigas de Santa María* (ed. Mettmann), 1:37–38.

52. As suggested, e.g., by Rodríguez Barral, *La imagen del judío,* 67–70. See also Espí Forcén, *Recrucificando al Cristo,* 95–107.

53. On this, see Carpenter, "Portrayal of the Jew," 19–20.

54. Kulp-Hill, *Songs of Holy Mary,* 19; Alfonso X, *Cantigas de Santa María* (ed. Mettmann), 1:37–38.

55. Berceo, *Miracles of Our Lady,* 86–87.

56. Ibid., 87. On anti-Judaism in Berceo's work, see Saugnieux, *Berceo y las culturas del siglo XIII,* 73–102.

57. A strong case for this is made by Gerli, "Poet and Pilgrim."

58. Raizman, "Rediscovered Illuminated Manuscript," 38.

59. For the text, see Kulp-Hill, *Songs of Holy Mary,* 4; Alfonso X, *Cantigas de Santa María* (ed. Mettmann), 1:7–8.

60. Valdeón Baruque, *Alfonso X el Sabio,* 103–5.

61. See Cantera Burgos, *El tratado "Contra caecitatem iudeorum";* see also Monsalvo Antón, *Teoría y evolución de un conflicto social,* 216, and Valdeón Baruque, *Los judíos de Castilla,* 16–17; and Baer, *History of the Jews in Christian Spain,* 1:128–29.

62. Rubin, *Corpus Christi,* esp. 12–82.

63. Ibid., 67–70. For Innocent's letter on wet nurses, see Grayzel, *Church and the Jews,* 1:115. This seems to have become a concern in Iberia too: in 1258 in Valladolid, the Cortes passed a law preventing all nurses from breastfeeding children of different faith communities; see Dillard, *Daughters of the Reconquest,* 207.

64. As Kulp-Hill observes, the caption describes him as having bitten the man, but the text's use of the word "adobou" (to "soak" or "marinate") implies that it urinated on him; see Kulp-Hill, *Songs of Holy Mary,* 346; see also Alfonso X, *Cantigas de Santa María* (ed. Mettmann), 3:89–90.

65. Rubin, *Gentile Tales,* 24; such surrogacy is especially clear in the thirteenth-century story of Adam of Bristol, discussed by Stacey, "From Ritual Crucifixion to Host Desecration," esp. 17.

66. Kulp-Hill, *Songs of Holy Mary,* 11.

67. Latin text from Boyd, "Little Clergeon's *Alma Redemptoris Mater,*" 10–11.

68. Kulp-Hill, *Songs of Holy Mary,* 12; Alfonso X, *Cantigas de Santa María* (ed. Mettmann), 1:23.

69. Gautier de Coincy, *Les miracles de Nostre Dame* 4:42–72; Dahan, "Les juifs dans les Miracles de Gautier de Coincy," 41–48 and 59–68, 47–48 and 59–60.

70. As also observed by Rodríguez Barral, *La imagen del judío,* 67.

71. Rodríguez Barral has also commented on this connection in the *Cantigas de Santa María* ("Dialéctica texto-imagen," 215–18).

72. Kulp-Hill, *Songs of Holy Mary,* 136; Alfonso X, *Cantigas de Santa María* (ed. Mettmann), 2:25–26.

73. Kulp-Hill, *Songs of Holy Mary,* 110; Alfonso X, *Cantigas de Santa María* (ed. Mettmann), 1:246–48.

74. Kulp-Hill, *Songs of Holy Mary,* 140; Alfonso X, *Cantigas de Santa María* (ed. Mettmann), 1:247, line 50.

75. Rodríguez Barral, *La imagen del judío,* 73–74.

76. "Como o judeo deitóu a omage de Sancta María na privada per consello do demo." See ibid., 70.

77. These include a tale from John of Garland's *Stella Maris,* in which a group of Jews attacks an image of Christ that they find in a house purchased from a Christian, and the *Legenda aurea's* account of a Jew's attack on a crucifix in Hagia Sophia in Constantinople, a Catalan illustration of which was described in chapter 3. See John of Garland, *Stella Maris,* 117 and 177–78. Despite this, Rodríguez Barral argues that Cantiga 34 should be understood primarily in light of a concern over image desecration (*Imagen del judío,* 70).

78. Berceo, *Miracles of Our Lady,* 114–22.

79. Kulp-Hill, *Songs of Holy Mary,* 34; Alfonso X, *Cantigas de Santa María* (ed. Mettmann), 1:70–75.

80. *Contra* the view of Klein ("Moros y judíos en las 'Cantigas' de Alfonso el Sabio," 349), who reads into this *cantiga* greater negativity of expression and gesture.

81. See, e.g., the edition of Gil de Zamora's miracle in Fita, "Cincuenta leyendas por Juan Gil de Zamora," 112–13; see also John of Garland, *Stella Maris,* 141–42.

82. Kulp-Hill, *Songs of Holy Mary,* 369–70; Alfonso X, *Cantigas de Santa María* (ed. Mettmann), 3:133–35.

83. Alfonso acceded to the demand for lower interest rates in 1268, dropping the original rate of 33 1/3 percent to 25 percent. See Monsalvo Antón, *Teoría y evolución de un conflicto social,* 209; Valdeón Baruque, *Alfonso X el Sabio,* 200–201; and Valdeón Baruque, *Los judíos de Castilla,* 17–18. On the involvement of Jews in Alfonso's tax system, see O'Callaghan, "Cortes and Royal Taxation," esp. 390–91.

84. Baer, *History of the Jews in Christian Spain,* 1:117–36.

85. Caesarius of Heisterbach, *Dialogue on Miracles,* 2:112–15; see also Ferreiro Alemparte, "Fuentes germánicas en las 'Cantigas de Santa María,'" esp. 52–53.

86. For these *cantigas* see Kulp-Hill, *Songs of Holy Mary,* 129–30, 158–59, and 250; Alfonso X, *Cantigas de Santa María* (ed. Mettmann), 2:8–10 and 271–73.

87. Kulp-Hill, *Songs of Holy Mary,* 250; Alfonso X, *Cantigas de Santa María* (ed. Mettmann), 2:271.

88. A tendency noted also by Molina Filgueiras, "La imagen y su contexto," 75–76.

89. Kulp-Hill, *Songs of Holy Mary,* 135; Alfonso X, *Cantigas de Santa María* (ed. Mettmann), 2:23–24.

90. Carpenter, *Alfonso X and the Jews,* 33; see also Carpenter, "Sorcerer Defends the Virgin," 15–16.

91. Carpenter, "Sorcerer Defends the Virgin," 20.

92. Goldberg, "Literary Portrait of the Child," 15.

93. Kulp-Hill, *Songs of Holy Mary,* 114; Alfonso X, *Cantigas de Santa María* (ed. Mettmann), 1:257–59.

94. Nirenberg, "Conversion, Sex, and Segregation," 51. On child conversion more generally, see Jordan, "Adolescence and Conversion."

95. See Ray, *Sephardic Frontier,* 169.

96. Kulp-Hill, *Songs of Holy Mary,* 133–34; Alfonso X, *Cantigas de Santa María* (ed. Mettmann), 2:19–21. This *cantiga* has inspired a substantial bibliography, including Fradejas Lebrero, "La Cantiga CVII o de Mari Saltos"; Benaim de Lasry, "Marisaltos"; Tinnell, "Marisaltos"; Mirrer, "Beautiful Jewess"; and Prieto de la Iglesia and Sánchez Prieto, "La Cantiga 107 de Alfonso X."

97. Kulp-Hill, *Songs of Holy Mary,* 134; Alfonso X, *Cantigas de Santa María* (ed. Mettmann), 2:19, line 20.

98. Benaim de Lasry, "Marisaltos," 300; for a discussion of Cerrato's tale, see Prieto de la Iglesia and Sánchez Prieto, "La Cantiga 107 de Alfonso X," 165–70.

Epilogue

1. Geertz, "Thick Description," 4–5.

BIBLIOGRAPHY

Abelard, Peter. *A Dialogue of a Philosopher with a Jew, and a Christian.* Translated by Pierre J. Payer. Toronto: Pontifical Institute of Mediaeval Studies, 1979.

Abulafia, Anna Sapir. "Bodies in the Jewish-Christian Debate." In *Framing Medieval Bodies,* edited by Sarah Kay and Miri Rubin, 123–37. Manchester: Manchester University Press, 1996.

———. *Christians and Jews in Dispute: Disputational Literature and the Rise of Anti-Judaism in the West (c. 1000–1150).* Aldershot: Ashgate, 1998.

———. *Christians and Jews in the Twelfth-Century Renaissance.* London: Routledge, 1995.

———. "Jewish Carnality in Twelfth-Century Renaissance Thought." In Wood, *Christianity and Judaism,* 59–76.

Ainaud, Joan. "Viga del baldaquino." In *Museo de Cataluña: Arte románico.* Madrid: Editorial Orgaz, 1984.

Aita, Nella. "O códice florentino das Cantigas de Alfonso o Sábio." *Revista de Língua Portuguesa* 13 (1921): 187–99.

Aizenberg, Edna. "*Una judía muy fermosa:* The Jewess as Sex Object in Medieval Spanish Literature and Lore." *La Corónica* 12 (1984): 187–94.

Alcoy i Pedros, Rosa María. "Biga de la Passió." In *Prefiguració del Museu Nacional d'Art de Catalunya,* 168–71. Barcelona: MNAC, 1992.

———. "Canvis i oscil·lacions en la imatge pictòrica dels jueus a la Catalunya del segle XIV." In *Actes del primer col·loqui d'historia dels jueus a la corona d'Aragó,* edited by David Romano, 371–92. Lléida: Quaderns del Institut d'Estudis Ilerdencs, 1991.

Aldea Vaquero, Quintín, et al. *Diccionario de história eclesiástica de España.* 4 vols. Madrid: CSIC, 1972–75.

Alfonso X, King of Castile and Leon. *Cantigas de Santa María.* Edited by Walter Mettmann. 4 vols. Coimbra: Por ordem da Universidade, 1959–1972.

———. *Las Cantigas de Santa María: Edición facsímil del Códice T.I.1 de la Biblioteca de San Lorenzo el Real de El Escorial, siglo XIII.* 2 vols. Madrid: Edilán, 1979.

———. *Lapidario.* Edited by María Brey Mariño. Madrid: Castalia, 1968.

———. *Libro de ajedrez, dados y tablas.* Edited by Pilar García Morencos. 2 vols. Madrid: Patrimonio Nacional, 1987.

Alfonso X, King of Castile and Leon, et al. *Las Cantigas de Santa María: Edición facsímil del códice B.R. 20 de la Biblioteca Nazionale Centrale de Florencia, Siglo XIII.* Edited by Ana Domínguez Rodríguez, Agustín Santiago Luque, and María Victoria Chico Picaza. 2 vols. Madrid: Edilán, 1989–91.

Alfonso X: Toledo 1984. Toledo: Museo de Santa Cruz and Ministerio de Cultura, 1984.

Alsina, Teresa. "La imatge visual i la concepció dels jueus a la Catalunya medieval." *L'Avenç* 81 (April 1985): 54–56.

Anglés, Higinio. *La música de la Cantigas de Santa María.* 3 vols. in 4. Barcelona: Diputación Provincial de Barcelona, 1943–64.

Ansoleaga, Florencio. "Claustro de la Catedral de Pamplona: Puerta del Refectorio." *Boletín de la Comisión de Monumentos de Navarra,* 2nd ser., vol. 4 (1913): 41–44.

Aragonés Estella, Ezperanza. *La imágen del mal en el románico Navarro.* Pamplona: Gob. de Navarra, 1996.

Arbós Ayuso, Cristina. "Los judíos en la literature española (siglos XIII–XIV): Los judíos y la economía; protecciones y privilegios." *Actas de las jornadas de estudios sefardíes* (1980): 141–50.

Arnold, Thomas W., and Arnold Grohmann. *The Islamic Book: A Contribution to Its Art and History from the VII–XVIII Century.* Paris: Pegasus Press,1929.

Arte románico de Cataluña: Colecciones del Museu Nacional d'Art de Catalunya. Madrid: Centro Cultural del Conde-Duque, 2001.

The Art of Medieval Spain, A.D. 500–1200. New York: Metropolitan Museum of Art, 1993.

Assis, Yom Tov. *The Golden Age of Aragonese Jewry: Community and Society in the Crown of Aragon, 1213–1327.* London: Littman, 1997.

———. *Jewish Economy in the Medieval Crown of Aragon, 1213–1327: Money and Power.* Leiden: E. J. Brill, 1997.

———. "Synagogues in Medieval Spain." *Jewish Art* 18 (1992): 7–29

Astorga Redondo, María Jesús. *El Arca de San Isidoro: Historia de un relicario.* León: Diputación Provincial, 1990.

Augustine. *Answer to Faustus, a Manichaean.* Introduced and translated by Roland Teske. Edited by Boniface Ramsey. Hyde Park, N.Y.: New City Press, 2007.

———. *Treatises on Marriage and Other Subjects.* Translated by Charles T. Wilcox et al. Edited by Roy J. Deferrari. Washington, D.C.: Catholic University of America Press, 1955.

Avril, François, et al. *Manuscrits enluminés de la Bibliothèque Nationale: Manuscrits de la peninusule Ibérique.* Paris: Bibliothèque Nationale, 1982.

Baer, Eva. *Islamic Ornament.* New York: New York University Press, 1998.

Baer, Fritz. See Baer, Yitzhak.

Baer, Yitzhak. *A History of the Jews in Christian Spain.* Translated by Louis Schiffman. 2 vols. Philadelphia: Jewish Publication Society of America, 1961–66; repr., 1992.

———. *Die Juden im christlichen Spanien.* 4 vols. Berlin: Akademie-Verlag, 1929–36; repr., 2 vols. in 3, Amersham, UK: Demand Reprints, 1984. [Page references are to the reprint edition.]

Baert, Barbara. "New Observations on the Genesis of Girona (1050–1100): The Iconography of the Legend of the True Cross." *Gesta* 38, no. 2 (1999): 115–27.

Bagby, Albert. "Alfonso X, el Sabio compara moros y judíos." *Romanische Forschungen* 82 (1970): 578–83.

———. "The Figure of the Jew in the *Cantigas* of Alfonso X." In Katz and Keller, *Studies on the "Cantigas de Santa María,"* 235–45.

———. "The Jew in the *Cantigas* de Alfonso X, El Sabio." *Speculum* 46, no. 4 (1971): 670–88.

———. "The Moslem in the *Cantigas* of Alfonso X, el Sabio." *Kentucky Romance Quarterly* 20 (1973): 173–207.

Bale, Anthony. *The Jew in the Medieval Book: English Antisemitisms, 1350–1500.* Cambridge: Cambridge University Press, 2006.

Ballesteros Beretta, Antonio. *Alfonso X El Sabio.* Barcelona: Salvat, 1963; repr., Barcelona: El Albir, 1984.

Bango García, Clara. "Salero de pellizcos." In Bango Torviso, *Memoria de Sefarad,* 157.

Bango Torviso, Isidro, ed. *Memoria de Sefarad.* Madrid: SEACEX, 2002.

Bard, Rachel. *Navarra, the Durable Kingdom.* Reno: University of Nevada Press, 1982.

Barros, Carlos, ed. *Xudeus e conversos na historia: Actas do congreso internacional.* 2 vols. Santiago de Compostela: Editorial de la Historia, 1994.

Bartlett, Robert. *The Making of Europe: Conquest, Colonization, and Cultural Change, 950–1350.* Princeton: Princeton University Press, 1993.

———. "Medieval and Modern Concepts of Race and Ethnicity." *Journal of Medieval and Early Modern Studies* 31, no. 1 (2001): 39–56.

Baumgarten, Elisheva. *Mothers and Children: Jewish Family Life in Medieval Europe.* Princeton: Princeton University Press, 2004.

Bayo, Juan Carlos. "Las colecciones universales de milagros de la Virgen hasta Gonzalo de Berceo." *Bulletin of Spanish Studies* 81, nos. 7–8 (2004): 849–71.

Bell, Nicolas. *Music in Medieval Manuscripts.* London: British Library, 2001.

Benaim de Lasry, Anita. "Marisaltos: Artificial Purification in Alfonso el Sabio's *Cantiga* 107." In Katz and Keller, *Studies on the "Cantigas de Santa María,"* 299–311.

Berceo, Gonzalo de. "El Duelo de la Virgen." Edited by Germán Orduna. In *Gonzalo de Berceo: Obra completa,* coordinated by Isabel Uría, 797–857. Madrid: Espasa-Calpe, 1992.

———. *Miracles of Our Lady.* Translated by Richard Terry Mount and Annette Grant Cash. Lexington: University Press of Kentucky, 1997.

———. *Los milagros de Nuestra Señora.* Vol. 2 of *Obras completas.* Edited by Brian Dutton. London: Tamesis, 1971.

Berger, Anna Maria Busse. *Medieval Music and the Art of Memory.* Berkeley: University of California Press, 2005.

Bernard of Clairvaux. *Sancti Bernardi opera.* Edited by Jean Leclercq et al. 8 vols. in 9. Rome: Ed. Cistercienses, 1957–77.

Biller, Peter. "A 'Scientific' View of Jews from Paris Around 1300." In *Gli ebrei e le scienze / The Jews and the Sciences,* edited by Agostino Bagliani, 137–68. Micrologus: Nature, Sciences, and Medieval Societies 9. Florence: SISMEL Edizioni de Galluzo, 2001.

———. "Views of Jews from Paris Around 1300: Christian or 'Scientific'?" In Wood, *Christianity and Judaism,* 187–207.

Bindman, David, and Henry Louis Gates, eds. *The Image of the Black in Western Art.* 3 vols. in 4. New ed. Cambridge: Belknap Press of Harvard University Press, 2010.

Blair, Sheila S., and Jonathan Bloom. *The Art and Architecture of Islam, 1250–1800.* New Haven: Yale University Press, 1994.

Blasco García, Vicente. *San Ildefonso, De Virginitate Beatae Mariae: Historia de su tradición manuscrita, texto y comentario grammatical, y estilístico.* Madrid: CSIC, 1937.

Blasco Martínez, Asunción. "Jaime I y los judíos de Aragón." In *La sociedad en Aragón y Cataluña en el reinado de Jaime I (1213–1276),* edited by Esteban Sarasa, 97–134. Zaragoza: Institución Fernando el Católico, 2009.

Blumenkranz, Bernhard. "Ecriture et image dans la polémique antijuive de Matfre Ermengaud." *Cahiers de Fanjeaux* 12 (1977): 295–317.

———. "Géographie historique d'un thème de l'iconographie religieuse: Les representations de Synagoga en France." In *Mélanges offerts à René Crozet à l'occasion de son 70 anniversaire, par ses amis, ses collègues, ses élèves,* edited by Pierre Gallais and Yves-Jean Rion, 2 vols., 2:1141–57. Poitiers: Société d'études médiévales, 1966.

———. "Juden und Jüdisches in Christlichen Wundererzählungen: Ein unbekanntes Gebiet religiöse Polemik." *Theologische Zeitschrift* 10 (1954): 417–46.

———. *Le juif medieval au miroir de l'art chrétien.* Paris: Études Augustiniennes, 1966.

Bohigas, Pere. *La ilustración y la decoración del libro manuscrito en Cataluña: Contribución al estudio de la historia de la miniatura catalana.* 3 vols. Barcelona: Asociación de Bibliófilos de Barcelona, 1960–67.

Bolduc, Michelle. "The Breviari d'amor: Rhetoric and Preaching in Thirteenth-Century Languedoc." *Rhetorica* 24 (2006): 403–27.

Bonfil, Robert. "The Devil and the Jews in the Christian Consciousness of the Middle Ages." In *Antisemitism Through the Ages,* edited by Schmuel Almog, translated by Nathan H. Reissnel, 91–98. Oxford: Pergamon Press, 1988.

Bosch, Gulnar K., John Carswell, and Guy Petherbridge. *Islamic Bindings and Bookmaking.* Chicago: Oriental Institute, University of Chicago, 1981.

Bosom i Sern, Sebastià, and Salvador Galceran i Vigué. *Catàleg de protocols de Puigcerdà.* Col·lecció d'Inventaris d'Arxiús Notarials de Catalunya 4. Barcelona: Fundació Noguera, 1983.

Boyd, Beverly. "The Little Clergeon's *Alma Redemptoris Mater.*" *Notes and Queries* 202 (1957): 277.

———. *The Middle English Miracles of the Virgin.* San Marino, Calif.: Huntingdon Library, 1964.

Bradbury, Carlee. "Imaging and Imagining the Jew in Medieval England." Ph.D. diss., University of Illinois, 2007.

Brann, Ross, ed. *Power in the Portrayal: Representations of Jews and Muslims in Eleventh- and Twelfth-Century Spain.* Princeton: Princeton University Press, 2002.

Branner, Robert. *Manuscript Painting in Paris During the Reign of Saint Louis: A Study of Styles.* Berkeley: University of California Press, 1977.

Bucher, François. *The Pamplona Bibles.* 2 vols. New Haven: Yale University Press, 1970.

Burmeister, Heike. *Der "Judenknabe": Studien un Texte zu einem Mittelalterlichen Marienmirakel in deutscher Überlieferung.* Goppingen: Kummerle Verlag, 1998.

Burns, Robert I., ed. *Emperor of Culture: Alfonso X the Learned of Castile and His Thirteenth-Century Renaissance.* Philadelphia: University of Pennsylvania Press, 1990.

———. "Stupor Mundi: Alfonso X of Castile, the Learned." In Burns, *Emperor of Culture,* 1–13.

Butterfield, Ardis. "Introduction: Gautier de Coinci, *Miracles de Nostre Dame:* Texts and Manuscripts." In Krause and Stones, *Gautier de Coinci,* 1–18.

Caesarius of Heisterbach. *Dialogue on Miracles.* Translated by Henry von Essen Scott and Charles Cook Swinton Bland. 2 vols. London: Routledge, 1929.

Cahn, Walter. "The Expulsion of the Jews as History and Allegory in Painting and Sculpture of the Twelfth and Thirteenth Centuries." In Signer and Van Engen, *Jews and Christians in Twelfth-Century Europe,* 94–109.

Camille, Michael. "The Devil's Writing: Diabolic Literacy in Medieval Art." In *World Art: Themes of Unity in Diversity,* edited by Irving Lavin, 3 vols., 2:355–58. University Park: Pennsylvania State University Press, 1989.

———. *The Gothic Idol: Ideology and Image-Making in Medieval Art.* New York: Cambridge University Press, 1989.

———. *Image on the Edge.* New York: Reaktion, 1992.

———. "Labouring for the Lord: The Ploughman and Social Order in the Luttrell Psalter." *Art History* 10, no. 4 (1987): 423–54.

———. "Seeing and Lecturing: Disputation in a Twelfth-Century Tympanum from Reims." In *Reading Medieval Images: The Art Historian and the Object,* edited by Elizabeth Sears and Thelma K. Thomas, 75–87. Ann Arbor: University of Michigan Press, 2002.

Campo del Pozo, Fernando. "El monacato de San Agustín en España hasta la gran unión en el año 1256." In Melville, *Secundum regulam vivere,* 5–30.

Cantera Burgos, Francisco. *El tratado "Contra caecitatem iudeorum" de Fray Bernardo Oliver.* Madrid: CSIC, 1965.

Cantera Montenegro, Enrique. *Aspectos de la vida cotidiana de los judíos en la España medieval.* Madrid: UNED, 1998.

Carbonell i Esteller, Eduard. *Tresors medievals del Museu Nacional d'Art de Catalunya.* Barcelona: Lunwerg, 1997.

Cárdenas-Rotunno, Anthony J. "In Search of a King: An Alfonsine Bibliology." In Burns, *Emperor of Culture,* 198–208.

———. "The Theophilus Legend in Prose, Poetry and Miniatures in the Códice Rico of Alfonso X: Compacting with Hell and Closing the Devil's Gate." In McInnis, *Models in Medieval Iberian Literature,* 39–68.

Carpenter, Dwayne L. *Alfonso X and the Jews: An Edition of and Commentary on Siete partidas 7.24 "De los judíos."* Berkeley: University of California Press, 1986.

———. "The Portrayal of the Jew in Alfonso the Learned's *Cantigas de Santa María.*" In *In Iberia and Beyond: Hispanic Jews Between Cultures,* edited by Bernard Dov Cooperman, 15–42. Newark: University of Delaware Press, 1998.

———. "Social Perception and Literary Portrayal: Jews and Muslims in Medieval Spanish Literature." In Mann, Glick, and Dodds, *Convivencia,* 61–81.

———. "A Sorcerer Defends the Virgin: Merlin in the *Cantigas de Santa María.*" *Cantigueiros* 5 (1993): 5–24.

Cash, Annette Grant. "Holy Mary Intervenes for the Clergy in the *Cantigas* of Alfonso X and in the *Milagros* of Berceo: Observations Concerning the Implicit Audience." *Cantigueiros* 8 (1996): 3–13.

La Cataluña judía. Barcelona: Museu d'Historia de Catalunya, 2002.

Castro, Américo. *España en su historia: Cristianos, moros, y judíos.* Buenos Aires: Ed. Losada, 1948.

La Chanson de Roland: The French Corpus. Edited by Joseph J. Duggan. Turnhout: Brepols, 2005.

Chazan, Robert. *Barcelona and Beyond: The Disputation of 1263 and Its Aftermath.* Berkeley: University of California Press, 1992.

———. *Church, State, and Jew in the Middle Ages.* New York: Behrman House, 1980.

———. *Daggers of Faith: Thirteenth-Century Missionizing and Jewish Response.* Berkeley: University of California Press, 1989.

———. *European Jewry and the First Crusade.* Berkeley: University of California Press, 1987.

———. *Medieval Stereotypes and Modern Antisemitism.* Berkeley: University of California Press, 1997.

———. *Reassessing Jewish Life in Medieval Europe.* New York: Cambridge University Press, 2010.

Chico Picaza, María Victoria. "'La arquitectura desde la miniatura,' una aproximación desde la baja edad media castellana." *Anales de Historia del Arte,* vol. extraordinario (2008): 57–71.

———. "Cronología de la miniatura Alfonsí: Estado de la cuestión." *Anales de Historia del Arte* 4 (1993–94): 569–76.

———. "Hagiografía en las *Cantigas de Santa María:* Byzantinismos y otros criterios de selección." *Anales de Historia del Arte* 9 (1999): 35–54.

———. "La relación texto-imagen en las *Cantigas de Santa María,* de Alfonso el Sabio." *Reales Sitios* 28, no. 87 (1986): 61–72.

———. "El scriptorium de Alfonso X el Sabio." In Bango Torviso, *Memoria de Sefarad,* 268–72.

———. "La teoría medieval de la música y la miniatura de las Cantigas." *Anales de Historia del Arte* 13 (2003): 83–95.

Cohen, Jeffrey Jerome. "On Saracen Enjoyment: Some Fantasies of Race in Late Medieval France and England." *Journal of Medieval and Early Modern Studies* 31, no. 1 (2001): 113–46.

———, ed. *The Postcolonial Middle Ages.* New York: St. Martin's Press, 2000.

Cohen, Jeremy. *Christ Killers: The Jews and the Passion from the Bible to the Big Screen.* New York: Oxford University Press, 2007.

———. *The Friars and the Jews: The Evolution of Medieval Anti-Judaism.* Ithaca: Cornell University Press, 1982.

———, ed. *From Witness to Witchcraft: Jews and Judaism in Medieval Christian Thought.* Wiesbaden: Harrassowitz, 1996.

———. "The Jews as Killers of Christ in the Latin Tradition: From Augustine to the Friars." *Traditio* 39 (1983): 1–27.

———. *Living Letters of the Law: Ideas of the Jew in Medieval Christianity.* Berkeley: University of California Press, 1999.

———. "The Muslim Connection, or On the Changing Role of the Jew in High Medieval Theology." In Cohen, *From Witness to Witchcraft,* 141–62.

Cohen, Mark R. *Under Crescent and Cross: The Jews in the Middle Ages.* Princeton: Princeton University Press, 1994.

Cohn, Samuel K. "The Black Death and the Burning of Jews." *Past and Present* 196 (August 2007): 3–36.

Coll i Rosell, Gaspar. "Les pintures murals del reracor de la Catedral de Tarragona: Arguments per a una filiació trescentista italianizant." *D'Art* 20 (1994): 253–65.

———. *Manuscrits jurídics i il·luminació: Estudi d'alguns codexs dels Ustages i Constitucions de Catalunya i del Decret de Graciá, 1300–1350.* Barcelona: Curial Edicions Catalanes, Publicacions de L'Abadia de Montserrat, 1995.

Cómez Ramos, Rafael. "El Alcázar de Sevilla en dos ejemplos de dominación cultural: Alfonso X el Sabio y Pedro I el Cruel." In *Spanien und der Orient im frühen und hohen Mittelalter,* 157–64. Madrider Beiträge 24. Mainz: Philipp von Zabern, 1996.

———. *Arquitectura Alfonsí.* Seville: Sevilla, 1974.

———. *Las empresas artísticas de Alfonso el Sabio.* Seville: Sevilla, 1979.

Companys Farrerons, Isabel, and Nùria Montardit Bofarull. *Embigats gótico-mudèixars al Tarragonés.* Tarragona: Excma. Diputació Provincial de Tarragona, 1983.

Constable, Olivia Remie. "Chess and Courtly Culture in Medieval Castile: The *Libro de ajedrez* of Alfonso el Sabio." *Speculum* 82, no. 2 (2007): 301–47.

Corbella i Llobet, Ramon. *L'aljama de jueus de Vic.* Vic: Tip. Católica de Sant Josep, 1909; repr., Vic: Institut d'Estudis Ausunencs, 1984.

Cothren, Michael. "The Iconography of Theophilus Windows in the First Half of the Thirteenth Century." *Speculum* 59, no. 2 (1984): 308–41.

Cowdrey, H. E. J. *The Cluniacs and the Gregorian Reform.* Oxford: Clarendon Press, 1970.

Crites, Danya. "Churches Made Fit for a King: Alfonso X and Meaning in the Religious Architecture of Post-Conquest Seville." *Medieval Encounters* 15 (2009): 391–413.

Cutler, Allan, and Helen Cutler. *The Jew as Ally of the Muslim: Medieval Roots of Anti-Semitism.* Notre Dame: University of Notre Dame Press, 1986.

Dahan, Gilbert. "Les juifs dans les Miracles de Gautier de Coincy." *Archives Juives* 16 (1980): 41–48, 59–68.

Dalmases Balañá, Nùria de, and Antonio José i Pitarch. *Els inicis i l'art romànic: Segles IX–XII.* Barcelona: Edicions 62, 1986.

Dangler, Jean. *Making Difference in Medieval and Early Modern Iberia.* Notre Dame: University of Notre Dame Press, 2005.

De Hamel, Christopher. *The Book: A History of the Bible.* New York: Phaidon, 2001.

———. *A History of Illuminated Manuscripts.* New York: Phaidon, 1977.

Delclaux, Federico. *Imágenes de la Virgen en los códices medievales de España.* Madrid: Dirección General de Bellas Artes, Ministerio de Educación y Ciencia, Patronato Nacional de Museos, 1973.

Delcor, Matthias. "Les juifs de Puigcerdà au XIIIeme siècle." *Sefarad* 26 (1966): 17–46.

Delgado Roig, Juan. "Examen médico-legal de unos restos históricos: Los cadáveres de Alfonso X y Beatriz de Suabia." *Archivo Hispalense* 9 (1948): 135–53.

Déroche, François. "Une reliure du Xe–XIe siècle." *Nouvelles des manuscrits du Moyen-Orient* 54 (1995): 1–9.

Despina, Sor María. "Las acusaciones de Crimen Ritual en España." *El Olivo* 9 (1979): 48–70.

Despres, Denise. "Mary of the Eucharist: Cultic Antijudaism in Some Fourteenth-Century English Devotional Manuscripts." In Cohen, *From Witness to Witchcraft,* 375–401.

Dexter, Elise Forsyth. "Sources of the Cantigas of Alfonso el Sabio." Ph.D. diss., University of Wisconsin, 1926.

Dillard, Heath. *Daughters of the Reconquest: Women in Castilian Town Society, 1100–1300.* New York: Cambridge University Press, 1984.

Dodds, Jerrilynn D. *Architecture and Ideology in Early Medieval Spain.* University Park: Penn State University Press, 1990.

———."Islam, Christianity, and the Problem of Religious Art." In *Art of Medieval Spain,* 27–37.

———. "Mudejar Tradition and the Synagogues of Medieval Spain." In Mann, Glick, and Dodds, *Convivencia,* 113–31.

———. "The Mudejar Tradition in Architecture." In Jayyusi, *Legacy of Muslim Spain,* 592–98.

Dodds, Jerrilynn D., María Rosa Menocal, and Abigail Krasner Balbale. *The Arts of Intimacy.* New Haven: Yale University Press, 2008.

Domínguez Bordona, Jesús. *Diccionario de iluminadores españoles.* Madrid: Maestre, 1957.

Domínguez Ortiz, Antonio. *Los judeoconversos en la España moderna.* Madrid: Editorial Mapfre, 1992.

Domínguez Rodriguez, Ana. *Astrología y arte en el Lapidario de Alfonso X el Sabio.* Madrid: Edilán, 1984.

———. "En torno al Árbol de Jesé (siglos XI–XIII): Tres ejemplos en las *Cantigas de Santa María.*" In Parkinson, *Cobras e Son,* 72–92.

———. "Filiación estilística de la miniatura alfonsí." In *España entre el Mediterráneo y el Atlántico,* 2 vols., 2:345–58. Actas del XXIII Congreso Internacional de Historia del Arte, Granada, 1973. Granada: Universidad de Granada, 1976–78.

———. "Iconografía evangélica en las *Cantigas de Santa María.*" In Katz and Keller, *Studies on the "Cantigas de Santa María,"* 53–79.

———. "La miniatura del 'Scriptorium Alfonsí.'" In *Estudios Alfonsíes: Lexicografía, lírica, estética y política de Alfonso el Sabio,* edited by Juan Vernet Ginés, José Mondéjar Cumpián, and Jesús Montoya Martínez, 127–61. Granada: Universidad de Granada, 1985.

———. "Texto, imagen y diseño de la página en la miniatura de Alfonso el Sabio." In *Imágenes y promotores en el arte medieval: Miscelánea en homenaje a Joaquín Yarza Luaces,* edited by Maria Luisa Melero Moneo et al., 313–26. Bellaterra: Universidad Autónoma de Barcelona, 2001.

Domínguez Rodríguez, Ana, and Pilar Treviño Gajardo. *Las Cantigas de Santa María: Formas e imagines.* Madrid: A y N Ediciones, 2007.

———. "Tradición del texto y tradición de la imagen en las *Cantigas de Santa María.*" *Reales Sitios* 164, no. 2 (2005): 2–17.

Ducrot-Granderye, Arlette P. *Etudes sur les Miracles de Nostre Dame de Gautier de Coinci.* Helsinki: Suomalainen Tiedeakatemia, 1932.

Ecker, Heather. *Caliphs and Kings: The Art and Influence of Islamic Spain.* Washington, D.C.: Freer Gallery of Art and Arthur M. Sackler Gallery, 2004.

———. "How to Administer a Conquered City in Al-Andalus: Mosques, Parish Churches, and Parishes." In Robinson and Rouhi, *Under the Influence,* 45–65.

Elukin, Joshua. "From Jew to Christian? Conversion and Immutability in Medieval Europe." In *Varieties of Religious Conversion in the Middle Ages,* edited by James Muldoon, 171–89. Gainesville: University Press of Florida, 1997.

Emmerson, Richard K. *Antichrist in the Middle Ages: A Study of Medieval Apocalypticism, Art, and Literature.* Seattle: University of Washington Press, 1981.

Ermengaud, Matfre. *Le Breviari d'amor de Matfre Ermengaud.* Edited and introduced by Peter T. Ricketts. 5 vols. London: Westfield College, 1976–2004.

Escandell Proust, Isabel. "La Biblia de 1268 del archivo episcopal de Vic." *Anuario del Departamento de Historia y Teoría del Arte* (UAM) 2 (1990): 103–15.

Espí Forcén, Carlos. "El corista de 'Engraterra': ¿San Guillermo de Norwich, San Hugo de Lincoln o Santo Dominguito del Val de Zaragoza?" *Miscelánea Medieval Murciana* 32 (2008): 51–64.

———. *Recrucificando a Cristo: Los judíos de la Passion Imaginis en la isla de Mallorca.* Mallorca: Objeto Perdido, 2009.

Ettinghausen, Richard. "Near Eastern Book Covers and Their Influence on European Bindings: A Report on the Exhibition 'History of Bookbinding' at the Baltimore Museum of Art, 1957–58." *Ars Orientalis* 3 (1959): 113–31.

Fábrega Grau, Angel. *Pasionario Hispánico (siglos X–XI).* 2 vols. Madrid: Instituto Enrique Flórez, 1953–55.

Falque Rey, Emma, Juan Gil, and Antonio Maya, eds. *Chronica Hispana saeculi XII.* Corpus Christianorum. Continuatio mediaevalis 71. Turnhout: Brepols, 1990.

Favà Monllau, Cèsar. "El retaule eucarístic de Vilafermosa i la iconografia del Corpus Christa a la Corona d'Aragó." *Locus Amoenus* 8 (2005–6): 105–21.

Feliciano, María Judith. "Muslim Shrouds for Christian Kings? A Reassessment of Andalusi Textiles in Thirteenth-Century Castilian Life and Ritual." In Robinson and Rouhi, *Under the Influence,* 101–31.

Feliciano, María Judith, Cynthia Robinson, and Leyla Rouhi, eds. "Interrogating Iberian Frontiers: Cross-Disciplinary Approaches to Mudéjar History, Religion, Art and Literature." Special issue of *Medieval Encounters* 12, no. 3 (2006).

Felsenstein, Frank. *Anti-Semitic Stereotypes: A Paradigm of Otherness in English Popular Culture, 1660–1830.* Baltimore: Johns Hopkins University Press, 1995.

Fernández, Laura. "Historia Florentina del Códice de las *Cantigas de Santa María,* MS. B.R. 20, de la 'Biblioteca palatina' a la 'Nazionale Centrale.'" *Reales Sitios* 164, no. 2 (2005): 18–29.

Ferreira, Manuel Pedro. "The Stemma of the Marian *Cantigas:* Philological and Musical Evidence." *Cantigueiros* 6 (1994): 58–98.

Ferreiro Alemparte, Jaime. "Fuentes germánicas en las 'Cantigas de Santa María' de Alfonso el Sabio." *Grial* 31 (1971): 31–62.

Ferrer García, Felix A. "El santo y la serpiente: Leyenda y realidad en el cenotafio de los mártires Vicente, Sabina y Cristeta de Ávila." *Cuadernos Abulenses* 29 (2000): 11–59.

Fidalgo Francisco, Elvira. "Consideración social de los judíos a través de las *Cantigas de Santa María.*" *Revista de literature medieval* 8 (1996): 91–104.

Filgueira Valverde, José. *Cantigas de Santa María: Códice Rico de El Escorial, MS escurialense T.I.1.* Madrid: Castalia, 1985.

———. "El texto: Introducción histórico-crítico, transcripción, version castellana y comentarios." In Alfonso X et al., *Las Cantigas de Santa María,* 44–48.

———. "Os xudeos nas *Cantigas de Santa María.*" In Barros, *Xudeus e conversos na historia,* 1:245–63.

Filgueira Valverde, Xosé. See Filgueira Valverde, José.

Fita, Fidel. "Cincuenta leyendas por Juan Gil de Zamora combinadas con las *Cantigas* de Alfonso el Sabio." *Boletín de la Real Academia de la Historia* 7 (1885): 54–144.

———. "Treinta leyendas por Gil de Zamora." *Boletín de la Real Academia de la Historia* 13 (1888): 187–225.

Flórez, Enrique, et al. *España sagrada: Theatro geographico-historico de la iglesia de España: Origen, divisiones y limites de todas sus provincias: Antiguedad, traslaciones, y estado antiguo y presente de sus sillas, en todos los dominios de España, y Portugal.* 51 vols. Madrid: M. F. Rodríguez, 1754–1879.

Flory, David. "Berceo's *Milagros* and the *Cantigas de Santa María:* The Question of Intended Audience." *Cantigueiros* 8 (1996): 15–28.

———. *Marian Representations in the Miracle Tales of Thirteenth-Century Spain and France.* Washington, D.C.: Catholic University Press, 2000.

Foster, Elisa A. "The Writing on the Wall: The Presence of Arabic Inscription in the Synagogue of El Tránsito." M.A. thesis, Southern Methodist University, 2004.

Fradejas Lebrero, José. "La Cantiga CVII o de Mari Saltos." *Fragmentos* 2 (1984): 20–32.

Freire, José L. "The *CSM:* Social Perception and Literary Portrayal of Jews and Muslims, and Historical Reality." In McInnis, *Models in Medieval Iberian Literature,* 9–38.

Friedman, Jerome. "Jewish Conversion, the Spanish Pure Blood Laws, and Reformation: A Revisionist View of Racial and Religious Antisemitism." *Sixteenth-Century Journal* 18 (1987): 3–31.

Frojmovic, Eva, ed. *Imagining the Self, Imagining the Other: Visual Representation and Jewish-Christian Dynamics in the Middle Ages and Early Modern Period.* Leiden: E. J. Brill, 2002.

Fryer, Alfred C. "Theophilus the Penitent as Represented in Art." *Archaeological Journal* 92 (1935): 287–333.

Fuchs, Eduard. *Die Juden in der Karikatur: Ein Beitrag zur Kulturgeschichte.* Munich: Albert Langen, 1921.

Gacek, Adam. "Arabic Bookmaking and Terminology as Portrayed by Bakr al-Ishbīlī in His *Kitāb al-taysīr fī ṣinaʿat al-tasfīr.*" *Manuscripts of the Middle East* 5 (1990–91): 106–13.

Gallego, María Ángeles. "The Languages of Medieval Iberia and Their Religious Dimension." *Medieval Encounters* 9, no. 1 (2003): 107–39.

Garabito Gregorio, Godofredo. "Escultura castellano-leonesa en la Colección Godia." *Boletín de la Real Academia de Bellas Artes de la Purísima Concepción* 26 (1991): 53–72.

García Arenal, Mercedes. "Los moros en las *Cantigas* de Alfonso X." *Al-Qantara* 6 (1985): 133–51.

García Cuadrado, Ámparo. *Las Cantigas: El códice de Florencia.* Murcia: Universidad de Murcia, 1993.

García Gainza, María Concepción, et al. *Catálogo monumental de Navarra.* Vol. 5, *Merindad de Pamplona,* pt. 2, *Imoz-Zugarramurdi.* Pamplona: Gobierno de Navarra, 1996.

García Morencos, Pilar. *Libro de ajedrez, dados y tablas de Alfonso X el Sabio.* Madrid: Patrimonio Nacional, 1987.

García Serrano, Francisco. *Preachers of the City: The Expansion of the Dominican Order in Castile, 1217–1348.* New Orleans: University Press of the South, 1997.

Gaster, Moses. "The Letter of Toledo." *Folk-Lore* 13 (1902): 115–31.

Gautier de Coincy. *Les miracles de Nostre Dame.* Edited by V. Frederic Koenig. 4 vols. Geneva: Droz, 1955–70.

Geertz, Clifford. "Thick Description: Toward an Interpretive Theory of Culture." In *The Interpretation of Cultures: Selected Essays,* 3–30. New York: Basic Books, 1973.

Gerli, Michael. "Poet and Pilgrim: Discourse, Language, Imagery, and

Audience in Berceo's *Milagros de Nuestra Señora*." In *Hispanic Medieval Studies in Honor of Samuel G. Armistead*, edited by Michael Gerli and Harvey L. Sharrer, 140–51. Madison, Wis.: Hispanic Seminary of Medieval Studies, 1992.

Gil de Zamora, Juan. *De preconiis Hispaniae: Estudio preliminar y edición crítica.* Edited by Manuel de Castro y Castro. Madrid: Universidad de Madrid, 1955.

Gilman, Sander. *The Jew's Body.* London: Routledge, 1991.

Ginio, Alisa Meyuhas. *La forteresse de la foi: La vision du monde d'Alonso de Espina, moine espagnol (?–1466).* Paris: Les Éditions du Cerf, 1998.

Glick, Thomas F. "Convivencia: An Introductory Note." In Mann, Glick, and Dodds, *Convivencia,* 1–9.

———. *Islamic and Christian Spain in the Early Middle Ages.* Princeton: Princeton University Press, 1979.

Godia, Francisco, and Liliana Godia Guardiola. *Románico y Gótico de la colección Francisco Godia.* Barcelona: Fundación Francisco Godia, 2001.

Goldberg, Harriet. "Literary Portrait of the Child in Castilian Medieval Literature." *Kentucky Romance Quarterly* 27 (1980): 11–27.

Goldschmidt, Werner. "Sepulcro de San Vicente, en Avila." *Archivo Español de Arte y Arqueologia* 12 (1936): 161–70.

González Jiménez, Manuel. "Alfonso X, Rey de Castilla y León (1252–1284)." In Montoya Martínez and Domínguez Rodríguez, *El scriptorium alfonsí,* 1–15.

———. "¿Re-Conquista? Un Estado de la Cuestión." In *Tópicos y Realidades de la Edad Media,* edited by Eloy Benito Ruano, 155–78. Madrid: Real Academia de la Historia, 2000.

Grabar, Oleg. *The Mediation of Ornament.* Princeton: Princeton University Press, 1995.

———. "Two Paradoxes in the Art of the Spanish Peninsula." In Jayyusi, *Legacy of Muslim Spain,* 583–91.

Grauert, Hermann. "Meister Johann von Toledo." *Sitzungsberichte der Königliche Bayerischen Akademie der Wissenschaften, Philosophisch-Philologische und Historische Classe* 2 (1901): 111–325.

Grautoff, Gwendollyn Gout. "*Vidal mayor:* A Visualisation of the Juridical Miniatures." *Medieval History Journal* 3, no. 1 (2000): 67–89.

Grayzel, Solomon, ed. and trans. *The Church and the Jews in the XIIIth Century: A Study of Their Relations During the Years 1198–1254, Based on the Papal Letters and the Conciliar Decrees of the Period.* Philadelphia: Dropsie College, 1933; rev. ed., New York, Hermon Press, 1966.

Greenblatt, Stephen. *Renaissance Self-Fashioning from More to Shakespeare.* Chicago: University of Chicago Press, 1980.

Gregorio Sirem, Daniel. "Las lecturas de las *Cantigas de Santa María.*" *De Arte: Revista de Historia del Arte* 6 (2007): 57–74.

Gudiol i Cunill, Josep, and Salvador Sanpere i Miquel. *La pintura mig-eval catalana.* 2 vols. in 5. Barcelona: S. Babra, 1926–55.

Guerrero Lovillo, José. *Las Cántigas: Estudio arqueológico de las miniaturas.* Madrid: CSIC, 1949.

Harris, Anne F. "The Performative Terms of Jewish Iconoclasm and Conversion in Two Saint Nicholas Windows at Chartres Cathedral." In Merback, *Beyond the Yellow Badge,* 119–41.

Harris, Julie A. "Good Jews, Bad Jews, and No Jews at All: Ritual Imagery and Social Standards in the Catalan Haggadot." In *Church, State, Vellum, and Stone: Studies in Honor of John Williams,* edited by Therese Martin and Julie Harris, 275–96. Leiden: E. J. Brill, 2005.

Hatton, Angus, and Vikki McKay. "Anti-Semitism in the *Cantigas de Santa María.*" *Bulletin of Hispanic Studies* 61 (1983): 189–99.

Heng, Geraldine. *Empire of Magic: Medieval Romance and the Politics of Cultural Fantasy.* New York: Columbia University Press, 2003.

———. "The Romance of England: *Richard Coeur de Lyon,* Saracens, Jews, and the Politics of Race and Nation." In Cohen, *Postcolonial Middle Ages,* 135–71.

Herbert, James. "Visual Culture / Visual Studies." In *Critical Terms for Art History,* edited by Robert S. Nelson and Richard Schiff, 452–64. Chicago: University of Chicago Press, 2003.

Hering Torres, Max Sebastián. "'Limpieza de Sangre': ¿Racismo en la Edad Moderna?" *Tiempos Modernos* 9 (2003–4): 1–16.

Hillgarth, Jocelyn N. *The Spanish Kingdoms, 1250–1516.* Oxford: Clarendon Press, 1978.

Hofmeister, Wernfried. "Das Jüdel im Kontext mittelhochdeutscher literarischer Kindesdarstellungen." In *Die Juden in ihrer Mittelalterlichen Umwelt,* edited by Alfred Ebenbauer and Klaus Zatloukal, 91–103. Cologne: Bohlau, 1991.

The Holie Bible Faithfully Translated into English out of the Authentical Latin. 2 vols. Douay: Laurence Kellam, 1609–10.

Hourihane, Colum, ed. *Spanish Medieval Art: Recent Studies.* Tempe, Ariz.: MRTS; Princeton, N.J.: Index of Christian Art, 2007.

Hsia, Ronnie Po-chia. *The Myth of Ritual Murder: Jews and Magic in Reformation Germany.* New Haven: Yale University Press, 1988.

Iogna-Prat, Dominique. *Order and Exclusion: Cluny and Christendom Face Heresy, Judaism, and Islam.* Translated by Graham Robert Edwards. Ithaca: Cornell University Press, 2002.

Jackson, Deirdre F. "Depictions of Theophilus in Devotional Books: Remarks Based on a Miniature in Alfonso X's *Cantigas de Santa María.*" In *Under the Influence: The Concept of Influence and the Study of Illuminated Manuscripts,* edited by Alixe Bovey and John Lowden, 75–88. Turnhout: Brepols, 2007.

———. "Shields of Faith: Apotropaic Images of the Virgin in Alfonso X's *Cantigas de Santa María.*" *RACAR: Revue d'Art Canadienne* 24, no. 2 (1997): 38–46.

Jacobus de Voragine. *The Golden Legend: Readings on the Saints.* Translated by William Granger Ryan. Princeton: Princeton University Press, 1993.

Jayyusi, Salma Khadra, ed. *The Legacy of Muslim Spain.* Leiden: E. J. Brill, 1992.

Jochum, Herbert, ed. *Ecclesia und Synagoga: Das Judentum in der christlichen Kunst.* Essen: Alte Synagoge; Saarbrücken: Regionalgeschichtliches Museum, 1993.

John of Garland. *The Stella Maris of John of Garland.* Edited by Evelyn Faye Wilson. Cambridge, Mass.: Medieval Academy of America, 1946.

Jordan, William Chester. "Adolescence and Conversion in the Middle Ages." In Signer and Van Engen, *Jews and Christians in Twelfth-Century Europe,* 77–93.

———. "The Last Tormentor of Christ: An Image of the Jew in Ancient and Medieval Exegesis, Art, and Drama." *Jewish Quarterly Review* 78 (1987): 21–47.

———. "Marían Devotion and the Talmud Trial of 1240." In *Religionsgespräche im Mittelalter,* edited by Bernard Lewis and Friedrich Niewöhner, 61–76. Wiesbaden: Harrassowitz, 1992.

———. "Why 'Race'?" *Journal of Medieval and Early Modern Studies* 31, no. 1 (2001): 166–73.

Jung, Jacqueline. "The Passion, the Jews, and the Crisis of the Individual on the Naumburg West Choir Screen." In Merback, *Beyond the Yellow Badge,* 145–77.

Junyent, Eduardo. "Le scriptorium de la cathedrale de Vich." *Cahiers de Saint-Michel de Cuxa* 5 (1974): 65–69.

Kagay, Donald J., ed. *Usatges de Barcelona: The Fundamental Law of Catalonia.* Philadelphia: University of Pennsylvania Press, 1994.

Kaplan, Paul. "Introduction to the New Edition." In Bindman and Gates, *Image of the Black in Western Art,* vol. 2, pt. 1, 1–30.

Katz, Israel, and John Esten Keller, eds. *Studies on the "Cantigas de Santa María": Proceedings of the First International Symposium on the "Cantigas de Santa María" of Alfonso X El Sabio (1221–1284).* Madison, Wis.: Hispanic Seminary of Medieval Studies, 1987.

Kauffmann, Charles M. "Ein spanisches Gesetzbuch aud dem XIII. Jahrhundert in Aachener Privatbesitz." *Aachener Kunstblätter* 29 (1964): 108–38.

Keller, John Esten. "Daily Living as Presented in the *Cantigas* of Alfonso the Learned." *Speculum* 33 (1958): 484–89.

———. "Some Remarks on Visualization in the *Cantigas de Santa María.*" *Ariel* (April 1974): 7–12.

———. "Verbalization and Visualization in the *Cantigas de Santa María.*" In *Oelschläger Festschrift,* 221–26. Estudios de la Hispanófila 36. Chapel Hill, N.C.: Estudios de Hispanófila, 1976.

Keller, John Esten, and Annette Grant Cash. *Daily Life as Depicted in the Cantigas de Santa María.* Studies in Romance Languages 44. Lexington: University Press of Kentucky, 1998.

Kessler, Herbert, and David R. Nirenberg, eds. *Judaism and Christian Art: Aesthetic Anxieties from the Catacombs to Colonialism.* Philadelphia: University of Pennsylvania Press, 2011.

Kinoshita, Sharon. *Medieval Boundaries: Rethinking Difference in Old French Literature.* Philadelphia: University of Pennsylvania Press, 2006.

Kisch, Guido. "The Yellow Badge in History." *Historia Judaica* 4 (1942): 95–144.

Klein, Elka. *Jews, Christian Society, and Royal Power in Medieval Barcelona.* Ann Arbor: University of Michigan Press, 2006.

Klein, Peter K. "Der Ausdruck unterschiedlicher Konflikte in der Darstellung der Juden und Mauren in den 'Cantigas' Alfons des Weisen von Kastilien un León." In *Bereit zum Konflikt: Strategien und Medien Konflikterzeugnungen und Konfliktbewältigung im europäischen Mittelalter,* edited by Oliver Auge et al., 67–86. Ostfildern: Jan Thorbecke, 2008.

———. "'Jud, dir kuckt der Spitzbub aus dem Gesicht!' Traditionen Antisemitischer Bildstereotype oder die Physiognomie de 'Juden' als Construct." In *Abgestempelt: Judenfeindliche Postkarten,* edited by Helmut Gold et al., 43–78. Heidelberg: Umschau, 1999.

———. "Kunst und Feudalismus zur Zeit Alfons de Weisen von Kastilien und Leon (1252–1284): Die Illustration der *Cantigas.*" In *Bauwerk und Bildwerk: Anschauliche Beiträge zur Kultur und Social-Geschichte,* edited by Karl Clausberg et al., 169–212. Giessen: Anabas, 1981.

———. "Moros y judíos en las 'Cantigas' de Alfonso el Sabio: Imágenes de conflictos distintos." In *Simposio internacional "El Legado de Al-Andalus": El arte andalusi en los reinos de León y Castilla durante la edad media,* edited by Manuel Valdés Fernández, 341–64. Valladolid: Fundación del Patrimonio Histórico de Castilla y León, 2007.

Kogman-Appel, Katrin. *Illuminated Haggadot from Medieval Spain: Biblical Imagery and the Passover Holiday.* University Park: Pennsylvania State University Press, 2006.

———. *Jewish Book Art Between Islam and Christianity: The Decoration of Hebrew Bibles in Medieval Spain.* Leiden: E. J. Brill, 2004.

Kosmer, Ellen, and James F. Powers. "Manuscript Illustration: The *Cantigas* in Their Contemporary Art Context." In Burns, *Emperor of Culture,* 46–71.

Kraus, Henry. *The Living Theatre of Medieval Art.* London: Thames and Hudson, 1967.

Krause, Kathy M., and Alison Stones, eds. *Gautier de Coinci: Miracles, Music, and Manuscripts.* Turnhout: Brepols, 2006.

Kruger, Steven. "The Bodies of Jews in the Late Middle Ages." In *The Idea of Medieval Literature: New Essays on Chaucer and Medieval Culture in Honor of Donald R. Howard,* edited by James M. Dean and Christian K. Zacher, 301–23. Newark: University of Delaware Press, 1992.

———. "Medieval Christian (Dis)identifications: Muslims and Jews in Guibert of Nogent." *New Literary History* 28, no. 2 (1997): 185–203.

———. *The Spectral Jew: Conversion and Embodiment in Medieval Europe.* Minneapolis: University of Minnesota Press, 2005.

Kulp-Hill, Kathleen. "The Captions to the Miniatures of the 'Códice Rico' of the *Cantigas de Santa María.*" *Cantigueiros* 7 (1995): 3–64.

———. *Songs of Holy Mary of Alfonso the Wise.* Tempe, Ariz.: Medieval and Renaissance Texts and Studies, 2000.

Kupfer, Marcia. ". . . lectres . . . plus vrayes: Hebrew Script and Jewish Witness in the Mandeville Manuscript of King Charles V." *Speculum* (2008): 58–111.

———. "Medieval World Maps: Embedded Images, Interpretive Frames." *Word and Image* 10, no. 3 (1994): 262–88.

Lacarra Ducay, María Carmen. "Las miniaturas del *Vidal mayor:* Estudio histórico-artístico." In *Vidal mayor,* edited by Antonio Ubieto Arteta, 2 vols., 1:113–66. Huesca: Instituto de Estudios Altoaragoneses, 1989.

Langmuir, Gavin I. "L'absence d'accusation de meurtre rituel a l'ouest du Rhone." In *Juifs et judaïsme de Languedoc, XIIIe siècle–début XIVe siècle,* edited by Marie-Humbert Vicaire and Bernhard Blumenkranz, 235–49. Toulouse: Privat, 1977.

———. "Historiographic Crucifixion." In *Les Juifs au regard de l'Histoire: Mélanges en l'honneur de Bernhard Blumenkranz,* edited by Gilbert Dahan, 109–27. Paris: Picard, 1985.

———. "Thomas of Monmouth: Detector of Ritual Murder." *Speculum* 59, no. 4 (1984): 820–46.

Lapostolle, Christine. "Images et apparitions: Illustrations des 'Miracles de Nostre Dame.'" *Médiévales* (1982): 47–67.

Laske-Fix, Katja. *Der Bildzyklus des Breviari d'amor.* Munich: Schnell & Steiner, 1973.

Lasker, Daniel J., and Sarah Stroumsa. *The Polemic of Nestor the Priest. Quiṣṣat mujādalat al-Usquf and Sefer Nestor ha-Komer.* Jerusalem: Ben-Zvi Institute for the Study of Jewish Communities in the East, 1996.

Lazar, Moshe. "The Lamb and the Scapegoat: The Dehumanization of the Jews in Medieval Propaganda Imagery." In *Anti-Semitism in Times of Crisis,* edited by Sander Gilman and Steven T. Katz, 38–80. New York: New York University Press, 1991.

———. "Theophilus: Servant of Two Masters; The Pre-Faustian Theme of Despair and Revolt." *Modern Language Notes* 87, no. 6 (1972): 31–50.

Le Goff, Jacques. *Your Money or Your Life: Economy and Religion in the Middle Ages.* New York: Zone Books, 1988.

León Tello, Pilar. *Judíos de Ávila.* Ávila: Diputación Provincial de Ávila, Instituto "Gran Duque de Alba," 1963.

Lerner, Robert E. *The Powers of Prophecy: The Cedar of Lebanon Vision from the Mongol Onslaught to the Dream of the Enlightenment.* Berkeley: University of California Press, 1983.

Leroquais, Victor. *Les sacramentaires et les missels manuscrits des bibliothèques publiques de France.* 4 vols. Paris: Protat, 1924.

Leroy, Beatrice. *The Jews of Navarre.* Jerusalem: Magnes Press, 1985.

Lewis, Bernard. *Race and Color in Islam.* New York: Harper and Row, 1971.

———. *Race and Slavery in the Middle East: An Historical Enquiry.* New York: Oxford University Press, 1990.

Liaño Martínez, Emma. "Elementos de orígen islámico en el claustro de la catedral de Tarragona." *Universitas Tarraconensis* 9 (1987): 141–49.

Linaje Conde, Antonio. "Vida canonical en la "Repoblación" de la Península Ibérica?" In Melville, *Secundum regulam vivere,* 73–85.

Linehan, Peter. *Spain, 1157–1300: A Partible Inheritance.* Malden, Mass.: Blackwell, 2008.

Lipton, Sara. *Images of Intolerance: The Representation of Jews and Judaism in the Bible Moralisée.* Berkeley: University of California Press, 1999.

———. "The Jew's Face: Vision, Knowledge, and Identity in Medieval Anti-Jewish Caricature." In *Late Medieval Jewish Identities: Iberia and Beyond,* edited by Carmen Caballero-Navas and Esperanza Alonso, 259–87. New York: Palgrave Macmillan, 2010.

———. "The Temple Is My Body: Gender, Carnality, and Synagoga in the Bible Moralisée." In Frojmovic, *Imagining the Self, Imagining the Other,* 129–63.

———. "Unfeigned Witness: Jews, Matter, and Vision in Twelfth-Century Christian Art." In Kessler and Nirenberg, *Judaism and Christian Art,* 45–73.

———. "Where Are the Gothic Jewish Women? On the Non-iconography of the Jewess in the *Cantigas de Santa María.*" *Jewish History* 22 (2008): 139–77.

Little, Lester K. *Religious Poverty and the Profit Economy in Medieval Europe.* Ithaca: Cornell University Press 1978.

Llop i Jordana, Irene. "Aportacions a l'estudi de l'aljama de jueus de Vic al segle XIII." *Ausa* 21, no. 152 (2003): 143–50.

———. "Jewish Moneylenders from Vic According to the *Liber Judeorum* 1341–1354." *Hispania Judaica* 2 (1999): 75–87.

Llull, Ramon. *See* Ramon Llull.

Lourie, Elena. "Anatomy of Ambivalence: Muslims Under the Crown of Aragón." In *Crusade and Colonisation: Muslims, Christians, and Jews in Aragón,* 1–77. Aldershot: Variorum, 1990.

———. "Cultic Dancing and Courtly Love: Jews and Popular Culture in Fourteenth-Century Aragón and Valencia." In *Cross-Cultural Convergences in the Crusader Period: Essays Presented to Aryeh Grabois on his Sixty-Fifth Birthday,* edited by Michael Goodich Menache and Sylvia Schlein, 151–82. New York: Peter Lang, 1995.

———. "A Plot Which Failed? The Case of the Corpse Found in the Jewish Call of Barcelona." *Mediterranean Historical Review* 1 (1986): 187–220.

Lowden, John. *The Making of the Bibles Moralisées.* 2 vols. University Park: Pennsylvania State University Press, 2000.

Maccoby, Hyam. *Judaism on Trial: Jewish-Christian Disputations in the Middle Ages.* London: Littman, 1996.

MacDonald, Robert A. "Law and Politics: Alfonso's Program of Political Reform." In *The Worlds of Alfonso the Learned and James the Conqueror,* edited by Robert I. Burns, 150–98. Princeton: Princeton University Press, 1985.

Mann, Janice. *Romanesque Architecture and Its Sculptural Decoration in Christian Spain, 1000–1120.* Toronto: University of Toronto Press, 2009.

Mann, Vivian B. *Art and Ceremony in Jewish Life: Essays in the History of Jewish Art.* London: Pindar Press, 2005.

———, ed. *Uneasy Communion: Jews, Christians, and the Altarpieces of Medieval Spain,* New York: Museum of Biblical Art, 2010.

Mann, Vivian B., Thomas F. Glick, and Jerrilynn D. Dodds, eds. *Convivencia: Jews, Muslims, and Christians in Medieval Spain.* New York: Braziller, 1992.

Marcais, Georges, and Louis Poinssot, *Objets kairouanais, IXe au XIIIe siècle: Réliures, verreries, cuivres et bronzes, bijoux.* Tunis: Tournier, 1948.

Marcus, Ivan G. "Images of the Jews in the Exempla of Caesarius of Heisterbach." In Cohen, *From Witness to Witchcraft,* 247–56.

Márquez Villanueva, Francisco. *El concepto cultural alfonsí.* Madrid: Editorial Mapfre, 1994.

Marullo, Teresa. "Osservazioni sulle Cantigas de Alfonso e sui *Miracles* de Coincy." *Archivum Romanum* 18 (1934): 495–539.

McCulloch, John M. "Jewish Ritual Murder: William of Norwich, Thomas of Monmouth, and the Early Dissemination of the Myth." *Speculum* 72, no. 3 (1997): 698–740.

McInnis, Judy B., ed. *Models in Medieval Iberian Literature and Their Modern Reflections: Convivencia as Structural, Cultural, and Sexual Ideal.* Newark, Del.: Juan de la Cuesta, 2002.

McMichael, Steven J. *Was Jesus of Nazareth the Messiah? Alphonso de Espina's Argument Against the Jews in the Fortalitium Fidei (c. 1464).* Atlanta: Scholars Press, 1994.

Melero Moneo, María Luisa. "El Diablo en la Matanza de los Inocentes: Una particularidad de la escultura románica hispana." *D'Art* 12 (1986): 1–15.

———. "Eucarístia y polémica antisemita en el retablo y frontal de Vallbona des Monges." *Locus Amoenus* 2 (2002–3): 21–40.

———. *La pintura sobre tabla del gótico lineal: Frontales, laterales de altar y retablos en el reino de Mallorca y los condados catalanes.* Barcelona: Museu Nacional d'Art de Catalunya and Edicions i Publicacions de la Universitat de Barcelona, 2005.

Mellinkoff, Ruth. *The Mark of Cain.* Berkeley: University of California Press, 1981.

———. *Outcasts: Signs of Otherness in Northern European Art in the Later Middle Ages.* 2 vols. Berkeley: University of California Press, 1993.

Melville, Gert, ed. *Secundum regulam vivere: Festschrift für P. Norbert Backmund.* Windberg: Poppe-Verlag, 1978.

Menéndez Pidal, Gonzalo. "Las Cantigas: La vida en el siglo XIII según la representación iconográfica (I)." *Cuadernos de la Alhambra* 14 (1978): 87–98.

Menéndez Pidal, Gonzalo, and Carmen Bernis. "Las Cantigas: La vida en el siglo XIII según la representación iconográfica (II): Traje, aderezo, afeites." *Cuadernos de la Alhambra* 15–17 (1979–81): 89–174.

Menéndez Pidal de Navascués, Faustino, Mikel Ramos Aguirre, and Esperanza Ochoa de Olza Eguiraun. *Sellos medievales de Navarra: Estudio y corpus descriptivo* Pamplona: Gobierno de Navarra, 1995.

Menocal, María Rosa. *Ornament of the World: How Muslims, Jews, and Christians Created a Culture of Tolerance in Medieval Spain.* Boston: Little, Brown, 2002.

Merback, Mitchell B., ed. *Beyond the Yellow Badge: New Approaches to Anti-Judaism and Antisemitism in Medieval and Early Modern Visual Culture.* Leiden: E. J. Brill, 2007.

Mettmann, Walter. "Algunas observaciones sobre la génesis de la colección de las *Cantigas de Santa María* y sobre el problema del autor." In Katz and Keller, *Studies on the "Cantigas de Santa María,"* 355–56.

Meyerson, Mark D. *Jews in an Iberian Frontier Kingdom: Society, Economy, and Politics in Morvedre, 1248–1391.* Leiden: E. J. Brill, 2005.

Miquel i Rosell, Francesc X. *Cataleg dels llibres manuscrits de la Biblioteca del Monestir de Sant Cugat del Vallès existents a l'Arxiu de la Corona d'Aragó.* Barcelona: Imprenta de la Casa de Caritat, 1937.

Miranda García, Carlos. "Consideraciones sobre el judío y el hereje en occitania a través del ciclo de images de la historia de la 'ceguera de los judíos' del *Breviari d'amor* de Matfre Ermengaud de Beziers: Escorial MS S.I.3." *Archivo Español de Arte* 67, no. 267 (1994): 257–67.

Mirrer, Louise. "The Beautiful Jewess: Marisaltos in Alfonso X's Cantigas de Santa María." In *Women, Jews, and Muslims in the Texts of Reconquest Castile,* 31–44. Ann Arbor: University of Michigan Press, 1996.

———. "The Jew's Body in Medieval Iberian Literary Portraits and Miniatures: Examples from the *Cantigas de Santa María* and the *Cantar de mio Cid.*" *Shofar* 12, no. 3 (1994): 17–30.

Mitre Fernández, Emilio. *Los judíos de Castilla en tiempo de Enrique III: El pogrom de 1391.* Valladolid: Universidad de Valladolid, 1994.

Molina Filgueiras, Joan. "La imagen y su contexto: Perfiles de la iconografía antijudía en la España medieval." In *Els jueus a la Girona medieval,* XII ciclo de conferencias Girona a l'Abast, 33–85. Girona: Bell-lloc, 2008.

———. "Las imágenes del judío en la España medieval." In Bango Torviso, *Memoria de Sefarad,* 373–79.

Moncada, Juan Luis de. *Episcopologio de Vich, escrito a mediados del siglo XVII.* 3 vols. Vic: R. Anglada, 1894–1901.

Monreal Agustí, Luis. *El Conventet II: Colección de escultura.* Barcelona: Publicaciones Reunidas, 1972.

Monsalvo Antón, José María. "Mentalidad antijudía en la Castilla medieval." In Barros, *Xudeus e conversos na historia,* 1:21–84.

———. *Teoría y evolución de un conflicto social: El antisemitismo en la Corona de Castilla en la Baja Edad Media.* Madrid: Siglo XXI, 1985.

Monteira Arías, Inés. "Los musulmanes como verdugos de los personajes sagrados en la iconografía románica: Una interpretación actualizada de las escrituras para combatir el Islam en la Edad Media." *Codex Aquilarensis* 23 (2007): 67–87.

Montoya Martínez, Jesús. "El códice de Florencia: Una nueva hipótesis de trabajo." *Romance Quarterly* (1986): 323–29.

———. *Las colecciones de milagros de la Virgen en la Edad Media (El milagro literario).* Colección Filológica 29. Granada: Universidad de Granada, 1981.

———. "Judíos y moros en las *Cantigas de Santa María.*" *Historia del derecho* 2 (1980): 69–90.

———. "El milagro de Teófilo en Coinci, Berceo y Alfonso el Sabio." *Berceo* 87 (1974): 152–85.

Montoya Martínez, Jesús, and Ana Domínguez Rodríguez, eds. *El scriptorium alfonsí: De los Libros de Astrología a las Cantigas de Santa María.* Cursos de verano de El Escorial. Madrid: Editorial Complutense, 1999.

Moore, R. I. *The Formation of a Persecuting Society: Authority and Deviance in Western Europe, 950–1250.* Rev. ed. Oxford: Wiley Blackwell, 2007.

Moralejo Álvarez, Serafín. "Artistas, patronos y público en el arte del Camino de Santiago." *Compostellanum* 30 (1985): 395–430.

———. "On the Road: The Camino de Santiago." In *Art of Medieval Spain,* 175–83.

Mussafia, Adolf. "Studien zu den mittelalterlichen Marienlegenden." *Sitzungsberichte der Kaiserlichen Akademie der Wissenschaft in Wien* 113 (1886): 917–94; 115 (1887): 5–93; 119 (1889): fasc. ix, 1–66; 123 (1890): fasc. viii, 1–85; 139 (1898): fasc. viii, 1–74.

Nirenberg, David R. *Communities of Violence: Persecution of Minorities in the Middle Ages.* Princeton: Princeton University Press, 1996.

———. "El concepto de la raza en la España medieval." *Edad Media: Revista de Historia* 3 (Spring 2000): 39–60.

———. "Conversion, Sex, and Segregation: Jews and Christians in Medieval Spain." *American Historical Review* 107, no. 4 (2006): 1065–93.

———. "Enmity and Assimilation: Jews, Christians, and Converts in Medieval Spain." *Common Knowledge* 9, no. 1 (2003): 137–55.

———. "Race and the Middle Ages: The Case of Spain and Its Jews." In *Rereading the Black Legend: The Discourses of Religious and Racial Difference in the Renaissance Empires,* edited by Margaret Rich Greer, Walter Mignolo, and Maureen Quilligan, 71–87. Chicago: University of Chicago Press, 2007.

Nissen, Theodor. "Zu den ältesten Fassungen der Legende vom Judenknaben." *Zeitschrift für französische Sprache und Literatur* 62 (1939): 393–403.

Norris, Michael Byron. "Early Gothic Illuminated Bibles at Bologna: The 'Prima Maniera' Phase, 1250–1274." Ph.D. diss., University of California at Santa Barbara, 1993.

O'Callaghan, Joseph F. *Alfonso X and the Cantigas de Santa María: A Poetic Biography.* Leiden: E. J. Brill, 1998.

———. "The Cortes and Royal Taxation During the Reign of Alfonso." *Traditio* 27 (1971): 379–98.

———. *A History of Medieval Spain.* Ithaca: Cornell University Press, 1975.

———, trans. *The Latin Chronicle of the Kings of Castile.* Tempe: Arizona Center for Medieval and Renaissance Studies, 2002.

———, ed. *The Learned King: The Reign of Alfonso X of Castile.* Philadelphia: University of Pennsylvania Press, 1993.

———. *Reconquest and Crusade in Medieval Spain.* Philadelphia: University of Pennsylvania Press, 2003

Ollich i Castanyer, Inmaculada. "Aspectes economics de l'activitat dels jueus de Vic, segons els 'Libri iudeorum' (1266–1278)." *Miscel·lània de Textos Medievals* 3 (1985): 3–118.

———. "Les entitats eclesiàstiques de Vic al segle XIII." *Ausa* 8, no. 84 (1976): 90–101.

———. "Un nou document sobre la 'scola seu sinagoga iudeorum' de Vic (vers 1278)." *Ausa* 8, nos. 87–88 (1978): 257–67.

Ortega Martínez, Ana Isabel. "Pavimento: Azulejos." In Bango Torviso, *Memoria de Sefarad,* 140.

Palomera Plaza, Santiago. "Bocado de caballo" and "Pieza de cinturón." In Bango Torviso, *Memoria de Sefarad,* 127–30.

Parker, Elizabeth C. "Editing the Cloisters Cross." *Gesta* 45, no. 2 (2006): 147–60.

Parker, Elizabeth C., and Charles T. Little. *The Cloisters Cross: Its Art and Meaning.* New York: Metropolitan Museum of Art, 1994.

Parkes, James. *The Jew in the Medieval Community: A Study of His Political and Economic Situation.* London: Soncino Press, 1938.

Parkinson, Stephen, ed. *Cobras e Son: Papers on the Text, Music, and Manuscripts of the Cantigas de Santa María.* Oxford: European Humanities Research Centre, University of Oxford, 2000.

———. "The First Reorganization of the CSM." *Cantigueiros* 1 (1988): 91–97.

Parkinson, Stephen, and Deirdre Jackson. "Collection, Composition, and Compilation in the *Cantigas de Santa María.*" *Portuguese Studies* 22, no. 2 (2006): 159–72.

Patton, Pamela A. "The Cloister as Cultural Mirror: Anti-Jewish Imagery at Santa María la Mayor in Tudela." In *Der mittelalterliche Kreuzgang: Architectur, Funktion und Programm,* edited by Peter Klein, 317–32. Regensburg: Schnell & Steiner, 2003.

———. "Constructing the Inimical Jew in the *Cantigas de Santa María:* Theophilus's Magician in Text and Image." In Merback, *Beyond the Yellow Badge,* 233–56.

———. "An Islamic Envelope-Flap Binding in the Cloister of Tudela: Another 'Muslim Connection' for Iberian Jews?" In Hourihane, *Spanish Medieval Art,* 65–88.

———. "The Little Jewish Boy: Afterlife of a Byzantine Legend in Thirteenth-Century Spain." In *Images and Afterlife: Essays in Honor of Annemarie Weyl Carr,* edited by Lynn Jones. Aldershot: Ashgate, forthcoming.

———. *Pictorial Narrative in the Romanesque Cloister: Cloister Imagery and Religious Life in Medieval Spain.* New York: Peter Lang, 2004.

Pavón Maldonado, Basilio. *Tudela, ciudad medieval: Arte islámico y mudéjar.* Madrid: Instituto Hispano-Árabe de Cultura, 1978.

Pedro Ferreira, Manuel. "The Stemma of the Marian *Cantigas:* Philological and Musical Evidence." *Cantigueiros* 6 (1994): 58–98.

Pelizaeus, Theodor. "Beiträge zur Geschichte der Legende vom Judenknabe." Inaugural dissertation, University of Halle-Wittenberg, 1914.

Perarnau i Espelt, Josep. "Els quatre sermons catalans de sant Vicent Ferrer en el manuscript 476 de la Biblioteca de Catalunya." *Arxiú de Textos Catalans Antics* 15 (1996): 109–340.

Peter the Venerable. *The Letters of Peter the Venerable.* Edited and introduced by Giles Constable. 2 vols. Cambridge, Mass.: Harvard University Press, 1967.

Petrus Alfonsi. *Dialogue Against the Jews.* Translated by Irven M. Resnick. Fathers of the Church, Mediaeval Continuation, 8. Washington, D.C.: Catholic University of America Press, 2006.

Petzold, Andreas. "'Of the Significance of Colors': The Iconography of Colour in Romanesque and Early Gothic Book Illumination." In *Image and Belief: Studies in Celebration of the Eightieth Anniversary of the Index of Christian Art,* edited by Colum Hourihane, 125–34. Princeton: Princeton University Press, 1999.

Pick, Lucy. *Conflict and Coexistence: Archbishop Rodrigo and the Muslims and Jews of Medieval Spain.* Ann Arbor: University of Michigan Press, 2004.

Plenzat, Karl. *Die Theophiluslegende in den Dichtungen des Mittelalters.* Berlin: E. Ebering, 1926; repr., Nendeln, Liechtenstein: Kraus Reprint, 1967.

Porter, A. Kingsley. *Romanesque Sculpture of the Pilgrimage Roads.* Boston: Marshall Jones, 1923; repr., New York: Hacker Art Books, 1966.

Prado-Vilar, Francisco. "The Gothic Anamorphic Gaze: Regarding the Worth of Others." In Robinson and Rouhi, *Under the Influence,* 67–100.

———. "*Iudeus sacer:* Life, Law, and Identity in the 'State of Exception' Called 'Marian Miracle.'" In Kessler and Nirenberg, *Judaism and Christian Art,* 115–42.

Presilla, Maricel. "The Image of Death and Political Ideology in the *Cantigas de Santa María.*" In Katz and Keller, *Studies on the "Cantigas de Santa María,"* 403–59.

Prieto de la Iglesia, Remedios, and Ana Belén Sánchez Prieto. "La Cantiga 107 de Alfonso X y el proceso de transformación de la leyenda de María de Salto." *Estudios Segovianos* 38, no. 95 (1997): 155–226.

Procter, Evelyn. *Alfonso X of Castile: Patron of Literature and Learning.* Oxford: Clarendon Press, 1951.

Prudentius. Edited and translated by H. J. Thomson. 2 vols. Cambridge, Mass.: Harvard University Press, 1949–53.

Quinn, Malcom. *The Swastika: Constructing the Symbol.* London: Routledge, 1994.

Raizman, David. "The Church of Santa Cruz and the Beginnings of Mudejar Architecture in Toledo." *Gesta* 38, no. 2 (1999): 128–41.

———. "A Rediscovered Illuminated Manuscript of St. Ildefonsus's *De Virginitate Beatae Maríae* in the Biblioteca Nacional in Madrid." *Gesta* 26, no. 1 (1987): 37–46.

Ramon Llull. *Doctor Illuminatus: A Ramon Llull Reader.* Edited and translated by Anthony Bonner. Princeton: Princeton University Press, 1993.

Ray, Jonathan. "Beyond Tolerance and Persecution: Reassessing Our Approach to Medieval Convivencia." *Jewish Social Studies* 11, no. 2 (2005): 1–18.

———. *The Sephardic Frontier: The Reconquista and the Jewish Community in Medieval Iberia.* Ithaca: Cornell University Press, 2007.

Remensnyder, Amy G. "Christian Captives, Muslim Maidens, and Mary." *Speculum* 82, no. 3 (2007): 642–77.

Resnick, Irven. "Medieval Roots of the Myth of Jewish Male Menses." *Harvard Theological Review* 93, no. 3 (2000): 241–63.

Ricard, Prosper. "Reliures marocaines du XIIIe siècle, notes sur des specimens d'époque et de tradition almohades." *Hespéris* 17 (1933): 109–27.

———. "Sur un type de reliure des temps Almohades." *Ars Islamica* 1 (1934): 74–79.

Ricketts, Peter T. "The Hispanic Tradition of the *Breviari d'amor* of Matfre Ermengaud of Béziers." In *Hispanic Studies in Honour of Joseph Manson,* edited by Dorothy M. Atkinson and Anthony H. Clarke, 227–53. Oxford: Dolphin, 1972.

Rico Camps, Daniel. "A Shrine in Its Setting: San Vicente de Ávila." In *Decorations for the Holy Dead: Visual Embellishment on Tombs and Shrines,* edited by Stephen Lamia and Elizabeth del Alamo, 57–76. Turnhout: Brepols, 2002.

Riera i Sans, Jaume. "Los tumultos contra las juderías de la corona de Aragón en 1391." *Cuadernos de Historia* 8 (1977): 213–25.

Rincón García, Wifredo. "La devoción a San Dominguito de Val en el Archivo Capitular de la Iglesia Metropolitana de Zaragoza. Culto e iconografía." In *Memoria Ecclesiae XXI: Religiosidad popular y archivos de la iglesia santoral hispano-mozárabe en las diocésis de España,* edited by Augustín Hevia Ballina, 127–48. Oviedo: Asociación de Archiveros de la Iglesia en España, 2002.

Robert, Ulysse. "Étude historique et archéologique sur la roue des Juifs depuis le XIIIe siècle. I." *Revue des études juives* 6 (1882): 81–95.

———. "Étude historique et archeologique sur la roue des Juifs depuis le XIIIe siècle. II." *Revue des études juives* 7 (1883): 94–102.

———. "The Yellow Badge in History." *Historia Judaica* 19 (1957): 89–146.

Robinson, Cynthia. *In Praise of Song: The Making of Courtly Culture in Al-Andalus and Provence, 1005–1134 A.D.* Leiden: E. J. Brill, 2002.

———. *Three Ladies and a Lover: Mediterranean Courtly Culture Through the Text and Images of the "Hadîth Bayâd wa Riyâd," an Andalusî Manuscript.* London: Curzon-Routledge, 2006.

Robinson, Cynthia, and Leyla Rouhi, eds. *Under the Influence: Questioning the Comparative in Medieval Castile.* Leiden: E. J. Brill, 2005.

Rodríguez Barral, Paulino. "*Contra caecitatem iudeorum:* El tópico de la ceguera de los judíos en la plástica medieval hispánica." *Ilu: Revista de Ciencias de las Religiones* 12 (2007): 181–209.

———. "La dialéctica texto-imagen: A propósito de la representación del judío en las *Cantigas de Santa María* de Alfonso X." *Anuario de estudios medievales* 37, no. 1 (2007): 213–43.

———. "Eucaristía y antisemitismo en la plástica gótica hispanica." *Boletín del Museo e Instituto "Camón Aznar"* 97 (2006): 279–348.

———. *La imagen del judío en la España medieval: El conflicto entre cristianismo y judaísmo en las artes visuales góticas.* Barcelona: Universitat de Barcelona, 2009.

Romano, David. "Los judíos y Alfonso X." *Revista de Occidente* 43 (December 1984): 203–17.

Roth, Cecil. "Portraits and Caricatures of Medieval English Jews." In *Essays and Portraits in Anglo-Jewish History,* 22–25. Philadelphia: Jewish Publication Society, 1962.

Roth, Norman. *Conversos, Inquisition, and the Expulsion of the Jews from Spain.* Madison: University of Wisconsin Press, 1995.

———. "Jewish Collaborators in Alfonso's Scientific Work." In Burns, *Emperor of Culture,* 59–71.

Rowe, Nina. "Idealization and Subjection at the South Façade of Strasbourg Cathedral." In Merback, *Beyond the Yellow Badge,* 179–202.

———. "Synagoga Tumbles, a Rider Triumphs: Clerical Viewers and the Fürstenportal of Bamberg Cathedral." *Gesta* 45, no. 1 (2006): 15–42.

———. *The Jew, the Cathedral, and the Medieval City: Synagoga and Ecclesia in the Thirteenth Century.* New York: Cambridge University Press, 2011

Rubin, Miri. *Corpus Christi: The Eucharist in Late Medieval Culture.* New York: Cambridge University Press, 1991.

———. "Desecration of the Host: The Birth of an Accusation." *Studies in Church History* 29 (1992): 169–85.

———. *Gentile Tales: The Narrative Assault on Late Medieval Jews.* Philadelphia: University of Pennsylvania Press, 1999.

Ruggles, D. Fairchild. "The Alcazar of Seville and Mudejar Architecture." *Gesta* 43, no. 2 (2004): 87–98.

———. "Representation and Identity in Medieval Spain: Beatus Manuscripts and the Mudejar Churches of Teruel." In *Languages of Power in Islamic Spain,* edited by Ross Brann, 77–106. Bethesda, Md.: CDL Press, 1997.

Ruiz, Teófilo F. *From Heaven to Earth: The Reordering of Castilian Society, 1150–1350.* Princeton: Princeton University Press, 2004.

———. *Spain's Centuries of Crisis, 1300–1474.* Oxford: Blackwell, 2007.

Russakoff, Anna. "The Role of the Image in an Illustrated Manuscript of *Les Miracles de Nôtre-Dame* by Gautier de Coinci: Besançon, Bibliothèque Municipale 551." *Manuscripta* 47–48 (2003–4): 136–44.

Sainz de la Maza, Carlos. "Los judíos de Berceo y los de Alfonso X en España de last tres religiones." *Dicenda: Cuadernos de Filología Hispánica Arcadia* 6 (1987): 209–15.

Sánchez Ameijeiras, Rocío. "Church Reform and the Poetics of Gothic Sculpture in Burgos and Amiens." In Hourihane, *Spanish Medieval Art,* 155–86.

———. "La fortuna sevillana del códice florentino de las *Cantigas:* Tumbas, textas e imagines." *Quintana* 15 (2002): 257–73.

———. "Imaxes e teoría da imaxe nas *Cantigas de Santa María.*" In *As Cantigas de Santa María,* edited by Elvira Fidalgo, 246–301. Vigo: Xerais de Galicia, Ediciones, 2002.

Sánchez Real, José. "La judería de Tarragona." *Sefarad* 11 (1951): 339–48.

———. "Los judíos de Tarragona." *Boletín Arqueológico: Órgano de la Real Sociedad Arqueológica Tarraconense* 49 (1949): 15–45.

Sánchez Ucón, María José. "El niño mártir Dominguito de Val: A la Santidad a través de la leyenda." In *Muerte, religiosidad y cultura popular, siglos XIII–*

XVIII, edited by Eliseo Serrano Martín, 119–50. Zaragoza: Institución Fernando el Católico, 1994.

Sansy, Danièle. "Chapeau juif ou chapeau pointu? Esquisse d'un signe d'infamie." In *Symbole des Alltags, Alltag der Symbole: Festschrift für Harry Kühnel zum 65. Geburtstag,* edited by Gertrud Blaschitz and Harry Kühnel, 349–75. Graz: Akademische Druck- und Verlagsanstalt, 1992.

———. "Jalons pour une iconographie medieval du juif." In Barros, *Xudeus e conversos na historia,* 1:135–70.

Santiago Luque, A. "Marco histórico y texto." In Alfonso X et al., *Las Cantigas de Santa María,* 2:11–22.

Saugnieux, Joël. *Berceo y las culturas del siglo XIII.* Logroño: Servicio de Cultura de la Excma. Diputación Provincial, 1982.

Scarborough, Connie L. "A Summary of the Research on the Miniatures of the *CSM.*" *Cantigueiros* 1, no. 1 (1987): 41–50.

———. "Verbalization and Visualization in MS T.I.1 of the *Cantigas de Santa Maria:* The Theme of the Runaway Nun." In Katz and Keller, *Studies on the "Cantigas de Santa María,"* 135–54.

Schaffer, Martha E. "Los códices de las *Cantigas de Santa María:* Su problemática." In Montoya Martínez and Domínguez Rodríguez, *El scriptorium alfonsí,* 126–48.

———. "The 'Evolution' of the *Cantigas de Santa María.*" In Parkinson, *Cobras e Son,* 186–213.

Schapiro, Meyer. *The Parma Ildefonsus, a Romanesque Illuminated Manuscript from Cluny and Related Works.* New York: College Art Association, 1964.

Schefer, Jean Louis. *L'hostie profanée: Histoire d'une fiction théologique.* Paris: P.O.L., 2007.

Scholem, Gershom. "The Star of David: History of a Symbol." In *The Messianic Idea in Judaism and Other Essays in Jewish Spirituality,* translated by Michael Meyer, 257–81. New York: Schocken Books, 1971.

Schreckenberg, Heinz. *The Jews in Christian Art: An Illustrated History.* Translated by John Bowden. London: SCM Press, 1996.

Schroeder, Henry Joseph. *Disciplinary Decrees of the General Councils: Text, Translation and Commentary.* St. Louis: B. Herder, 1937.

Seiferth, Wolfgang S. *Synagogue and Church in the Middle Ages: Two Symbols in Art and Literature.* Translated by Lee Chadeayne and Paul Gottwald. New York: Ungar, 1970.

Shalom, Ram Ben. "Between Official and Private Dispute: The Case of Christian Spain and Provence in the Late Middle Ages." *AJS Review* 27, no. 1 (2003): 23–71.

Sharot, Stephen. "Jewish Millenarianism: A Comparison of Medieval Communities." *Comparative Studies in Society and History* 22, no. 3 (1980): 394–415.

Shatzmiller, Paul. *La deuxième controverse de Paris: Un chapitre dans le polémique entre chrètiens et juifs au Moyen Age.* Paris: E. Peeters, 1994.

Sicroff, Albert A. *Les controverses des status de "pureté de sang" en Espagne du XVe au XVIIe siècle.* Paris: Didier, 1960.

Las siete partidas. Edited by Robert I. Burns. Translated by Samuel Parsons Scott. Philadelphia: University of Pennsylvania Press, 2001.

Signer, Michael A., and John H. van Engen, eds. *Jews and Christians in Twelfth-Century Europe.* Notre Dame: University of Notre Dame Press, 2001.

Silva Maroto, Pilar. "Fernando Gallego and the Altarpiece of Ciudad Rodrigo." In *Fernando Gallego and His Workshop: The Altarpiece from Ciudad Rodrigo,* edited by Amanda Dotseth et al., 39–70. Dallas: Meadows Museum, 2008.

Silva y Verasteguí, Soledad de. *La miniatura medieval en Navarra.* Pamplona: Gobierno de Navarra, 1988.

Simonsohn, Schlomo. *The Apostolic See and the Jews.* Toronto: Pontifical Institute of Medieval Studies, 1988.

Snow, Joseph T. "Alfonso as Troubadour: The Fact and the Fiction." In Burns, *Emperor of Culture,* 126–40.

———. "The Central Role of the Troubadour Persona of Alfonso X in the *Cantigas de Santa María.*" *Bulletin of Hispanic Studies* 56 (1979): 305–15.

———. "The Current Status of Cantigas Studies." In Katz and Keller, *Studies on the "Cantigas de Santa María,"* 475–86.

———. "Trends in Scholarship on Alfonsine Poetry." *La Corónica* 11, no. 2 (1983): 248–57.

———. *The Poetry of Alfonso X: A Critical Bibliography.* Research Bibliographies and Checklists 19. London: Grant and Cutler, 1977.

Sobrequés i Callicó, Jaume, ed. *Llibre verd de Barcelona.* 2 vols. Barcelona: Editorial Base, 2004.

Soler Ferrer, María Paz. "Salero de pellizcos." In Mann, Glick, and Dodds, *Convivencia,* 227.

Southern, Richard. "The English Origins of the 'Miracles of the Virgin.'" *Medieval and Renaissance Studies* 4 (1958): 176–216.

Stacey, Robert C. "From Ritual Crucifixion to Host Desecration: Jews and the Body of Christ." *Jewish History* 12, no. 1 (1998): 11–28.

Stahl, Harvey. *Picturing Kingship: History and Painting in the Psalter of Saint Louis.* University Park: Pennsylvania State University Press, 2007.

Stones, Alison. "Illustrated Miracles de Nostre Dame Manuscripts Listed by Sigla." In Krause and Stones, *Gautier de Coinci,* 369–72.

Strickland, Deborah Higgs. *Saracens, Demons, and Jews: Making Monsters in Medieval Art.* Princeton: Princeton University Press, 2003.

Stroll, Mary. *The Jewish Pope: Ideology and Politics in the Papal Schism of 1130.* Leiden: E. J. Brill, 1987.

Sureda, Joan. *La pintura románica en Cataluña.* Madrid: Alianza, 1981.

Synan, Edward A. *The Popes and the Jews.* New York: Macmillan, 1965.

Szirmai, Janós Alexander. *The Archaeology of Medieval Bookbinding.* Aldershot: Ashgate, 1999.

Teensma, Benjamin N. "Os Judeus na Espanha do século XIII, segunda as *Cantigas de Santa María* de Alfonso X o Sábio." *Occidente* 79 (1970): 85–102.

Tilander, Gunnar, ed. *Vidal mayor: Traducción aragonesa de la obra "In excelsis Dei thesauris" de Vidal de Canellas.* 3 vols. Lund: H. Ohlssons, 1956.

Timmerman, Achim. "The Avenging Crucifix: Some Observations on the Iconography of the Living Cross." *Gesta* 40, no. 2 (2001): 141–60.

Tinnell, Roger. "Marisaltos and the 'Salt de la Bella Donna.'" *Cantigueiros* 2 (1988–89): 69–77.

Tolan, John V. *Petrus Alfonsi and His Medieval Readers.* Gainesville: University Press of Florida, 1993.

———. *Saracens: Islam in the Medieval European Imagination.* New York: Columbia University Press, 2002.

Tomasch, Sylvia. "Postcolonial Chaucer and the Virtual Jew." In Cohen, *Postcolonial Middle Ages,* 243–60.

Torres Balbás, Leopoldo. *Arte almohade: Arte nazarí: Arte mudéjar.* Ars Hispaniae 4. Madrid: Editorial Plus-Ultra, 1949.

———. "El mudéjar como constante artística." In *Actas del Ier Simposio Internacional de Mudejarismo,* 29–40. Teruel: Diputación Provincial, 1981.

Trachtenberg, Joshua. *The Devil and the Jews: The Medieval Conception of the Jew and Its Relation to Modern Antisemitism.* New Haven: Yale University Press, 1943; repr., Philadelphia: Jewish Publication Society, 1983.

Trivison, Mary Louise. "Prayer and Prejudice in the CSM." *Cantigueiros* 1 (1988): 119–27.

Valdeón Baruque, Julio. *Alfonso X el Sabio: La forja de la España moderna.* Madrid: Ediciones Temas de Hoy, 2003.

———. *Los judíos de Castilla y la revolución Trastámara.* Valladolid: University of Valladolid, 1968.

Vazquez de Parga, Luis. "El maestro del refectorio de Pamplona." *Príncipe de Viana* (1948): 3–18.

Verkerk, Dorothy Hoogland. "Black Servant, Black Demon: Color Ideology in the Ashburnham Pentateuch." *Journal of Medieval and Early Modern Studies* 31, no. 1 (2001): 57–77.

La vida judía en Sefarad: Sinagoga del Tránsito, Toledo, noviembre 1991–enero 1992. Madrid: Ministerio de Cultura, 1991.

Vila da Vila, Margarita. "La iconografía de San Vicente y sus hermanas en la arquitectura medieval abulense de los siglos XII y XIII." In *Parentesco, familia y Matrimonio en Galicia,* edited by José Bermejo, 255–68. Santiago: Tórculo Edicions, 1988.

Vivancos Pérez, Juan. "Biga de la Passió." In *Introducció a l'estudi de l'art romànic Català, fons d'art romànic Català del Museu Nacional d'Art de Catalunya,* edited by Federico Mayor and Antonio Pladevall Font, 406–8. Catalunya románica 1. Barcelona: Fundació Enciclopèdia Catalana, 1994.

Vose, Robin. *Dominicans, Muslims, and Jews in the Medieval Crown of Aragon.* New York: Cambridge University Press, 2009.

Warner, George F. *Descriptive Catalogue of Illuminated Manuscripts in the Library of C. W. Dyson Perrins.* 2 vols. Oxford: Oxford University Press, 1920.

Watson, Andrew G. *Catalogue of Dated and Datable Manuscripts c. 700–1600 in the Department of Manuscripts, the British Library.* London: British Library, 1979.

Weber, Annette. "Die Entwicklung des Judenbildes im 13. Jahrhundert und sein Platz in der Lettner- und Tympanon-Skulptur: Fragen zum Verhaltnis von Ikonographie und Stil." *Städel-Jahrbuch* 14 (1993): 35–54.

———. "'. . . Maria die ist juden veind.' Antijüdische Mariendarstellungen in der Kunst des 13–15 Jahrhunderts." In *Maria Tochter Sion? Mariologie, Marienfrömmigkeit und Judenfeindschaft,* edited by Johannes Heil and Rainer Kampling, 69–110. Paderborn: Schöningh, 2001.

Webster, Jill. *Els Menorets: The Franciscans in the Realm of Aragon from Saint Francis to the Black Death.* Toronto: Pontifical Institute of Medieval Studies, 1993.

Weiss, Daniel. *Art and Crusade in the Age of Saint Louis.* New York: Cambridge University Press, 1998.

Werckmeister, Otto Karl. "The Islamic Rider in the Beatus of Gerona." *Gesta* 36, no. 2 (1997): 101–6.

Williams, John W. "Cluny and Spain." *Gesta* 27 (1988): 93–101.

Williams, John W., and Daniel Walker. "Reliquary of Saint Isidore." In *Art of Medieval Spain,* 239–44.

Wisch, Barbara. "Vested Interest: Redressing Jews on Michelangelo's Sistine Ceiling." *Artibus et Historiae* 24, no. 48 (2003): 143–72.

Wolf, Kenneth. "*Convivencia* in Medieval Spain: A Brief History of an Idea." *Religion Compass* 3, no. 1 (2009): 72–85.

Wolff, Philippe. "The 1391 Pogrom in Spain: Social Crisis or Not?" *Past and Present* 50 (February 1971): 4–18.

Wollesen, Jens T. "Sub specie ludi . . : Text and Images in Alfonso El Sabio's *Libro de acedrex, dados e tablas.*" *Zeitschrift für Kunstgeschichte* 53 (1990): 277–308.

Wolter, Eugen. *Der Judenknabe.* Halle: M. Niemeyer, 1879.

Wood, Diana, ed. *Christianity and Judaism.* Studies in Church History 29. Cambridge, Mass.: Ecclesiastical History Society, 1992.

Wulstan, David. "The Compilation of the *Cantigas* of Alfonso el Sabio." In Parkinson, *Cobras e Son,* 154–85.

Yarza Luaces, Joaquín. "Del alfaquí sabio a los seudo-obispos: Una particularidad iconográfica gótica." *Sharq al-Andalus* 10–11 (1993–94): 749–76.

———. "La il.lustració." In Sobrequés i Callicó, *Llibre verd de Barcelona,* 2:257–318.

Yerushalmi, Yosef Hayim. *Assimilation and Racial Anti-Semitism: The Iberian and the German Models.* New York: Leo Baeck Institute, 1982.

INDEX

Page numbers in *italics* indicate figures.